Philosophical Problems and Arguments: An Introduction

Philosophical Problems and Arguments: An Introduction

FOURTH EDITION

James W. Cornman
formerly University of Pennsylvania

Keith Lehrer
University of Arizona

George S. Pappas
Ohio State University

Hackett Publishing Company
Indianapolis/Cambridge

To Betty, Adrienne, and Chris

For further information, please address
  Hackett Publishing Company, Inc.
  P. O. Box 44937
  Indianapolis, Indiana 46244-0937

The paper used in this publication meets minimum requirements of American
National Standard for Information Sciences—Permanence of Paper for Printed
Library Materials, ANSI Z39.48-1984

Library of Congress Cataloging-in-Publication Data

Cornman, James W.
   Philosophical problems and arguments: an introduction / James W.
Cornman, Keith Lehrer, George S. Pappas.—4th ed.
     p.   cm.
   Includes bibliographical references and index.
   ISBN 0-87220-125-2 (alk. paper)
   ISBN 0-87220-124-4 (pbk.)
       1. Philosophy—Introduction. I. Lehrer, Keith. II. Pappas, George
Sotiros. 1942- . III. Title
   BD21.C66 1991
     100—dc20
                                                          91-21663
                                                             CIP

Preface to the 4th Edition

Gratified by the reception of a third edition, we have set out to provide an up-to-date fourth edition, with improvements suggested by our students, colleagues, and teachers of the earlier editions. We have made a serious attempt to make the fourth edition more accessible to the student and have eliminated some of the more difficult sections. The first three chapters were revised by Lehrer, with the assistance of Leopold Stubenberg, and the last three by Pappas, though we collaborated on the entire effort. All the chapters have been changed to bring them up to date in terms of the current literature and to make them less difficult to follow. Chapter One has been considerably shortened, with some new introductory material on the nature of philosophy added at the beginning to engage the interest of the student. Chapters Two and Three, though dialectical in character, have a new and simpler organization which the students should find easier to handle. Chapter Two contains some new material on reliabilism and causal theories of knowledge as well as a novel resolution of the problem of skepticism. Chapter Three contains some new argumentation for incompatibilism derived from Van Inwagen and some new argumentation for compatibilism derived from Frankfurt and Dennett.

□ Chapters Four, Five, and Six have been changed in a number of important ways for this edition. In Chapter Four, the discussion of dualistic interactionism has been shortened, despite the addition of some new material to that section. Also, greater attention to eliminative materialism is provided, with a focus on some of the arguments of Paul Churchland. Moreover, functionalism is brought into the discussion, as are some criticisms of that theory. Chapter Five has been changed in two principal ways: there is an extended discussion of Alston's account of perceiving God, and the discussion of the argument from evil has been greatly expanded, resulting in a rather different conclusion to that chapter from earlier editions. Chapter Six includes new material on an act-deontological theory, and some slight additional material on ethical relativism and ethical skepticism. Otherwise, Chapter Six has been changed by deletion, most notably of some of the discussion of psychological egoism.

□ We wish to thank Leopold Stubenberg for assisting with the shortening and reorganization of the first three chapters, Barbara Hannan for her comments on the first three chapters, Angelo Corlett for assistance with bibliographical work, and Diana Raffman for her helpful comments on the mind-body problem. We should also thank Lois Day for keying in the chapters into a word processor. We are especially grateful for the assistance of Paul Coppock who, as copy editor, helped us in many ways to improve the style and content of the book.

Keith Lehrer and George Pappas

Preface to the 1st Edition

Joseph Conrad said that his aim in writing was "before all, to make you *see*." Ours is, above all, to make you *think*. We want to make you think about the problems that philosophers have discussed. We also hope this introduction to philosophy will set you thinking about other problems. To achieve our aim, we have concentrated on five basic philosophical problems and tried to give a careful and thorough presentation and examination of the most plausible reasons for and against the solutions philosophers have proposed for these problems.

□ Each problem is discussed in a separate and virtually independent chapter. Each discussion, however, does rely on the material of the first chapter, where the nature of reasoning and argument is discussed and where certain basic philosophical terms are explained. Thus the first chapter is vital for a thorough grasp of the chapters that follow it, and it should be read before, or together with them.

□ At the conclusion of each chapter we have presented a solution to the problem discussed. But because of the very nature of the problems, and because this is an introductory book, none of these solutions should be considered as final. They are, we claim, the most reasonable conclusions to reach on the basis of the material presented. But we have not, nor has anyone else, presented and examined all the material needed to solve these problems once and for all. To emphasize that you should think about these solutions rather than accept them, some of the exercises at the back of each chapter raise questions to test your grasp of the material. For those whose appetite is whetted for more reading on the various topics, we have provided an annotated bibliography at the end of the text.

□ Committee efforts often produce compromise results. To avoid the pitfalls of such results, each of us has assumed complete responsibility for three chapters, Mr. Lehrer for the first three and Mr. Cornman for the last three. You will see differences in style, but we hope that you can also find an important common feature—the attempt to evaluate the subject matter dispassionately, fairly, and carefully.

□ Although we have divided responsibility, we are not divided in our thanks to many people who have read, criticized, and contributed to this book. Two we must especially thank are Lewis W. Beck and John D.

Moore, both of whom carefully read and helpfully criticized the entire book. Others whose help in various ways deserves mention are Jean Hopson, Loretta Kopelman, Joel Levinson, Natalie Tarbet, and Peter van Inwagen.

J. W. C.
K. L.

Contents

TWO
The Problem of Knowledge and Skepticism   39

THREE

FOUR

FIVE

ONE

The Content and Methods of Philosophy

WHAT IS PHILOSOPHY?

Some Philosophical Questions

What is philosophy? Philosophy is the collection of fundamental intellectual questions. What are they? That is one. Let us illustrate others. Consider the problem of knowledge and skepticism. People dogmatically assert that they know things. One person asserts that she knows something, another denies this. It occurs to a philosophical eavesdropper to wonder what knowledge is and whether anyone really knows. Are we not often wrong when we claim to know something? At one time people claimed that they knew the earth was flat. But now? At one time, not so long ago, people claimed they knew that the idea of a person walking on the moon was a mere fiction. But now? At the present time, people claim to know that no one can travel backward in time. But later? Who knows?

Doubt explodes. Are we not often wrong about what we see before us? "Never!" we retort, until memory reminds of the pleasures of the house of mirrors and other visual illusions. What about the stick that appears bent when immersed in water? What about the cold water that feels warm to chilled flesh? What about the illusion of water covering the highway ahead, receding as we approach the sunbaked stretch? And to bring the illusions right up to our nose, what about the illusion of the pair of pencils a few inches from our nose, when we stare into the distance holding a

1

single pencil a few inches before our nose? (Try it!) The senses are full
of deception, and yet we depend on them to know what we see and feel.
We trust them, but should we?

Once doubt enters the philosophical mind, it explodes and becomes
philosophical. It occurs to us that we depend not only on our senses, on
sight and touch, but on the nerves and brain to which they are attached.
We remember reading of experiments in which some surgeon obtains direct
contact with the brain of a patient and, upon applying gentle stimulation,
causes the person to have a sensory experience exactly like seeing an object
before him, when nothing is there. The sensory experience is caused from
the inside by stimulating the brain, rather than from the outside by some
object seen: mere illusion. And then it occurs to one that in dreams
something similar happens. One dreams that one sees, but the cause is
inside, not outside. One does not see what one dreams one does. Again,
illusion.

Can sensory experience be the stuff of which knowledge is made? Can
knowledge and illusion be made of the same stuff? Of course not. But
our knowledge of the world, if such there be, must be made of the stuff of
sense. For how could we know what the world is like except by the use
of our senses, of our eyes and ears? The smiling skeptic within cheerfully
replies, "We know nothing. Illusion duplicates reality and ignorance
replaces knowledge."

The skeptic within makes one a philosopher. How can we possibly know
anything if illusion duplicates reality? How can we know the real thing
from illusion? And what is knowledge anyway? When you ask these
things you have taken the philosophical turn. You have entered the
problem of knowledge and skepticism, the subject of our second chapter.

You might think that, having raised the question whether you know
anything at all, and taken it seriously, you have questioned enough. But
philosophy asks all the fundamental questions. The question whether you
want to follow the path of philosophy or turn back suggests that it is up to
you which way you go. The question suggests that you are free to study
philosophy or not. But are you? It may seem to you that you are, but our
brief reflections on the illusions of the senses have made us sensitive to the
distinction between illusion and reality. It may appear to you that you
have some freedom in many matters, though not in all, and the study of
philosophy appears to be one in which you are free. If the course is
required for a degree, you cannot obtain the degree without taking the
course. Still, you could have chosen not to take the course. You could
have chosen not to take the degree. You could have chosen not to pursue
higher education at all. It is, after all, completely up to you. You are
completely free.

A doubt creeps in. Suppose the course is required for law school, and
you wanted to be a lawyer for as long as you can remember; since you
were a small child, perhaps. You really cannot imagine pursuing another

course of study. Were you free to choose not to be a lawyer? Could you really have chosen to be something entirely different? A tailor? You may conclude that you could no more have chosen to be a tailor than jump to the moon. Why? Well, that is just the way you are. You have always wanted to be a lawyer and never even considered the possibility of being a tailor. But why are you the way you are? Is that just an accident? Did it just happen? Or did your background contain a cause? Perhaps you met a lawyer, or watched one on television, or have a relative who is a lawyer, and that is how you got the idea. Some experience caused the idea to arise in you. Once you got the idea, other experiences reinforced it until it became inevitable that you would study law. The outcome was causally determined by the history of your experience. If the outcome was determined, however, you are not free. You could not have done otherwise.

The doubt readily explodes. Surely whatever you do, whenever you do it, has a causal history. Though we may be ignorant of the causal history of our actions, especially trivial ones, they all have causes, don't they? Moreover, the things that cause our actions themselves have causes, because everything has a cause. That is the thesis of determinism. Everything is caused, or everything is causally determined. If everything is caused, however, then everything is the inevitable causal outcome of a history that extends far into the remote past. It seems to us that we are free. But are we? If all your actions and choices, desires and convictions, are the inevitable result of an unbroken causal chain, how can you be free? How can it be up to you whether you study philosophy or not, when your studying philosophy was causally determined? Should you conclude that you are free, as you seem to be, and that the action is not causally determined? Or should you accept that the action, like all others, is causally determined and that freedom is an illusion? Or is there some way of combining freedom and determinism after all? What is freedom, anyway? Freedom and determinism are the subject of the third chapter. It contains answers to these questions.

As you think about these philosophical problems, you may begin to think about your thoughts. You might, finding that you understand these philosophical issues, decide you have a good brain. What, though, is the connection between your thoughts and your brain? Does the brain cause the thoughts? Are the thoughts nothing but conditions of the brain? But thoughts seem so unlike states of the brain. Suppose someone could look inside your skull and observe the neural activity. Compare that to what you experience when you think of a trip through the country. You think of greening and blooming, of winding and walking, of pleasure and peace. That is how your thoughts appear to you, completely unlike the neural activity of a gelatinous mass in your head. How can things that appear to be so different be the same? Remember, though, things are not always what they appear to be. Maybe your thoughts are not what they appear to be. Maybe there is nothing but the neural activities. Or maybe the thoughts and brain states are identical, even though they do not appear to be so. But could not my thoughts occur in a different sort of brain, or even in a computer? How then can my thoughts be identical with states of my actual brain? What is the relation between thoughts and brains, between the mind and the body? That is the problem of our fourth chapter, on the mind-body problem.

It may never have occurred to you to question the existence of knowledge, freedom, and surely not your own thoughts. If, however, you have thought of religious matters, of claims concerning the existence of God, for example, then you are familiar with the arguments and counter-arguments concerning the existence of God. Theists will point to the remarkable order and organization of the universe as a sign of design and the existence of a divine designer. They will argue that there must be some first cause. Atheists will reply that there is no need of a first cause, because everything may be explained in terms of the causation of ante-cedent events. They will find disorder in the form of evil and argue that this is incompatible with the existence of a perfectly good, all-knowing, and all-powerful being. Is the appearance of design illusory? Is the appearance of evil illusory? Which arguments are sound and which fallacious? Is it reasonable to believe in the existence of God, or is it not? Those are the questions discussed in the fifth chapter.

It will probably also have occurred to you to question the claims of morality, the claims that some actions are right and others wrong. How can you tell whether an action is right or wrong? Again, some actions clearly appear to be wrong, but are they really? What is the rule or criterion of right and wrong action? Is it the command of God? Is it merely our own interests? Is it some basic principle? One cannot help but notice the conflict between people over what is right and wrong. Does such conflict or disagreement show that there is no rule of right and wrong? Consider people who think it right to kill their parents, after a certain age, to prevent them from deteriorating. We obviously disagree with them. But how could we resolve that disagreement? Does the disagreement show that the assumption that some actions are right and some are wrong is mere illusion? If not, what is the basis of right and wrong, good and evil, justice and injustice? These are familiar questions. We investigate their merits in the last chapter of our book.

We have briefly considered some of the most important questions of philosophy. To answer them, you must think and reason. No elegant experiment can settle any of these questions. You must look at the arguments and learn to discern sound and valid arguments from unsound and invalid ones. You will learn how to do this in this chapter. Then you will have some chance to find the answers to these questions. They are among the most fundamental questions you can raise. To answer them you must undertake the philosophical journey.

The Nature of Philosophy: Science or Speculation?

Generally, the most satisfactory way to discover what an academic subject is about, whether it is in the sciences or the humanities, is to absorb oneself in the study of questions and problems characteristic of the field. General descriptions of a field are often either so abstract as to be uninformative or so idiosyncratic as to be misinformative. Nevertheless, now that you are briefly acquainted with some questions and problems of the subject, it is worthwhile to attempt some characterization of philosophy, if only an historical one, to give you a better understanding of the nature of philosophical inquiry. One principal reason is to explain the predominant role of disputation and argument in the study of philosophical problems. To this end we shall, without pretending to offer a precise definition, present some information about philosophy as a discipline in order to provide a general orientation toward the field you are about to study.

First, a few words about the historical development of philosophy as a field. Not too long ago, all scientific subjects were considered part of philosophy. *Philosophy concerning matter* encompassed what we now think of as physics and chemistry; *philosophy concerning mind* covered the subject of psychology and adjacent areas. In short, philosophy was once construed so broadly as to cover any field of theoretical inquiry. Any subject matter for which some general explanatory theory might be offered would have been a branch of philosophy. However, once a field of study came to be dominated by some main theory and developed standard methods of criticism and confirmation, then the field was cut off from the mother country of philosophy and became independent.

For example, philosophers once advanced a variety of theories to explain the nature of matter. One suggested that everything was made of water; another, somewhat closer to current conceptions, proposed that matter was composed of tiny, homogeneous, indivisible atoms. Once certain theories of matter, as well as experimental methods for testing such theories, became well established in the community of scholars, the philosophy of matter became the sciences of physics and chemistry. Another example of a philosophical problem that has been converted to a scientific one is the problem of the nature of life. At one time, life was conjectured to be an entity that enters the body at birth and departs at death. Currently, the nature of life is explained in terms of biochemistry.

Thus, it is a peculiarity of philosophy that, once argument and disputation have brought us to some theory, accompanied by a methodology, adequate to cope successfully with some issues in philosophy, the theory and methodology become separated from philosophy and are considered part of another discipline. Certain subjects are currently in transition. One such example is the field of linguistics, and, more particularly, the subject of semantics within that field. Philosophers have articulated a variety of theories to explain how words and other representations can have meaning, and what constitutes the meaning of words and other representations. In semantics, there is no sharp distinction between a philosopher and a linguist. In a field in transition, whether an investigator is a philosopher or a scientist characteristically becomes a moot question. In philosophy the successful development of an area often leads to the independence and autonomy of the developed part. For this reason, any specification of philosophy in terms of subject matter is likely to be both controversial today and out of date tomorrow.

The preceding considerations illustrate one relatively constant feature of philosophy, however: the fundamental character of the questions asked. No experimental technique is available to answer these questions. Instead, the questions studied in philosophy are approached through dialectical methods of argument and counterargument. And a student can sometimes feel that, after a long and arduous inquiry, nothing has been settled. This impression is partly due to the fact that, at any given time, philosophy will be found to deal with those intellectual problems that have not yet been articulated in such a way that any single theory and methodology can be fastened upon to solve them. Where the human intellect is grappling with some complex, fundamental philosophical problem, the search for a solution is at the same time a search for a special methodology. The search is carried forth by the perennial methodology of argumentation and the evaluation of argumentation.

The preceding characterization should not lead you to think that *all* philosophical problems are potentially exportable through successful processing. Some questions and problems resist such exportation by virtue of their general and fundamental character. The questions we have raised concerning knowledge, freedom, morality, and the existence of God are examples. In all fields of inquiry, people seek knowledge. It is in philosophy that one asks what knowledge is and whether there is any such thing at all. In some fields—economics and politics, for example—people study the causal consequences of various actions and policies. In philosophy one asks what general features make actions and policies right or wrong. Other questions we have briefly considered, about the character of freedom, of mind, and of God, appear to be the perennial subject matter of philosophy because they are both very basic and very general questions.

Moreover, the successful treatment of a problem within one field can generate quite new problems. For example, an explanation of physical phenomena in terms of laws and theories raises the question whether the movement of human bodies, which are part of the physical universe, takes place in a purely mechanical way that makes a sham of our impression that we are free agents determining our own destiny by deliberation and decision. Similarly, the success of neurophysiology in explaining our behavior raises the question whether thoughts and feelings are anything more than physical processes. We have no way of answering these questions by direct appeal to experiment or firmly established theory.

Instead, we must rely on the methods of philosophical investigation—the careful examination of arguments offered in defense of divergent positions and the analysis of important terms contained therein.

There need be no fear of famine in philosophy. The subject matter of philosophy is limited only by the capacity of the human mind to ask new questions and to reformulate old ones in some novel way. By so doing, additional content is provided to the one field that welcomes all those intellectual orphans rejected by other disciplines because of their unruly and difficult ways. Philosophy is the home of those intellectual problems with which others cannot cope. As a result, it is filled with the intellectual excitement of controversy and disputation taking place at the frontiers of rational inquiry.

THE TOOLS OF THE TRADE

Before discussing the problems just outlined, we must consider the methods and techniques of philosophy. Sometimes philosophy is said to be a dialectical discipline, meaning that philosophy proceeds through arguments and counterarguments. Of course, all disciplines depend on arguments to some extent, but in philosophy logical reasoning plays an especially prominent role. The explanation is that philosophy strives to answer such fundamental questions that specific empirical facts can seldom resolve the issues. When two people disagree about some philosophical matter, the only avenue of progress open to them is to consider and evaluate the arguments and objections on both sides. Therefore, philosophical inquiry must be critical and logical if any gain is to result. To facilitate such inquiry, we must learn to ask critical questions about the arguments we encounter, and to examine the answers with logical acumen. These are questions of logic and semantics. We shall present a brief introduction to logic and semantics, in order to approach the challenging problems of philosophy with the logical skills that are needed for intelligent and rigorous inquiry.

Deductive Logic
The field whose subject is *argument* is known as logic, or formal logic. The first question to answer in this field is: What is an argument? For our purposes, an argument is a group of statements of which one, the *conclusion*, is claimed to follow from the others. For example, consider the following argument: Everything is caused and, that being so, no one acts freely. This argument, the merits of which we shall consider in Chapter Three, might be stated more formally as follows:

1. If everything is caused, then no one acts freely.

2. Everything is caused.

Therefore

3. No one acts freely.

The word 'Therefore' above statement (3) indicates that what falls beneath it is the conclusion that is claimed to follow from the statements above. Statements (1) and (2) are the reasons given for concluding (3), and such statements are called *premises*. Thus, every argument consists of a conclusion and one or more premises from which the conclusion is claimed to follow.

Soundness and validity
There are, in general, two kinds of arguments, *inductive* and *deductive*. We shall consider inductive arguments subsequently, but first let us concentrate on deductive arguments, an example of which was just presented. A *deductive* argument is said to be *sound* when the premises of the argument are true and the argument is *valid*. Saying that an argument is valid is equivalent to saying that it is logically impossible that the premises of the argument are true and the conclusion false. A less precise but intuitively clear way of putting this is to say that, in a valid argument, *if* the premises are true, then the conclusion must be true. By this definition, it is easy to see that the preceding argument is valid, and, if the premises are true, then it must be sound as well. For *if* the premises

1. If everything is caused, then no one acts freely.

and

2. Everything is caused.

are both true, then it must also be true that

3. No one acts freely.

As a simple matter of logic, it is impossible that premises (1) and (2) should both be true and conclusion (3) be false. It is important to notice that the fact that this argument is valid does not prove that the conclusion is true. Validity is a hypothetical or conditional characteristic; it assures us that the conclusion of the argument is true *if* the premises are.

The argument may also be said to be valid in virtue of its *form*. We can represent the form of the preceding argument by the following schema:

If P, then Q
P
Therefore
Q

This argument form is called *Modus Ponens*. Every argument of this form is valid, and thus we may say that the argument form itself is valid. Consider the following argument:

If God exists, then there is no evil.

God exists.

Therefore

There is no evil.

This argument, like the preceding one, is valid because it has the form of *Modus Ponens*. We can obtain these arguments from *Modus Ponens* by substituting the appropriate English sentences for the letters *P* and *Q* in the argument form. If we substitute the sentence 'God exists' for the letter *P* and the sentence 'There is no evil' for the letter *Q* in the argument form, we will obtain the valid argument just cited. Whenever an argument form is valid, then we obtain a valid argument if we substitute in this way.

The following are other valid argument forms:

Modus Tollens

If *P*, then *Q*
Not *Q*
Therefore
Not *P*

Disjunctive Syllogism

Either *P* or *Q*
Not *P*
Therefore
Q

Hypothetical Syllogism

If *P*, then *Q*
If *Q*, then *R*
Therefore
If *P*, then *R*

Contraposition

If *P*, then *Q*
Therefore
If not *Q*, then not *P*

This list of argument forms is not complete or definitive. However, by considering various arguments of these forms, we can obtain an intuitive idea of what a valid argument is like. Many arguments can be shown to be valid by making the proper substitutions in the preceding arguments forms. In some cases, we will have to appeal to more than one argument form to show that an argument is valid. For example, consider the following argument:

If God does not exist, then everything is permitted.

If murder is not permitted, then not everything is permitted.

Murder is not permitted.

Therefore

It is not the case that God does not exist.

To show that this argument is valid, first notice that from

If murder is not permitted, then not everything is permitted.

and

Murder is not permitted.

we may conclude by *Modus Ponens* that

Not everything is permitted.

We may now take this statement, which is the conclusion of the foregoing argument, and use it as a premise in another argument. From the premise

If God does not exist, then everything is permitted.

and the new premise

Not everything is permitted.

we may conclude by *Modus Tollens* that

It is not the case that God does not exist.

This shows that from the original premises we could validly deduce the conclusion of the original argument by appealing to the argument forms previously listed. A lesson to be learned from the argument just considered is that anything validly deduced from a set of premises, such as the statement

Not everything is permitted.

may be added to the original premises for the purpose of making further deductions.

EXERCISES

All of the following arguments can be shown to be valid by appealing to the argument forms previously listed. Decide what argument form each of the following arguments has:

1. If the brain is needed for thought, then thought always occurs in the head.

    If thought always occurs in the head, then no spirit without a body ever thinks.

    Therefore

If the brain is needed for thought, then no spirit without a body ever thinks.

2. If reasons are the causes of actions, then all rational actions are caused.

    Therefore

    If not all rational actions are caused, then it is not the case that reasons are the causes of actions.

3. Either wars are avoided or the innocent suffer.

    Wars are not avoided.

    Therefore

    The innocent suffer.

4. If all people could be mistaken in what they believe, then all people lack knowledge.

    All people could be mistaken in what they believe.

    Therefore

    All people lack knowledge.

Show that each of the following arguments is valid by appealing to valid argument forms:

5. Either wars are avoided or the innocent suffer.

    If wars are avoided, then all people love peace.

    Not all people love peace.

    Therefore

    The innocent suffer.

6. If no actions are free, then no one is responsible for his or her actions.

    If no one is responsible for his or her actions, then no one deserves to be punished.

    No actions are free.

    Therefore

    No one deserves to be punished.

7. If the innocent suffer, then the world is not perfect.

If God exists, then the world is perfect.

Therefore

If the innocent suffer, then God does not exist.

Other valid argument forms

We obtain some valid argument forms by substituting into the form expressions that are not sentences. To see why this is so, consider the following argument:

All right actions are actions that produce good consequences.

All actions that produce good consequences are actions that maximize happiness and minimize pain.

Therefore

All right actions are actions that maximize happiness and minimize pain.

Brief reflection will convince you that if the premises of this argument are true, then the conclusion must also be true. This argument is not of the form of *Modus Ponens*, or any of the other forms considered earlier. The argument is valid in virtue of being an argument of the following form:

All *X* are *Y*.
All *Y* are *Z*.
Therefore
All *X* are *Z*.

All arguments of this form are valid. We get an argument of this form by substituting expressions describing classes of things for the letters *X*, *Y*, and *Z*. If we substitute the expression 'right actions' for *X*, 'actions that produce good consequences' for *Y*, and 'actions that maximize happiness and minimize pain' for *Z*, then we will obtain the argument just considered. Other valid argument forms of this kind are

No *X* are *Y*.   All *X* are *Y*.   All *X* are *Y*.
All *Z* are *X*.   Some *X* are *Z*.   Some *X* are not *Z*.
Therefore   *Therefore*   *Therefore*
No *Z* are *Y*.   Some *Y* are *Z*.   Some *Y* are not *Z*.

Such arguments are known as *categorical syllogisms*.

Validity and truth

Arguments of a valid form are valid even if they are completely absurd. For example, the following argument is valid:

All women are tigers.

All tigers are men.

Therefore

All women are men.

This argument has false premises and a false conclusion. That it is valid brings out the hypothetical character of validity. What the validity of such an argument amounts to is that it assures us that the conclusion must be true *if* the premises are true.

If an argument can be valid and yet have a preposterously false conclusion, what good is validity? Why should we be concerned with validity at all? The answer is that a valid argument is *truth-preserving*. Truth in the premises of a valid argument is preserved in the conclusion. Of course, if the premises are not true to begin with, then even a valid argument cannot ensure that the conclusion is true. But *only* valid arguments are truth-preserving. An analogy might help to clarify this point. Roughly, valid arguments preserve truth as good freezers preserve food. If the food you place in a freezer is spoiled to begin with, then even a good freezer cannot preserve it. But if the food placed in a good freezer is fresh, then the freezer will preserve it. Good freezers and valid arguments preserve fresh food and truth, respectively. But, just as the former cannot preserve food when the food is spoiled, so the latter cannot preserve truth when the premises are false. Garbage in, garbage out. Nevertheless, food freezers and valid arguments are worth having because they do preserve something good when one has it, and without them one may wind up with something rotten even when beginning with something impeccable. Thus, validity is to be desired and invalidity is to be eschewed.

The method of counterexample and possible worlds

We have considered several valid argument forms. However, these forms are only a few among many. For our purposes, it is not necessary, even if it would be useful, to know all of the valid argument forms. Instead we shall rely on a more intuitive test for validity. First, we need a test for *invalidity*, that is, a method of showing that the conclusion of an argument does *not* follow validly from the premises. The technique we shall adopt is known as the *method of counterexample*.

Finding a counterexample to an argument is a matter of imagining a *possible world* in which the premises are true and the conclusion false. The possibility of such a world shows the argument is invalid. You can think of possible worlds as variants of our actual world. For every way in which our actual world could have been different than it is, there exists a possible world that is different in this way. For example: The Iraq crisis might have led to the outbreak of the third world war; therefore, there exists a possible world in which the crisis led to the war. Reagan might not have been shot; therefore, there exists a possible world where he was not shot. Your parents might never have met; therefore, there is a world in which you were never born. The expression, 'possible world,' is just a fancy way of talking about the way things might be but actually are not. Possible worlds are easily constructed: whenever you imagine some possible alteration of the actual world, you construct a possible world that differs in the altered respect from the actual world. Finding a counterexample to a purportedly valid argument is a matter of constructing a possible world in which the premises of the argument come out true and the conclusion comes out false. This shows that it is possible for the premises to be true and the conclusion false.

You can give your imagination wings in thinking up such worlds and such examples, but you must not fly beyond the possible. A counterexample need not be an example of anything that has ever happened or of anything at all likely to happen. Just as long as the example clearly describes something possible, a clearly possible world in which the conclusion is false and the premises true, the argument's claim to validity is refuted. You can refute invalid arguments by the use of your imagination. Let us try this out. Consider the following argument:

All Communists are opposed to capitalism.

Jones is opposed to capitalism.

Therefore

Jones is a Communist.

It is perfectly easy to describe a counterexample that shows that the conclusion of this argument does not follow from the premises. Imagine a possible world in which Jones is a person who believes that all wealth and property should be owned and controlled by his family and passed on by inheritance. Thus, he rejects both capitalism and communism in favor of Jonesism, a heretofore unknown economic doctrine which states that everything should belong to the Joneses. What is described in this example is a possible world, and, supposing that both the first and second premises are true, it is an example in which the premises are true and the conclusion false. This counterexample shows that it is possible for the premises of the argument to be true and for the conclusion to be false. The argument has been shown to be invalid. Imagination triumphs over invalidity. The argument is destroyed.

The foregoing remarks illustrate the method of counterexample as it applies to arguments. It is essentially a method for establishing invalidity. We also have some tests for validity. If the argument is in one of the valid argument forms cited above, then it is a valid argument. Moreover, an argument may be shown to be valid by the repeated use of the argument forms. Yet some arguments are obviously valid, even though they are not in any of the argument forms discussed. For example, from a statement such as

Jill is criminal lawyer.

we may obviously validly conclude

Jill is a lawyer.

Since there are valid arguments not covered by any of the argument forms noted here, we need a procedure for deciding whether an argument is valid. Our procedure will be as follows. We will regard an argument as innocent until proven guilty. That is, we accept an argument as valid until we think of some counterexample to prove that it is invalid. Of course, this procedure must not be applied thoughtlessly or uncritically. We must ask ourselves if it is at all possible that this argument can be shown to be invalid by counterexample. We must stretch our imaginations across possible worlds. If, after careful reflection, we conclude that no such examples are to be found, we may tentatively accept the argument as valid. This is the procedure we will adopt.

EXERCISES

Find counterexamples to the following arguments. Use your imagination! Remember that a valid argument may have false premises, so an example showing a premise to be false does *not* constitute a counterexample showing the argument to be invalid.

1. If Smith is the thief, then Jones was involved in the crime.

   Smith is not the thief.

   Therefore

   Jones was not involved in the crime.

2. All people apply for well-paying jobs.

   Jane is a person who has a job she applied for.

   Therefore

   Jane has a well-paying job.

3. Social change always produces violence.

   Violence is bad.

Therefore

Social change is bad.

4. If a person knows something, then he must have an idea of it.

   Therefore

   All a person ever knows are his own ideas.

5. Scientists are constantly discovering that all sensations are caused by neurological processes.

   Therefore

   Sensations are nothing but physical processes.

6. I know for certain that I exist.

   I do not know for certain that any physical thing exists.

   Therefore

   I am not a physical thing.

7. No argument has been found to prove that God exists.

   Therefore

   God does not exist.

Question-begging arguments

Other features of an argument, some of which we have already noted, might lead us to reject an argument even though we consider it valid. For example, we might know that the premises of the argument are false. Another important reason for rejecting an argument is that we can see that the argument *begs the question*. An argument begs the question when a premise of the argument is simply a restatement of the conclusion.

Suppose a philosopher is arguing that no involuntary act should be punished. The following argument blatantly begs the question:

All acts that should be punished are voluntary.

Therefore

All acts that should be punished are not involuntary.

In this argument, the conclusion and the premise are different ways of saying the same thing. Thus, if the conclusion of the argument is what is at issue, then the argument begs the question.

Sometimes the premise which restates the conclusion in a question-begging argument is better disguised. Consider the following argument:

An act without the volition of the agent should not be punished.

An involuntary act is an act without the volition of the agent.

Therefore

An involuntary act should not be punished.

This argument is discovered to be question-begging when we ask what it means to say an act is "without the volition of the agent," because once we reflect on that curious expression, it becomes obvious that it means no more or less than "involuntary." Thus, the first premise of the argument, when we understand what it means, is seen to assert precisely the same thing as the conclusion.

An example of an argument that is *not* question-begging and that has the same conclusion is the following:

No involuntary act is wrong.

An act should not be punished unless it is wrong.

Therefore

No involuntary act should be punished.

Neither of these premises is a disguised reformulation of the conclusion. To say that an act is voluntary is quite different from saying that it is wrong, because many voluntary acts are perfectly all right. The premises of this valid argument might be challenged. But that is the only way that a disputant could escape the conclusion.

Further remarks on truth and validity

We have already noted that a valid argument may have false premises and thereby fail to establish the truth of its conclusion. However, it is equally essential to notice that an unsound argument, though it fails to establish the truth of its conclusion, may have a true conclusion nonetheless. Consequently, by showing that an argument is unsound because it has some false premises, one does not prove that the conclusion of the argument is false.

To illustrate these points let us consider two arguments, one a theistic argument and the other an atheistic argument, which, though valid, have contrary conclusions. The argument of the theist is the following:

The world exhibits conclusive evidence of design.

If the world exhibits conclusive evidence of design, then the world has a designer, who is God.

Therefore

The world has a designer, who is God.

The second argument is one an atheist might put to use.

If God exists, there is an all-powerful, all-knowing, and perfectly good being who created the world.

If there is an all-powerful, all-knowing, and perfectly good being who created the world, then the world is free of evil.

The world is not free of evil.

Therefore

God does not exist.

These two arguments have diametrically opposed conclusions. The conclusion of the first is inconsistent with the conclusion of the second; thus, one of the arguments must have a false conclusion. Both arguments are perfectly valid. The conclusion of each must be true *if* the premises are true. Therefore, one of the arguments, though valid, must be unsound. At least one of the premises of one of the arguments must be false; or both arguments might contain some false premises, and in that case both of these valid arguments would be unsound. This illustrates the fact that the unsound character of an argument does not show its conclusion to be false. One of the arguments might have a true conclusion even if *both* of them are unsound. By attacking an argument, we can only establish that it is unsound. We cannot thereby show that its conclusion is false. On the other hand, by presenting an argument that is sound and not question-begging, we can establish that the conclusion of the argument is true. Hence, constructing sound arguments, though more difficult than laying bare the fallacies of the arguments of others, is the task that yields the richer result.

Modality

Possibility, analyticity, and consistency

In defining the notion of validity, we often use the word 'impossible.' This term has many uses, but so far we have been concerned with a single use of this term. We have indicated this usage by speaking of logical impossibility. The intuitive idea of *logical* impossibility is as follows: Some things can be shown to be impossible by appealing to nothing more than logic and the meaning of terms. These things are logically impossible. It is logically impossible that God both exists and does not exist, for it is a mere truth of logic that nothing both exists and does not exist. To say that a statement describes something logically impossible is equivalent to saying that the statement is contradictory or inconsistent. The following are examples of contradictory statements:

1. Jones will pass Philosophy 100 and Jones will not pass Philosophy 100.

2. All soccer players are athletes but some soccer players are not athletes.

3. Any brother is a female.

Taken literally, none of these statements could possibly be true. But slightly different considerations are needed to show this in each case. The first statement is a perfectly explicit contradiction. The second conjunct of this conjunction denies with the word 'not' what the first conjunct asserts. The second statement, though obviously contradictory, differs from the first one. In the second statement, what is asserted in the first conjunct is not denied in the second conjunct *simply* by the use of the word 'not.' To show that the second statement is contradictory we need to consider the meaning of the words 'some' and 'all' as well as the word 'not.' These three words occur in the lexicon of the logician and are considered "logical words" because they appear in the valid argument forms of formal logic.

The third statement, though again contradictory, raises a somewhat different issue. To show that it is contradictory, one must, in addition to appealing to formal logic, also consider the meaning or definition of the term 'brother,' that is, one must know that a person to whom that term applies is by definition male and not female. Once this is clear, we can see that the statement asserts that some people both are and are not female. As a sheer matter of logic, this is impossible. However, the term 'brother' is not a term of formal logic; it is a descriptive term. Some philosophers deny that anything of philosophical importance turns on the distinction between terms of logic and descriptive terms, because they maintain that, in the last analysis, the distinction turns out to be arbitrary and artificial. For our purposes, it will suffice to notice that, in order to show that certain statements are contradictory, such as the preceding statements (2) and (3), we must consider the meaning or definition of key terms within the statement.

Necessity and analyticity

Statements that describe something logically impossible are contradictory and hence may be shown to be false by appealing to nothing more than logic and the meaning of terms. Other statements may be shown to be *true* by appealing to nothing more than logic and the meaning of terms. Such statements describe something logically necessary and are often called analytic statements.

For example, it is logically necessary that either God exists or God does not exist. The *denial* of any logically impossible statement is a logically necessary statement, and vice versa. For example, the statement

1a. It is not true both that Jones will pass Philosophy 100 and that Jones will not pass Philosophy 100.

is the denial of statement (1) and it is logically necessary.   Similarly, statements

2a. It is not true both that all soccer players are athletes and that some soccer players are not athletes.

and

3a. It is not the case that any brother is a female.

which are the denials of (2) and (3), respectively, are both logically necessary or analytic. The necessity of these statements can be made even more readily evident by reformulating them. For example, (1a) and (2a) are equivalent to

1b. Either Jones will pass Philosophy 100 or Jones will not pass Philosophy 100.

and

2b. Either all soccer players are athletes or some soccer players are not athletes.

respectively.   Fairly obviously, all of these statements are logically necessary.   The necessity of statements such as (2b) and (3a) could be made even more explicit by considering the definitions of the terms 'all,' 'some,' 'brother,' and 'female.' To understand precisely how this would be accomplished, we must consider the subject of definitions, which we shall do below. Before doing so, however, we shall consider a simple test for determining necessity and impossibility.

Possible worlds: A test of possibility and necessity
There is a test of logical possibility or impossibility and logical necessity that may prove useful and amusing. It is the imagination of possible worlds. To decide whether something is logically necessary, ask yourself whether you can imagine a possible world in which the statement would be false without changing the meaning of any of its words. Finding such a possible world is like finding a counterexample. It is a possible case that refutes the claim that something is logically necessary. To consider an example, you may think it obviously true that all thought occurs in brains. Perhaps this is true in our world. It is, however, easy to imagine a world in which there are beings, disembodied souls, for example, who think. You do not need to agree that there actually is any such world, only that it is possible, to refute the claim that it is logically necessary that all thought occurs in brains. Thus, even though it might be true in our world that all thought occurs in brains, it is not logically necessary that all

thought occurs in brains. We can imagine possible worlds in which beings think without brains. Heaven is one such imagined world, and, alas, so is hell.

Thus, we have a test, a kind of imagination experiment, to test the claim that some statement is logically necessary. If you can conceive of a possible world in which the statement is false, then it is not logically necessary. This is because the claim that something is logically necessary is equivalent to the claim that it is true in all possible worlds and false in none. The appeal to possible worlds is also useful when considering whether a statement is logically impossible. Try to imagine a possible world, one which might be quite different from the actual world, in which the statement is true. If you can think of such a world, then you will have refuted the claim that the statement is logically impossible. That is because the claim that a statement is logically impossible is equivalent to the claim that there is no possible world in which it is true. Hence, finding a possible world in which the statement is true refutes the claim that it is logically impossible. Consider the claim that it is logically impossible for cats to speak English. No cat in our world speaks English, of course, but we can imagine a world in which cats evolve in such a way that they can learn to speak, and that some of them speak English. Instead of meowing plaintively at the door, cats in this world say, "I would like to go outside now, please." It won't happen, but the imagined world is possible and amusing to contemplate. That suffices to refute the claim that it is logically impossible that cats should speak English.

Thus, you can test whether a statement is logically impossible by asking yourself whether you can think of a possible world in which the statement is true. If you can, then the statement is not logically impossible. Claims that some statement is necessary or impossible are implicitly claims about the truth or falsity of the statement in all possible worlds. The claim that a statement is logically necessary is equivalent to the claim that it is true in all possible worlds, while the statement that it is logically impossible is equivalent to the claim that it is false in all possible worlds. That is the reason the test works.

Thinking about possible worlds can afford you considerable pleasure because you can give full reign to your imagination rather than being confined to consideration of what the world is actually like. Be careful, however. Imagination can outrun the possible as well as the actual. If you imagine a world in which there are round squares conversing with numbers, you have imagined a world that is not possible. There is no possible world which contains round squares because such objects would be both round and not round, square and not square. If the world you imagine is implicitly contradictory in this way, it is not a possible world. So the test must be used with caution. It is nevertheless useful to philosophers as a standard method for determining what is called the *modality* of statements; that is, their necessity, impossibility or possibility.

May we appeal to possible worlds to show that a statement is logically necessary, or that a statement is logically impossible, rather than just attempting to refute such claims? If you have attempted to imagine possible worlds in which a statement is false, and after a judicious effort can find none, you may conclude tentatively that the statement is necessary. Similarly, if you have attempted to imagine possible worlds in which a statement is true, and after careful deliberation you can find none, you may conclude tentatively that the statement is impossible. You may only conclude *tentatively* that a statement is necessary or impossible, as a result of your search for a possible world; for the claim of necessity or impossibility is a claim about *all* possible worlds. You may, of course, overlook some possible world in your consideration. As you become a seasoned possible world explorer, you will become more trustworthy in discovering possible worlds. Consequently, your use of the test will become more trustworthy, and you will become a more skilled philosopher.

To determine whether a statement is logically necessary or logically impossible, it is important to understand the meaning of the statement as clearly as possible. Indeed, to determine whether you have described a counterexample or a possible world, you must often reflect on the meaning of the words in your description to insure that no contradiction is concealed in it. Definitions tell us what a word means, and so we shall now turn to a consideration of definitions.

Meaning

Definition
There are many ways to explain the meaning of a word. Sometimes one can do it by example, or by telling a story, or in any number of other ways. But one very important way to express the meaning of a word is to give a definition of it. When a word is defined, certain other words are supplied which together have the same meaning as the word to be defined. For example, we might define the word 'brother' by using the words 'male sibling,' that is, the word 'brother' is equal by definition to the words 'male sibling.'

Reportive definitions
Such a definition is a report of an ordinary meaning of a word. We shall accordingly call such definitions *reportive*. If a reportive definition is accurate, then one may substitute the defining words for the word defined in most sentences without changing the meaning of the sentence. For example, consider the sentence

Joan's brother will inherit the money.

Because the word 'brother' may be defined as 'male sibling,' we may substitute the latter for the former in the foregoing sentence and obtain

Joan's male sibling will inherit the money.

which is equivalent in meaning to the first. It is easy enough to see why such substitution should not alter the meaning of a sentence. If the only change we make in a sentence is to replace one word in the sentence with another having the same meaning, then we expect the meaning of the sentence to be unchanged.

In one case, however, substituting the definition of a word for the word itself in a sentence will change the meaning of the sentence. Philosophy is full of surprises. For example, in the true sentence

The word 'brother' has seven letters.

the word 'brother' occurs in quotation marks, in order to assert something about the word 'brother,' rather than about a brother. In cases where a word occurs in quotation marks, we may change the meaning of the sentence by substituting some other words for the word that occurs in quotation marks, even if the words substituted are equal by definition to the original word. For example, if we substitute 'male sibling' for 'brother' in the sentence above, we get

The word 'male sibling' has seven letters.

which is false and differs in meaning from the original. So we must not substitute the definition of a word for the word itself when the word occurs in quotation marks.

Definitions and possible worlds
How can we test the correctness of reportive definitions? Notice that the term 'brother' is equal by definition to 'male sibling' just in case the statement

Something is a brother if and only if it is a male sibling.

is analytic or logically necessary. That is, the definition is correct just in case there is no possible world with a brother who is not a male sibling or vice versa. We adopted a procedure for deciding whether certain things are logically impossible, namely, the method of counterexample or consideration of possible worlds. We employ the same method for testing reportive definitions. We said earlier that we will conclude tentatively that a statement is logically impossible if, after careful reflection, we can think of no possible world in which it is true. Similarly, here we shall conclude tentatively that a definition is satisfactory if, after careful reflection, we can think of no possible world in which either the defined word truly applies to something but the defining words do not, or vice versa. When we can think of such a possible world, then we have found a counterexample to the alleged definition, showing that we do not have an accurate reportive definition. If we can find no such possible world, then we may regard the definition as innocent until proven otherwise.

An example or two should help to clarify this. We shall not be able to find any possible world with a person who is a brother but not a male sibling, or vice versa. So the definition is correct. Suppose, however, someone foolishly alleges that we may define 'brother' simply as 'sibling.' The term 'sibling' applies to many people to whom the term 'brother' does not apply; namely, to all female siblings. Thus we have many counterexamples to this definition. When a definition is defective, in that the defined term does not apply to something to which the defining terms do apply, as in the case just considered, then the definition is said to be too broad. On the other hand, if someone alleges that we may define 'brother' as 'married male sibling,' so that the defining terms would not apply to things to which the defined term does apply—namely, unmarried brothers— then the alleged definition is said to be too narrow.

A definition may have the unhappy defect of being both too broad and too narrow. For example, if someone suggests we define 'brother' as 'tenth oldest sibling,' then this definition would be at once too narrow and too broad. Obviously, the definition is too narrow, because some brothers are not tenth oldest siblings. However, the definition is certainly also too broad. For, whatever the facts of life, it is at least possible that a tenth oldest sibling should be female and hence not a brother. Remember that to provide a counterexample, we need to find an example in a logically possible world. The example need not be of anything in the actual world. Thus, the definition of 'brother' as 'tenth oldest sibling' is both too broad and too narrow. An accurate reportive definition is one that is neither too broad nor too narrow.

EXERCISES

Find counterexamples to the following reportive definitions:

1. 'Religion' equals by definition 'a system of basic values.'

2. 'Communism' equals by definition 'a system in which the government controls the economy.'

3. 'Science' equals by definition 'the search for truth.'

4. 'Good newspaper' equals by definition 'a newspaper that prints all the news that's fit to print.'

5. 'Good music' equals by definition 'music of which the critics approve.'

6. 'Desirable' equals by definition 'something that is desired.'

7. 'Father' equals by definition 'a parent who is never pregnant.'

8. 'Water' equals by definition 'H_2O.'

Stipulative definitions

A second kind of definition, not to be confused with reportive definitions, plays a major role in philosophical writing. This kind of definition is not intended to be an accurate report of actual usage. Instead, it stipulates a special or technical usage. Sometimes, it is convenient and fruitful to use some word in a technical way for precision or clarification. In such cases, one may simply stipulate the special meaning assigned to the word. We shall call definitions of this kind *stipulative*.

Almost every book on a technical subject employs stipulative definitions. A book on chemistry defines 'mixture' and 'solution' in technical ways because it is useful to do so in chemistry. We have defined 'validity' in a technical way because it is useful to do so for our purposes. So long as stipulative definitions are not confused with reportive definitions, they are perfectly legitimate and useful conventions. It is important to recognize that a stipulative definition cannot be rejected by producing a counterexample. When a person stipulates that she is going to define a term in a certain way—for example, if she stipulates that she is going to define 'straight line' as 'the path of light'—then that is what she means by the term 'straight line.' By her stipulation, the defined term and the defining terms apply to exactly the same things. There are no counterexamples to stipulative definitions. Plainly, stipulation is a convenient device.

The redefinist fallacy: An abuse of stipulation

One way of misemploying stipulative definitions in an argument is so common and fallacious, however, that it deserves special consideration. The technique consists in making some controversial statement true, indeed, analytic, by stipulating a definition for some key term and then claiming to have shown the *original* statement to be true. When this happens, a stipulative definition is masquerading as a reportive one. We shall refer to this dubious procedure as the *redefinist fallacy*.

Here is an example of the fallacy. Philosophers have debated the thesis that every event has a cause. Defenders of this thesis are known as *determinists*. Suppose that a determinist argues that every event has a cause by first defining the word 'event' as 'occurrence having a cause,' and then concluding that every event has a cause. This strategy would hardly fool anyone. The determinist has, by stipulating a special meaning for the word 'event,' changed the meaning of the controversial thesis. As he is using the word 'event,' the thesis reduces by substitution to the trivially true statement that every occurrence having a cause has a cause. This was hardly the subject of controversy.

The antidote to this procedure is to show that, by changing the meaning of the statement, the stipulative definition has simply diverted the discussion from the controversial thesis at issue to some trivial truth that was never in question.

Meaning, definition, and reference

So far, we have considered one aspect of semantics, or theory of meaning, namely, definition. However, in addition to the definition of a word, it is often important also to consider its reference. Meaning and reference are not the same. A term may have a meaning that we may be able to define but not actually refer to anything that exists. For example, the term 'unicorn' is a term that we may define and which has a meaning but, if there are no unicorns, then the term 'unicorn' does not refer to anything that exists. Two expressions that have the same meaning, such as 'brother' and 'male sibling,' refer to the same objects. Two expressions may refer to the same existing objects, however, even if they do not have the same meaning. Suppose that humans and only humans laugh. Then the expressions 'human being' and 'laughing animal' refer to the same objects, even though the two expressions differ in meaning.

Sometimes, a philosophical dispute rests on the issue of whether two expressions refer to the same thing when they differ in meaning. Consider the claim of a materialist that mental events are cerebral events. One might be tempted to object that the expressions 'mental event' and 'cerebral event' differ in meaning, but this fact leaves the materialist a ready reply in terms of the distinction between meaning and reference. The materialist replies that the expressions 'mental event' and 'cerebral event' refer to the same thing even though they differ in meaning. The question whether, in fact, the two expressions refer to the same thing is controversial, and we shall return to this dispute in Chapter Four. Here we shall be satisfied to note that the difference in meaning leaves open the question of whether the terms refer to the same objects. Questions of sameness of reference extend beyond questions of meaning and definition.

Entailment

It is essential at this juncture to introduce a term that occurs very frequently in philosophical writing. It is the term 'entails.' It is used in a technical sense in philosophy to describe a relation between statements, and may be defined in terms of the notion of validity. To say that one or more statements entail some conclusion is equivalent to saying that the conclusion follows validly from those statements. More precisely, 'P entails Q' is equal by definition to 'Q is validly deducible from P.' Thus, for example, the statements

If all people are wicked, then no person is to be trusted.

and

All people are wicked.

together entail the statement

No person is to be trusted.

because the latter is validly deducible from the former. On the other hand, the statement

All people are wicked.

does not entail

No person is to be trusted.

because the latter is not validly deducible from the former. It is at least logically possible that some wicked people are to be trusted. We can imagine a possible world in which that is so. Try it!

The various terms that we have introduced are interrelated in a number of ways. We can explore some of these relations, while at the same time further elucidating the notion of entailment, by considering the various equivalent ways in which we might define the term 'entails.' By investigating these equivalent formulations, we shall be able to summarize and perhaps clarify the discussion up to this point.

The following are equivalent ways of defining entailment. 1. It is logically impossible that the premises should be true and the conclusion false. 2. There is no possible world in which the premises are true and the conclusion is false. 3. It would be contradictory to assert that the premises are true and the conclusion is false. 4. It is logically necessary that if the premises are true then the conclusion is also true. 5. In all possible worlds in which the premises are true, the conclusion is true as well. 6. The statement affirming that if the premises are true then the conclusion is true is analytic. All these ways of defining the term 'entails' are equivalent, given the way we have defined the terms 'logically impossible,' 'logically necessary,' 'contradictory,' and 'analytic.' It would be a useful exercise for you to explain precisely why this is so. Please try it.

The A Priori and the Empirical

Once we establish that an argument is valid, our attention must turn to the statements constituting the premises. How are we to determine whether they are true? The truth of some statements must be determined empirically, that is, by observation. Others may be determined without appeal to observation. These are called *a priori* statements. An a priori statement is sometimes described as a statement whose truth or falsity may be known prior to any appeal to experience. However, this characterization is not intended to suggest that experience is irrelevant to discovering or learning what the statement means. Once the meaning of an a priori statement is understood, however, no evidence drawn from observation is needed to justify the claim to know whether the statement is true or false. When we have learned enough to understand the meaning of such statements and the words contained therein, we can know whether they are true without any appeal to empirical evidence. Such statements are ones whose truth or falsity can be known a priori. The analytic and contradictory statements considered earlier on pp. 19-20 are all examples of such statements.

In contrast to a priori statements are all those statements that can be known to be true or false only on the basis of evidence obtained from observation. These are *a posteriori*, or empirical, statements. The following are examples of empirical statements:

1. I have a head.
2. The moon has craters.
3. Some mushrooms are poisonous.
4. All mules are sterile.

These statements are not only empirical but are also thought to be true. If you substitute the word 'tail,' 'vineyards,' 'apples,' and 'cows' for the terms 'head,' 'craters,' 'mushrooms,' and 'mules,' respectively, in the preceding four statements, you will obtain four empirical statements that are considered false.

A priori/a posteriori, analytic/synthetic, necessary/contingent

In this chapter we have learned of three ways to characterize statements that are of particular interest to the philosopher: each statement is (i) either necessary or contingent, (ii) either analytic or synthetic, (iii) either a priori or empirical (or a posteriori). We shall now take a brief look at how these three distinctions are interrelated.

First, notice that these three distinctions pertain to three distinct aspects of a statement. The necessary/contingent distinction concerns the *modal status* of a statement. To say that a statement is necessarily true is to say that it must be true or that it is true in all possible worlds. A statement is contingently true in case it just happens to be true because of the way the actual world is. The analytic/synthetic distinction concerns *the basis of a statement's truth or falsity*. To say that a statement is analytically true is to say that its truth is grounded solely in the meaning of its terms and the laws of logic. A statement is synthetically true just in case its truth is not grounded exclusively on the meaning of its terms and on the laws of logic. The a priori/a posteriori distinction concerns the *epistemic status* of a statement. To say that a statement is true a priori is to say that its truth can be known without appeal to experience. A statement is true a posteriori just in case its truth can only be known by relying on experience.

Having noted the differences between these three distinctions, consider their similarities. The most striking observation about these three distinctions is that they seem to divide up the set of statements into exactly the same subclasses. That is, we can use each one of the three distinctions to divide the set of statements into two classes: the one consists of necessary, analytic, and a priori statements; the other contains contingent, synthetic, and a posteriori statements. But this neat division of statements into two groups is not universally accepted. The most notable dissenters have been Immanuel Kant and, in our times, Saul Kripke. Kant argued that some statements are necessary, synthetic and a priori; for example, "Every event has a cause." Ever since, "the problem of the synthetic a priori" has occupied a fairly central position on the philosophical stage. Recently, Kripke argued that some statements are necessary, synthetic, and a posteriori. "Water is H_2O," "Heat is mean molecular energy," and other such theoretical identifications are examples of such a posteriori necessities.

Induction
Arguments that are not valid deductive arguments and that are not necessarily truth-preserving are traditionally called inductive arguments. When we consider the vast number of things we believe, we will soon discover that induction is the warrant of most of them. It is rare to elicit premises from observation from which one can validly deduce the truth of those a posteriori statements one believes. The deduction almost always fails, but the powers of human reason refuse to be restrained by the limits of deductive reasoning. When a deductive argument is not forthcoming to defend our beliefs, but the evidence seems strong nonetheless, then induction is called upon to meet our needs. Hence, we must obtain some understanding of this variety of argumentation.

Inductive cogency
In an inductive argument, the premises are evidence for the conclusion or hypothesis. Unlike a sound deductive argument, in which the premises entail the conclusion, the evidence of a sound inductive argument does not entail the hypothesis inferred from it. What, then, is a sound inductive argument? One condition of soundness is that the evidence must consist of true statements. This is a condition shared with sound deductive arguments. But if the evidence does not logically entail the hypothesis inferred from it, what virtue of inductive arguments corresponds to the condition of validity in the case of deductive ones?

Some philosophers doubt that there is any satisfactory answer and, consequently, repudiate the idea of inductive logic altogether. However, having noted the controversy that imbues this subject, we shall nevertheless attempt to formulate a second condition of soundness for inductive arguments.

Even if an inductive inference from evidence to hypothesis is not necessarily truth-preserving—that is, even if it is logically possible that the evidence is true and the conclusion false—such an inference is nonetheless sound if it is reasonable to think that the inference is truth-preserving; that is, if it is reasonable to think that the hypothesis is true if the evidence is. A sound deductive argument is one in which the premises are true and in which, if the premises are true, the conclusion must be true. A sound inductive argument is one in which the statement of the evidence is true and in which, if the premises are true, then it is reasonable to accept the hypothesis as true. So the second condition of soundness of an inductive argument, which we shall call inductive cogency, may be put as follows: If the evidence is true, it is reasonable to accept the hypothesis as true also. A sound inductive argument is one in which the statement of the evidence is true and which is inductively cogent.[1]

Truth and reasonable belief

The term 'reasonable' is used here in a special sense. Whether it is reasonable to think that a statement is true depends on one's purposes. It may make someone happy to think it is true that God exists, and, if his purpose is to obtain happiness by thinking such things, perhaps for this end it is reasonable for him to think it true that God exists. But this has nothing whatever to do with inductive arguments or the kind of reasonableness they require for their soundness. Instead, the kind of reasonableness required for a sound inductive argument must have truth and the avoidance of error as the only ends. A sound inductive argument must be one in which, if the statements of evidence are true, then accepting the inferred hypothesis as true is reasonable for the purposes of accepting true hypotheses and avoiding the acceptance of false ones.

It should, however, be noted that the ends of accepting true statements and avoiding the acceptance of false ones are somewhat at odds. For the simplest way to avoid accepting false statements is not to accept any statement. By so doing, one accepts nothing false. On the other hand, to accept what is true, the simplest way is to accept all statements, because by so doing one will accept every true statement. Of course, the trouble with accepting all statements, even if one could do it, is that one would be accepting as many false statements as true ones. Similarly, the trouble with accepting no statements is that one thereby forgoes the chance of accepting true statements. The problem is to strike a balance between

---

1. This account of induction diverges from but is indebted to Isaac Levi, *Gambling with Truth: An Essay on Induction and the Aims of Science*. (New York: Alfred A. Knopf, Inc., and London: Routledge & Kegan Paul, Ltd., 1967.)

these two ends of accepting what is true and, at the same time, avoiding acceptance of what is false.

Cogency and competition

An inductive argument thus always runs the risk of failing to preserve truth, that is, of leading to error. What makes the risk of error worth taking is the chance of accepting a hypothesis which is true instead of some competing hypothesis which is false. We may obtain an improved account of inductive cogency by noting the importance of the concept of competition among hypotheses as a feature of induction. Whether it is reasonable to accept a statement as true depends on what other statements it competes with, as well as on the probability of the statement on the evidence.

Let us consider an inductive argument that once led philosophers and scientists to the conclusion that the universe was designed by some agent. To appreciate the inductive reasoning leading to this conclusion, recall that before the theory of evolution was conceived, the existence of human beings constituted a fundamental intellectual problem. Even if one had theories of matter adequate to account for many features of the physical universe, the existence of human beings remained puzzling. The existence of animals presented a striking contrast to inert matter, but, although some philosophers were willing to look upon animals as complex physical mechanisms, to draw the same conclusion concerning human beings was repugnant. Perhaps the principal reason for this aversion was the existence of conscious thought and rational cogitation. A philosopher who willingly rejected the idea that lower animals think and reason could not very well deny that he himself was thinking and reasoning while engaged in those very activities. So the existence of humans, thinking and reasoning beings, constituted a problematic phenomenon indeed. Naturally, the question arose how to explain it.

We can frame this question by asking what hypothesis it would be reasonable to accept as true by induction from the evidence. To some thinkers, there seemed to be only two competing hypotheses. One was that human beings came to exist as a sheer matter of cosmic chance or accident. The other was that human beings came to exist as a result of some design or plan. Hence, as these thinkers considered the matter, the following two hypotheses were the competitors for acceptance in this context:

1. Human beings came to exist by chance.

2. Human beings came to exist by design.

Not surprisingly, given that these were the hypotheses from which to choose, the second rather than the first was considered more probable on the evidence. It seemed extremely unlikely that anything so remarkably intricate and complex as a human being should come to exist by chance. Indeed, the intricate and complex organization of human beings appeared strikingly analogous to the intricate and complex characteristics of objects designed by human beings. This argument by analogy, which we shall consider again later (Chapter Five), was inductive, of course, but it was also based on a rather limited set of alternative hypotheses. With competition limited in this way, it is not at all surprising that some of the most acute and critical thinkers of the past regarded hypothesis (2) as the one to be inductively inferred from the evidence.

Now, the astute reader may have noticed that, strictly speaking, a person who considers hypotheses (1) and (2) should, to be completely judicious, consider one other hypothesis as well, namely, the hypothesis that neither (1) nor (2) is correct. Thus, we could also consider the following negative hypothesis:

3. Human beings came to exist by something other than chance or design.

The omission of this hypothesis from the competition was justified because of its uninformative nature. It offers no explanation at all of the observed phenomena. Though it may well be true, if one is seeking a hypothesis to explain the existence of man, hypothesis (3) does not compete for that role.

A much smaller proportion of philosophers and scientists would today consider cogent the inductive inference of hypothesis (2) from the evidence. But one reason for this is that today we do not consider these two hypotheses to be the only competing alternatives. There is of course the evolutionary hypothesis

4. Human beings came to exist by evolution.

Here it is most important not to confound the informative hypothesis (4) with the uninformative hypothesis (3). Hypothesis (3) is logically implied by (4), but the justification of (3) depends entirely on the cogency of inductive argument in favor of (4). Once the evolutionary hypothesis was conceived, the competition included not only (1) and (2) but also (4). Since many scientists and philosophers, perhaps most, would consider hypothesis (4) to be the most probable of the competing three, they consider the induction of that hypothesis from the evidence to be cogent.

It is important to notice the difference between hypothesis (3) and hypothesis (4). The former is negative and does not explain the phenomenon in question, the existence of human beings. The latter, by contrast, offers a very sophisticated and comprehensive theory, the theory of evolution, as an explanation for that phenomenon. For that reason, a person who would not consider hypothesis (3) as a competitor would consider hypothesis (4) to be a competitor, and, indeed, a successful competitor. The preceding arguments lead to a number of important conclusions. First, the cogency of an inductive argument depends, in part, on what other statements the hypothesis of the argument competes with. Second, what statements a hypothesis competes with itself depends on what hypotheses have been conceived and, in this way, on the context of inquiry.

Inductive cogency as successful competition

We conclude that inductive cogency depends essentially on the evidential and conceptual context of reasoning. We can give a definition of inductive cogency in terms of the notion of competition, as follows: An inductive argument from evidence to hypothesis is inductively cogent if and only if the hypothesis is that hypothesis which, of all the competing hypotheses, has the greatest probability of being true on the basis of the evidence. Thus, whether it is reasonable to accept a hypothesis as true, if the statements of evidence are true, is determined by whether that hypothesis is the most probable, on the evidence, of all those with which it competes.

The conclusion we have reached supplies us with a methodology for checking the cogency of an inductive argument. Confronted with an inductive argument, one should pose two critical questions:

1. What statements does the hypothesis of the argument compete with?

2. Is the hypothesis more probable than all of those hypotheses with which it competes?

Only if the answer to the second question is affirmative may we consider the argument cogent. Moreover, there is no automatic test or formal rule by which one provides an answer to either of these questions. To answer the first, we must make use of all the intellectual resources at our command. The failure to consider some competitor for a hypothesis may lead us to accept some hypothesis it is quite unreasonable to accept. However, if we have diligently searched for competitors and seriously considered the probability of each, then we may, tentatively, consider an argument inductively cogent when the conclusion is the most probable of all the competitors we can conceive.

The search for a more probable competitor to disprove inductive cogency is like the search for a counterexample to disprove deductive validity. The failure to find a counterexample does not prove there is none. Similarly, the failure to find a more probable competing hypothesis does not prove there is none. Moreover, these methods of refutation are no more effective than the person who employs them. In the end, when deciding on whether to accept an argument as deductively valid or inductively cogent, we shall depend not on any automatic procedure, but on our intelligence and integrity. This is not a defect. For all progress in science and the humanities depends ultimately on these elements. No methodology transcends or overrides the human intellect.

EXERCISES

(Note: Exercises marked with an * are thought-problems not explicitly solved in the text.)

1. Of what does an argument consist? What is a valid argument? What is a valid argument form? How is a valid argument derived from a valid argument form? What is a sound argument?

2. Consider the following argument:

    Validity is of no importance. An argument can have false premises and still be valid. In fact, it can have false premises and a false conclusion, yet still be valid. Therefore, there is no connection between truth and validity. Thus, validity is irrelevant to truth and therefore to philosophical inquiry.

    How would you reply to this argument? Which statements of the argument are correct and which incorrect?

3. How does the method of counterexample serve as a test of invalidity? Why does a counterexample show an argument to be invalid? Why is an argument valid if there are no counterexamples to it? What procedure is proposed for deciding whether to accept an argument as valid? What is the relevance of considering possible worlds? Do you think it is a sensible procedure? Why?

4. What is a question-begging argument? Why are they to be eschewed?

5. Can an unsound argument have a true conclusion? Why? Can an unsound but valid argument have a true conclusion? Why?

6. Consider the following argument:

    Theists and theologians have offered any number of arguments to prove the existence of God. However, none of these is sound. Some have false premises, and others are invalid, but all have one or the other of these defects. Therefore, we may validly conclude that God does not exist.

    Is this argument sound? Why? Suppose that all the statements preceding the conclusion are true. Would the argument be sound, given that supposition? Why?

7. What is a logically impossible statement? What is a logically necessary statement? In what way are these two kinds of statements related? How are impossibility and necessity related to truth and falsity in possible worlds? Which kind of statement is contradictory and which is analytic?

8. What is a reportive definition? What principle of substitution is warranted by a reportive definition? How must such a principle be qualified? What procedure may we adopt for testing definitions? When is a definition too broad and when is it too narrow? Can a definition have both of these defects? How?

9. What is a stipulative definition? Why cannot a stipulative definition be rejected by finding a counterexample? How is a stipulative definition misemployed in the redefinist fallacy? What is that fallacy and how is it to be dealt with?

10. Consider the following argument:

Some people contend that socialism is a system that helps the poor. However, the meaning of the word 'socialism' is quite different from the meaning of the words 'system that helps the poor.' Therefore, the former word does not refer to the same thing as the latter group of words. We may thus conclude that socialism is not a system that helps the poor.

What is the matter with this argument? Does the sentence beginning with the word 'therefore' follow from the sentence that precedes it? Why?

11. How is the word 'entails' defined? What alternative ways are there of defining this word? Why are all these definitions equivalent?

12. What is an a priori statement? What is an a posteriori statement?

13. What is an inductive argument? How is induction distinguished from deduction? How is inductive cogency defined? How does it differ from validity?

14. What method for testing the cogency of inductive argument is proposed? How are the concepts of competition and probability embodied in the method? How can inductive cogency be disproved?

15.* Consider the following argument:

What matters in philosophy is that one obtains the truth. If your opinion is true and correct, then it matters little whether you can defend it with argument or reply to the arguments of others. On the other hand, if your opinion is false, then you will only be compounding your errors by defending your opinion with argument and attacking the arguments of more enlightened persons who have the truth. Thus argument is irrelevant to philosophical inquiry.

Discuss this argument.

16.* Has the notion of competition introduced in the text been adequately characterized? Can analytic statements be competitors of contingent statements? Can self-contradictory statements be competitors? If two statements compete with one another, should they be related to one another in some fashion? For instance, should they contradict one another?

17.* It would seem possible for more than one statement among those that compete to come out tied for being most probable among the competitors. Is this a problem that needs to be dealt with? How should it be handled if it is a problem?

Suggestions for Further Reading

Textbooks on logic

Bergmann, Merrie, James Moor, and Jack Nelson, *The Logic Book* (New York: Random House, 1980).

Black, Max, *Critical Thinking* (Englewood Cliffs: Prentice-Hall, Inc., 1962).

Church, Alonzo, *Introduction to Mathematical Logic I* (Princeton: Princeton University Press, 1956).

Clark, R. and P. Welsh, *Introduction to Logic* (New York: Van Nostrand Reinhold Company, 1962).

Copi, Irving, *Introduction to Logic*, 5th Edition (New York: Macmillan Publishing Co., Inc., 1978).

Mates, Benson, *Elementary Logic* (New York: Oxford University Press, 1965).

Quine, W. V. O., *Methods of Logic* (New York: Holt, Rinehart & Winston, Inc., 1959).

Salmon, Wesley C., *Logic*, 2nd Edition (Englewood Cliffs: Prentice-Hall, Inc., 1973).

Skyrms, Brian, *Choices and Chance: An Introduction to Inductive Logic*, 2nd Edition (Belmont: Dickenson Publishing Company, 1975).

Suppes, Patrick, *Introduction to Logic* (New York: Van Nostrand Reinhold Company, 1960).

Contemporary texts and collections

Bradley, R. and N. Swartz, *Possible Worlds: An Introduction to Logic and Its Philosophy* (Indianapolis: Hackett, 1979).

Copi, Irving M. and James A. Gould, *Readings on Logic* (New York: Macmillan Publishing Co., Inc., 1972).

Gorovitz, Samuel and Ron G. Williams, *Philosophical Analysis* (New York: Random House, Inc., 1965).

Lehrer, Adrienne and Keith, *Theory of Meaning* (Englewood Cliffs: Prentice-Hall, Inc., 1970).

Quine, W. V. O., *From a Logical Point of View* (New York: Harper & Row, 1953).

Russell, Bertrand, *The Problems of Philosophy* (New York: Oxford University Press, 1912).

Sleigh, Robert, *Necessary Truth* (Englewood Cliffs: Prentice-Hall, Inc., 1970).

TWO

The Problem of Knowledge and Skepticism

ABOUT SKEPTICISM

We briefly confronted the skeptic and felt her power in Chapter One. A skeptic denies that we know what we think we do. She may, however, limit her skepticism to some vulnerable domain. For example, most people suppose that they have knowledge by means of the senses. They suppose that they see, touch, feel, hear, smell, and taste things, and that they thus know of the existence of these things by means of sensory perception. You would maintain, prior to your exposure to philosophy, that you see a book now and know there is a book before you. You would claim to have gained knowledge of the existence of the book, as well as its shape and color, on the basis of visual perception. But do you really know these things? "Yes," you say? Skeptics deny that you know. If you are going to become a philosopher, you must follow the skeptical turn and decide on its merits.

The Motives of Skepticism
You may well wonder what motive a philosopher might have for denying that we know what we think we do. The most direct motivation arises from theory and speculation. When philosophical inquiry leads a philosopher to

conclusions that conflict with what people ordinarily claim to know, she will be inspired to undermine adverse claims, to clear the way for her theory. Plato was a speculative philosopher who arrived at the conclusion that reality, the proper object of knowledge, could not be perceived by the senses because it consisted of intelligible objects apprehended by the intellect.[1] These intelligible objects included the objects of mathematics (numbers, triangularity, and congruence), of morality (justice, goodness, and honor), and other equally abstract items. He argued that these intelligible objects were unchanging and eternal, in contrast to the constantly changing and evanescent objects of sense experience. The objects of sense experience are, he alleged, like mere shadows of the reality of intelligible forms. Hence Plato was led to deny that we have knowledge of sensory objects such as tables, stars, or even specks of dirt. His skepticism was an ingredient in his speculative theory concerning the intelligible nature of reality.

Current forms of skepticism often emerge from scientific theory and speculation. For example, light takes a number of years to reach us from a distant star. When we view the sky on a clear evening and think that we are seeing a star as it is at the moment of viewing, and, consequently, know at least something about how the star now looks, we are quite mistaken. The star might no longer exist at all, because what we see now is light that emanated from the star a number of years ago. Now, reflecting on this fact, Bertrand Russell noted that even nearby objects, say a chair a few feet in front of one, are also seen as a result of light waves striking the eye, and those light waves take some time to travel from the object to the surface of the eye. Hence, Russell argued, if we suppose that we are seeing the object just as it is and that we know something about how the object now looks, we may certainly be mistaken. Even in that very short time required for the light emanating from the object to reach the eye, the object may undergo some change or even disappear altogether. Russell concludes that we do not know that the objects are the way they look, that the chair is black, for example, or, for that matter, that the objects we think we see now exist.[2] Just as an object can change in the short time it takes for the light waves to reach our eyes, so the object can cease to exist altogether in that time. Thus, a scientific theory, one concerning light waves and the physiology of perceptual processes, provides the premises for skeptical argumentation.

Another instance of scientific theory leading to skeptical conclusions is to be found in the writings of Wilfrid Sellars. Sellars thinks that our commonsense convictions conflict with scientific conclusions concerning

---

1. Plato, *The Republic*, 476-79, 504-09, 509-11. (Page numbers are the marginal numbers commonly given in Plato's texts.)

2. Bertrand Russell, *The Analysis of Mind* (London: Allen & Unwin, 1921), 124-36.

the color of objects. Suppose we have a transparent pink glass cube which appears to be pink through and through. We ordinarily would take the cube to be a homogeneous pink cube. Not so, according to Sellars. Science tells us the cube is made up of colorless atoms. There is no characteristic of the cube, considered at the atomic level, that the cube has homogeneously, through and through. Because of the explanatory power of science, Sellars concludes that we should accept atomic theory and reject the idea that the cube is homogeneously pink, through and through.[3] Thus Sellars would be led to reject the commonsense knowledge claim concerning the homogeneous color of objects.

Whether or not one agrees with these arguments, they illustrate a fundamental feature of most skeptical philosophy, namely, that it receives support from speculation concerning other matters. We have mentioned philosophical and scientific theories that guided philosophers down the path to skepticism. But religious theories have evoked skeptical machinations as well. A fundamentalist, or anyone who believes in the revelation of truth from supernatural sources, may be led to reject commonsense claims to knowledge. For example, if one believes from biblical interpretation that the earth has existed for only a few thousand years, one will be led to reject for the sake of faith those assumptions, which most people suppose they know, sustaining the conclusion that the earth has existed for millions of years.

Skepticism and Dogmatism
However, skepticism is worth considering quite apart from theories that serve the ends of speculation, whether philosophical, scientific, or religious. Whether we are skeptics or not is likely to influence the way we discourse and how we inquire after truth. If a person says that he knows the answer to some question or problem, and then tells us what he knows, his claim to know is intended to end debate on the topic. If we are wondering whether all liquids expand when they freeze, as water does, or whether that is a special feature of water, and someone claims to know that this is a special feature of water and that other liquids do not behave in a similar manner, he is making a claim intended to terminate inquiry in this matter. Often we welcome relief from uncertainty, but it is worth asking whether such relief from doubt is philosophically warranted.

Once we note that a knowledge claim is intended to terminate inquiry, we may become wary of such claims, for fear of falling prey to uncritical conviction; in other words, to dogmatism. Knowledge claims are dogmatic, though we may not notice this, perhaps because we like to think ourselves enlightened and undogmatic in our own knowledge claims. But are we? Once we raise fundamental issues, dogma and knowledge become

---

3. Wilfrid F. Sellars, *Science, Perception and Reality* (NY: Humanities, 1963), 121-23.

inextricably intertwined.   Our convictions concerning the source of knowledge, how we know, are dogmatic. At one time it was dogma that knowledge comes from revelation. A person accepting such dogma might think she knows that someone is possessed by the devil, by observing alterations in her personality and behavior that constitute demonic possession. Starting from different assumptions, we might deny that such people observed demonic possession. Notice how dogmatic our competing claims are! We begin with a different dogma, crudely put, that empirical science rather than revelation is the source of knowledge. Having adopted that dogma, we reject those knowledge claims based on competing assumptions, those of revelation, for example. So which dogma is correct? The religious one? The scientific one? To ask is to enter the debate with the skeptic, who answers with a question, "Who knows?" Her smile reveals her conclusion. No one knows.

In an effort to understand our empiricist dogma that knowledge of the world is gleaned from perception and observation, we shall study skepticism with regard to the senses. We suppose that we know of the existence and characteristics of objects by means of the senses, by perception. Perceptual belief is the best source of knowledge, or so we dogmatically assume. But do our perceptual beliefs constitute knowledge? The skeptic denies this. She does not deny that we have perceptual beliefs. She does not even deny that some them are true. She denies that we know that our perceptual beliefs are true. Her denial is an affirmation of the openness of inquiry. If she is right, no one can stop inquiry with a dogmatic claim to know. We lose something, she reassures us, if we become skeptics, namely, our dogmatism and the illusion of finality. We gain something, freedom to inquire unbound by dogmatism. We cannot, however, total up the losses and gains to decide whether to become skeptics. We must reflect on the reasons and arguments of the skeptic. She is ready to examine her doctrine in the cool light of reason. Let us reason with her.

An Analysis of Knowledge

Before examining arguments for skepticism, and those concerning perceptual knowledge in particular, let us consider briefly what is meant by saying that a person knows something. Our strategy is to begin by defining knowledge in line with the assumptions of common sense. Starting with this conception of knowledge, we shall turn to the claims of the skeptic. If a sound skeptical argument can be built on this conception of knowledge, then the skeptic will have shown that there is no knowledge in the ordinary sense of the word. What, then, is the ordinary sense of the word 'know'? To answer this clearly, we must first specify more precisely what is being asked, for the word 'know' has a great variety of uses and meanings. For example, a person might be said to know how to play golf, she might also be said to know Paris, and finally, she might be said to know that the University of San Marcos is the oldest university in the Western Hemisphere. The latter use of the word 'know' is the one most directly related to the concept of truth and is the familiar object of skeptical criticism. To say that a person knows that the University of San Marcos is the oldest university in the Western Hemisphere is equivalent to saying that she knows it is true that San Marcos is the oldest in the Western Hemisphere. This sort of knowledge is sometimes called theoretical or discursive. However, the distinguishing feature of such knowledge is that truth is its object: it is knowledge of the truth.

Such knowledge claims may be formulated either by saying a person knows that X, or by saying he knows it is true that X. These two ways of stating such knowledge claims are equivalent. Thus truth is a necessary condition of such knowledge; if a person knows that something is so, then it must be true that it is so. A person may claim to know something is true when it is not; but then, contrary to his claim, he does not know. He is ignorant of the truth. For example, if a person claims to know that Harvard University is the oldest college in the United States, he would be mistaken, because this is not true. He does not know what he claims to know. We have now seen that one necessary condition of a person knowing something is that it be true. Another necessary condition is that a person must at least believe the thing in question. Obviously, a person does not know that something is true if he does not even believe it is true.

May we then simply equate knowledge with true belief? Absolutely not! To see why not, consider a person who has a hunch and thus believes that the final score of next year's Army-Navy football game will be a 21–21 tie. Moreover, suppose that the person is quite ignorant of the outcome of past contests and other relevant data. Finally, imagine that, as a mere matter of luck, he happens to be right. That it is a mere matter of luck is illustrated by the fact that he often has such hunches about the final scores of football games and is almost always wrong. His true belief about the outcome of the Army-Navy game should not be counted as knowledge. It was a lucky guess and nothing more.

How is knowledge to be distinguished from mere true belief? Most philosophers, skeptics included, have argued that whether true belief is to be counted as knowledge depends on how well justified the person is in believing what he does. The person who has a true belief about the Army-Navy game is quite unjustified, for he really has no reason or justification for believing the score will be a 21–21 tie. On the other hand, a person watching the game, who hears the final gun as play ends, is completely justified in that belief and hence knows that the final score is twenty-one points apiece. Thus, we may assume that a person lacks knowledge unless he is justified, and indeed completely justified, in believing what he does. Moreover, what will ordinarily determine whether a person is well enough justified is the quality of the evidence that forms the basis for his belief.

The evidence of the person in the stands watching the game is quite adequate, whereas the evidence of the person who guesses is exceedingly paltry.

A further qualification is required. A person may be quite well justified in what she believes, even though her justification is based on some false assumption.[4] For example, if a person parks her car in a public parking lot for a few hours, she is quite well justified, when she returns to her car and does not observe any alteration, in assuming that the engine of the car remains under the hood. Of course, if someone has stolen the engine while she was away, then her belief that there is an engine under the hood falls short of knowledge simply because it is untrue that the engine is there. However, imagine that after the engine was stolen a friend came along, and, noticing the engine had been removed, arranged to have it replaced with another before the owner returned, so as to relieve her of the agony of finding her engine stolen. Then the owner will be quite correct in her belief that there is an engine under the hood of her car when she returns. Moreover, she is quite well justified in this belief as well. However, the owner's belief will be based on a false assumption, namely, that the engine that was under the hood of her car when she left remains there now. This false assumption leads her to the true conclusion that there is an engine under her hood. But since the only justification she has for believing this is based on the false assumption, we should not say that she knows that there is an engine under the hood of her car.

We must require not only that a person be well justified in what he or she believes, but also that his or her justification not depend essentially on any false assumption; otherwise, a person cannot be said to know. This qualification may be articulated in a variety of ways. We shall require that a person be completely justified in believing something, in order to know what he or she believes is true; and also that his or her justification must be undefeated by any false assumption on which it essentially depends.

We conclude that a person knows something just in case his or her belief is true, completely justified, and the justification is undefeated. A skeptic building her case on this analysis of knowledge may argue, concerning things people commonly assume they know, either (1) that we do not even believe those things, (2) that they are not true, (3) that we are not completely justified in believing them, or (4) that our justification, though complete, is defeated by some false assumption on which it essentially depends. The most promising place for the skeptic to get a foothold is condition (3). A skeptic who wishes to defend some very extensive form of skepticism, for example, by contending we do not know that any of our perceptual beliefs are true, will do best to argue that condition (3) in the analysis is never satisfied by such beliefs. "Are we completely justified in

---

4. Edmund Gettier, "Is Justified True Belief Knowledge?" *Analysis* 23 (1963), 121-23.

our perceptual beliefs?" The skeptic says, "No!" and sets out to convince her dogmatic detractors of the merits of her skepticism.

Dogmatism and Epistemism

Earlier in this chapter we spoke of different forms of dogmatism and of different dogmas. A *dogma*, as we are using the term, is an assumption one makes uncritically, with no attempt at reflective justification, and which one feels is perfectly evident, something which stands in no need of serious examination. The unquestioned assumption that we gain knowledge of the existence and characteristics of ordinary objects by means of perception is a dogma.

A person who thinks we get knowledge of objects by means of perception need not be a dogmatist, however. Such a person might well be quite critical and reflective about this assumption and maintain, in fact, that good arguments support it. Let us coin a new word for such a person and call him an *epistemist*. We will say that an epistemist (e-pis-tem-ist) regarding perceptual knowledge is one who not only accepts the claim that we gain knowledge of objects by means of perception, but who also thinks that there are good reasons in favor of this claim. The skeptic, by contrast, insists that there are good, indeed better, reasons for denying the assumption. We will understand the following discussion as a dispute between the epistemist and the skeptic.

SKEPTICISM WITH REGARD TO THE SENSES

We shall now examine the skeptical argument with respect to perceptual belief. By so doing we shall consider seriously and at length a challenge to one of the most fundamental assumptions of the current intellectual milieu, namely, that we obtain knowledge of the world by means of sense experience, by observation and perception. The initial stages of the argument may strike you as weird and disorienting. This is to be expected. When our fundamental assumptions and presuppositions are brought before the court of evidence and pronounced unfit, we feel abandoned in our uncertainty with nothing to sustain us. We may be inclined to repudiate the court as unjust. Such a response is natural but unwarranted. A skeptic claiming that our perceptual beliefs fall short of knowledge need not suggest that they be abandoned. As long as those beliefs remain more probable than those with which they compete, it is reasonable enough to maintain them. But if skepticism wins the day, then we must regard even those quite reasonable perceptual beliefs with an open mind and generously expose them to criticism and debate. Doing so, though initially discomforting, like exposing one's flesh to the elements, soon becomes routine and, moreover, provides an invigorating sense of well-being. With these words of reassurance, we embark on our quest for skepticism with regard to the senses.

Our perceptual beliefs about what we hear, touch, and see are based on evidence. This might not seem obvious at first, because such evidence is rarely formulated in words. We do not ordinarily justify our perceptual beliefs—for example, my belief that I see a red apple in my hand—by appealing to any other belief or statement. However, these beliefs are not without evidence. It is the unformulated evidence of our senses, the direct and immediate evidence of sensory experience, of the way things appear, that seems to justify our perceptual beliefs. For example, imagine a person who believes that she sees a red apple. We generally assume that what justifies this belief is the visual experience she is then having, the visual appearance of a red apple. We do not ordinarily formulate and state such "evidence," because we have no reason to do so. We do assume that this "evidence" justifies our perceptual beliefs, however. The question we must now consider is whether this "evidence" provides complete justification for these beliefs.

The Skeptical Argument from the Relativity of Observation

One argument for skepticism is based on the relativity of the observer. Suppose some object stimulates my sense organs, and I see something red. It might happen that the object also stimulates the sense organs of someone else, who sees an object of a different color, for example, green. Imagine that the object is in fact white, but that there is a transparent red plastic shield between the object and me, and a green one between the object and the other observer. If neither of us knows of the presence of these shields, then each of us might be entirely convinced that he sees the object's true color.

This rather contrived example has quite general implications. For if we pay close attention to what we see, it becomes plausible to claim that no two people see the same object in exactly the same way. For example, consider a square envelope. Pay very close attention to what you see when you look at this object. If the envelope remains stationary while you move about, or is moved while you remain stationary, what you see will constantly change. When you see the envelope from one angle you will see something perfectly square, but as you move away to one side and see the envelope from a more oblique angle you will see something that is not quite square. Thus two people seeing the envelope from different angles will not see the same thing. These are familiar facts of perceptual experience. How can they be used to serve the purposes of the skeptic?

The example of the envelope may be taken to show that at least one of the two persons involved does not see the envelope as it really is. The envelope cannot be both perfectly square and not square at one and the same time. Thus, if each person comes to have a perceptual belief, one to the effect that she sees some square object and the other to the effect that she sees an object that is not square, then at least one of them will be mistaken. Hence, at least one of them will not know, on the basis of his or her perception, that his or her perceptual belief is true. One person may have a true belief. Thus, the person who views the envelope from directly above and sees a square object, will form the true perceptual belief that he sees a square object. The fact that perception is relative, however, that what one sees depends on a variety of constantly changing factors (position of the observer, lighting, condition of the observer, and the like), is enough to show that any perceptual belief may be a mistake, for our perceptual beliefs are often in error.

To obtain the skeptical conclusion, we need another premise: that if a person knows something and is thus completely justified in believing it, he or she cannot possibly be mistaken in his or her belief. If a person says that he or she believes something but admits that he or she could be mistaken, then he or she has thereby admitted that he or she is not completely justified in his or her belief and does not know that what he or she believes is true. Similarly, if a person could be mistaken, then the person lacks knowledge about the matter. Even when a person is not mistaken, if the person could be mistaken, the person does not know what they believe is true. Thus a person knows something only if the person could not be mistaken.

The relevance of the preceding comments is straightforward. We noted that sometimes a person's perceptual belief will be in error, in part because of the relativity of perception. When in error, surely, a person does not gain perceptual knowledge. This shows that it is possible for a person to be mistaken in his or her perceptual belief. Since people are, in fact, sometimes mistaken in such beliefs, then clearly it is possible for them to be mistaken in those beliefs. Moreover, we are perfectly justified in arguing from the premise that people are sometimes mistaken when they believe what they see (or otherwise perceive) to the general conclusion that this is always possible. For either the premise that a person has a perceptual belief that he perceives a thing with a certain sensible quality, such as being red or round, entails that there is a thing with that quality or it does not. Because we sometimes make mistakes in perceptual beliefs of this sort, obviously the entailment does not hold. If the entailment does not hold, then it is always at least logically possible that a person should have a perceptual belief and that the belief is nonetheless mistaken.

Having established the preceding points, we may now reconstruct the argument for skepticism. Whenever a person believes what he or she sees, it is possible that he or she is mistaken. If a person knows something, then it is not possible that he or she is mistaken. Therefore, when a person believes what he or she sees, he or she does not know it. This conclusion is correctly derived from the premises antecedently defended.

Moreover, the argument employed to show that no one ever knows an object to have some sensible quality, one perceived by the senses, can be cogently generalized to show that no one even knows that the object itself exists. For, just as we sometimes see something as having some sensible quality, when it does not have that quality, so we sometimes see some sensible object when it does not even exist. Hallucinations are experiences of this sort. A person who has delirium tremens, or one who has taken a heavy dose of LSD, sometimes sees things—for example, pink rats—when there are no such things. Thus a person might believe that what he or she sees exists and be completely mistaken in this belief. Seeing an object does not constitute knowing that that object exists. A person who knows something cannot be mistaken.

Summary of the argument
We may now formulate an argument for skepticism as follows:

1. We are sometimes mistaken in our perceptual beliefs.

2. If we are sometimes mistaken in our perceptual beliefs, then it is always logically possible that our perceptual beliefs are false.

3. If it is always logically possible that our perceptual beliefs are false, then we never know that any of our perceptual beliefs are true.

Therefore

4. We never know that any of our perceptual beliefs are true.

This conclusion is validly deduced from the three premises which were just defended.

An epistemist objection to the second premise:
Some actual errors don't prove that we could always be mistaken
The skeptic has illicitly adopted the premise

2. If we are sometimes mistaken in our perceptual beliefs, then it is always logically possible that our perceptual beliefs are false.

In those cases in which our perceptual beliefs are false, it is obviously possible that they are false. But how does that prove that it is always possible that our perceptual beliefs are false? It may be that there are some true perceptual beliefs which could not possibly be false. Until we have some reason for thinking otherwise, we are surely justified in asserting there are such true perceptual beliefs and, consequently, in rejecting premise (2) of the skeptical argument. We may also then reject the skeptical conclusion.

A skeptical rejoinder:
Erroneous and veridical experience are subjectively indistinguishable

How can we sustain the skeptical claim that it is always logically possible that our perceptual beliefs are false, in the face of the preceding objection? The answer arises from considering the evidence that we have for our perceptual beliefs. The evidence that we have for any perceptual belief, no matter how plausible, can be duplicated by evidence for an exactly similar perceptual belief which is, in fact, mistaken.

To clarify this point, suppose that two people are looking through different windows. The first person reports that there is a sphere on a table outside her window; she sees the sphere to be green. She sees this no matter from what vantage point she views things. Suppose further that the second person, looking through her own window, sees and reports the very same thing. Each person has exactly the same justification for claiming to know that there is a green sphere outside his window. Each is in just as good a position to know this as the other. Surely, the only correct conclusion to reach is that either each person knows there is a green sphere outside her window or that neither of them knows this. It would be entirely arbitrary, and hence unreasonable, to say that one person knows this and the other does not.

However, it is perfectly possible that one of these people is mistaken and the other is not. Suppose the first person sees what she does because there is a green sphere outside her window. On the other hand, suppose the second sees what she does because she is being tricked with mirrors and drawings—there is no green sphere outside her window at all. Moreover, the deception is so excellent that from behind the windows no one could detect any difference in what is seen through each. This shows that the first person, who is in fact not mistaken, could have been mistaken. The second person was mistaken, and the first person had no better evidence for what she believed than the second person did. Since having this evidence did not keep the second person from being mistaken, the first person, too, could have been mistaken. What was so in the one case could have been so in the other. The only reasonable conclusion is that neither person has knowledge.

What we have just imagined has perfectly general implications. The experiences a person has, when he or she sees something that really exists, can always be duplicated by the experiences of another person who is being deceived. Because the experiences in question provide the only evidence a person has for believing what she does, if one person fails to know what she believes, so must the other. If one is mistaken in believing something, then another person who has a similar belief based on similar experiences surely could have been mistaken—even if in fact she is not. Since this duplication of experiences is always possible, it is always possible that a perceptual belief based on sensory experience is mistaken. The argument for skepticism requires no other assumption.

The Modified Skeptical Argument

We may conclude, then, with a slightly modified formulation of the argument for skepticism. The first two premises of the argument, which differ from the initial premises of the preceding skeptical argument, are as follows:

1. The experiences of a person who has a true perceptual belief may be exactly duplicated by the experiences of a person whose perceptual belief is exactly similar but false.

2. If the experiences of a person who has a true perceptual belief may be exactly duplicated by the experiences of a person whose perceptual belief is exactly similar but false, then it is always logically possible that our perceptual beliefs are false.

The next premise is the same as in the earlier argument:

3. If it is always logically possible that our perceptual beliefs are false, then no one ever knows that any of our perceptual beliefs are true.

From these three premises we can deduce the skeptical conclusion.

4. No one ever knows that any of our perceptual beliefs are true.

An epistemist objection to the first premise of the modified argument: A single example cannot support a general conclusion

The preceding argument might be challenged on the grounds that a general conclusion is drawn from a particular example. It is true that the two people looking through their respective windows might have almost exactly the same experiences, even though one of them is mistaken and the other correct. Perhaps this shows that both of these people could have been mistaken and that neither of them knows what she believes. However, to concede this point is not to concede the more general conclusion that whenever anyone sees something which is in fact the case, his experiences may be exactly duplicated by the experiences of another person who sees the same thing, though in fact he is mistaken. For example, consider a person holding the object he sees directly in front of him. How could his experiences be duplicated by the experiences of someone who is not confronted with such an object? If they could not, then premise (1) of the preceding skeptical argument may be rejected.

The first skeptical rejoinder: The argument from hallucinations

We noted in our experiment that both people view what they believe to be a green sphere from behind a window. But taking away the window, though it might help those two people to discover the trick that has been played on one of them, will not alter the primary force of the argument. For all of us view the world through the 'window' of our senses, and, as a result, a person who sees something that does exist may in general have the same experience as one who sees something that does not exist. The clearest example of what the skeptic is trying to prove is supplied by Lady Macbeth. At one time, after the murder of Duncan, she sees and feels blood on her hands. Her hands seem to be covered with Duncan's blood. She goes mad. Part of her madness consists of seeing and feeling blood on her hands. Of course, this is a hallucination. But the experiences she has when she is hallucinating might be exactly similar to the experiences she had when there really was blood on her hands. Because she could be mistaken, at the later time, in believing there is blood on her hands—indeed, she is mistaken—she could also be mistaken in believing the same thing at the earlier time. She had the same experiences to rely on in both cases. Consequently, it would be arbitrary, unreasonable, and epistemologically undemocratic to suppose that Lady Macbeth knows that she has blood on her hands at the earlier time but not at the later.

In addition to being misled by visual experience, the subject of hallucinations may also be misled by tactual experience and the experience of the other senses as well. We may imagine that, when mad, Lady Macbeth not only sees but also feels and smells blood on her hands, though there is none there. Such a hallucination is complete and systematic with respect to all the senses. Thus, our defense of the premise

1. The experiences of a person who has a true perceptual belief may be duplicated by the experiences of a person whose perceptual belief is exactly similar but false.

is that such duplication of experiences may always result from hallucinations. Erroneous perceptual beliefs based on hallucinatory experience obviously do not constitute knowledge, and correct perceptual beliefs are no better corroborated by experience. Therefore, perceptual beliefs in general, whether true or in error, never constitute knowledge.

Again, we must guard against misunderstanding. By distinguishing between those cases that involve hallucinations and those that do not, the skeptic is not contradicting herself. She is not supposing that we know which cases are which. We may, with perfect consistency, both agree that there is a distinction between hallucinatory experience, which evokes false perceptual belief, and ordinary experience, which evokes true perceptual belief, and yet deny that we know which kind of experience we are having. That is the position adopted here by the skeptic.

An epistemist objection to the skeptical rejoinder: Some actual hallucinations don't prove that we might always be hallucinating

The preceding argument suffers from the same defect as the skeptic's argument about the two green spheres: a general conclusion is drawn from a particular example. The skeptic produces an example: Lady Macbeth with and without bloody hands. The experiences she has when she sees something that exists are duplicated in hallucinations when she sees something that does not exist. The skeptic concludes that, when a person sees something that exists, her experiences may well be exactly duplicated in hallucinations when she sees something that does not exist. But how does this general conclusion follow from that one example? By what means does the skeptic prove that it is always possible to duplicate in hallucinations the sense experiences we have when our perceptual beliefs are true? How does she demonstrate that hallucinations are always possible no matter what our experiences are like? So far no such demonstration has been given; therefore we have no reason to accept the skeptic's conclusion.

A skeptical rejoinder: There are no grounds for holding that some experiences are immune to hallucination

Where does the burden of proof lie? If one concedes that a hallucination like Lady Macbeth's is possible, what reason is there for denying that hallucinations are always possible? When we believe we see something on our own hands, that is the kind of belief that we ordinarily accept with the greatest confidence and equanimity. When we believe we see something at a distance, or when our vision is obscured in some other way, we may have some doubt. But when we see something on our very own hands and feel it and smell it as well, then we have no doubt. Instead we feel certain that the thing exists. If experiences of this kind may be produced by hallucinations, and the resultant perceptual beliefs be in error, then how can we reasonably deny that all experiences can be produced by hallucinations, and consequently be accompanied by mistaken perceptual beliefs? Surely we cannot deny this. The range of experiences that hallucinations might possibly produce is without limit. And the argument for skepticism is perfectly sound.

An epistemist objection: Coherence and the testimony of others as criteria for non-hallucinatory experience

The argument for skepticism just stated assumes that complete and systematic hallucinations are always possible. This is the premise we shall now critically examine. Sometimes hallucinations mislead us concerning what is in our very hands. But we are not entirely at the epistemological mercy of such hallucinations, for we do have ways of discovering when our experiences are hallucinatory. But if we have some way of telling whether or not we are suffering a hallucination, then there must be some perceptual beliefs that are accompanied by experiences that rule out the possibility of hallucinations. In this case the experiences on which our belief is based could not be hallucinatory.

Moreover, it is not difficult to explain what kind of experiences rule out the possibility of hallucinations. We need only ask how we in fact discover that we are suffering a hallucination. One way is through the testimony of other people who know that our experiences are hallucinatory. Many people were in a position to tell Lady Macbeth that her experiences were hallucinatory, and although in her madness she would not accept such information, it was entirely available to her. Because we are not primarily concerned with madness but rather with normality, it is quite relevant that a normal person may discover that some of his experiences are hallucinatory through the help of others. Moreover, when one is in the company of others, and all agree concerning what they see, it is altogether reasonable to assume that no hallucination is taking place. Nonetheless, one qualification is necessary. Sometimes, in unusual circumstances, we know that a whole group of people is susceptible to hallucinations. For example, suppose they have taken a drug known to produce hallucinations, or suppose they have suffered some acute physical hardship, like being deprived of drink or sleep. Such conditions might produce group hallucinations. However, if people and circumstances are altogether ordinary, as they usually are, then an agreement in perceptual belief rules out the possibility of hallucinations.

Hallucinations are detected in another way, which does not require the testimony of others. It concerns the coherence among our experiences. A person who suffers from the hallucination of drinking water, when none is available to him, may see, feel, and even taste water which, because of his hallucination, he mistakenly believes exists. However, if he has been long deprived of water, he will soon notice that his thirst has not at all abated. People have, in fact, concluded from such experiences that they were suffering a hallucination. They were subsequently no longer misled. Thus, in this case there is a failure of experiential coherence. By drinking water one expects to quench one's thirst; and when one has the experience of seeing, feeling, and drinking water, but one's thirst is not quenched, then the experiences seem incoherent, and incomprehensible. Incoherence is therefore a sign of hallucinations, and coherence is, on the other hand, a sign of reality. Indeed, experiences that are sufficiently coherent exclude the possibility of hallucinations.

Finally, these criteria of nonhallucinations, or of veridical experiences, may be satisfied together and may thereby mutually reinforce each other. Often our experiences are entirely coherent, and our perceptual beliefs completely agree with the beliefs of others in our company.

A skeptical rejoinder:
Appeals to coherence and testimony merely beg the question
The appeal of the foregoing argument to the testimony of others as a safeguard against being misled by hallucinations begs the question. For to know what the testimony of another is, we must first know that we are confronted by another and know what he or she is saying. But to know these things is to know something by seeing or otherwise perceiving that they are so. The argument rests squarely on the assumption that perceiving such things constitutes knowledge. Of course, this assumption is precisely what the arguments for skepticism are intended to refute.

Moreover, the second argument, based on experiential coherence, has the same weakness. Some hallucinations do make themselves manifest to their victim by some kind of incoherence, but such a hallucination is partial or incomplete. Some expected experiential feature does not turn up, and the experience shows itself to be hallucinatory by being a bit too surprising. But why must we assume that hallucinations always expose themselves in this way? What proof is there that coherent and systematic experiences cannot possibly result from hallucinations? There is no reason to suppose that such hallucinations are impossible. Therefore, we are again justified in concluding that the experiences that a person has, when his perceptual beliefs are true, may be exactly repeated in hallucinations when his perceptual beliefs are false. Consequently, such beliefs never constitute knowledge.

The second skeptical rejoinder: The braino argument

However, we must pause long enough over the epistemist's argument to ensure that the skeptic is not again accused of passing too quickly from the particular example to a general conclusion. To rid ourselves of this recurring objection, let us indulge in a bit of science fiction and by so doing prove once and for all that skepticism is the tenable and correct position. Imagine that a superscientist invents a machine—we shall call it a "braino,"—that enables him to produce hallucinations in certain subjects. The machine operates by influencing the brain of a subject who wears a special cap, called a "braino cap." When the braino cap is placed on a subject's head, the operator of the braino can affect his brain so as to produce any hallucination in the subject that the operator wishes. The braino is a hallucination-producing machine. The hallucinations produced by it may be as complete, systematic, and coherent as the operator of the braino desires to make them.

What does the possibility of such a machine prove? It proves that the experiences a person has when his perceptual beliefs are true could be duplicated in hallucinations when the same perceptual beliefs are false. This shows that no mark or sign in experience distinguishes true perceptual beliefs from false ones resulting from hallucinations.

An analogy helps to illustrate the importance of the preceding considerations. Suppose that you are confronted with a barrel full of apples some of which are rotten and others of which are not. Usually there will be some sign or mark by which you can tell the rotten apples from the good ones. The rotten apples will be brown or soft, or they will have some other visible defect by which you can detect their condition. On the other hand, the good apples will be firm, red, and otherwise appear desirable. We suppose we can tell the difference between a good apple and a rotten one because we have signs to guide us.

However, suppose we are confronted with a barrel of apples that are quite indistinguishable in appearance, though some of the apples are rotten at the core. We are now presented with an apple from this barrel and prohibited from cutting it open. In this predicament, if someone should ask us whether the apple is rotten or good, the only thing to reply is, "I don't know." We might add, "There is no way to tell."

Similarly, because there is no mark or sign in experience by which we can distinguish true perceptual beliefs of ordinary experience from false ones arising in hallucinations, if someone should ask us whether a perceptual belief of ours is true or false, the only thing to reply is, "I don't know." We might add, "There is no way to tell." Just as there is no way to tell whether the apples in the second barrel are rotten, because we have no experiential signs to guide us, so there is no way to tell whether our perceptual beliefs are true, because we have no experiential signs to guide us. With only experience to guide us, we have no way to rule out the possibility of error. Even when our perceptual beliefs happen to be true, we could just as well have been mistaken. Indeed, when a perceptual belief is true, this is more a matter of good luck than good sense. Of course, no belief that turns out to be true as a matter of luck can reasonably be counted as knowledge.

An epistemist objection:
The skeptic's fallacious argument from possibility to actuality
In the first arguments we examined, the skeptic argued from a single example of hallucinations to a general conclusion, which is surely a fallacy, but, having now avoided this fallacy, she argues from possibility to actuality, which is no less of a fallacy. The present argument starts from the premise that the braino is a logical possibility, and consequently that it is a logical possibility that there should be hallucinations that are coherent, complete, and systematic in every way. From this premise of logical possibility, she arrives at the conclusion that we in fact have no way of telling whether or not we are hallucinating. By what line of reasoning may such a factual conclusion be derived from a premise concerning mere possibility? Even if it is logically possible that hallucinations should be coherent, complete, and systematic, hallucinations are not in fact so hard to detect. Therefore, experience does in fact enable us to tell whether our perceptual beliefs are true or false.

A skeptical rejoinder: How to pass from possibility to actuality
The contention that "hallucinations are not in fact so hard to detect" is the very heart of the issue. If the braino is a logical possibility, then how can we tell that hallucinations are not in fact so hard to detect? On the contrary, we may suffer hallucinations that we cannot detect. If it is logically possible that hallucinations should be coherent, complete, and systematic in every way, then there is no way of detecting at any moment that we are not suffering from a hallucination. Our critic supposes we can detect many hallucinations, but this is beside the basic point. The problem

is to explain how we can tell that we are not hallucinating. Our braino argument was intended to establish that we can never tell this, even if we can sometimes tell that we are hallucinating.

Sometimes we can tell that we are hallucinating, but we have no way of telling that we are not. Our argument to support this claim is best put in the form of a challenge. Consider some perceptual belief that you would maintain does not result from hallucinations. What experiences guarantee this? Indeed, what experiences provide you with any evidence of it? Notice that whatever experience you indicate, the braino argument will be quite sufficient to prove that such an experience is no guarantee against hallucination. All we need do is imagine that you have, unknown to yourself, the braino cap on your head. The operator of the braino is producing the very experiences you claim guarantee that you are not hallucinating!

The passage, from the possibility of hallucinations to the conclusion that there is in fact no way of telling that one is not hallucinating, is legitimate, because the former possibility may be used to reject any experience that is so impertinent as to present itself as a sure sign of reality. Any experience can be shown to be unequal to this task, on the grounds that it can be produced in hallucinations.

A skeptical argument:
The evil operator argument—another route from possibility to actuality

The preceding argument may be reinforced if we let our examples become even more fanciful than we have heretofore. Imagine that all people are controlled by the braino and that the machine is run by some evil being, Dr. O, who plots to keep us completely in error through hallucinations. Dr. O does not wish to be detected, so he supplies hallucinations that are coherent, complete, and systematic. Indeed, the hallucinations he produces in us are a perfect counterfeit of reality. Our experiences fulfill our expectations and contain no more surprises than we would expect from reality. But it is not reality we experience; our perceptual beliefs about the world are quite mistaken, for the source of our experiences is a mere machine, the braino, which creates hallucinations. In such a predicament we might have just the sort of perceptual beliefs we now have, based on experiences exactly similar to those we now have. But our perceptual beliefs would be altogether false.

The imagined situation is exactly similar to ours with respect to the reasons or evidence we would have for our perceptual beliefs. Experience is virtually the same in both cases. Consequently, if we lack knowledge in one situation, we must surely lack it in the other. Obviously, we lack knowledge when we are controlled by the braino, for then our perceptual beliefs are false. Hence, we also lack knowledge in our present situation. More precisely, our perceptual beliefs fail to constitute knowledge in either case.

We believe that we are not controlled by such a machine, and if we are fortunate in this belief, then no doubt many of our perceptual beliefs are true. It is, however, good fortune and not good evidence that we should thank for the correctness of these beliefs. We are just lucky if there is no Dr. O controlling us with a braino; and from that good fortune may result the further good fortune that most of our perceptual beliefs are true. It is just a matter of luck, however, and nothing epistemologically more glorious than that. If a belief is true as a result of luck, then it is a lucky guess—not knowledge.

Summary of the Modified Skeptical Argument
Earlier we defended skepticism by employing an argument the first premise of which was

1. The experiences of a person who has a true perceptual belief may be exactly duplicated by the experiences of a person whose perceptual belief is exactly similar but false.

From this premise and the following two premises

2. If the experiences of a person who has a true perceptual belief may be exactly duplicated by the experiences of a person whose perceptual belief is exactly similar but false, then it is always logically possible that any of our perceptual beliefs are false.

and

3. If it is always logically possible that any of our perceptual beliefs are false, then no one ever knows that any of our perceptual beliefs are true.

we deduced the skeptical conclusion

4. No one ever knows that any perceptual belief is true.

Premise (1) of the argument was called into question by the opponents of skepticism, and we have now derived this premise from the following premises:

5. The braino hypothesis is logically possible.

6. If the braino hypothesis is logically possible, then any experience may be duplicated in hallucinations.

7. If any experience may be duplicated in hallucinations, then the experiences of a person who has a true perceptual belief may be exactly duplicated by the experiences of a person whose perceptual belief is exactly similar but false.

From these premises, premise (1) may be validly deduced.

An epistemist objection:
The meaninglessness of the perfect-hallucination hypothesis

Let us examine the situation in which we are all deceived by the evil genius, Dr. O, who is busy supplying hallucinations to us with his braino. Is this situation really possible? Consider it in very concrete terms. Imagine Dr. O contriving to deceive us. Moreover, let us concentrate on the experience of one man, whose name is Tom, as Dr. O goes about deceiving him.[5] Dr. O will supply our experiences by using the braino. Because it is the braino that produces hallucinations, we need not suppose that there are any of the usual things around in the world at all when Dr. O deceives his victims. Therefore let us suppose that all those things are destroyed. We may thus imagine that Tom stands alone on a barren world, a braino cap firmly attached to his skull. He is, of course, quite oblivious to his predicament, for Dr. O, true to his plan, is supplying Tom with hallucinations that exactly duplicate the experiences of his usual existence.

The success of the evil genius is quite complete. What he has destroyed he deceives Tom into believing exists by causing Tom to hallucinate. Tom's hallucinating experiences exactly duplicate the experiences he would have if the things destroyed still existed. It is an extraordinarily clever deception, but in spite of this apparent success, Dr. O has more nearly succeeded in fooling himself than Tom. Why is this so? Let us return to the supposedly barren scene of the drama.

Imagine that Dr. O, having deceived Tom, grows weary of his unacknowledged success and wishes, while continuing the deception, to have Tom acknowledge this accomplishment. The next day, when Tom is, for example, having the experience of entering a room where flowers stand, Dr. O. tactfully suggests to Tom that there are no flowers. Tom then has the experience of raising the flowers to his nose, smelling them, and touching them. Tom is reassured. He denies there is deception. After all, having looked, sniffed, felt, with satisfying results, what could Dr. O. possibly mean by saying he is deceived? To this Dr. O. replies, "Your flowers are nothing but a hallucination." But Tom is unpersuaded. His flowers are perfect. A hallucination? Never!

At this point in the drama Dr. O is sorely tempted just to throw the switch on the braino and expose the fraud to Tom. But to do so is to give up the deception, which he does not want to do because of all his labors. So the evil genius, not feeling so ingenious now, is faced with a dilemma. Either he can maintain the deception—in which case Tom, refusing to acknowledge the deception, will deny that it exists—or he can alter his plan—in which case Tom, detecting that he has been fooled, will convert a perfect deception into a perfect farce. Either way Dr. O will fail to

---

5. This story is adapted, with mechanical contrivances, from O. K. Bouwsma, "Descartes' Evil Genius," *The Philosophical Review*, Vol. 58 (1949), 141-42.

attain his goal. For if the deception continues, how is Dr. O to make any sense of the idea to Tom?

From Tom's standpoint, the perfect deception is no deception at all. Once all the usual experiences are made to occur, the suggestion that Tom is suffering a hallucination is made senseless. Tom can make no sense of it. It is just as senseless to suppose such a deception is being worked on us. When a person is hallucinating, there must be ways to detect that this is so, even if the victim, like Lady Macbeth, fails to detect the hallucination in these ways. Once all the appropriate tests are made in order to ensure that one is not hallucinating, the suggestion that one might still be hallucinating is meaningless. What we mean by saying that a person is hallucinating is that some such tests will fail. The perfect hallucination is a bubble of semantic incongruity that disappears under the pressure of semantic scrutiny.

The defect in the skeptic's argument is that she assumes that a perfect hallucination is possible. Imagination, when it works overtime, might convince one this is so, but it cannot be. For something to be possible it must be meaningful. However, imagination is not restricted by bonds of meaningfulness. There is little difficulty in imagining something when the very idea of it is completely meaningless. We can imagine a cat in a tree with the parts of the cat disappearing one by one, first the tail, then the paw, then the body, until finally all that is left of the cat in the tree is a feline grin. We can imagine this, but the idea of the grin without a head is perfectly meaningless. The remarkable scope of the human imagination is a joy in life, but it is a trap for philosophical reflection. This is true precisely because it is so easy to suppose that whatever is imaginable is possible. The worldless hallucination of a world is precisely like the catless grin of a cat. We can imagine both but neither is literally meaningful.

Thus our reply to skepticism is a semantic one. The evil genius argument of the skeptic proceeds from the premise that a perfect hallucination is possible. But the idea of a perfect hallucination is meaningless, and hence such a hallucination is not possible. Because the argument of the skeptic proceeds from a false premise, it must be rejected.

A skeptical rejoinder:
The charge of meaninglessness rests on confusion
Why does it seem so plausible to contend that the perfect-hallucination hypothesis is meaningless? The explanation stems from an ambiguity in such terms as 'nonsense' and 'meaningless.' All these terms are used in both a semantic and an epistemic sense. A sentence is nonsense, or meaningless, in the semantic sense of the term only if the sentence asserts nothing, and consequently is neither true nor false. A perfect example of such a sentence is 'Pirots carulize elactically.' That sentence asserts nothing; it is neither true nor false. It is not made up of meaningful

words. An example of a sentence that is meaningless in the semantic sense, but that is made up of meaningful words, is 'Verb at do fog Joe.' The defect of this sentence is that it is ungrammatical. We can even have a sentence that is grammatical and composed of meaningful words, but that is nevertheless meaningless in the semantic sense. An example is 'Worms integrate the moon by C# homogeneously when moralizing to rescind apples.' This sentence, like the preceding ones, asserts nothing.

All the sentences we have considered are nonsense and meaningless in that they are either semantically or grammatically defective in such a way that a person who uttered them would, in ordinary circumstances, be asserting nothing. In contrast to this semantic sense of the terms 'nonsense' and 'meaningless,' there is an epistemic sense. Sometimes we say that a sentence is meaningless because, though it asserts something, what is asserted is preposterous. If a man says, "Everyone has died," we might reply, "Nonsense," or alternatively, "What do you mean?" or possibly even, "That is meaningless." It is not that the sentence asserts nothing; on the contrary, it is because the sentence asserts something patently false that we reply as we do. The sentence uttered is perfectly meaningful; what is nonsensical and meaningless is the fact that the person has uttered it. To put the matter another way, we can make sense of the sentence; we know what it asserts. But we cannot make sense of the man uttering it; we do not understand why he would utter it. Thus, when we use terms like 'nonsense' and 'meaningless' in the epistemic sense, the correct use of them requires only that what is uttered seem absurdly false. Of course, to seem preposterously false, the sentence must assert something, and thus be either true or false.

These remarks are directly relevant to the perfect-hallucination hypothesis. The perfect-hallucination hypothesis seems to be 'nonsense' and 'meaningless' in just the epistemic sense of these terms: the hypothesis seems preposterously false. And even the skeptic may concede, it should be remembered, that the hypothesis seems false. However, for the hypothesis to seem false, it must be meaningful; it must assert something in order to seem false.

If the perfect-hallucination hypothesis is meaningful in the semantic sense—that is, if it asserts something—then the fact that it is not meaningful in the epistemic sense is irrelevant to the contentions of skepticism. As we pointed out earlier, the skeptic may, with perfect consistency, concede that the perfect-hallucination hypothesis seems false. She may even believe that it is false. All people, whether skeptics or not, presumably believe this. But though we all believe the hypothesis is false, the skeptic argues that no one knows it is false. She concludes that because no one knows it is false, no one knows that any of his perceptual beliefs are true. Therefore, such beliefs do not constitute knowledge.

An epistemist objection to the third premise: The skeptic's failure to distinguish probable judgments from lucky guesses
Suppose that epistemist concedes, for the sake of avoiding an impasse, that the perfect-hallucination hypothesis does assert something, that it is either true or false. Further, we shall concede that the evidence we have from sense experience is always such that it is logically possible that our perceptual beliefs based on this evidence are false.

If we make these concessions, must we also concede the day to skepticism? Let us examine once again the logical structure of the argument for skepticism and see if we can find a defect. The argument is as follows:

1. The experiences of a person who has a true perceptual belief may be exactly duplicated by the experiences of a person whose perceptual belief is exactly similar but false.

2. If the experiences of a person who has a true perceptual belief may be exactly duplicated by the experiences of a person whose perceptual belief is exactly similar but false, then it is always logically possible that any of our perceptual beliefs are false.

3. If it is always logically possible that any of our perceptual beliefs are false, then no one ever knows that any of our perceptual beliefs are true.

Therefore

4. No one ever knows that any of our perceptual beliefs are true.

By defending the possibility of a perfect hallucination, the skeptic has substantiated premise (1). Moreover, let us concede the truth of premise (2) as well. To extricate ourselves from the consequences of skepticism we shall now direct our attack against premise (3).

The skeptic's defense of premise (3) can be found in her statement of the evil-operator argument (pp. 56–57), where she attributes the truth of perceptual beliefs to luck. This enables her to derive premise (3) from

8. If it is logically possible that any of our perceptual beliefs are false, then a perceptual belief that turns out to be true is nothing more than a lucky guess.

and

9. If any perceptual belief that turns out to be true is nothing more than a lucky guess, then no one ever knows that any of our perceptual beliefs are true.

Although the deduction of premise (3) from (8) and (9) is valid, premise (8) should be rejected. In this way we can avoid accepting premise (3).

In premise (8), the skeptic has assumed that if it is logically possible for a belief to be false, then, when the belief turns out to be true, it is nothing more than a lucky guess, and hence not something we know. For convenience, let us label as *corrigible* any belief of such a kind that it is logically possible for a belief of that kind to be false. Almost all our beliefs about subjects outside logic and mathematics are corrigible.

The skeptical contention that corrigible belief leaves us entirely at the mercy of luck—as premise (8) asserts—is not difficult to refute. Evidence that does not exclude the logical possibility of error may greatly reduce the probability of error. Moreover, when our evidence reduces the probability of error to a point where it is negligible, it is preposterous to say that escaping from error is nothing but luck. To believe what is extremely probable, and to disbelieve what is immensely improbable, is completely reasonable. When a person believes something that is rendered exceedingly probable by the evidence on which he bases his belief, then it is no mere matter of luck if he is right and his belief is true. Beliefs that are sufficiently probable, even if corrigible, should be considered knowledge whenever they are true.

A skeptical rejoinder: The employment of the notion of probability begs the question against the skeptic

Every attempt to escape skepticism knocks, sooner or later, on the door of probability. But there is no help behind the door. Indeed once we pass through it, we shall find ourselves securely locked in the very den of skepticism. Let us consider how to bolt the door.

If the appeal to probability is to succeed, the epistemist must go beyond claiming that our corrigible beliefs are based on evidence that renders them highly probable. It is not enough that a belief be highly probable; the one who has the belief must know this to be so, or the belief will again, if true, be so merely as a matter of luck. To see this, let us turn to the example of the gaming table. Imagine that a person is invited to play a game of "Millee," which is played as follows: There is a machine with a window, which, when a button is pushed, closes and subsequently opens to display either a red or a green square. Moreover, part of the definition of the game involves the following rule: the machine must be set so that the green square appears only once in a million plays. Thus the odds are one in a million that the red square will fail to appear when the window opens.

Imagine that a person is invited to play Millee but is not told the odds. He might choose to bet that the red square will appear when the window opens, and of course he is correct. In spite of the odds in his favor, we would be entirely justified in saying that his belief that the red square would appear was, from his point of view, a lucky guess. The reason is that he does not know that the odds are a million to one in his favor. Indeed, for all he knows, the odds might be anything at all. In the absence of such knowledge, his being right is nothing more than luck.

Now suppose that a person believes that there really is a tomato in front of her, and that this belief is based on the evidence of sense experience, or any other inductive evidence you please. The odds might be a million to one that her hypothesis will turn out to be true when based on such evidence. But if the person does not know that these are the odds, and if, moreover, for all she knows the odds may be anything at all, then were she right, this would be nothing more than luck. In both this case and the case of the person at the gaming table, being right is a matter of luck, even though the odds are fantastically in favor of both being right. It is a matter of luck because both of them are ignorant of the odds.

Of course, both the gambler and the perceptual believer would be in an entirely different position if they knew the odds. Then, neither would correctly be described as being right merely through luck. The question to be answered by the skeptic is the following: Need we suppose that the perceptual believer is ignorant of the odds in favor of her belief? Could not a person who based her belief on evidence that rendered her belief highly probable also know how probable her belief is? To establish the case for skepticism, we must prove that the perceptual believer is inescapably ignorant of such probabilities.

As a first step, let us consider briefly how we ever know anything about probabilities. The term 'probability' is interpreted in a number of different ways, but the idea that seems most relevant in this context is concerned with truth frequency. If a person is to convert his perceptual beliefs to epistemic gold by his knowledge of probability, he must know that his belief, based on the evidence he has, is the kind of belief that is more frequently—indeed, much more frequently—true than false, when based on the evidence he has. The perceptual believer must know that perceptual beliefs based on the usual evidence of sense experience are much more frequently true than false.

But we cannot know any such thing; for consider the problem a person faces who wishes to establish that perceptual beliefs based on the evidence of sense experience are much more frequently true than false. To find this out he would have to find a sample of perceptual beliefs and determine how many of them were true. The information about such a sample would be absolutely essential to his finding out that beliefs of this kind are much more frequently true than false. But how is he to acquire this information? To obtain such knowledge, he must be able to determine how many of the beliefs in his sample are true. To do this, he must know which of them constitute knowledge and which do not.

However, this requirement is calamitous, because we have already shown that a perceptual belief can constitute knowledge only if the person knows that beliefs of this kind are much more often true than false. We have now concluded that in order to know that beliefs of this kind are frequently true, we must first know which beliefs of this kind are true and which false. Therefore, before we can know that any perceptual belief is true, we must first know that certain perceptual beliefs are true. This is an altogether pernicious epistemic situation. Moreover, the only alternative is skepticism. In short, either we know that certain perceptual beliefs are true before we know any perceptual beliefs are true, which is absurd, or we do not know that any perceptual beliefs are true. It is obvious the latter alternative must be accepted.

Let us review the argument briefly. In order to escape skepticism concerning corrigible beliefs, it must be shown that such beliefs are based on evidence which renders them highly probable, and also that we know those beliefs are highly probable. To know the latter, we must know that such beliefs, when based on evidence of a specified sort, are much more frequently true than false. However, to find out that such beliefs are much more frequently true than false, we must consider a sample of such beliefs and determine what percentage of the beliefs in the sample is true. To determine what percentage of the beliefs is true, we must know which of a certain sample are true.

Therefore before a person can know that any corrigible belief based on inductive evidence is true, he must know that a certain probability statement is true. But he cannot know such a statement is true unless he already knows that certain corrigible beliefs based on inductive evidence are true. Therefore, no one can know that any corrigible belief based on inductive evidence is true. The escape route via probability is, in fact, an expressway to skepticism.

An epistemist objection: An externalist account of justification undermines the skeptic's argument against probability

The skeptic assumed the premise

8. If it is always logically possible that any of our perceptual beliefs are false, then a perceptual belief that turns out to be true is nothing more than a lucky guess.

We attacked the premise on the grounds that if a perceptual belief, like my belief that there is a book in front of me, is of a kind that is much more frequently true than false, then that belief is more than a lucky guess. If the odds are extraordinarily in favor of my being right, as they surely are, then my belief, assuming it to be true, is no mere lucky guess. That is the epistemist argument.

What has the skeptic replied? She has said that if a person does not know the odds are in her favor, then the person's belief, if true, remains a lucky guess. But is the reply plausible? There is one kind of epistemist doctrine, *externalism*, that affirms, contrary to the skeptic, that a true belief that is externally related to the truth in the appropriate way is knowledge. It is not merely a lucky guess, even if we are ignorant of the existence of the external relationship. To see the point of externalism, suppose for the moment that our experiences are veridical rather than hallucinatory, and that the external world is what we suppose it to be. Suppose, as I believe, that there is a book in front of me. My belief that there is a book in front of me arises because of this truth. The fact that there is a book before me causes me to have the experience of seeing a book, which in turn causes me to believe that there is a book in front of me. This process is a perfectly reliable one which gives me information about the existence of an object in the external world, the book before me. When I am correct in believing that there is a book before me, that is not merely luck! My belief is the product of a very reliable process. To say that the process is reliable is to say that the process most frequently produces true beliefs and very rarely produces false ones.   A belief resulting from such processes, when it is true, is no mere lucky guess. The process connects us with the external world.

The critical point, contrary to the skeptic, is that I need not know that the belief in question arises from such a process to avoid mere guessing. It suffices that the process reliably produces true beliefs. In the case of the game of Millee, luck favors my belief, but the process producing my belief is not reliable. I see a red square on the first play of the game, and believe that I will see a red square on the second play of the game. I am right, but the process of forming a belief that the previous outcome in a game of chance will repeat itself is, in general, not a reliable belief-forming process.   Note the contrast with perception.   Perception is a reliable belief-forming process, even if it is always logically possible that our perceptual beliefs are mistaken, for, in fact, our perceptual beliefs are reliably produced and not mere guesses. The logical possibility of being mistaken in our perceptual beliefs fails to yield the consequence that such beliefs, if true, are mere lucky guesses.   They may be the products of reliable processes which connect us to the external world in a way required to obtain knowledge. Premise (8) is dissolved by the application of the solvent of externalism.[6]

A skeptical rejoinder:
The externalist begs the question against the skeptic

The epistemist, embracing the doctrine of externalism, has argued that beliefs arising from a reliable belief-forming process are, when true, not lucky guesses but knowledge. The problem with the argument is that the epistemist has assumed that there are reliable belief-forming processes when he is not entitled to that assumption in our dispute. If the story about Dr. O were true, then our belief-forming processes would be unreliable, and we would have no way of knowing that this is so. Since the story about Dr. O represents a logical possibility, our processes may be unreliable and our beliefs, if true, may be mere lucky guesses. We must,

---

6. This form of externalism was developed by Alvin I. Goldman, in *Epistemology and Cognition* (Cambridge: Harvard University Press, 1986).

however, concede one point to the epistemist. The argument from the logical possibility of perceptual error to the conclusion that true perceptual beliefs are lucky guesses is not logically valid. The possibility that such beliefs are the results of reliable belief-forming processes is a counter-example.

Skepticism is, however, dialectically fertile and readily gives birth to a new premise to supplant the old one. Suppose, for the moment, that a belief is the product of a reliable belief-forming process, but we do not know that the process is reliable. In that case, though our beliefs may be more than lucky guesses, we will not know this. Consider a fanciful example. A young child, Alice, who is eight, is endowed with a peculiar ability. When someone asks her what the social security number of a named person is, Dane Taylor, for example, a number immediately occurs to her, 598-81-9908. She has no idea why or how the number occurs to her, but she believes it is the social security number of the person in question, Dane Taylor. Now suppose that the process is a reliable one, perhaps arranged by a Dr. O who has gained access to the braino on Alice's head and the register of social security numbers, but that Alice has no idea that the process is a reliable one. As far as she can tell, her beliefs about social security numbers are mere guesswork. But then she does not know that her beliefs about social security numbers are true!

This fanciful example is a counterexample to the externalist assumption that a true belief that is the product of a reliable belief-forming process is knowledge. That assumption is false, precisely because a person might, like Alice, be ignorant of the fact that her belief is the product of such a process. Moreover, the logical possibility that our perceptual beliefs might be in error insures that even if our belief-forming processes are connected with the external world in a reliable manner, we shall be ignorant of this fact and, therefore, be ignorant of the truth of those beliefs. We, like Alice, may have beliefs that are the products of such processes, but we, again like her, cannot tell that this is so, because of the logical possibility of the deceptions of Dr. O.

Our skeptical reply to the epistemist incorporates two new premises

10. If it is always logically possible that any of our perceptual beliefs are false, then we cannot tell whether or not a perceptual belief that turns out to be true is a lucky guess.

11. If we cannot tell whether or not a perceptual belief that turns out to be true is a lucky guess, then we never know that any of our perceptual beliefs are true.

From these two premises we deduce premise (3) of our argument

3. If it is always logically possible that any of our perceptual beliefs are false, then we never know that any of our perceptual beliefs are true.

From this premise, together with the premise that it is always possible that any of our perceptual beliefs are false, which follows from the logical possibility of the story about Dr. O, we derive our skeptical conclusion that we never know that any of our perceptual beliefs are true.

The preceding argument against the externalist defense admits of terse summary. Contrary to the externalist, we have to know that our beliefs are not lucky guesses in order to know that they are true. To know that our perceptual beliefs are the products of reliable belief-forming processes and not lucky guesses, we would have to know that those processes produce beliefs that are very frequently true and very infrequently false. So our excursion through externalism leaves the epistemist in his original quandary. He must assume that we know that our perceptual beliefs are frequently true in order to show that we know that any of them are true. To assume that is shamelessly to beg the question.

An epistemist objection:
The principle of charity supports externalism
Can an externalist justify assuming that our perceptual beliefs are frequently true, and the products of reliable belief-forming systems, without begging the question against the skeptic? There is an argument that says that a principle of charity dictates this result. The principle of charity says that when we interpret the speech of another we should interpret it in such a way as to maximize the true beliefs we ascribe to others on the basis of what we believe to be true.[7] Suppose I see the sun shining and you say to me, "Sunny day, isn't it?" It would be perverse of me to suppose that you believe it is raining and interpret your use of the word 'Sunny' to mean 'Rainy.' Why? I cannot prove you believe it is sunny, but, given what I believe about the weather, that is the most charitable interpretation for me to make of what you believe. On the basis of what I believe about the weather, your belief about the weather would be true if my belief about the weather is true. Notice that this argument appeals only to what the interpreter believes to be true. When I am charitable toward you, I should interpret what you say in such a way as to maximize the true beliefs I ascribe to you, based on what I believe to be true. It does not presuppose that I know what is true. Therefore, application of the principle of charity to perceptual beliefs of others does not presuppose that we know that our perceptual beliefs are true. So appeal to the principle does not beg the question.

The principle of charity tells us to be charitable toward others concerning the truth of their beliefs. If we follow the principle of charity, we will interpret the perceptual beliefs of others in such a way that their perceptual

---

7. The principle of charity is defended by Donald Davidson in *Inquiries into Truth and Interpretation* (Oxford, Clarendon Press, 1984).

beliefs very frequently turn out to be true and very infrequently turn out to be false, at least in terms of what we believe. So the principle of charity yields exactly the conclusion we want concerning others, namely, that their perceptual beliefs are frequently true, indeed, almost always true. We may, moreover, apply the principle to ourselves by following the dictum that charity begins at home and conclude that our perceptual beliefs are also frequently true. Whether we apply the principle of charity to ourselves as well as to others, as it seems only equitable to allow, we obtain the desired conclusion that perceptual beliefs are almost always true.

A skeptical rejoinder: Charity without knowledge

The principle of charity may be a useful method for interpreting the remarks of others in some cases, but it is useless as a defense of the epistemist. What it tells us, in effect, is to assume that others have beliefs about what is true that correspond as fully as possible with our beliefs about what is true. Sometimes this is unreasonable, for example, when I know that you hold some peculiar metaphysical view, like that of Leibniz, who held that everything was made up of minds and that matter did not exist. It would be distinctly uncharitable to Leibniz to interpret him in such a way as to assume that he did not believe that everything was made up of minds. Even in those cases in which we have no reason to think that the belief system of the other is peculiar, and where application of the principle of charity does seem appropriate, it only warrants me in so interpreting the beliefs of the other that they accord as fully as possible with my own beliefs. Thus, to say that I should interpret the beliefs of others in such a way as to maximize the truth of those beliefs is just to say that I should interpret their beliefs in such a way as to maximize correspondence with my own beliefs.

The application of the principle of charity to myself is therefore redundant. My beliefs already correspond to my beliefs, and so the application of the principle to myself adds nothing whatsoever to my beliefs. It leads me to believe that my beliefs are true, but, of course, I already believe that my beliefs are true, because to believe something is just to believe that it is true. To believe that I see my nose is just to believe that it is true that I see my nose. The principle of charity is, therefore, ineffective in proving that our perceptual beliefs are frequently true. In general, therefore, the epistemist has failed to show that our perceptual beliefs and our corrigible beliefs based on inductive evidence are even probable. To show that they are even probable, the epistemist must show that they are very frequently true and very infrequently false. This the epistemist cannot do, without begging the question by assuming that we know such beliefs are true in order to prove that we know precisely this.

An epistemist objection: Internalism and complete justification

The skeptic's reply to externalism has proven it to be an insufficient bulwark against skepticism. Fortunately, externalism is no more necessary than it is sufficient for a defense of the epistemist position. To show that our perceptual beliefs and other corrigible beliefs are probable, we do not need to show or know anything about frequencies. The skeptic lured the epistemist into her den by converting the discussion of probability into a discussion about frequency. What is required for knowledge is justification for our beliefs, and probabilities are adequate to provide such justification. The justification arises, however, not from a connection with the external world, as the skeptic alleges and her externalist opponent unwisely conceded. Justification arises, instead, from internal standards of evidence. It is, therefore, *internalism* not externalism that provides a defense against skepticism.   It is the internal connection between our beliefs and our internal standards of evidence and justification that support the edifice of knowledge. Let us go inside for a defense of knowledge.

An internalist critique of skepticism will focus on the skeptical premise (10) above.

10. If it is always logically possible that any of our perceptual beliefs are false, then we cannot tell whether or not a perceptual belief that turns out to be true is a lucky guess.

Complete justification is a condition of knowledge. If we can tell that we are completely justified in believing something, that there is a book before me, for example, then we can also tell that the belief is not a guess and, if true, not a lucky guess. The internalist thesis is as follows: Though it is always logically possible for any perceptual or corrigible belief to be false, we can often tell that the belief is not a guess, because we can tell that it is a completely justified belief. Moreover, we can know that our corrigible beliefs are completely justified without first knowing how frequently such beliefs are true. We can know this by appeal to internal principles or standards of justification.[8]

The very character of some beliefs stamps them as epistemically abhorrent and unjustified. A contradictory belief is one example, and a belief that flies in the face of overwhelming evidence is another. A person who refuses, in ordinary circumstances, to believe what her senses would lead her to believe, and who, moreover, believes quite the opposite instead, is an epistemically wanton and unreasonable person. On the other hand, a person who believes precisely what the evidence of her senses leads her to believe, is completely justified in terms of our internal standards of epistemic justification.

---

8. The primary defender of internalism is R. M. Chisholm, *Theory of Knowledge*, 4th ed. (Englewood Cliffs: Prentice-Hall, 1990).

We can see that this is true by considering our predicament in the most desperate epistemic situation, namely, one in which Dr. O is constantly deceiving us. Even in this situation, we can distinguish between justified and unjustified belief by appeal to our internal standards of justification. I, being presented with experiences that duplicate those of seeing a book and no reason to doubt that there is a book before me, believe that there is a book there. Another, having exactly the same experiences, believes that the great pumpkin stands before her, even though her experiences duplicate those of seeing a book, and she has no reason to think that the great pumpkin stands before her, nor any reason to doubt that there is a book before her. However amusing her beliefs may be, it is clear that she is epistemically unjustified in her odd belief and that I am completely justified in mine. Given the deceptions of Dr. O, both of our beliefs are in error, but mine is completely justified by the standards of epistemic justification, and hers is not. Our internal standards of epistemic justification suffice to tell us that certain kinds of beliefs are completely justified no matter what the external world is like.

In summary, our internal standards of evidence and justification ensure that at least some of our corrigible beliefs, perceptual beliefs, for example, are completely justified. Thus, though such beliefs are corrigible, we can easily tell by appeal to such internal standards that such beliefs are more than guesses, and, if true, more than mere lucky guesses.

A skeptical rejoinder:
Satisfaction of internal standards is not a guide to truth

The internalist speculations of the epistemist rest on an appeal to internal standards. Such appeals are the common refuge of all who seek to escape from the pains of inquiry and criticism. It is time to expose this form of reasoning as the intellectual protector of the status quo. Having exposed it, we can then elaborate a skeptical alternative to the dogmatic conservation of accepted opinion.

Let us lay out the internalist argument of the epistemist with greater care than he has been wont to do. It is as follows:

1. Some of our beliefs are completely justified in terms of our internal standards of epistemic evaluation.

2. If any of our beliefs are completely justified in terms of our internal standards of epistemic evaluation, then those beliefs are completely justified even if beliefs of that kind almost always turn out to be false.

Therefore

3. Some of our beliefs are completely justified even if beliefs of that kind almost always turn out to be false.

This is the argument, and surely it need only be stated this baldly to be rendered ineffective for the purpose of refuting skepticism. The internalist, in presenting an epistemist argument, has very cleverly attracted our attention to premise (1). But his strategy is doomed by the inadequacy of premise (2), which is needed to bring us to the epistemist conclusion.

The problem for the epistemist is that it does not at all follow, from the fact that something is completely justified in terms of our standards of evaluation, that it is completely justified for the purpose of attaining knowledge. This is especially clear when the kind of belief in question almost always turns out to be false. What does it mean to say that some belief is completely justified in terms of our internal standards of evaluation? What it means, surely, is that we accept a principle according to which beliefs of that kind are completely justified. But the fact that some principle is accepted in no way shows that it is true. Hence, when such a principle tells us that a belief is completely justified, we still may reasonably ask whether the principle is correct. If it is not, then the beliefs it certifies as completely justified may be absolutely counterfeit; that is, they may not be completely justified at all.

To conclude that some belief is completely justified, because it is so justified in terms of some internal standard of evaluation we accept, is to offer an argument without any merit whatever. For it simply does not follow in any way that we are completely justified in some belief merely because that belief conforms to some internal standard of evaluation. The standard itself may be totally defective. Every standard of evaluation is intended to fulfill some purpose. What purpose are our internal epistemic standards supposed to fulfill? Obviously, they are supposed to lead us to obtain truth and avoid error. What then if conformity to our internal epistemic standard makes us fall into error? Then they are defective, a snare and delusion, and we should set them aside.

The point may be further illustrated, and usefully so, by considering a controversial epistemological claim. Imagine that some person is entirely convinced that she has some extrasensory powers, and, more specifically, that she can tell what cards are drawn from a deck, even though she does not see the cards, by concentrating in a special way. She then repeatedly claims to know what card is drawn from the deck. When we challenge her claim to know, she says her claim is completely justified in terms of her internal epistemic standards. We then note that she is much more often incorrect than correct in such claims; indeed, we might even note that she is no more often correct in what she says than one would expect by chance. She then regards us with disdainful incredulity and remarks that apparently we have not understood. She informs us that her beliefs in such matters are completely justified in terms of her internal standards of epistemic evaluation, and hence her beliefs are completely justified, even if those beliefs are mostly false. Those are her standards, and there is an end to it.

No one would accept that argument as having any credibility whatever. It obviously does not follow from the fact that a belief is completely justified in terms of her internal standards that such a belief is completely justified. This point remains cogent when generalized. No matter what her internal standard might be, it does not follow from the fact that the belief is completely justified according to her internal standard, that the belief is epistemically justified. It might not be epistemically justified at all.

We are likely to overlook this point when we accept the standards in question. But the internalist argument of the epistemist is no better than the argument of our self-acclaimed mistress of extrasensory powers. The objective of epistemic justification is the attainment of truth and the avoidance of error. When an internal epistemic standard is useless for this purpose, it fails to yield the complete justification required by our epistemic enterprise. The appeal to internal epistemic standards is but one more ineffective attempt to evade skepticism. An external connection with truth is not, as the externalist claimed, sufficient for epistemic justification, but it is necessary to that end. The epistemist must show that his internal standards of justification are connected with truth, that perceptual beliefs, for example, are more frequently true than false, or candidly concede defeat.

An epistemist objection: Innocent justification

It may be conceded that our appeal to internal epistemic standards is ineffective if some argument is required to show that such standards are connected with truth. But is any such argument needed? The skeptic continually supposes that we have to know that certain frequencies obtain, or that certain frequencies do not obtain, if we are to know that our corrigible beliefs are true. But she has put the shoe on the wrong epistemic foot. Certain corrigible beliefs—for example, cautious perceptual beliefs and distinct memory beliefs—we need not justify by antecedently establishing that beliefs of this kind are more frequently true than false. On the contrary, unless there is some reason to believe that such beliefs are more frequently false than true, we are completely justified in such beliefs. One way of putting the matter is to say that such beliefs are epistemically innocent until proven guilty. They are justified unless they are shown to be unjustified.

Moreover, often our perceptual beliefs are so completely justified that it would be epistemically pointless, and indeed unreasonable, to attempt to justify them by arguing that such beliefs are more frequently true than false. For example, if I see my index finger and feel it there as well, my belief that there really is such a finger is not one that could reasonably be defended by such an argument. This belief is so completely justified that any such argument mustered in defense of it would surely proceed from premises less evident than the conclusion they support. Such an argument would be epistemically useless. For, to justify a conclusion, some of the premises of the argument must be more evident than the conclusion, and none of the premises may be any less evident. Only such an argument can add epistemic weight to the conclusion. Unless some of the premises are initially more evident than the conclusion, there will be no more reason for accepting the premises than there was originally for accepting the conclusion. Thus, for an argument to justify the conclusion deduced from the premises, at least some of the premises must be more evident, more reasonable to accept, than the conclusion.

However, the belief about my index finger is so completely justified that there is no belief that is more reasonable or evident. When I see something that I also touch and feel, in the absence of evidence to the contrary, the belief that such a thing exists is so evident, so reasonable, that it would be pointless to seek a frequency argument to justify the belief. To what premises could I appeal? Surely, any premise to which I might appeal would be less evident, or at least no more evident, than the very belief I was attempting to justify. The belief is so completely justified that no such argument to justify it could reasonably be given.

A skeptical rejoinder: Appeal to innocent justification does not rid the epistemist of the burden of proof

The primary defect of this defense of epistemism is the manner in which all equity and fairness in disputation are set neatly aside for the convenience of epistemism. We begin by questioning whether perceptual beliefs are completely justified. And what is the response to our query? It is the bold assertion that these beliefs are so evident and completely justified in themselves that no argument can even be offered to sustain them. But this reply constitutes a most immediate and obvious begging of the question against skepticism. The epistemist has simply laid it down that what seems most evident and completely justified to him must be conceded to be completely justified without argument or debate. We agree that the beliefs in question may seem completely justified to the epistemist, indeed, so completely justified that no argument could serve to render those beliefs any more evident to him. What we deny is that those beliefs are com-pletely justified, and what we require is some argument to convince us that those beliefs are so justified. The epistemist has become desperate with his dubious appeals to innocence, and we are left unsatisfied.

If matters remain at the level of denial and simple assertion, we have arrived at an impasse, and neither party to the dispute can claim victory. It is essential that we move beyond this level of argumentation. How should we proceed? With impartiality, of course. A principle of impartiality requires that until some justificatory argument is offered, we shall not assume that the claims of either party are justified or unjustified. But here is the crux: this principle of impartiality curiously favors the skeptic. If the claims of neither the epistemist nor the skeptic are assumed to be completely justified, then the perceptual beliefs of the epistemist must not be assumed to be completely justified. Therefore, they must not be assumed to constitute knowledge either. In this way, simple fairness and impartiality in discourse and disputation sustain the case for skepticism. We must assume at the outset that the beliefs in question, including those perceptual beliefs cited by the epistemist, are not completely justified until some argument is presented to justify them. If skepticism is treated fairly before the bar of evidence, the burden of proof must rest entirely with the epistemist.

An epistemist objection:
An argument to the best explanation provides the required proof

The reply to the skeptic, ingenious as she is proving to be, is to shoulder the burden of proof and provide a justification for our corrigible beliefs, perceptual beliefs, for example, without begging the question. The burden is not a heavy one. We need only compare the fanciful hypothesis of the skeptic to our modest perceptual beliefs to notice the superiority of the latter. To avoid begging the question, however, let us consider our most modest perceptual beliefs as mere hypotheses and compare them to the skeptical hypotheses. Let us proceed scientifically, and ask which hypothesis we should accept.

Certain experiences lead me to believe that a book is before me. Here are two hypotheses. The epistemist hypothesis is that I have the experiences I do because there is a book before me which I see. The skeptical hypothesis is that I have the experiences that I do because there is a braino attached to my head, controlled by Dr. O, who is attempting to deceive me into believing that there is book before me when there is not. How should we decide which hypothesis to accept? Surely the choice is not a difficult one, if we proceed scientifically. We need only ask which hypothesis provides the best explanation, the epistemist hypothesis or the skeptical hypothesis. When confronted with competing hypotheses, a scientist asks which hypothesis provides the better explanation of data, the observed path of the planets, for example. The better explanation, the Copernican hypothesis that the planets revolve around the sun, rather than the Ptolemaic hypothesis that the sun revolves around the earth, is the one the scientist accepts.

Now compare the hypothesis that there is book before me to the skeptical hypothesis that a braino controlled by Dr. O is attached to my head. Which is the best hypothesis to explain my experiences? The epistemist hypothesis, without a doubt. It is a better explanation to suppose that there is a book before me than to accept in the fanciful story of Dr. O. Justification and knowledge arise from an inference to the best explanation of the experiences from which we began. We are completely justified in our perceptual beliefs precisely because they provide the best explanation of our perceptual experiences.[9] I have all the familiar experiences of seeing a book before me. The explanation is that there is a book before me which I see. What could explain better? Nothing? Then the epistemist is right. We are completely justified. The conclusion easily bears the burden of proof against the skeptic.

A skeptical reply: Explanation without truth is worthless

Is the epistemist hypothesis a better explanation than the skeptical hypothesis, if the skeptical hypothesis is true and the epistemist hypothesis is false? On the contrary, if our perceptual experiences are caused by Dr. O, then that is the better explanation of those experiences. When the epistemist says that his explanation is best, he is not providing a justification for our perceptual beliefs; he is begging the question by appealing to his epistemist assumption that such beliefs are true. Of course, if a perceptual belief is true, if really I see a book, for example, as I believe I do, then the hypothesis that I see a book is a better explanation of my perceptual experiences than the hypothesis that my experiences are generated by Dr. O. If, however, my experiences are caused by Dr. O, then the best explanation of my experiences is that they were caused by Dr. O. It all depends on which explanation is true. The best explanation is the true one.

Sometimes we are not completely justified in accepting that one rather than the other of two conflicting hypotheses is true, when we judge that one explains some phenomena better than the other. For example, two conflicting hypotheses might explain the motions of some planet, say the irregular orbit of Mercury, and we might note that one is simpler than the other. If we do not know which of the hypotheses is true, we may regard the simpler hypothesis as the better explanation. In general, when we are unable to decide which of two hypotheses is true, we may appeal to some explanatory feature of the two hypotheses, such as simplicity, to decide which is better.

That one hypothesis is better than another in terms of some explanatory feature other than truth fails to provide a complete justification for accepting that the better explanation is true, however. One explanation may be better than another without our being completely justified in accepting that either of them is true, because neither of them is the best explanation of the phenomena in question. The best explanation must be a true explanation, simply because a true explanation is better than a false one. Moreover, this assumption is essential to the argument of the epistemist. If a best explanation could be false, then it would be useless

---

9. This theory of knowledge as inference to the best explanation is developed by Gilbert Harman in *Thought* (Princeton: Princeton University Press, 1973).

for the epistemist to argue that his hypothesis provides the best explanation. Whatever explanatory merits other than truth his hypothesis might have, they would fail to show that we are completely justified in accepting his hypothesis as true.

It is truth, not other explanatory merits, that is the objective of knowledge and complete justification. What the epistemist must prove, therefore, is that his hypothesis is true, and he cannot do this by appealing to other explanatory merits of his hypothesis. Explanation without truth is epistemically worthless. The epistemist appeal to the best explanation must beg the question by assuming the truth of such explanation or else become irrelevant to the reality of knowledge and complete justification. Thus, the appeal proves impotent against the skeptic.

Another Argument for the Skeptical Conclusion:
Complete Justification as Excluding the Chance of Error:
The Lottery Paradox

In fact, as we shall now prove, a completely justified belief must be one that leads to truth without any risk of error. We shall argue that a person is not completely justified in what she believes unless there is no chance whatever that she is mistaken. If there is some chance that she is mistaken, however small, then she is not completely justified in her belief, and therefore, she lacks knowledge. This thesis is highly contentious. People often say that they know, when there is obviously some chance that they are in error. So ordinary speech suggests that we should not require that all chance of error be excluded before a person may be said to know. However, as we shall prove by appeal to the lottery paradox, a contradiction results from assuming that a belief may be completely justified when some chance of error remains. Hence we shall conclude that this assumption must be rejected to save our conception of knowledge from inconsistency.

Suppose, for the sake of argument, that a belief could be completely justified without all chance of error being excluded. How great a chance of error is to be allowed? One chance in ten? One chance in a million? It won't matter. If there is one chance in n, whatever number n may be, we shall be led into contradiction. Imagine we say one chance in a million is acceptable. Now, suppose we set up a fair lottery with a million tickets numbered consecutively from 1, and that a ticket has been drawn but not inspected. Of course, there is only one chance in a million that the number 1 ticket has been drawn. So, by the current proposal, we would be completely justified in believing that the number 1 ticket was not picked. There is only one chance in a million of error. Hence we would be completely justified in claiming to know that the number 1 ticket was not picked.

Moreover, people really do speak this way about lotteries; they do say they know that the ticket they hold was not drawn because there is so little chance of it. However, a similar claim can be made concerning the number 2 ticket, for there is equally little chance that it was picked. So we can say that we know that the number 2 ticket was not picked. But then the same reasoning applies to each ticket in the lottery. Of each ticket in the lottery, we would be completely justified in believing, and, hence, in claiming to know, that the ticket has not been drawn. But the set of things we would thus claim to know is inconsistent. It is contradictory to claim that each of the tickets in a fair lottery with one winning ticket is not the winner. For if each is not the winner, then the lottery with one winning ticket has no winning ticket. Of course, requiring the chance of error to be less than one in a million will not help. However small the chance, we can find a large enough lottery to create the paradox. Since the assumption that a belief may be completely justified though there is some chance of error leads to contradiction, we must reject it. To analyze knowledge in terms of complete justification that allows for some chance of error is to render knowledge logically inconsistent.

We now have established a critical premise in our final argument for skepticism, namely, that if a person is completely justified in what he believes, then his justification must exclude all chance of error. There is some chance, however slight, that the braino hypothesis, or some other hypothesis of the same skeptical cut, is true; and therefore some chance that our ordinary perceptual beliefs are in error. Therefore those beliefs are not completely justified. Because they are not completely justified, we do not know that they are true.

Summary of the argument

The argument just advanced may be laid out as follows:

1. If anyone knows that any perceptual belief of his is true, then he is completely justified in his perceptual belief.

2. If anyone is completely justified in his perceptual belief, then his justification for his perceptual belief excludes all chance of error.

From these two premises we conclude

Therefore

3. If anyone knows that any perceptual belief of his is true, then his justification for his perceptual belief excludes all chance of error.

Having reached this conclusion, we appeal to material from an earlier argument to reach our skeptical conclusion.

4. If there is some chance that the braino hypothesis is true, then the justification anyone has for his perceptual belief does not exclude all chance of error.

5. There is some chance that the braino hypothesis is true.

Therefore

6. The justification anyone has for his perceptual belief does not exclude all chance of error.

From conclusions (3) and (6) we obtain our further skeptical conclusion

7. No one knows that any perceptual belief of his is true.

An epistemist objection:
The skeptic's braino hypothesis is a mere possibility
We may concede most of this argument without conceding the conclusion. For we may deny there is some chance the braino hypothesis is true. We have conceded that the braino hypothesis is logically possible. But the logical possibility of truth does not show there is any chance whatever that the hypothesis is true. To argue that a belief is not completely justified because some conflicting hypothesis is logically possible is to argue fallaciously. We have shown this earlier. So, if the skeptic attempts to argue from the logical possibility of the braino hypothesis to the conclusion that there is some chance that it is true, her argument will be ill-founded. There is no chance that the braino hypothesis is true; it is simply preposterous.

A skeptical rejoinder:
The survival hypothesis: A realistic skeptical hypothesis
We do not by any means concede that there is no chance that the braino hypothesis is true. After all, how do you know that it is false? Note that any alleged evidence of the falsity of the hypothesis could be explained in terms of the attempts of Dr. O to mislead us. However, again for the sake of argument, it will be useful to present a skeptical hypothesis that is more apt to obtain agreement from an impartial consideration. So we shall construct, ultimately, a hypothesis which obviously has some chance of being correct.

Since our capacity for scientific discovery is not matched by our capacity to use scientific discoveries wisely, our survival as a species may depend on our ignorance of the true nature of the world. There is at least some chance that if our perceptual beliefs were not slightly incorrect, then we would indeed destroy ourselves, as a result of scientific discovery and mishandled technology based upon it. Thus, we propose that there is at least some chance that erroneous beliefs have survival value, and, moreover, that the erroneousness of our perceptual beliefs has saved us from destroying ourselves long ago. There is some chance, however small, that the erroneousness of our perceptual beliefs has survival value.

Suppose, to illustrate, that there is some particular theory that is especially dangerous to humankind. Imagine that some discovery in physics would enable us to understand how to release vast amounts of energy in a simple way with common materials. If we imagine, moreover, that such devices might have the power of thermonuclear bombs and that anyone could easily learn how to construct them from materials to which we all have access, then we can see that such devices would place us all at the mercy of demented and desperate people willing to destroy themselves to destroy others. And then the holocaust would result from the madness of the few.

The foregoing is but one way in which the discovery of some principle might serve to destroy us. One might imagine countless others. If the discovery of such a principle would obliterate life, then the failure to discover it would be necessary for our continued existence. Now one way in which we might be prevented from discovering such a principle is by virtue of perceptual error. If we are misled at the perceptual level, our attempts to check those theories that might lead to the fatal one will be subverted at the level of observation. We shall, by dint of our defective observational beliefs, be encouraged to accept some slightly incorrect theories that are more probable, in terms of our slightly erroneous perceptual beliefs, than those correct but fatal theories we reject. In short, theory is based, either directly or indirectly, on observation, and, therefore, faulty observation, erroneous perceptual beliefs, can prevent us from arriving at correct theories. We propose that there is some chance, however small you might think it is, that our very survival at this moment depends on our failure to accept some correct theory, because of our erroneous perceptual beliefs. In this way, then, there is some chance that our perceptual beliefs are erroneous, and, indeed, that our survival has depended on it. If you ask how the error could have gone undetected, the answer is that, had it been detected, no one would be here now to report the result.

A bit of science fiction may help you to imagine how our survival might depend on perceptual error. Imagine that a group of very intelligent beings, living in a remote galaxy, have the means to observe the earth from a scientific spaceship concealed from our view. Let us call these beings *googols* after the number googol, which is ten to the hundredth power, because their intelligence is ten to the hundredth power greater than that of the most intelligent earthling. One googol scientist, John, reaches an alarming conclusion about the humans, namely, that their rate of scientific discovery will soon enable them to create very inexpensive weapons with sufficient power to destroy themselves. His computation leads him, moreover, to conclude that the weapons will actually be used within fifty years, due to the slow rate of moral development of humans and their inadequate understanding of how to control their aggressiveness. The humans are clearly an endangered species, and John places them on the urgent concern list, offering a prize to any googol who can find a method for saving the humans.

One googol genius, Mary, who has special fondness for the foolish humans, comes up with an elegant solution. It is possible to introduce a very small microbe that will live as a parasite on the brain tissue of humans, being passed from one to the other, which will produce a minor distortion in the way in which humans perceive the world so that their perceptual beliefs will all be slightly inaccurate. This will introduce errors into their scientific observations that will prevent them from making the scientific discoveries that would lead to the creation of the endangering weapons. There is a special elegance to the solution resulting from the fact that errors caused by the microbe will also prevent the humans from making the scientific discovery that would reveal the microbe itself. Mary points out that a minor modification of the microbe would reduce human fertility to a level that would be more compatible with resources of their habitat and proposes the modification be added.

After careful study as to whether the microbe would have harmful side effects, or whether the humans might discover the weapons by other means, it is concluded that Mary's solution will be effective and benign. Mary, revealing typical googol integrity, points out that, strictly speaking, all perceptual beliefs of the humans will be false once the microbe is introduced. Indeed, she insists that it is improper to describe the post-microbe-infestation perceptual beliefs of humans as merely inaccurate, for they will be erroneous, even if only very slightly so. Her point is thoughtfully considered by the referees, but her solution is deemed much less invasive than other alternatives, which range from turning the earth into a kind of human park for googol visitation to preserving a sample of living human brains in vats, and Mary wins the prize. The microbe is introduced undetected onto earth, it functions as predicted, and the humans are saved by their microbe-caused errors of observation. The googols extend Mary the prize of their esteem and celebrate the survival of the humans.

Summary of the Final Skeptical Argument

We now present a summary of the preceding argument. In our summary, we refer to the hypothesis that the erroneousness of our perceptual beliefs has survival value as *the survival hypothesis*. The argument then is as follows:

1. If anyone knows that any perceptual belief of hers is true, then her perceptual belief is completely justified.

2. If anyone is completely justified in her perceptual belief, then her justification for her perceptual belief excludes all chance of error.

Therefore

3. If anyone knows that any perceptual belief of hers is true, then her justification for her perceptual belief excludes all chance of error.

We continue our argument:

4. If no one knows that the survival hypothesis is false, then no one's justification for her perceptual belief excludes all chance of error.

5. No one knows that the survival hypothesis is false.

Therefore

6. No one's justification for her perceptual belief excludes all chance of error.

Finally, from statements (3) and (6) we conclude

7. No one knows that any perceptual belief of hers is true.

We have, by this argument, formulated our argument for skepticism. We shall rest the matter here. However, it is important to understand the implications of the doctrine. Standards of evidence and epistemic evaluation telling us that some beliefs are completely justified, beyond all risk and chance of error, must be laid aside in favor of a more skeptical and flexible theory of reasonable belief. We are not repudiating reason; instead, we are claiming that nothing is beyond its reach. Nothing is so secure or sacrosanct as to be beyond rational criticism. Hence we may always ask whether it is reasonable to accept some statement as evidence for a hypothesis. The question is not resolved by appeal to some infallible beliefs beyond all chance of error. It is settled instead, tentatively and subject to subsequent reconsideration, by appeal to the probabilities, to the very genuine risk of error we admit. The reasonable statement to accept is the one that is more probable than those with which it competes for the status of hypothesis or evidence. In this way, and by induction, we may proceed to reason in terms of evidence and hypothesis without dogmatism or pseudocertainties of knowledge.

In conclusion, it is important to point out that we are not disputing here over the mere use of the word 'know.' Our objection to the dogmatic contention that people know certain of their beliefs to be true is the roadblock to inquiry indigenous to such claims. If a person says he knows that something is true, then he intends his listener to take what he says as true on his authority. It is not a matter to be questioned. The word 'know' functions this way in ordinary discourse, and we consider this a defect of such discourse. We affirm the right and the need to submit any statement or belief to criticism and requisite justification. None are allowed exemption from this ordeal of reason. We concede, of course, that a person might succeed in using the word 'know' without such dogmatic implications. And if someone uses the word in some weaker sense, allowing for fallibility, the chance of error, and the appropriateness of criticism, then we wish him well.

NEW KNOWLEDGE AS UNDEFEATED JUSTIFICATION: A REVISIONIST ALTERNATIVE TO THE SKEPTIC AND THE EPISTEMIST

Let us reflect on the dispute between the skeptic and the epistemist. The skeptic has proven that our perceptual beliefs and corrigible beliefs generally are not completely justified in any way that guarantees the truth of those beliefs and excludes all chance of error. Must we concede the day to the skeptic? The arguments of the skeptic are formidable. What have we learned from her? We have learned that all justification runs some risk of error. Any justification for what we believe is fallible. When we seek a justification for what we believe, the best we can find will inevitably fall short of guaranteeing the truth of what we believe. Justification can aim at truth but cannot eliminate the risk of error. If our search for knowledge is the quest for complete justification and a guarantee of truth, we must admit our ignorance and concede the day to the skeptic. There is another way, however.

We can revise our conception of knowledge. We may redefine knowledge without committing the redefinist fallacy by admitting that our new conception is a revision. We can construct a new conception of knowledge and make this new knowledge the object of our philosophical quest. How can we do this? We begin by admitting that our justification for what we believe remains fallible and falls short of a complete justification. We continue by noting that the fallible justification we do have for our beliefs, the sort appealed to by the internalist, for example, may prove a trustworthy and reliable guide to truth. Such justification may lead us to truth without being based on any false premise or assumption. These reflections show us how to revise our conception of knowledge. The revisionist takes fallible justification rather than complete justification as the basis of knowledge, and affirms that when fallible justification for our beliefs does not depend on error and leads us to truth, we attain a new kind of knowledge. This kind of knowledge based on fallible justification becomes the legitimate object of philosophical and scientific inquiry. In this way, revisionism transcends epistemism and skepticism, combining the insights of both. We have not been able to prove the skeptical hypotheses to be false. We believe, however, that those hypotheses are fanciful, false constructions of the imagination, rather than a truthful account of our world. We believe that our perceptual beliefs about the objects we see, hear, and touch inform us in a trustworthy way about the truth of those objects. We believe, therefore, that beliefs that are justified by our internal standards of justification, though those standards be fallible guides to truth, are also externally connected with truth in a trustworthy and reliable manner. We believe all this.

Suppose, in fact, that our fallible internal justification for our perceptual beliefs and other corrigible beliefs does not rest on error but instead leads us to truth in some trustworthy and reliable manner, as the externalist maintains. Then a revised conception of knowledge lies shining before us. One component is fallibilism, which we take from the skeptic. Another component is internal justification, which we take from the epistemist and the internalist. The final component, which we take from the epistemist and the externalist, is that of justification that is undefeated by error and that connects us with truth in a trustworthy and reliable manner. It is easy to assemble the components, as we have seen, to obtain a revised conception of knowledge. Undefeated fallible justification is the new knowledge that we seek.[10]

It is the object of our inquiry. We cannot prove, as the skeptic has taught us, that our justification is undefeated by error. We have learned from her that some forms of error are invincible and beyond detection. If some skeptical hypothesis of invincible deception is true, then our justification is defeated and our perceptual beliefs are errors. In that case, our situation is epistemically desperate, and we must remain ignorant. If, however, we are right in thinking that our perceptual beliefs will lead us to truth in a trustworthy manner, as our internal standards of justification tell us, then our fallible justification is undefeated, and we have new knowledge. If there is an appropriate match between our beliefs about ourselves and our perceptual relation to the external world, then internal justification matches external justification, fallible justification goes undefeated, and we obtain a new kind of knowledge.

We must, in conclusion, thank the skeptic for undermining our dogmatism and our arrogance. She has shown us our fallibility. We may, nevertheless, seek reasoning and justification that lead us to truth in a reliable manner. The nobility of the goal of truth sustains the undertaking. We ennoble ourselves in seeking truth, even when we realize that we may fail to obtain that noble objective. If the justification we find does not rest on error and enables us to reach the truth, we shall have attained our revised kind of knowledge. This new knowledge is based on a fallible quest for truth without any guarantee of success; we may attain it, though we cannot prove that we will. To the skeptic who asks for proof that we shall succeed, we must put our hands over mouths in silence. We have no proof. We may, however, invite her to join our quest for truth and the new kind of knowledge we seek. Once we admit to the skeptic that she is right and we have no guarantee of success, she, being a woman of insight and character, who has, moreover, freed us of our dogmatism and arrogance, may join as a sympathetic friend in our noble undertaking. We

---

10. This conception of knowledge is developed by Keith Lehrer in *Theory of Knowledge* (Boulder: Westview Press, 1990).

may say to her, "Let us reason further with one another to find some fallible justification to lead us to the truth in what interests us, concerning freedom, mind, God and morals," and she, our brilliant adversary, will become a friend to our philosophical undertaking. The modesty resulting from a recognition of our own fallibility becomes us, opens the road to inquiry and removes the roadblocks to understanding. Revisionism combines the insights of skepticism and epistemism in harmony.

EXERCISES

Skepticism, Knowledge, and Truth

1. What is skepticism? Why have speculators also sometimes been skeptics? Are you a skeptic, a speculator, or both? Why?

2. Consider the following claim:

   We may define 'knowing' as 'having the right answer.' When a person knows the answer, then he has the right answer, and when he has the right answer, then he knows the answer. Thus, the definition given is exactly right.

   What is the matter with this definition?

3. Consider the following argument:

   No unjustified belief can be counted as a case of knowledge. On the other hand, every case of knowledge involves a justified belief. Thus, there is no difference between knowledge and justified belief.

   What is the matter with this argument?

4. It is sometimes said that knowledge and truth are one and the same. Would you agree to this? Explain and justify your answer.

Skeptical Arguments:
The Relativity of Observation and the Braino Hypothesis

5. Consider the following argument:

   When a person sees something, he does not have any evidence for believing what he sees. Therefore, perceptual beliefs are those for which we have no evidence.

   Is this contention correct? Why?

6. The skeptic contends that if we are sometimes mistaken in our perceptual beliefs, then it is always logically possible that our perceptual beliefs are false. How does he employ this premise to

support the skeptical conclusion that we never know that any of our perceptual beliefs are true? How is the premise challenged by the epistemist? Is the challenge successful?

7. In reply to an epistemist objection, the skeptical argument is modified. A major premise of the modified argument assumes that the experiences of a person who has a true perceptual belief may be exactly duplicated by the experiences of a person whose perceptual belief is exactly similar but false. How does the skeptic defend this premise? How does the epistemist question it? What other premises are needed for the deduction of the skeptical conclusion? Were any of these premises used in an earlier argument?

8. What skeptical premise is defended by an appeal to hallucinations? How does the skeptic attempt to prove that hallucinations are always possible? How does the skeptic reply to the epistemist objection that hallucinations can be detected by applying the tests of experimental coherence and the testimony of others?

9. Consider the following epistemist argument:

The appeal to hallucinations in defense of skepticism is entirely illegitimate. In describing some experiences as hallucinatory, the skeptic is tacitly assuming that we can tell the difference between experiences that are hallucinatory and those that are not. But if we can tell the difference, then skepticism is false. The skeptical use of hallucination is thus self defeating. What is the skeptical reply to this argument? Who is right? Why?

10. The braino argument is brought in by the skeptic to defend a premise of his argument and to meet an objection of the epistemist. What is the premise and what was the epistemist objection to it? What objection, involving the distinction between possibility and actuality, is raised by the epistemist against the braino argument? How does the skeptic think that we may legitimately pass from possibility to actuality?

11. Consider the following epistemist argument:

The idea that such a machine as the braino exists is nothing more than idle fantasy. It need not be taken any more seriously than tales of Santa Claus. Thus, the idea that we are controlled by the braino, which the skeptic puts forth as a serious hypothesis, may be rejected without further argument. Rejecting the idea allows us to reject the conclusion of skepticism as well.

What would the skeptic reply to these remarks?

Is the Skeptic's Hypothesis Meaningless?

12. The story of Tom and Dr. O is intended to refute a premise of the skeptic's argument. What is the premise? Why is the perfect deception said to be no deception at all? Why is the perfect hallucination said to be meaningless? Is what the epistemist says correct? Does it refute skepticism?

13. Consider the following skeptical argument:

No one can imagine what anything contradictory would be like. For example, no one can imagine what a round square would be like. Therefore, if we can imagine something, then it is logically possible and not contradictory. So the mere fact that we can imagine what a perfect hallucination would be like, as we did in the story of Tom and Dr. O, shows that such a hallucination is possible.

How might an epistemist reply to this argument? Would the reply be successful? Why?

14. What explanation of meaningfulness is provided by the distinction between an epistemic and a semantic sense of 'meaningless'? Does this distinction really help the skeptic's cause? How?

Complete Justification:
Probability, Externalism, Internalism, and Justification

15. To defeat skepticism, the epistemist contends that evidence which does not exclude the possibility of error may nonetheless greatly reduce the probability of error. What premise of the skeptic does the epistemist hope to refute by contending this? Why is it especially important, from the standpoint of epistemism, to defeat the premise of skepticism? Does the epistemist succeed?

16. What argument does the skeptic employ to show that the epistemist's appeal to probability will lead to skepticism? How does the question of establishing frequencies in a sample enter into the argument? Is any other premise of the skeptical argument vulnerable to attack?

17. The epistemist claims that some beliefs may be assumed to be completely justified until some argument to the contrary is offered. What is the skeptic's reply to this contention? What is the role of the principle of impartiality in the reply? Is the reply effective?

18. Explain the notion of externalism by pointing out how this notion is connected to the following notions: probability, frequency, lucky guessing, reliable process. How does the epistemist use externalism in his reply to the skeptic? How does the skeptic attack the epistemist's use of externalism?

19. Explain the principle of charity; use an example. What does the epistemist mean when he says, "Charity begins at home"? The skeptic maintains that some uses of the principle of charity might lead to most uncharitable results. Which kind of case does the skeptic have in mind? What, exactly, is the skeptic's argument for the claim that the epistemist's slogan "charity begins at home" is entirely useless for the epistemist's cause?

20. Explain how the epistemist tries to use the notion of internalism. Which skeptical premise does the epistemist hope to refute by an appeal to internalism? How does the skeptic challenge the epistemist's claim that conformity to internal standards of justification yields complete justification?

21. The epistemist appeals to the notion of competition in the attempt to refute premise (8). What is the epistemist's argument on this score? Does it succeed?

Justification of Excluding the Possibility of Error; and the Revisionist Account of Knowledge

22. Consider the following argument:

The skeptic argues that all chance of error must be excluded before we are completely justified in a belief. This leads to the conclusion that we never are so justified, and hence that we know nothing. But surely that conclusion is absurd. Consequently, it is most reasonable to reject the premise on which it was based. While we must admit that high probability will not suffice for complete justification, it is possible that high probability, plus some other factor, may suffice and also permit us to elude the lottery paradox. The only problem is to say what that other factor is.

What do you think of this argument? Is it plausible? Can you propose the missing factor?

23. The final skeptical argument is stated in terms of the survival hypothesis. The epistemist has no reply to this argument. Is there some reasonable response an epistemist might make that has been overlooked? How would a revisionist reply to the skeptic?

24. Consider the new skeptical argument:

In order for a person really to know something, he must be absolutely certain of it. Thus, in order for Sally to know that the liquid in the beaker is an acid, she must be absolutely certain that the liquid is an acid. But, in order for her to be absolutely certain of this, there must not be any imaginable grounds for doubting that the liquid is an acid. Surely, though, it is easy to imagine grounds for doubting this claim. Similarly, it is quite simple to imagine grounds for doubting any purported piece of perceptual knowledge. Hence, no perceptual belief is certain, and thus none counts as knowledge. Skepticism is vindicated.

Does this new argument succeed?

25. Explain as clearly as you can how the revisionist account of knowledge combines ingredients from the arguments of the epistemist, skeptic, internalist, and externalist. What is the role of fallible justification? What is the role of undefeated justification? If you were a skeptic, would you agree that the new kind of knowledge proposed by the revisionist can be obtained? Why?

Suggestions for Further Reading

Historical sources

Berkeley, George, *Three Dialogues Between Hylas and Philonous*, Colin M. Turbayne, editor (Indianapolis: Hackett, 1979).

Descartes, René, *Discourse on Method and Meditations*, in *The Philosophical Works of Descartes*, Elizabeth S. Haldane and G. R. T. Ross, editors (Cambridge: Cambridge University Press, 1982).

Hume, David, *An Enquiry Concerning Human Understanding*, Eric Steinberg, editor (Indianapolis: Hackett, 1977).

Plato, *Republic*, translated by G. M. A. Grube, (Indianapolis: Hackett, 1974).

Plato, *Theatetus*, translated by F. M. Cornford, in *Plato: The Collected Dialogues*, Edith Hamilton and Huntington Cairns, editors (Princeton: Princeton University Press, 1961).

Sextus Empiricus, *Outlines of Pyrrhonism*, in Volume 1 of *Sextus Empiricus* (London: Loeb Classical Library, 1933).

Contemporary texts and collections

Ammerman, Robert R. and Marcus Singer, editors, *Belief, Knowledge and Truth: Readings in the Theory of Knowledge* (New York: Charles Scribner's Sons, 1970).

Armstrong, David, *Belief, Truth and Knowledge* (New York: Cambridge University Press, 1973).

Audi, Robert, *Belief, Justification and Knowledge* (Belmont: Wadsworth Publishing Company, 1988).

Ayer, A. J., *The Problem of Knowledge* (Baltimore: Penguin Books, 1956).

Chisholm, Roderick, *Perceiving: A Philosophical Study* (Ithaca: Cornell University Press, 1957).

Chisholm, Roderick, *Theory of Knowledge*, 4th Edition (Englewood Cliffs: Prentice-Hall, Inc., 1990).

Cornman, James, *Skepticism, Justification and Explanation* (Dordrecht: Reidel, 1980).

Dretske, Fred, *Knowledge and the Flow of Information* (Cambridge: MIT Press, 1981).

Ginet, Carl, *Knowledge, Perception and Memory* (Dordrecht: Reidel, 1975).

Goldman, Alvin I., *Epistemology and Cognition* (Cambridge: Harvard University Press, 1986).

Harman, Gilbert, *Thought* (Princeton: Princeton University Press, 1972).

Kornblith, Hilary, editor, *Naturalizing Epistemology* (Cambridge: MIT Press, 1985).

Lehrer, Keith, *Knowledge* (London: Oxford University Press, 1974).

Lehrer, Keith, *Theory of Knowledge* (Boulder: Westview Press, 1990).

Moser, Paul and Arnold Vander Nat, editors, *Human Knowledge: Classical and Contemporary Approaches* (Oxford: Oxford University Press, 1987).

Pappas, George, editor, *Justification and Knowledge: New Studies in Epistemology* (Dordrecht: Reidel, 1979).

Pappas, George and Marshall Swain, editors, *Essays on Knowledge and Justification* (Ithaca: Cornell University Press, 1978).

Pears, David, *What Is Knowledge?* (New York: Harper & Row Publishers, Inc., 1971).

Pollock, John, *Contemporary Theories of Knowledge* (Totowa: Rowman, & Littlefield 1986).

Rescher, Nicholas, *Scepticism: A Critical Appraisal* (Oxford: Basil Blackwell, 1979).

Ross, G. and Michael Roth, editors, *Doubt* (Dordrecht: Kluwer, 1989).

Roth, Michael D. and Leon Galis, editors, *Knowing* (New York: Random House, 1970).

Slote, Michael, *Reason and Scepticism* (New York: Humanities Press, 1970).

Swain, Marshall, *Reasons and Knowledge* (Ithaca: Cornell University Press, 1981).

Tomberlin, James E., editor, *Philosophical Perspectives 2: Epistemology* (Atascadero: Ridgeview, 1988).

Unger, Peter, *Ignorance* (London: Oxford University Press, 1976).

Wittgenstein, Ludwig, *On Certainty*, G. E. M. Anscombe and G. H. von Wright, editors; translated by Paul, Denis and Anscombe (Oxford: Basil Blackwell, 1969).

Wolgast, Elizabeth, *Paradoxes of Knowledge* (Ithaca: Cornell University Press, 1978).

THREE

The Problem of Freedom and Determinism

THE NATURE OF THE PROBLEM

The problem of freedom and determinism is basically a paradox. A paradox arises when two equally evident assumptions lead to apparently inconsistent results. What paradox is connected with the problem of freedom and determinism? It is this. Determinism is the thesis of universal causation, the thesis that everything is caused. On the other hand, the doctrine of freedom maintains that some of our actions are free. Both of these things seem true. We believe both that everything is caused and that some of our actions are free. However, these two beliefs lead to results that are apparently inconsistent. For if everything is caused, then so are those actions we allege to be free. But then they are the result of some causes which made us perform the actions, and, therefore, the actions are not free. So in addition to believing that everything is caused and that some of our actions are free, we also believe that if our actions are caused, then they are not free. That is the paradox in our ordinary beliefs. To understand the puzzle more clearly, let us consider the case for determinism.

THE DETERMINIST POSITION

An Argument for Determinism: Something We All Believe

The first thing to notice about the thesis of determinism is that we all do believe that it is true. All of us believe, or at least are disposed to believe, that everything that happens has a cause. To see that you do believe this, consider what your reaction would be to the following situation: One morning you wake up and go out to start your new automobile. You put the key in the ignition, step on the gas pedal, push the starter, and nothing happens. Your automobile will not start. So you lift up the hood, look underneath, check the spark plugs, the carburetor, the battery, and so on; but everything seems to be in perfect order. Still, the fact remains: the car will not start. Somewhat disgruntled over this state of affairs, you call the local mechanic, who arrives on the scene teeming with confidence. He will fix the car so that it will start. He carefully looks it over, checks it with the thoroughness of an expert, but he too fails to find anything out of order.

Because the car is quite new, you become rather impatient at this point and call the factory representative. Shortly thereafter, he arrives with a clean white shirt, characteristic of his vocation, and begins to check your car. When he has finished a very thorough investigation, and his shirt is no longer white, you ask him, "What is the matter?" His reply is, "Nothing." Because your car still does not start, you decide to pursue the issue in different terms. "Well, what is the cause of the trouble?" you ask. At this point the factory representative straightens his tie and replies in an official voice, "There is no cause. There is nothing the matter with the car. It simply does not start." He continues, "This is one of those curious situations in which a problem really has no cause whatever. There is no cause for the failure of your car to start. It just won't start, and that is all there is to be said."

His report is preposterous. You would remain convinced that there must be some cause. From the fact that the factory representative has failed to find the cause of the trouble, it does not follow that there is no cause. There must be some cause which the man has been unable to discover. The reason you find the report unacceptable is that you are convinced that things have causes. You, like all people of good sense, believe that determinism is true.

Causes may be difficult to find, but to say that a cause is difficult to find is not to say that the cause does not exist. We are all convinced that the failure of the car to start has some cause. A similar argument could be used to show we believe all other things are caused too. Anything on which you focus your attention, anything about which you wonder, is a thing for which you might seek the cause. "Why did that happen?" you ask, and you expect a causal explanation. No matter what happens, you may always ask, "Why did it happen?" or alternatively, "What was the cause of that?" All of us believe that such questions must have an answer. This shows that we are all convinced that whatever happens is caused, even those of us who have not considered the matter in such general terms.

Of course, the fact that the thesis of determinism is believed by everyone does not make it true. Widespread belief of this sort just shows that the belief is part of common sense and, like other beliefs of common sense, it may be false. However, the belief that determinism is true is reasonable. In addition to being widely believed, determinism is a thesis that we all continue to believe after we think it over carefully, examine what it means, and unsuccessfully try to think of counterexamples to it. Let us suppose then that everything does have a cause. Why should this generate a paradox? What problem arises from this commonsense conviction?

The paradoxical consequences of determinism

Suppose that a person has a hereditary disease, and that the disease is the result of causal factors over which she has no control. Nothing she could have done would have prevented her from catching the disease. She does not have it of her own free will; it is the inevitable outcome of events and processes that were beyond her influence. Consequently, she could not reasonably be held responsible for having it. Another way of putting the matter is this: Having such a disease is not something a person does; it is not her action. It is something that happens to her.

What is the relevance of this example to the thesis of determinism? Common sense says that everything that happens is caused. It follows that everything I do must be caused, for among the things that happen in the universe are the actions that I perform. Imagine that I move my trigger finger. This must be caused. Moreover, whatever caused the movement must itself be caused by some earlier conditions and factors. Those conditions and factors must be caused by still earlier factors, and so on. This series of causal factors must extend backward indefinitely into the past. Thus, the movement of my finger is caused ultimately by factors that existed in the remote past, before I was born, factors over which I have no control.

If, however, it is a consequence of the thesis of determinism that a person's actions are the inevitable outcome of causal processes that began before he was born and over which he had no control, then, no matter what a person does, he could not have done otherwise. He could not have prevented his actions from occurring, nor could he have performed any other action instead. His action and inaction alike are the inevitable outcome of events and processes beyond his influence. Consequently, no person may reasonably be held responsible for any of his actions.

To see that this conclusion is inescapable, let us compare the case of the person who has a hereditary disease with that of a person who has just shot and murdered another human being. We said earlier that a person who has a hereditary disease may not reasonably be held responsible for having it, because it is not something she has of her own free will. But why not? The answer, of course, is that her disease is the inevitable outcome of causal factors over which she has no control. However, exactly the same thing must be conceded with respect to the murderer when we suppose that determinism is true. For his act of pulling the trigger on the murder weapon was as inevitable as contracting a hereditary disease. He could no more have prevented himself from moving the trigger than the diseased person could have prevented herself from having the disease. Moving the trigger and contracting the disease are both the inevitable outcome of causal processes extending back in time before the birth of either person. They are thus equally powerless. The murderer, like the diseased person, is really more passive than active. He has no choice, no free will, no real option. He is, in effect, more the one who is moved than the one who moves. Consequently, the murderer is no more responsible for pulling the trigger than the sick person is for contracting the disease.

It may seem that there is an important difference between the two cases, in that the murderer must have done many things to place himself in the position to shoot his victim. He had to obtain a gun, confront his victim, take careful aim, and so on. It might be said that the murderer could quite easily have avoided committing murder, simply by omitting any one of these preparatory actions. But this is sheer delusion. Each of these preparatory actions was itself the inevitable causal consequence of antecedent conditions that existed before the person was born and that, consequently, were entirely outside the scope of his control. By the same argument that we used to show that his pulling the trigger was something he was powerless to prevent, we could show that he was equally powerless to prevent any of the actions that led up to the climactic one. None of his actions are free. They are determined by things entirely beyond his control.

One further qualification is in order. We have spoken of the person as having no choice about what he does. This should not be taken to suggest that the person does not choose or decide to do the things he does. If this looks peculiar at first, remember that a person may choose to do something when, in fact, he has no choice. He can think he has options that do not actually exist. A classic case of this, derived from John Locke, is the following.[1] Suppose that a person is brought into a room while asleep, and that the door to the room, being the only way of escape, is locked from the outside. But the person does not know or even suspect that the door is locked. He awakens, finds himself in the room, and notices that he has very agreeable company. Not knowing that he is locked in, the

---

1. John Locke, *An Essay Concerning Human Understanding*, Book II, Chapter 21, Paragraph 10.

person might consider leaving but chooses to remain instead. Of course, the person really has no choice; he cannot leave, but he does truly choose. Occasionally, we choose to do something when we really have no choice.

This point is of importance to the *determinist position*. As we shall use the latter term, it refers not just to the thesis of determinism, but also to the claim that determinism entails that there are no free actions, and to the claim that, consequently, no actions are free. Spinoza was a determinist in this sense, and he put the point in the following manner: We think we are free because we are ignorant of the causes of our actions.[2] Like the prisoner, if we were but enlightened concerning the true nature of our situation, we would see that we are not free. Human conduct is determined in the same way as the trajectory of a projectile, according to the determinist position. If the projectile were conscious, it might say to itself as it flew through the air, "I am free to swerve to the left or right, but I choose to continue to travel in this path." Of course, this is just so much nonsense. The projectile has no choice. The path it takes is causally determined: it cannot swerve either to the left or to the right. According to Spinoza, such a projectile would be no more foolish than most people are, for the motions that people make are no more free than the motions of a projectile. We are no more free to swerve from the paths we take than the projectile is free to swerve from its path. Because we are conscious, and ignorant of the causal determination of our actions, we think that we are free to swerve to the left or right, but we choose not to swerve at all. Hence the delusion that we are free. We choose only because we fail to realize that we are not free. Choosing when one has no choice—when one is not free—is founded on ignorance.

It now seems quite clear that the thesis of determinism does have paradoxical consequences indeed. For if we accept that thesis, as we are all disposed to do, then we must accept the consequences that no human action is free and, therefore, that no one is responsible for the actions he performs. We are no more responsible for our actions than is a diseased person for having a hereditary disease, or a projectile for following the path it does.

This line of thought has led some people to social activism. For example, Clarence Darrow, a famous lawyer, often defended people on trial for crimes punishable by execution by appealing to the thesis of determinism.[3] His appeal was based on the common ground that we share with the criminal. For if the behavior of the criminal is the outcome of such causal factors as heredity and infantile environment, so is the behavior

---

2. Benedict De Spinoza, *Ethics*, Part One, Appendix, Paragraph Two, and Part Two, Proposition XXXV, Scholium.

3. For Darrow's views, see his speeches, collected in *Attorney for the Damned* ed. Arthur Weinberg (New York: Simon and Schuster, 1957).

of the person who sits in the jury box. Good deeds and misdeeds alike are causal consequences of things that happened in the remote past and were beyond the influence of the doer of the deed. We are the fortunate or unfortunate result of a causal chain of events that began before any of us existed. As such, we are not responsible for our deeds. It would be wrong to execute a person for a deed he has committed. Juries were often persuaded by Darrow's appeal. As we can see, he did not hesitate to raise curious metaphysical questions to save the life of his client.

Summary of the argument of the determinist

The determinist argument we have considered has seemed persuasive to many philosophers. It will be useful at this point to summarize its premises and assumptions. Obviously, one premise is

1. The thesis of determinism is true.

This amounts to the assertion of universal causation, that is, to the claim that everything is causally determined. A second premise is

2. If the thesis of determinism is true, then there are no free actions.

These two premises yield the conclusion

3. There are no free actions.

This conclusion taken together with the further premise

4. If there are no free actions, then no one is responsible for his actions.

yields the further conclusion

5. No one is responsible for his actions.

The determinist, as we are construing that position, accepts all five of the foregoing statements.

Some terminology:
Determinism, libertarianism, compatibilism, and incompatibilism

Notice that premise (2) of the preceding argument is quite independent of premise (1). Either premise might be true while the other is false. Thus, a person who wishes to deny conclusion (3), that is, to affirm that some actions are free, might deny either premise. Premise (2) does not assert that determinism is true. It is merely a hypothetical statement about what would be the case if determinism were true. In this respect, premise (2) is like the statement 'If it rains, we shall get wet!' A person who makes this statement has not asserted that it will rain or that we shall get wet; her statement is merely a hypothetical one about what will happen if it rains. So premise (1) might be true and premise (2) false. It might be that, although the thesis of determinism is true, there are some free actions. Similarly, premise (2) might be true and premise (1) false. It might be that, although the thesis of determinism is not true, if it were true, then there would be no free actions.

Premise (2) asserts the incompatibility of free action with universal causation. Thus the position we have been considering so far rests not only on the premise that determinism is true, but also on the premise that determinism and free action are incompatible. Certain philosophers who have rejected statements (3) and (5) have been led to reject premise (1) and accept premise (2), and others have rejected premise (2) and accepted premise (1). The only position we have considered so far, that of the determinist, is one that is committed to both premise (1) and (2). To furnish ourselves with some labels for alternative views, let us call a person who rejects premise (2) (and consequently, who affirms the compatibility of the free action and universal determinism) a *compatibilist*. Then one who accepts premise (2) we can call an *incompatibilist*. Therefore a determinist, as we are using the term, is an incompatibilist who accepts the thesis of determinism. Finally, let us call a person who rejects premise (1) a *libertarian*. Contrary to the argument we have considered so far, the libertarian affirms that there is free action, but, because he accepts premise (2), he denies the truth of determinism. We can see what the different positions come to with the help of the following chart:

Steps of Argument Immediately Preceding	Determinist	Libertarian	Compatibilist
step (1) Thesis of determinism	accepts	rejects	accepts
step (2) If the thesis of determinism is true, then there are no free actions.	accepts	accepts	rejects
step (3) There are no free actions.	accepts	rejects	rejects
step (4) If there are no free actions, then no one is responsible for his or her actions.	accepts	accepts	accepts
step (5) No one is responsible for his or her actions.	accepts	rejects	rejects

The first three steps are clearly crucial, since all three positions accept step (4). It is also clear that both the determinist and the libertarian are incompatibilists, since both accept step (2). Finally, we may note for future reference that only the compatibilist position accepts both claims endorsed by common sense, namely, (1) and the denial of (3). The libertarian position is the one we shall next consider.

THE LIBERTARIAN POSITION

We have examined the arguments advanced by the determinist to show that there is no free action. What is there to be said for the libertarian view? The libertarian holds that people do have free will, that there is free action, and that, consequently, the thesis of determinism is false. So the libertarian denies that all human actions are caused. We have already noted that the thesis of determinism seems to be a plain matter of common sense. We all do seem to believe that everything is causally determined. How then can one reasonably hold, without flying in the face of common sense, that there are free actions? The answer advanced by certain libertarians—for example, Thomas Reid and C.A. Campbell—is quite compelling. According to both Campbell and Reid, it is every bit as much a matter of commonsense conviction to believe that we act freely as it is to believe the thesis of universal determinism.

A Libertarian Argument:
Deliberation and the Belief That We Are Free
In order to see why these and other philosophers have thought it a plain matter of common sense to believe that people perform free actions, it will be useful to examine with some care the notion of a free action. We remarked earlier that, according to the determinist, we are all powerless to act otherwise than we do. Thus, according to the determinist, whenever we act, it is not in our power not to act, and whenever we do not act, it is not in our power to act. The libertarian holds the contrary views. He maintains that sometimes when we act, it is in our power not to act; and sometimes when we do not act, it is in our power to act. In short, it is sometimes within our power to act otherwise than we do. Putting it another way, sometimes it is up to us whether or not we perform the actions we do. When this is true, then our actions are free actions. Thus, to say that an action is free is to say that we could have done otherwise, that we were free to do otherwise, or that it was in our power to do otherwise. According to the libertarian, we all believe that we perform free actions; consequently, the belief that we perform free actions is as much a part of common sense as the belief that the thesis of determinism is true. How can the libertarian show that we do all believe this?

One way is to reflect upon the nature of deliberation. At some time or other, each of us does deliberate. Some of us may deliberate for only a very short time; others of us may deliberate at great length. Sometimes our deliberations may be foolish and sometimes wise, but it is a familiar fact that deliberation does indeed occur. How does this fact show that we believe that we are free? The argument is quite simple. Part of what is involved in deliberation is the belief that we are free. If I deliberate about whether or not to perform some act, I must believe that it is in my power to perform the action and that it is also in my power not to perform it. If I believed that I was powerless with respect to performing or not performing the action, it would be absurd for me to deliberate about whether or not to perform it. Indeed, it would not even make sense to say that I was deliberating. I might be deliberating about whether or not to perform the action *if* it were in my power. But to deliberate about what one would do if one were not powerless is not the same thing as to deliberate about what to do.

To clarify the relation between deliberation and the belief that we are free, consider a concrete example. Suppose a person is deliberating about whether or not to pay her rent. She weighs the considerations on both sides. For example, she remembers that the landlord did not turn on the heat until rather late in the evening; she remembers that the landlord did not fix the leak in her bathroom; she remembers that the landlord did not shovel the walk after the last snowstorm; and so forth. On the other side, she remembers that the landlord was rather patient when, because of long illness she was unable to pay her rent last winter, and that the landlord himself has not been in very good health recently. After weighing the pros and cons, she finally reaches a decision. She decides that, all things considered, she ought to pay her rent. If she is a conscientious person, she will then, of course, pay her rent if she is able to, for that is what duty requires. This is a perfectly ordinary example of deliberation. Moreover, all that we have imagined might well have taken place even though the person was not able to pay her rent. Imagine that her bank account was depleted, although she did not know it, and that she would be unable to get hold of enough money to pay her rent. In this case, though she might deliberate about whether or not to pay her rent, it is not up to her whether or not it is paid. It is perfectly possible that a person should deliberate about whether or not to do something, like paying her rent, even though one of the alternatives is not within her power.

However, it is important to notice that a person must not know or believe that she is unable to pay her rent, if she is to be properly described as deliberating about the matter. If we modify the example and imagine that the person knows that her bank account is depleted, and that she cannot get any money, then we could not correctly describe her as deliberating about whether or not to pay her rent. For her to deliberate about whether or not to pay her rent, she must at least believe that she can pay it, and, of course, she must believe that she could leave the rent unpaid. She must believe that it is up to her whether or not the rent is paid. This case of deliberation is typical in this respect. A person who deliberates about whether to do *A* or *B* must believe that it is in her power to do *A* and in her power to do *B*. If she *believes* that one of these things is not in her power, then she is not deliberating about whether to do *A* or *B*. Therefore, deliberation implies the belief that we are free. All people who deliberate must believe, at the time of deliberation, that they perform free actions.

Because all people deliberate at some time, it is a conviction of common sense that we perform free actions. Thus, the libertarian argues that merely by introspecting we can discern that we often believe that we perform free actions. Sometimes we feel this in prospect, when we are considering some future action, and sometimes we feel it in retrospect, when we consider some past action. Moreover, in both sorts of cases, a libertarian would argue, the belief that we are free is a matter of reflective common sense. If we carefully think about such cases and consider whether we could have done otherwise, we find that we do then believe that we could have done so.

Objections to the preceding argument:
Acting from the strongest motive

Some determinists have challenged these purported data of introspection. For example, Adolf Grünbaum, a determinist, argues as follows:

> Let us carefully examine the content of the feeling that on a certain occasion we could have acted other than the way we did in fact act. What do we find? Does the feeling we have inform us that we could have acted otherwise *under exactly the same external and internal motivational conditions*? No, says the determinist, this feeling simply discloses that we were able to act in accord with our strongest desire at that time, and that we could indeed have acted otherwise if a different motive had prevailed at that time.[4]

The point of this argument is that, whenever we reflect on a past action, we do not discover that we believe we could have acted differently than we did, but rather that we always act from our strongest desire.

C. A. Campbell has replied that there are some cases in which we can discover by introspection that we do not act from our strongest desire, namely, when we "rise to duty" through moral effort. Campbell maintains that when I am in a situation where doing my duty, *X*, conflicts with satisfying my strongest desire, *Y*, I find that I cannot help believing that I *can* rise to duty and choose *X*; the "rising to duty" being effected by what is commonly called "effort of will." And I further find, if I ask myself just what it is I am believing when I believe that I "can" rise to duty, it is

---

4. Adolf Grünbaum, "Causality and the Science of Human Behavior," reprinted in part in *Philosophic Problems*, ed. by Maurice Mandelbaum et al. (New York: Macmillan, 1957) 336.

that it lies with me, here and now, quite absolutely, which of two genuinely open possibilities I adopt; whether, that is, I make the effort of will and choose X or, on the other hand, let my desiring nature, my character so far formed, "have its way" and choose Y, the course "in the line of least resistance."[5]

Campbell's reply is typical of the libertarian rejoinder to the sort of contention that Grünbaum has made. When we are faced with a situation of moral conflict, according to the libertarian we must be convinced that no matter how we choose, we could have chosen to act differently in exactly that situation, that is, under exactly the same external and internal motivational conditions. In such situations, we must be convinced that both actions are in our power and that the action we perform is up to us. Thus, the libertarian argues, introspection shows that we are sometimes convinced that we are not acting from our strongest desire and, moreover, that we believe our action is free.

Notice at this point that the claim that we always act from our strongest desire may be construed in such a way that it is simply true by definition. Suppose that by the words 'strongest desire' we simply mean that desire from which a person acts. In that case it will be true by definition that a man always acts from his strongest desire, provided he acts from a desire at all. However, if it is true by definition, or rather if it is made true by definition, then that contention will be irrelevant to the truth or falsity of determinism. In fact, we shall be faced with the redefinist fallacy mentioned in Chapter One. We can see this by considering two definitions:

1. 'strongest desire' $=_{df}$ 'that desire, among those a person has at a time, which has the greatest intensity.'

2. 'strongest desire' $=_{df}$ 'desire from which one acts.'

Definition (1) gives both the ordinary meaning of the term and the meaning relevant to the libertarian argument. The determinist circumvents the libertarian argument only by switching to definition (2). However, as we noted in Chapter One, no genuine victory in argumentation is achieved by redefining a crucial term in an argument. The determinist claim that one's strongest desire is the desire from which one acts cannot be established by definition. The question whether or not a particular desire caused a person to act as he did is a question of contingent fact. It is not true by *definition* that the desire caused him to perform that action. But it could be made true by definition that the desire on which he acted is the one we shall call

---

5. C. A. Campbell, "Is the Problem of Free Will A Pseudo-Problem?" reprinted in *A Modern Introduction to Philosophy*, rev. ed. by Paul Edwards and Arthur Pap (New York: The Free Press, 1965) 73.

'strongest.' Then it would be true by definition that he acted from his strongest desire, but it is not true by definition that any one of his desires caused him to act as he did. In short, it is not true by definition that a person's desires or anything else *cause* the action that he performs, and no amount of juggling of the definition of the phrase 'strongest desire' will alter this fact in any way.

Thus, we may conclude that it is in fact a datum of introspection that each of us does believe at some time that we have free will and that some of our actions are free. Indeed, Campbell's emphasis upon situations of moral conflict is needless. It is not only in cases of moral conflict that we believe there are genuine alternatives before us and that it is up to us which of two actions we perform. We believe it in all serious deliberation. Sometimes we deliberate concerning a pair of alternatives when no serious moral question is involved. It may be a situation where our decision will affect only ourselves, (and in a morally insignificant way), but which nonetheless seems to merit serious deliberation. Thus, even in such situations where no question of duty versus desire arises, we find that there is deliberation and, consequently, the belief that we are free.

Summary
Let us take stock of our results. The determinist claims that it is a plain matter of common sense to believe that the thesis of determinism is true. We have now discovered from examining the libertarian position that it seems to be every bit as much a matter of common sense to believe that we are free. Where does this leave us?

It leaves us with our original paradox. Let us return briefly to the argument we considered earlier. It had two premises:

1. The thesis of determinism is true.

2. If the thesis of determinism is true, then there are no free actions.

From these premises, the conclusion follows:

3. There are no free actions.

Both the libertarian and the determinist accept the second premise of this argument; but, whereas the determinist accepts the first premise, and, consequently, the conclusion that there are no free actions, the libertarian holds that there are free actions, and, consequently, rejects the first premise. We have now seen that common sense favors neither side, since it accepts the first premise but rejects the conclusion. Are there any considerations to show whether it is more reasonable to accept the thesis of determinism, or more reasonable to accept the belief that we perform free actions? So far, we have noted that it is as much a matter of common sense to believe that there are free actions as it is to believe the thesis of determinism, and vice versa. But now we must consider seriously the question we have just asked. Leaving aside the question of what we do in fact believe, we must turn to the question of what it is reasonable to believe when logical consistency forces us to sacrifice one of our beliefs. Let us first see what sort of evidence might show that it is reasonable to sacrifice our belief in determinism and to retain our belief that we perform free actions.

A Libertarian Argument:
Introspective Evidence for Freedom

The libertarian must show the evidence for her position to be stronger than the evidence for determinism. How can the libertarian establish this? To answer this question it will be useful to clarify to some extent the libertarian's position. We have spoken of the conviction that we are free, that we perform free actions, that we are free to do otherwise, and so forth. For the sake of economy as well as clarity, let us fix our attention upon some one locution that we can use to express the idea that people perform free actions. Perhaps the word best suited to accomplish this task is the little word 'can.' All the other ideas that the libertarian seeks to express may be expressed by using this word in its various tenses. For example, the libertarian sometimes formulates his views by saying that if a person is free with respect to some action A, then it is in his power to do A and it is also in his power not to do A. This idea can easily enough be expressed by saying that the person can do A and also that he can, instead, not do A. Another way of putting the libertarian position is to say that when a person is free, when her action is free, then it is up to her whether or not she performs that action. Again this idea can be expressed by saying that the person can perform the action and also that she can, if she wishes, not perform it. Still another way of expressing the libertarian idea is to say that a person is free when she has a choice. Now if a person really has a choice, it must be that, whatever she chooses to do, she could have done otherwise. Thus we may express the idea that a person has performed a free action by saying that although she did the action, and, obviously, could do it, it is also true that she could have done something else instead. Thus, a person performs a free action if and only if she could have done something else instead.

Whether we have evidence that people are free, outweighing the evidence that we have for the thesis of determinism, depends on how strong our evidence is for the hypothesis that a person could have done something other than what he did do on some occasion. How strong is this evidence?

The data of introspection

We do in fact all deliberate, and this means that all of us do, at some time or other, believe that we could have done otherwise. Thus, it must be taken as an undeniable fact of introspection that we do believe that we could have done otherwise. The question we must now consider is this:

does our believing this constitute evidence that it is true? We often believe things that are false, and our believing them does not constitute evidence that they are true. However, sometimes the reverse is true. Occasionally the mere fact that a person believes something does constitute some evidence for the truth of what he believes. For example, if I am the eyewitness to a killing, and I believe that Little Joe is the killer, then my belief would constitute evidence, indeed, perhaps very strong evidence, that Little Joe is in fact the killer. In this case, my believing something is so provides adequate evidence for concluding that it is so. Does our belief that we are free constitute adequate evidence that we are in fact free?

Before we try to answer this question, some important distinctions must be drawn. Consider again the eyewitness to a killing; what is his evidence that a killing took place? Well, one might say, his evidence is his actual visual experience, the fact that he actually sees the killing occur. Thus, the eyewitness's belief that a killing occurred is based on evidence of the senses. What about the rest of us who did not witness the killing? Our belief that a killing took place is based on the fact that one person is, and is known or reasonably believed by us to be, an actual eyewitness. The analogy the libertarian would use is this. A given individual, let us say A, has evidence for his belief that he is free, namely, a certain sort of feeling of freedom. This feeling is analogous to the visual experience of the eyewitness. The rest of us also have evidence that A is free, namely, the evidence that this is believed by A, and that he has or has had the appropriate feeling. What is crucial for the libertarian, however, is the first sort of evidence, what we might call "personal evidence." Any given person, such as A, has personal evidence that he is free whenever he has the relevant feeling of freedom, the feeling of being free to act in different ways or not to act at all.

A determinist rejoinder: The fallibility of introspection
Some determinists have argued that this feeling or belief that we are free constitutes no evidence whatsoever for believing that we are free, or that determinism is false. For example, Carl Hempel argues as follows:

> As for the first objection to determinism which refers to a stubborn feeling of freedom of choice, . . . it cannot count as evidence against determinism, for this kind of feeling can surely be deceptive. Indeed I think that the feeling is irrelevant to the question of causal determination. For in order to decide whether a given kind of choice is causally determined, we have to judge whether there is an antecedent event with which the choice is *connected by a general law* of simple form. And surely the data obtainable by introspection, especially the stubborn feeling of freedom, have no bearing on this question. The timid man in a hypnotist's audience, for example, who gets up to make a speech, may truthfully protest a feeling of complete freedom in choosing to do so: this

is quite compatible with the possibility that his choice was causally determined (via general laws concerning the effects of hypnosis) by the instruction he received earlier under hypnosis.[6]

It is important to notice that Hempel is not questioning what we find by introspecting. He concedes that we may discover by introspecting that we have this belief that we are free, but he denies that this belief constitutes any evidence for the claim that we are free. Therefore, the libertarian conviction that we sometimes could have done otherwise is, Hempel contends, not at all supported by the fact that we do believe this is so. His basic argument is that such a belief can be deceptive; the datum of introspection is not adequate evidence for the claim that we could have done otherwise, because we can be deceived by introspection. For this reason he contends that the datum of introspection has no bearing on the question of whether our actions or choices are causally determined by some antecedent event.

A libertarian reply:
Fallibility does not discredit introspection as a source of evidence
In spite of the persuasiveness of Hempel's argument, the libertarian might well reject it. In the first place, it does not follow from the fact that a person can be deceived in accepting a hypothesis on the basis of some experience, that her having that experience fails to give her adequate evidence for accepting the hypothesis. The experiences that give us adequate evidence for accepting hypotheses about any number of things are experiences that can be deceptive. For example, suppose that I see a chair in front of me. The experiences that I am having provide me with adequate evidence for believing that a chair is there. No one would deny that those experiences I have do constitute adequate evidence for that hypothesis. Nevertheless, as we noted in Chapter Two, this experience might be deceptive. For instance, a hypnotist might generate in me experiences of just this sort when there is no chair in front of me. Thus just as the hypnotist deceives a person into believing that he is free when he is not, so the hypnotist might deceive him into believing that there is a chair in front of him when there is not. Yet both experiences might constitute adequate evidence for the hypotheses the person accepts.

The argument we have just considered may be generalized. The experiences that give us adequate evidence for accepting a hypothesis about some physical object, such as that there is a chair before us, about some other person, such as that he is speaking to us, or about some past event, such as that we were married yesterday, are all experiences that can be

---

6. Carl G. Hempel, "Some Reflections on 'The Case For Determinism'," in *Determinism and Freedom In The Age Of Modern Science*, ed. by Sidney Hook (New York: New York University Press, 1958), 161.

deceptive. They are experiences that a hypnotist can use to deceive us. Just as the hypnotist deceives a person into believing that he is free when he is not, so the hypnotist deceives him into believing that there is a chair in front of him when there is not, that he is talking to another person when he is not, and that he was married yesterday when he was not. Yet the experiences the person is having do give him adequate evidence for accepting the hypotheses, even though the hypotheses are false.

The reason that such experiences give a person adequate evidence for his beliefs is that those experiences are not different in character from the experiences that we have when we see a chair in front of us, talk to another person, or remember that we were married yesterday.

As we have seen in Chapter Two, there is some chance that we are in error when we believe almost anything. And this may be considered grounds for denying that we *know*, when knowledge is construed as requiring that all chance of error be excluded. But even if we conclude that the evidence we have in these cases does not give us knowledge, as the skeptic avers, we may still fairly maintain that the evidence makes it reasonable for us to accept the hypotheses in question. Hypotheses *may* be false in spite of our evidence, but some are reasonable nonetheless. From the fact that the evidence may deceive us, it by no means follows that the evidence is inadequate to make our beliefs reasonable. The argument that the evidence may be deceptive does not prove, in the case of physical objects, other minds, past events, or free action, that our experiences have no bearing on, or relevance to, the question of whether it is reasonable to believe such things. To argue that, because an experience may be deceptive, it does not provide adequate evidence for accepting a hypothesis, is to commit oneself to a nihilistic position according to which almost nothing would be reasonable.

Moreover, it will not be legitimate for the determinist to reply to the foregoing argument that the case of free will is different from the other cases, in that we have good evidence that some human actions and choices are connected to preceding events by a law of nature, that is, are causally determined. For this reply employs the same logic as the preceding argument. That some of our actions are causally determined by preceding events fails to prove that our introspective datum is not adequate evidence for believing that we sometimes could have done otherwise. Similarly, that people sometimes suffer from hallucinations fails to prove that our senses do not give us adequate evidence for believing in the existence of material objects. Finally, that we are sometimes mistaken about past events fails to prove that memory does not give us adequate evidence for believing in the existence of past events. From the premise that in particular cases we are not free, we cannot validly argue to the general conclusion that introspection does not give us adequate evidence that we are free, just as from the premise that in particular cases we are misled by our senses and memory, we cannot validly argue to the general conclusion that our senses and our memory do not give us adequate evidence for the beliefs they lead us to accept.

A determinist rejoinder: A poor analogy

What has the libertarian offered as evidence for her belief that she is free? This evidence, it will be recalled, consists in a person's feeling of freedom. It is supposed to justify the person's belief that she is free, much in the way that the eyewitness's visual experience serves to justify his belief that a killing occurred. But consider the alleged analogy more closely. Is a feeling of freedom really analogous to a visual experience, or even to any sort of perceptual experience? To see that the answer is no, we need only observe that a perceptual experience, such as the visual experience of the killing, is one thing, and the belief that the killing occurred is another. The fact that there are two distinct events here, one of seeing and one of believing, is essential if one is to be the evidence for the other. A feeling of freedom, on the other hand, is not at all distinct from a belief that one is free. Hence, it is not analogous to a visual experience of an eyewitness. Rather, it is analogous to the belief that the eyewitness forms on the basis of his experience. No *independent* evidence has really been produced. What initially seemed to be that sort of evidence, namely a feeling of freedom, turns out on closer examination to be nothing more than the very belief that one is free. That, surely, does not qualify as independent evidence for the belief itself.

Is there any independent evidence that we are free? By independent evidence we mean evidence for the belief other than the belief itself, that is, some independent evidence in the form of things that we know to be true and that support the belief. The libertarian must supply such independent evidence to justify her claim that we have strong evidence that we are free.

A Third Libertarian Argument:
Empirical Evidence That We Could Have Done Otherwise

The libertarian might well argue that we do in fact have such independent evidence. It is quite clear that we sometimes have sufficient evidence for the hypothesis that a person can do something, for we often see a person do something, and when we see him do it, then, of course, we assume that he can do it. Indeed, that a person does something entails that he can do it. The crucial question is whether we can have adequate independent evidence for the hypothesis that a person can do something, when we do not see him do it and, moreover, when he does not do it. First, let us examine the question of whether we can have independent evidence that a person can do something when we do not see him do it. How are we to get such evidence?

To see a person do something at some other time is one way to get evidence that he can do it when we do not actually see him do it. That is, if a person does something today, and if he did it yesterday and the day before, and if his capacity to do this has not been altered negatively, then, when tomorrow rolls around, we may infer that he can still do it, even if we do not see him do it then.

Let us imagine that we are trying to set up an experiment to prove that a person can do otherwise at a certain time. Moreover, let us take a very simple action, the lifting of an arm, so as to avoid any irrelevant complications. Now we are to set up an experiment to show that at a certain time the person could do otherwise. We find a subject that is normal in every way and investigate when our subject can and cannot perform the very simple action involved. For example, we might first instruct him to lift his arm whenever we tell him to, and then observe that he does it. We might then instruct him to lift his arm whenever we tell him not to, observing that he does this. We might then tell him to heed or not to heed our instructions as he wishes and see that he sometimes lifts his arm when we tell him to, and sometimes does not. We might then run this same experiment under a variety of circumstances, indoors and outdoors, under stress and under relaxed conditions, with a weight attached to his arm, without impediment, and so on. Moreover, we might keep careful records on the condition of the subject throughout our experiments; finally, we might vary the condition of the subject by means of drugs, hypnotism, and so forth.

Now suppose we instruct our subject to heed or not to heed our directions as he wishes, and ensure that the condition of the subject, as well as the situation in which he is placed, are those that we have found to be most propitious for arm lifting. Moreover, suppose we watch him lift his arm, and then we avert our eyes for a moment and, subsequently, see him lift his arm again. Under these circumstances, we would have sufficient empirical evidence to support the hypothesis that the agent could have lifted his arm during that brief period when we did not see him lift it. We would be quite justified in claiming that the hypothesis is true. Therefore it is perfectly possible for us to acquire evidence, perfectly sound empirical evidence, for the hypothesis that a person could have done otherwise.

Reflecting upon this imagined experiment should show us that many actions—both familiar and unfamiliar, simple and complex—are such that, when a person performs them, we have adequate evidence to support the claim that he could have done otherwise. For most unfamiliar and complex actions contain, as essential parts, familiar and simple actions. For example, let us return to the murderer. Suppose that the weapon that he uses is a gun, that he aims carefully at his victim and then squeezes the trigger. The deed is then done; his victim has been shot. Notice that one crucial element or constituent of his action is pulling the trigger. If he could have held that finger still, he could also have avoided shooting his victim and thereby committing murder. Thus, if he could have done otherwise with respect to the action of moving his finger, the act of murder could have been avoided.

Of course, the act of moving a finger is very simple and familiar, one that we have often seen performed under a great variety of circumstances and conditions. It might well be argued that those complex actions that we judge the agent could have avoided performing each contain as an element some simple and familiar action that we know, on the basis of empirical evidence, the agent could have avoided performing. Thus, our judgments that a person could have done otherwise may all ultimately rest upon the empirical evidence that we have for the hypothesis that familiar and simple actions could have been avoided—that, though the agent performed them, he could have desisted. Moreover, we have additional evidence to show that a person could have done something he did not do. The evidence consists of our knowing whether a person tried to do something. The question of whether or not a person could have done otherwise, may rest entirely upon whether or not he tried to. To see that this is so, let us return to our imaginary experiment. Suppose that, after he has been injected with a special drug, our experimental subject does not raise his arm when we tell him to. We then wonder whether he could have raised his arm or not. The best way to find out is to ask him whether or not he tried to do so. If he says he made no attempt to move his arm, then the mere fact that his arm did not move provides no evidence that he could not have moved it. So, if a person does not try to do something, then his not doing it fails to provide evidence that he could not do it. On the other hand, if he says that he tried as hard as he could to move his arm and failed nonetheless, that is exceedingly strong evidence that he could not have moved it.

Therefore, one kind of evidence that we can accumulate to show that an agent could have done something is the agent's testimony about what he tried to do. For if the agent testifies that when his arm did not move he did not try to move it, his not moving it provides no evidence that he could not have moved it. Moreover, this evidence is crucial. We might have evidence that a person could do something because the conditions of the libertarian thought experiment might all be well satisfied, but we nevertheless might fail to have adequate empirical evidence that he could have done otherwise. For we might also have evidence that the person tried as hard as he could and failed nevertheless. However, when the conditions of the thought experiment are all well satisfied, and when in addition we have evidence that the agent did not try, and subsequently fail, to perform the action, then surely we have impressive empirical evidence that he could have done what he did not do. Therefore our belief—a belief that all people of common sense accept—that we often could have done otherwise, is strongly supported by empirical evidence.

Summary of the argument

To see the force of this libertarian argument, let us consider how the conclusion is derived from the premises we have defended. First, we have argued

1. We sometimes have adequate empirical evidence that we could have done otherwise.

Secondly, because we have said that when a person could have done otherwise, then his action is free, we may add the premise

2. If we sometimes have adequate empirical evidence that we could have done otherwise, then we also sometimes have adequate evidence that we perform free actions.

Moreover, because we have also said that if we perform free actions, then the thesis of determinism is false, we may also accept the premise

3. If we sometimes have adequate empirical evidence that we perform free actions, then we have adequate empirical evidence that the thesis of determinism is false.

From these three premises we may validly deduce the conclusion.

4. We have adequate empirical evidence that the thesis of determinism is false.

Of course, from the first two premises alone it follows that we sometimes have adequate empirical evidence that we perform free actions.

Objection by the determinist: Ancestral determination

What should the determinist reply? Recall that determinism entails not only that a given event is causally determined, that is, that there are earlier conditions that determine the event, but also that these conditions are themselves causally determined by earlier events, that those conditions are in turn determined by still earlier events, and so forth into the indefinite past. A person's behavior is, therefore, not merely causally determined but also, let us say, *ancestrally* determined by a chain of events stemming from the indefinite past. So the determinist rejoinder is going to hinge upon the fact that determinism implies not only that behavior is causally determined, but that it is ancestrally determined as well.

The argument is simply this. One might have the sort of evidence that we imagined in our experiment to support the hypothesis that a person could have raised his arm when, in fact, his behavior is not only causally determined, but ancestrally determined. The state of a person's arm is determined by the state of certain muscles within his body. We assume that the state of those muscles is determined by certain physical processes that go on in the body, and these physical processes are no doubt causally determined by earlier physical processes, and those by yet earlier ones, and so on into the indefinite past. Consequently, if the motion of his arm is not only causally determined, but ancestrally determined as well, then it is determined by conditions that existed before he was born and over which he had no control. Therefore, whether he moves his arm must be determined by conditions that he could not control.

The preceding remarks assume that determinism is true. But the crucial point is that the evidence we have from the libertarian's experiment is perfectly consistent with the motion of the subject's arm being ancestrally determined. It is perfectly consistent with the truth of determinism. If the evidence for the hypothesis that a person could have done otherwise is consistent with the ancestral determination of the person's behavior, then obviously the evidence is not adequate to establish the hypothesis that the person could have done otherwise. For if the evidence from our experiment is consistent with the hypothesis that the motionless state of the subject's arm was ancestrally determined, then it is also consistent with the hypothesis that he could not have done otherwise. Because the evidence fails to show that his behavior was not ancestrally determined, it also fails to show that he could have done otherwise. Therefore the evidence of the libertarian's experiment is inadequate to support her libertarian position.

A libertarian rejoinder: Justification without deduction

The libertarian reply to this argument resembles her reply to the determinist objection against the evidence of introspection. The determinist's objection to the claim that we have evidence adequate to establish that a person could have done otherwise is that all such evidence is logically consistent with the claim that the person in question could not have done otherwise. The determinist concluded that the evidence has no bearing on or relevance to the hypothesis that the person could have done otherwise.

The way the determinist argues would be rejected as unacceptable in other contexts. The determinist's only complaint against the evidence cited by the libertarian is that it is logically consistent with the denial of the hypothesis that it is meant to establish. Thus, the determinist presupposes that no amount of evidence is sufficient to justify a claim or belief that a person could have done something if the evidence does not entail that conclusion. This would seem to commit him to the quite untenable general thesis that no amount of inductive evidence, evidence that does not entail its conclusion, is adequate or sufficient to sustain any conclusion. This is surely absurd. All the hypotheses we accept about the future and the past are based on inductive evidence for those hypotheses. The only evidence we have about the past (for example, that a person was married yesterday) or about the future (for example, that there will be an eclipse of the sun at some specific time) is inductive. The evidence for these hypotheses surely does not entail that they are true. Nevertheless, inductive evidence may be perfectly adequate and sufficient to sustain them.

Moreover, we can see that the determinist's objection is mistaken by reflecting upon a case in which a person performs an action, thus proving that she could perform it, where we have only inductive evidence to show that she did so. For example, if we see a person standing with her finger on the only button that can ring a bell, and, though we do not see her push the button, we hear the bell ring, then we have adequate evidence for the hypothesis that she did, and hence could, push the button. The evidence that we have does not entail that conclusion, but it might well be adequate nonetheless. In short, the determinist's objection to the acceptance of the evidence in question as adequate for the hypothesis that a person could have done otherwise rests upon the inadequate premise that the evidence does not entail the hypothesis. That premise is much too weak. The evidence might well be sufficient to sustain the hypothesis inductively even if it is perfectly consistent with the denial of the hypothesis, that is, even though it does not entail that the hypothesis is true. To deny this is to head pell-mell down the road of irrationalism.

The Determinist reply:
Something must be wrong with the libertarian argument
The determinist replies hitherto presented have been ineffective. There is still a potent reply available to the determinist, however. Recall exactly what the thesis of determinism amounts to. It is basically the thesis of universal causation, that is, the claim that everything that happens has a cause. Thus, if the foregoing libertarian argument is correct throughout, what has really been produced is good empirical evidence that some action is *not caused*. However, the determinist insists, nothing of the kind has been produced. The evidence from the libertarian experiment does not show or even strongly support the claim that something which happens or fails to happen is uncaused. Remember the nature of the experiment, the determinist will urge. After witnessing the person raise and lower his arm a number of times and in a number of conditions, we then concern ourselves with whether this same person could have raised his arm when he in fact let it at rest. Surely, when his arm is motionless, various conditions of the person's muscles were causally sufficient for his arm to remain that way. To this the libertarian must agree, for these are the facts of anatomy. What is crucial is that the condition of his muscles at that moment was *causally sufficient* for his arm to remain at rest. For, if indeed his arm does remain at rest, then there was a cause for this, namely, the condition of his muscles. So, it has hardly been shown that it is reasonable to think that some action (here, the action of the arm remaining at rest) is *uncaused*. In fact, it does not really matter whether the libertarian conceded anything. It is manifestly true that the condition of the various muscles was causally sufficient for the arm to remain at rest. And, since the arm remained at rest, it was caused to do so by the

condition of the muscles. Thus, the experiment does not show that it is reasonable to believe that the action lacks a cause.

Now the determinist may go on the offensive in a novel sort of way. No good empirical evidence has been offered in support of the claim that some action is uncaused. But, if the libertarian argument were correct, then evidence in support of the claim that determinism is false *would* support the claim that some action is uncaused. Determinism just is the thesis that everything that happens has a cause. Hence, the determinist argues that something or other is wrong with the libertarian argument, even if we cannot pinpoint exactly what it is. That argument, if correct, would issue in a conclusion—that there is good empirical evidence for the claim that some action is uncaused—which is clearly not established. So something must be amiss in the libertarian argument.

A libertarian reply: A final word

The reply of the libertarian to this criticism consists in reiterating her original claim. She originally held that this evidence was adequate to support the thesis that a person could have done otherwise. The determinist has argued that this evidence does not seem to be the kind that could refute the thesis of determinism. The libertarian replies that the reason for this is that the hypothesis that a person could have done otherwise is not obviously incompatible with the thesis of determinism. The evidence showing that a person could have done otherwise also shows that any hypothesis incompatible with this one must be false. However, it might well be the case that some hypothesis is actually incompatible with the hypothesis that a person could have done otherwise, but does not appear to be incompatible with it. In that case, the conclusive evidence that a person could have done otherwise might not appear to be conclusive evidence to refute the other hypothesis, but it is conclusive, nonetheless.

An analogy should help to clarify this point. A person might see a die resting on her desk and thus have conclusive evidence that there is a die on her desk. Now a die is by definition a cube, and a cube is something that has twelve edges. That is, from the fact that something is a cube we may validly deduce that it has twelve edges. However, suppose that the person who observes the die on her desk and knows that it is a cube, does not realize that it follows, from the fact that something is a cube, that it has twelve edges. Though it would be apparent to this person that she has adequate evidence that there is a cube on her desk, it might not be apparent to her that she has adequate evidence that something on her desk has twelve edges. But the evidence that she has is adequate for the latter, nonetheless. Her seeing a die on her desk gives her evidence sufficient to establish that the thing on her desk has twelve edges. The fact that her evidence would not seem to her to be sufficient is beside the point. The evidence is sufficient whether or not she realizes that this is so. Similarly, if the statement that a person could have done otherwise is such that we can validly deduce from it that the person's behavior was not ancestrally determined and, therefore, that the thesis of determinism is false, then the evidence that we have to support the hypothesis that a person could have done otherwise is also evidence supporting the hypothesis that determinism is false.

A person who does not realize that one may validly deduce the falsity of determinism from the statement that a person could have done otherwise will not take evidence for the truth of the latter statement to be evidence for the falsity of determinism. But it is evidence, and sufficient evidence, for the latter, and therefore for the falsity of determinism. So the evidence that we have obtained from our imaginary experiment, and the evidence available to us from the uncontrolled but abundant resources of everyday life, is sufficient to show that a person could have done otherwise and, therefore, that the thesis of determinism is false.

THE COMPATIBILIST POSITION

One could plausibly contend that there is some merit to the final remarks of both the libertarian and the determinist. The determinist claims with some plausibility that the evidence that a person could have done otherwise is not adequate to refute the thesis of determinism. Indeed, this seems to be true, since if determinism were false, then something that happens would lack a cause, and the evidence produced from the imaginary experiment does not seem to show that any action lacks a cause. On the other hand, we must surely agree with the libertarian that there is very strong evidence for the hypothesis that a person could have done otherwise. But if that hypothesis entails the falsity of determinism, then we seemingly should agree with the libertarian that we have sufficient evidence for the falsity of determinism.

We began by noticing an apparent paradox: Common sense supports the thesis of determinism and also the thesis that some actions are free. Thus, it is reasonable to believe each of these claims. However, the two claims seem to be logically inconsistent. In the attempt to decide between the claims in question, we have been led, in effect, to another apparent paradox, namely, that there is strong empirical evidence sufficient to refute determinism, but that the same evidence does not seem to entail, or even inductively support, the claim that some action is uncaused. The fact that there seems to be merit in both the libertarian and the determinist positions has led some to search for an alternative view. Since our attempt to adjudicate between the libertarian and the determinist has led to another apparent paradox, we have additional reason to seek an alternative position that will resolve the paradoxes and retain what seem to be libertarian and determinist good points.

The libertarian and the determinist share a common premise: if determinism is true then there is no free action, or, if there is free action then determinism is not true. In other words, determinism and free action are incompatible. Consequently, we can easily see that someone might equally reject both the determinist's and the libertarian's position by denying their common premise. Philosophers who do so we shall call *compatibilists*, in contrast to determinists and libertarians, to whom we shall refer jointly as *incompatibilists*. (See the chart presented earlier in the chapter.)

The position of a compatibilist is philosophically tempting. We said earlier that the problem of freedom and determinism presents a paradox, because the thesis of determinism, as well as the hypothesis that people sometimes act freely, are both things a person of common sense accepts as evident. That two beliefs which are perfectly evident from the standpoint of common sense should turn out to be inconsistent, is a paradox indeed. The alleged inconsistency, according to the compatibilist, is only apparent and not real. Moreover, the other apparent paradox will also be dissolved. For, as we shall see, the compatibilist position will allow us to maintain that, while we do have empirical evidence that some person could have done otherwise, this is not empirical evidence for the falsity of determinism, and so is not empirical evidence that some action has no cause.

How is the compatibilist position defended? It does seem implausible to suggest that a person could have done otherwise, even though his behavior was determined causally by conditions existing before he was born and over which he had no control. Nevertheless, this is precisely the view that compatibilists defend. Their line of defense has taken two directions. In the first place, some compatibilists have tried, by analyzing the notion of causal determination, to show that the thesis of causal determinism implies nothing incompatible with free action. The most famous defender of this idea is perhaps John Stuart Mill, but many philosophers have followed this line of thought. Secondly, some compatibilists have tried to show that the idea of free action, that is, the idea that a person could have done otherwise, does not imply anything incompatible with determinism. These two approaches are really two sides of the same coin. For, of course, if the idea of free action implies nothing incompatible with the thesis of causal determinism, then the thesis of causal determinism can imply nothing incompatible with free action. However, from a methodological point of view, one might start by analyzing either notion in an effort to establish this compatibility. Finally, one might attempt to prove the compatibility of free action and determinism without offering an analysis of either. That may appear to be the least promising route, but it is one we must also investigate.

A Compatibilist Argument: Causation as a Constituent of Action

Certain arguments advanced to prove the compatibility of free action and determinism are distinctive because they try to prove compatibility by showing that determinism is indispensable to free action. This view has taken a number of forms. One is an argument that the distinction between action and mere passivity has itself to do with causation. Earlier, when we were examining the determinist case, we noticed that, according to the determinist, the truth of determinism implies that people are more passive than active. If human action is the inevitable outcome of causal forces beyond the person's control, it would seem that he is more acted upon than actor. The person who pulls the trigger on the murder weapon appears active, appears to perform an action. But, according to some determinists, he is not really active; instead, he is passively responding to causal forces that lie entirely outside of his influence. According to certain compatibilists, this is a complete inversion of the truth. For, as they see it, the difference between passive response and action must itself be delineated in causal terms.

What is the difference between a simple action (such as raising one's arm) and a mere movement of the body (one's arm going up), which is not an action? One compatibilist answer to this question is that when I raise my arm, something happening within me causes my arm to go up. My performing the simple action of raising my arm involves my arm going up in response, causal response, to something that takes place within me. Compatibilists have described this thing that goes on within me in various ways. For example, it has sometimes been referred to as a *volition*, the idea being that my raising my arm consists of my arm going up as a causal consequence of a volition occurring within me. The volition might well be described as an "arm-going-up volition," or something of the sort. However, this event, so described, is one whose very existence may be, and indeed has been, doubted. It is by no means evident that any such thing as a volition occurs within a person whenever she raises her arm. A volition would have to be some kind of occurrence, some episode that occurs within the person, but is not identifiable through introspection. For it is not at all clear that when a person raises her arm she can ever detect, by introspection, such a volition occurring. The theory of volition may, however, be stated in a form impervious to problems of this sort. The volition might consist of some well-known and familiar kind of psychological state. For example, it may be argued that when my arm goes up because I want it to go up, I have raised my arm. My doing something thus consists of a certain arm movement taking place because I want it to. This view requires that there be some connection between my wanting to perform the action and its occurrence. The obvious connection, suggests the compatibilists, is a causal one. The wanting causally produces the doing. If this view, or any variation of it, is correct, then my doing something requires its being caused by some psychological state that occurs within me.   Consequently, action, and therefore free action, must be compatible with causal determination, since it involves causal determination as a constituent.

An incompatibilist rejoinder: What controls the cause?

There are defects in this compatibilist argument. In the first place, it is by no means obvious from introspection that, whenever a person performs an action, his action is accompanied by some antecedent want, wish, desire, or any other specific psychological state. Actions occur under a variety of circumstances and subsequent to any number of different kinds of psychological states. Thus it is initially implausible to suggest there is any one introspectable kind of psychological state that is a constituent of every human action. However, even if we accept a notion of volition that is not an introspectable state, and allow for the possibility that every human action might have, as a necessary constituent, some such ingredient of which none of us is aware, the compatibilist will still not have won the day.

To see this, let us suppose that every action does have, as a necessary constituent, some state that causes the action to occur. It is by no means clear that what we are here supposing is at all intelligible. The idea has certain internal defects. For example, if the state in question is said to be a volition, then we must ask what the volition is a volition of. Suppose I raise my arm. Is the volition which is a constituent of this action a volition that my arm go up? If so, then is that volition itself an action? And if the volition is itself an action, then must there be another volition which in turn is a necessary constituent of this action? In that case, when I raise my arm, there would have to be a volition that my arm go up and, that volition itself, being an action, would have to have as a necessary ingredient a further volition, and so on. This would imply that an infinite series or regress of volitions must occur for me to raise my arm, and that is impossible. This regress cannot be avoided by a compatibilist who affirms that volitions are actions, and that all actions have volitions as a constituent.   Hence, the compatibilist rejoinder based on an appeal to volitions fails.

The compatibilist reply: Reasons and causes

The compatibilist contention is not only that actions are caused, but that they are caused by something not itself an action. Perhaps the paradigm of action, and of free action in particular, is rational action. A rational action is one for which the agent has reasons. Now suppose that a person not only performs an action, but has reasons for performing it. These reasons explain why she did it. Thus, if a person is asked why she raised her hand, and she replies that she wished to answer the question asked, then she has performed an action for which she has a reason.   The reason—that she wished to answer the question—explains the act. Reasons often imply a cause, but this is not to say that every reason is a cause. If somebody presents an argument, then she gives reasons for the conclusion of the argument, but in so doing she obviously has not caused the conclusion. However, there must be some connection between the content of a reason and the action for which it is a reason, or the reason would have absolutely nothing to do with the action. The reason is manifestly connected with the action in some way.

The most plausible way of explaining the connection between action and reason is to say it is a causal relation. It might be quite difficult to explain just how a person's reason is connected causally with his action. For example, it seems somewhat implausible to suggest that when a person raised her hand because she wished to answer a question, there occurred within her a wish to raise her hand, which in turn caused her arm to go up. Surely that would be a very inadequate causal account of why her arm went up. An adequate account of the way in which the wish was causally related to this action might contain a reference to a very complex set of conditions, other than those immediately apparent, which existed at the time. A helpful analogy is that of striking a match to light it. No one doubts that striking a match is causally connected with its lighting, but to say that the striking of the match caused its lighting is to give a very inadequate causal account. We know very well that striking matches is not sufficient to make them light. All sorts of additional conditions must prevail: there must be adequate oxygen, the pressure on the match must be heavy enough, the match must be dry, and so forth. Nevertheless, to say that the match lighted because it was struck is intelligible, because there is some, perhaps indirect, causal connection between striking a match and its lighting. Similarly, to say that a person raised her hand because she wished to answer a question is intelligible, because there is some, perhaps indirect, causal connection between her wishing to answer the question and the raising of her arm.

All this taken together provides the basis for a proof of the compatibility of rational action and determinism that escapes the preceding argument of the incompatibilist. The argument is this. The reasons that a person has for performing a certain action are not themselves actions. Having certain reasons for performing an action is not also something performed. Indeed, it is nonsense to speak of performing reasons. Moreover, a person may have no control over whether certain reasons occur to him. For example, a person might see something happen that provides him with a reason for some action, when his having that reason is beyond his control. If we see something happen that provides a reason for action, then we cannot help having that reason for doing what we do. However, this fails to show the resultant action to be unfree. It might be perfectly free, although the reasons for which it was performed are reasons the person could not help having. Suppose I see that a beam is about to fall on a person's head and I warn him. My reason for acting was that I saw the beam was about to hit the person on the head. Although I could not help having that reason, the action is nevertheless free. Therefore, an action may result from having a reason that one could not help having, that is, a reason that one was not free not to have, and the action might nevertheless be free. This shows that a free action may causally result from some condition the agent was powerless to prevent.

This, however, means the collapse of the argument for the incompatibility of free action and determinism. That argument depends upon the assumption that if an action is causally determined by some condition beyond the control of the agent, then the agent could not help doing what she did. It depends upon the premise that if a person's action is ancestrally determined, it is not a free action. But the way to refute this premise is now clear. If an action is causally determined by some reason that a person could not help having, then she is performing an action causally determined by conditions beyond her control. But such an action may nevertheless be free. My warning someone that a beam is about to strike his head is an example of a free action of just this sort. Therefore the rejoinder to the incompatibilist is simply that an action may be free even if it is ancestrally determined, and therefore causally determined by conditions over which the agent has no control. Because the thesis of determinism implies nothing, except that an action is ancestrally determined, that even appears to be incompatible with the idea that the action is free, we may conclude that free action and determinism are indeed compatible.

Summary of preceding arguments
To pinpoint the weakness in the incompatibilist argument, let us restate the premise from which he derives his conclusion. First he says, quite correctly,

1. If determinism is true, then some conditions that causally determine actions are beyond the control of the agent.

but then he contends,

2. If some conditions that causally determine actions are beyond the control of the agent, then there are no free actions.

from which premises he validly deduces the incompatibilist conclusion.

3. If determinism is true, then there are no free actions.

But we have now shown that premise (2) of the argument is equivalent to the false claim that if an action is free, then all conditions that causally determine the action must be within the control of the agent. In fact, as we have seen, there are free actions that are determined by conditions some of which are beyond the agent's control.

THE INCOMPATIBILIST POSITION

In reply, let us formulate the strongest argument for incompatiblism. Formerly, we noticed that determinism implies not only causal determination but ancestral determination as well. This point bears reformulation and reiteration in terms of a more precise conception of determinism and causation. Let us consider a concept of causation that is closely related to science, and more specifically to scientific explanation.

The most common model of scientific explanation is deductive. Suppose we want to explain some phenomenon, say that a piece of iron sinks in water. We then seek some antecedent condition and some law of nature from which we can deduce the thing to be explained. In the case of the iron sinking in water, the antecedent condition is that the given volume of iron weighs more than the same volume of water, that is, the specific gravity of iron is greater then that of water. The law is that whenever a solid object is placed in a liquid and the specific gravity of the solid is greater than the specific gravity of the liquid, the solid object sinks below the surface of the liquid.

Another way of putting this would be to say that the condition of the solid object having a greater specific gravity than the liquid is a sufficient condition for the solid object's sinking when placed in the liquid. Thus, if E is explained by virtue of the fact that there are certain conditions C and a law of nature L such that E is deducible from C in conjunction with L, then we shall say that C is causally sufficient for E.

According to the present formulation of determinism, it amounts to the thesis that there are antecedent sufficient conditions for everything that happens. Suppose that the thesis is true and that some event E occurs. We may conclude that there is some antecedent set of conditions C_1 that is sufficient for E. But we may also conclude that there is some set of antecedent conditions C_2 sufficient for C_1, and so on. However, the important thing to notice is that if C_2 is antecedent to and sufficient for C_1, and C_1 is antecedent to and sufficient for E, then C_2 is antecedent to and sufficient for E. This is evident from our definition of 'sufficient.' To say that X is sufficient for Y is to say that Y is deducible from X together with a premise stating the appropriate laws. Thus, if we can deduce E from C_1 together with one or more laws of nature L_1, and we can deduce C_1 from C_2 together with one or more laws of nature L_2, then we can deduce E from C_2 together with one or more laws of nature. All we need to do is to take C_2 together with L_1 and L_2, and we can obviously deduce E.

What does all this fancy logic show? Consider the consequences for the classroom example of my raising my hand. Suppose that determinism as characterized above is true. Could I have done otherwise? For example, could I have refrained from raising my hand? It might seem so upon first consideration, until we notice a simple but disastrous consequence of concluding that I could have done otherwise.

What is the disastrous consequence? It is one noticed by Peter van Inwagen.[7] If I could have done otherwise and, hence, not raised my hand, then I could have rendered false either the law *L* or the antecedent conditions *C*. Why? My raising my hand is the result of the law and the antecedent conditions. If I could have rendered false the statement that I raise my hand, by refraining from raising it, then I could have rendered false either the law or the conditions, because they together imply that I raise my hand. The point is that if I can render some statement false, then I can render false any statement implying that the statement is true. This point resembles arguments of the form of *modus tollens*, which you recall has the form

If *p* then *q*
Not *q*
Therefore,
Not *p*.

The law tells us that if *L* and *C*, then *A*. Suppose I could have brought it about that not *A*, that is, I could have rendered it false that *A*. If not *A*, then by *modus tollens*, not both *L* and *C*, that is, either not *L* or not *C*. Thus, I could have brought it about that either not *L* or not *C*, that is, I could have rendered it false that *L* or I could have rendered it false that *C*. In short, if I could have done otherwise, then I could have rendered false either the law *L* or the antecedent conditions *C* determining what I did.

Why is this disastrous for compatiblism? Simply because no one can render false a law of nature. Consider the law of gravity. It is a law, a scientific law, and no one can do anything about that. Thus, if I raise my hand now, and this is a consequence of a law of nature and antecedent conditions, I could not have rendered the law of nature false. No one can render a law of nature false. So, if I could have done otherwise, then it must be the statement of the antecedent conditions that I could have rendered false.

So, you might be inclined to think, what is disastrous about that? Suppose the antecedent conditions include my wanting to do something, to ask a question, for example. I could have rendered false the statement that I wanted to ask a question by simply not wanting to ask a question. But it is important to recall what our logical reasoning revealed above: that determinism tells us that these antecedent conditions also have antecedent

7. P. van Inwagen, "The Incompatibility of Free Will and Determinism," *Philosophical Studies* 27 (1975): 185-99.

sufficient conditions. So, if I do A, and determinism is true, then there is a law L_1 and a set of antecedent conditions C_1 such that from L_1 and C_1 we can deduce A. Similarly, however, if determinism is true, then C_1 is determined, which means there is some law L_2 and antecedent conditions C_2 such that from L_2 and C_2 we can deduce C_1. Of course, C_2 is also determined by some law and antecedent conditions C_3, and so forth backward in time to some condition C_N that existed before I was even born. Now for the disastrous consequence for the compatibilist. Consider all the laws L_1, L_2 and so forth to L_N and the antecedent conditions C_N. From all these laws together with C_N we can deduce all of the later antecedent conditions in the chain, including, C_3, then C_2, then C_1, and finally the action A. So if we combine all the laws into a superlaw L^*, then, from L^* and C_N we can deduce A, my raising my hand.

So, if I could have refrained from raising my hand, I could have rendered false either C_N or L^*. We have already argued that I could not have rendered false any of the laws, so I could not have rendered false the law L^*. I could also not have rendered false the statement of antecedent conditions, C_N, however, because those conditions existed before I was even born.

Now we can draw the incompatibilist conclusion. If determinism is true, then whatever I do, I could not have done otherwise. Why not? We have seen the reason. If I could have done otherwise, then either I could have rendered false the laws of nature, or I could have rendered false statements of conditions that existed before I was born. Clearly, I could not have done either of these things. I am totally powerless to influence either the laws of nature or conditions that existed before I was born. Therefore, compatiblism is false.

Assuming, as we must, that we cannot render false the laws of nature, we can restate the incompatibilist argument in terms of our lack of control over conditions that existed before we were born. If determinism is true and I perform an action A, then there is a set of antecedent conditions that is sufficient for my performing A, and there is a set of antecedent conditions sufficient for those conditions, and so on, back in time to conditions that existed before I was born. Actions that are determined in this way, we said earlier, are not only causally determined, they are ancestrally determined. In the light of the preceding reasoning, we may conclude that any of those sufficient conditions, in the chain of sufficient conditions that resulted in my performing action A, is itself sufficient for my performing A. Because some of those conditions existed before I was born, we may conclude that if determinism is true, then there are antecedent conditions sufficient for my performing A which existed before I was born and over which I had no control. Thus if determinism is true, and I perform action A, then not only is it true that nothing else could have happened, it is also true that nothing else could have happened because of conditions over which I had no control. That is the crucial point.

For it is correct to say that a person could have done otherwise, when there are antecedent conditions sufficient for his performing the action he did, only if he had control over some part of the conditions themselves. Consequently, if determinism is true, and my actions are ancestrally determined, then there will always be conditions, sufficient for my performing the action, that existed before I was born and over which I had no control. But if, when I perform an action, it is true that nothing else could have happened, because of antecedent conditions *over which I have no control*, then obviously I could not have done otherwise. All the means for having done otherwise were rendered unavailable to me by conditions that preceded my birth.

A Compatibilist Rejoinder: Further Reflections on 'Could'
The question at the heart of the dispute is the following: Is the statement that a person could have done otherwise compatible with the statement that there are sufficient conditions for his action over which he has no control? To simplify the discussion, let us use the word 'could' only in the sense related to freedom. Now let us consider how we might analyze the meaning of the statement that a person could have done otherwise. By analyzing this statement, we shall be able to prove that the answer to our question is affirmative.

The statement that a person could have done otherwise may be analyzed hypothetically. To say that a person could have done otherwise means no more or less than that he would have done otherwise if some specific condition had existed. For example, suppose I say that a person could have lifted a dumbbell. What does that mean? Surely what it means is that he would have succeeded in lifting the dumbbell if he had tried to lift it. Now consider the latter statement. The statement that a person would have succeeded in performing an action if he had tried to perform it is perfectly compatible with the statement that, determinism being true, his behaving in some contrary way was determined by conditions that existed before he was born. For the former statement asserts that, had antecedent conditions been different (that is, had his trying to perform the action been among the antecedent conditions), then the total result would have been different. This is perfectly compatible with the statement that antecedent conditions being what they actually were, it was determined that he would not perform the action. Thus, determinism is again shown to be compatible with free action.

One qualification is needed. Sometimes we say that a person could have performed an action when it would not make much sense to say that the person tried to perform the action. For example, if we say of a normal person that he could have moved his trigger finger, it would be peculiar to analyze this statement as meaning that he would have succeeded in moving his trigger finger if he had tried; for it seems strange to speak of a normal person as trying to move his finger. Usually we move our fingers without trying. Such a statement might be better analyzed in terms of a different hypothetical statement—for example, as meaning that the person would have moved his finger if he had chosen to do so. We need not commit ourselves to one kind of hypothetical analysis for all statements about what a person could have done. But whenever there is a statement of the form '*S* could have done *A*,' this statement may always be analyzed in terms of some hypothetical statement of the form '*S* would have been done *A* if *C*.' The condition *C* might vary from context to context. All we need to assert is that some such hypothetical analysis is always possible, because, given such an analysis, it is easy to prove that free action and determinism are perfectly consistent.

An incompatibilist reply: Ifs, cans, and chains

If we were to accept the kind of analysis proposed, we could prove the compatibility of free action and determinism. But the analyses are unsatisfactory. Statements of the form '*S* could have done *A*' are not analyzable as statements of the form '*S* would have done *A* if *C*.' Moreover, statements of the latter form do not even imply the former. Suppose that a person is chained to a wall but would like very much to move. Suppose now that someone argues that the person could have moved, on the ground that the person would have moved if he were not chained. Surely this would be an absurd argument. Though the statement

The person would move if he were not chained.

is true, it does not imply the statement

The person could have moved.

which is false. The person could not have moved precisely because he was chained. Moreover, the reason that he could not have moved is that he cannot get unchained. The conditions that prevent his movement are entirely beyond his control.

So far we have only considered one hypothetical analysis of one statement about what a person could have done; and, though the hypothetical statement in question does not imply the latter statement, some *other* hypothetical statement may provide an adequate analysis. However, the argument can be generalized. For whether you say of a person that he would have moved if he was not chained, if he tried to, if he chose to, if he wanted to, or if anything else of the sort, what you say will still not imply that he could have moved. Why not? Because it remains possible that conditions entirely beyond the person's control prevent him from trying, choosing, or wanting to do the thing in question. For example, if a person is prevented from trying to do something by conditions beyond his control, then the fact that he would have done the thing if he had tried to do it fails to prove that the person could have done it.

Moreover, if determinism is true, then there are antecedent conditions sufficient for whatever happens; consequently, there are conditions sufficient to prevent whatever did not happen. Furthermore, those conditions extend indefinitely backward into the past. Therefore, if a person does not try to do something, then, if determinism is true, there were antecedent conditions sufficient to prevent his trying, and those antecedent conditions, because they existed before the person was born, are entirely beyond his control.

Thus, no statement of the form 'S could have done A' is implied by a statement of the form 'S would have done A if C,' because it is perfectly possible that there should be conditions that prevent C from occurring and that these conditions are entirely beyond the control of S. Consequently, it is possible that a statement of the latter form is true but the former is false. Moreover, if determinism is true, then this will always be the case when C does not occur, because there will be antecedent conditions sufficient to prevent it from occurring which are entirely beyond the control of S. In short, if determinism is true, then no matter what a person would have done had conditions been different, she could not have done the thing in question, because the conditions could not have been different, as a result of conditions in the remote past over which the person had no control. Thus, once again, if determinism is true, then a person could never have done otherwise. Consequently, determinism is incompatible with free action.

FINAL COMPATIBILIST ARGUMENT: EVIDENCE FOR FREEDOM RECONSIDERED

To see what the argument is, let us return to an argument employed earlier by the libertarian. It was argued by the libertarian that we have perfectly adequate empirical evidence to show that a person could have done otherwise, evidence that passes muster before the canons of scientific method. We imagined a carefully controlled experiment to investigate when a person could and when he could not lift his arm. We not only checked his capacities under a great variety of internal and external conditions, we also took note of his own reports of what he did or did not try to accomplish. We then supposed that he was exposed to conditions that are ideal for arm lifting, as far as our subject is concerned. Then we argued that if he does not lift his arm at such a time, and if we know from his report that he did not try to do so, and he is certain that he would have succeeded had he tried, then we have adequate evidence that he could have lifted his arm. Thus we have adequate evidence that a person could have done otherwise. To this argument of the libertarian, the determinist replied that such evidence is not adequate to prove the thesis of determinism false. For, argues the determinist, how could such evidence prove that anything is uncaused, or that there are not sufficient conditions for something that occurred? Obviously, it could not prove any such thing.

Now the compatibilist maintains that both parties to the dispute have said something correct. The libertarian is correct in claiming that the evidence is adequate to show that a person could have done otherwise, and the determinist is correct in claiming that the evidence is not adequate to refute the thesis of determinism. Both these claims are eminently reasonable, and we can enjoy the luxury of accepting both, for the small price of affirming the compatibilism of determinism and free action.

If the truth of determinism is compatible with the truth of the statement that a person could have done otherwise, then evidence that is adequate for the truth of the latter need not be adequate for the falsity of the former. Indeed, there is no reason why the evidence for the truth of the latter should be relevant to either the truth or the falsity of determinism. The statement that I am a philosopher is compatible with the statement that I am a male, but there is evidence for the former statement that is quite irrelevant to the question of whether or not I am a male. On the other hand, if the truth of determinism is incompatible with the truth of the statement that a person could have done otherwise, then evidence adequate for the truth of the latter will be evidence adequate for the falsity of determinism. Thus, there is only one way of accepting the position that there is evidence adequate to show that people perform free actions but not adequate to show that determinism is false, namely, by holding that the thesis that people perform free actions is compatible with the thesis of determinism. For that reason the position of the compatibilist should be accepted. Free action and causal determinism are not incompatible, as they might appear; they are perfectly compatible. Because this is so, problem and paradox are dissolved in the light of logical clarity.

To better understand this last argument for compatiblism, let us return to the libertarian argument in a somewhat more precise form. The first premise, of course, is this:

1. We have good empirical evidence that a person could have done otherwise.

The evidence in question derives from the imaginary experiment described and discussed earlier. Next, a premise that should be obvious is used, namely

2. A free action is, by definition, an action a person performs although he could have done otherwise.

From these two premises, we can conclude that:

3. We have good empirical evidence that some actions are free.

There is also the premise that is common to both the libertarian and the determinist position, namely

    4. If the thesis of determinism is true, then no actions are free.

and from (3) and (4) we may derive

    5. We have good empirical evidence that the thesis of determinism is not true.

Here, as we noted, the libertarian rests the argument; but it can plainly be continued along the following lines:

    6. The claim that the thesis of determinism is not true is equivalent to the claim that something that happens is uncaused.

We thus derive,

    7. We have good empirical evidence that the claim that something that happens is uncaused is true.

But (7), the determinist argued, is surely false. So there must be something wrong with the argument! The problem is easy to find. Statement (2) is true and statement (5) is false. The culprit is premise (4). Premise (4) tells us that freedom and determinism are incompatible. It is precisely that assumption that leads to paradox—and the compatibilist rejects it.

The compatibilist argument can now be set out. She agrees with the determinist that (7) is false. The imaginary experiment of the libertarian does nothing to show that the action of leaving one's arm at rest is uncaused. She agrees with the libertarian that (1) and (3) are true. The evidence from the imaginary experiment *is* strong empirical evidence that the person could have done otherwise. She disagrees with both the libertarian and determinist who both accept statement (4). Premise (4) is the key assertion of the incompatibilist, and this premise is the one the compatibilist rejects.

The compatibilist position includes basically three elements: (a) some actions are free; (b) the thesis of determinism is true; and (c) the claim that (a) and (b) are consistent. Her defense of (a) is taken from the libertarian. It consists in noting that (a) is supported by reflective common sense, and also supported by the evidence produced from the imaginary experiment. Her case for (b) is taken from the determinist. What is new and original in the compatibilist doctrine is her argument that these strong elements in the libertarian and determinist positions jointly lead directly to (c), and thus to the establishment of compatibilism. Thus, our initial apparent paradox is resolved; the two doctrines of reflective common sense are consistent.

If compatibilism consisting of (a), (b), and (c) is correct, then the positions of both the libertarian and the determinist contain a false premise or assumption. Perhaps the most original part of the final argument for compatibilism is that it shows that the plausible strong points of the libertarian and determinist positions, when taken together, expose the error of incompatibilism common to both positions.

Finale: Control, Transcendence, and Elbow Room

We have shown that freedom and determinism are compatible, but you may wonder how that is possible. How can our actions be free when they result from conditions some of which occurred before we were born? To take an expression from Daniel Dennett, how can we find some elbow room for freedom when everything is causally determined?[8] How can we have control over actions when our actions result from conditions that are beyond our control? Those are the questions we shall briefly attempt to answer.

Control over our actions results from the exercise of our power to accept or reject a motive. Consider an example. You are sitting in a class, and it occurs to you that you would like to raise your hand, and you do so. You are convinced that it was up to you whether you raised your hand. You had a motive for raising your hand, your desire to ask a question, but it was up to you whether you acted on the motive or not. It was up to you whether you accepted or rejected the motive and raised your hand as a result. That is what it is like to have control over your action. What are the ingredients of such control?

The first ingredient is one of supervision. When you have control over your actions, you supervise the decision and execution of the action. Your relation to your internal motives is like your relationship to external advice. When one or more people give you advice, you are in charge of the decision. It is up to you whether you accept or reject the advice. You are in the position of a supervisor deciding whether to enact any one of the policies proposed by your underlings who offer their advice. Similarly, in the case of motives, you are in charge of the decision. It is up to you whether accept or reject the motives. The advice or motives become the objects of higher-level thoughts about them. Thoughts about thoughts are called *metathoughts*, and the process is *metamental ascent*. When we supervise advice or motives, our thoughts and decisions about the advice and motives occur at a metalevel. Through metamental ascent, we transcend first-level motives and take control.

This had led some philosophers, Harry Frankfurt for example, to suppose that when we not only do what we desire but desire at a second level, a metalevel, to have the first-level desire and, consequently, fully do what we want to do, then we are free in the way that is required for moral

---

8. Daniel Dennett, *Elbow Room* (Cambridge, MIT Press, 1984).

responsibility.[9] Consider the case of the person brought into a room while asleep and, though he does not know this, locked in the room. Awaking to find himself in agreeable company, he desires to remain and, we might imagine, wants to have that desire. Such a person seems to bear some responsibility for remaining in the room, as Frankfurt contends. The person's freedom appears limited, however, contrary to Frankfurt's contentions. The person locked in the room does not bear responsibility for all the consequences of remaining in the room because he cannot leave. If someone injures his loved ones, because he is not there to protect them, though he had no reason to think they were in danger, he is not responsible for their suffering as a result of remaining in the room. Though he willingly stays and is responsible for his willingness, he is not morally responsible for the consequences of his being in the room at the time in question, because those consequences would have been the same had he attempted to leave.

Moreover, the person does not have the sort of freedom we ordinarily desire and believe ourselves to have. The man believes that it is up to him whether he stays or goes, and so believes that he is free. But he is not free. Though the person desires to remain in the room, desires at the higher level to have that desire, and so accepts that motive, he lacks freedom. Metalevel acceptance of a motive, though necessary, leaves something out.

What is missing? In the example, the power to leave. The man is deceived about his situation. He thinks he is free to leave, but he is not. He is not in charge, though he mistakenly believes that he is, for he is not able to leave the room. We require not only metamental transcendence of our motives but the power to determine the outcome. In order to be free, I must have both the metamental ability to consider my motives and the ability to determine which motive prevails. To have these abilities, I must have the internal power to accept or reject motives for action, and I must have the external power to perform, or refrain from performing, the considered action. I must, moreover, not be deceived about my powers. Unlike the man locked in the room who believes that he has the power to leave when he does not, we are free when we have the powers we conceive ourselves to have. If, contrary to my conception of my powers, someone else has the power to control my thoughts or movements, then I lack the powers that are necessary to freedom. Freedom is like knowledge in one respect. An undefeated match between the internal conception of our powers and the truth about those powers is essential to freedom.

To put the matter briefly, when my powers are as I conceive them to be, with respect to some action, that is, when my metalevel powers suffice to

9. Harry Frankfurt, "Freedom of the Will and the Concept of a Person," *Journal of Philosophy*, 68 (1971): 5-20.

determine whether I accept or reject the motives for action, and when my first-level powers suffice to determine whether I perform or refrain from performing the action, then the action is within my control. If I prefer to accept a motive and act upon it, then I do accept it and perform the action. If I prefer to reject the motive and not act upon it, then I do reject it and do not perform the action. What happens is within my control because I have the powers I conceive myself to have with respect to the action. In that case I am free with respect to the action.

Let's return to the original question. How can we find the elbow room for freedom, if determinism is true? How can our actions be free, if they result from conditions in the remote past that are beyond our control? The answer is a simple one. What matters for our freedom is what powers we have now. Of course, what powers we have as well as how we use those powers are explained by the laws of nature and antecedent conditions like everything else. But the explanation of how we came to have a power or we use those powers is perfectly compatible with reality of those powers. The crux is that your being free depends on what you are like now, not on how you got that way. Your freedom, to return to our example, to raise your hand and ask a question, or to leave your arm at your side and forgo asking the question, consists of your abilities, your powers, at this moment. What matters is whether you have those abilities, those powers at this moment. If you do, then you are free.

Perhaps you fear from earlier discussion that if determinism is true, you really lack those abilities or powers, your conception of them is a mere illusion. To relieve the fear, consider a thought experiment. Imagine that there is duplicate universe, exactly like the present one, atom for atom the same and indistinguishable, but with one difference. The duplicate universe has just popped into existence a few moments ago as a cosmic accident, a causally undetermined and random occurrence. In this other universe, you have a duplicate, exactly like you, atom for atom indistinguishable. Your duplicate thinks about asking a question, just as you do, and decides to do so. Your duplicate has no causal history, for the duplicate universe has just now sprung into existence. Whether your duplicate has freedom depends not on his or her causal history, but on what he or she is like now, on what abilities he or she now has. You need have no fear that his or her raising a hand to ask a question is not free on the grounds that the action is the result of conditions in the remote past. The duplicate universe has no past. You will not find any reason for denying, when your duplicate raises his or her hand to ask a question, that this is a free action. You will conclude it is free. But now consider. You are just the same, atom for atom, as your duplicate. Your internal and external conditions are indistinguishable. If your duplicate has an ability or power to accept or reject a motive to raise a hand, then you have that ability or power to raise a hand or not to raise it. It is your present abilities and powers that determine whether you are now free to perform an action. It does not matter to your being free whether those abilities and powers arose from cosmic accident or ancestral determination.   Your causal history does not deprive you of your freedom. Your freedom is the product of your causal history. There is your elbow room for freedom when everything is caused. You are caused to be free. Now, what are you going to do with it?

EXERCISES

Determinism and Its Paradoxical Consequences

1. What argument does the determinist offer to show that we all believe the thesis of determinism?   Does the argument justify accepting determinism? Why?

2. What problem or paradox arises if we accept the thesis of determinism? How did Darrow manage to reason from the truth of determinism to the conclusion that criminals are not responsible for their deeds?

3. What is the difference between the thesis of determinism and the determinist position?

4. Consider the following argument:

    Some philosophers and lawyers have argued that people are not responsible for their deeds because all human actions are causally determined by things in the remote past. This argument is easily refuted. The law tells us when people are responsible for their misdeeds; the law defines responsibility. It does not matter what the causal history of an act happens to be. If the action is of a kind specified by the law—as, for example, murder—then the agent is responsible for that deed and deserves the specified punishment, regardless of how the murderous act came to be committed. Therefore, it is useless to argue that people are exempt from responsibility because of the causal history of their crimes. A deed that is a crime under the law is one for which a person is responsible and liable to be punished.

    What do you think Darrow might reply to this argument? Is the argument sound?

5. Do ordinary people really believe the thesis of determinism? Isn't it a part of common sense to believe that there are chance occurrences? And isn't a chance event an event the occurrence of which is *not* determined? It would seem, then, that if ordinary

people believe in the existence of chance, as they surely do, then it is false to claim that ordinary people believe the thesis of determinism? What, if anything, is wrong with this argument?

6. Throughout the last two thousand years philosophers have argued that the thesis of determinism is indefensible. That is, the believer in determinism is not in a position to argue successfully against his indeterministic opponent. Here is a statement of the argument by Epicurus from the fourth Century B.C.:

He who says that all things happen of necessity cannot criticize another who says that not all things happen of necessity. For he has to admit that the assertion also happens of necessity.

And more than two thousand years later Sir John Eccles writes:

`. . . I state emphatically that to deny free will is neither a rational nor a logical act. This denial either presupposes free will for the deliberately chosen response in making that denial, which is a contradiction, or else it is merely the automatic response of a nervous system built by genetic coding and molded by conditioning. One does not conduct a rational argument with a being who makes the claim that all its responses are reflexes, no matter how complex and subtle the conditioning.

What do you make of these arguments? Are Epicurus and Eccles saying exactly the same thing? Might a theory that is indefensible nevertheless be a true theory?

Libertarianism versus Determinism

7. What argument is given by libertarians (for example, Campbell) to support the conclusion that our belief that we are free is a belief of common sense? How does the matter of deliberation enter the argument? In what way does Grünbaum object to this libertarian argument? Is Campbell's reply to Grünbaum adequate? Why?

8. Consider the following determinist argument:

It is easy to prove that every human action is caused. In the first place, every action must have a motive of some sort. Even the most seemingly fortuitous and inadvertent actions can be shown to have a motive, if one is not put off by appearances and investigates the matter in depth. Psychologists—Sigmund Freud, for example— discover motives behind such apparently accidental acts as a slip of the tongue. So every act has a motive. Now if we go on to ask whether an act is caused, the obvious answer is that it is caused by a motive which motivated the act. Which motive? Clearly the strongest one. Indeed, the very proof that a motive is the strongest is that it prevailed; it, rather than another motive, caused the action. Thus are all actions seen to be caused by the strongest motive.

What might a libertarian reply to this argument? Who is right?

9. What argument does the libertarian present to show that we can escape logical inconsistency only by rejecting determinism in favor of the doctrine of free action? How does he define free action? Is the definition sensible?

10. Consider the following argument:

At one point the libertarian appeals to the notion of logical consistency to defend his conclusion. This is his basic error. Consistency is of little or no importance. It is the hobgoblin of little minds. However, the whole problem of freedom and determinism results from the alleged inconsistency of the two doctrines. But what if they are inconsistent? Why let that concern us? Let us boldly admit the inconsistency and say we shall accept both doctrines nonetheless. Thus is the problem of freedom and determinism laid to rest.

What is the matter with this bold suggestion? Does the determinist's rejection of the libertarian argument from logical consistency (mentioned in the preceding question) commit him to the view that logical consistency is unimportant? Why?

11. What argument, based on the data of introspection, is offered by the libertarian to show we have adequate evidence for free action? What objection does Hempel raise against this argument? Is the libertarian reply to this objection cogent? Why?

12. What argument does the libertarian put forth to prove that we have independent evidence to justify the belief that we perform free actions? Why is this argument required in addition to the argument based on the data of introspection? What objections are raised by the determinist against the libertarian argument for independent evidence of free action? What premise in the determinist's argument against the alleged evidence required reformulation? Why? Is the reformulated argument decisive?

13. Consider the following libertarian argument:

The determinist argues that we should accept the doctrine of determinism and reject the doctrine of freedom. But in so doing, he reveals that even he does not believe the thesis he defends. For suppose we are not free but determined, that we cannot help doing what we do. In that case, it would be pointless to argue that we should accept one doctrine rather than another, for we cannot help accepting the doctrine we do accept, whatever that might be. Thus if the determinist is serious in his attempt to persuade us to accept determinism, then he must believe that we could accept that doctrine even if, in fact, we do not. So he must believe that we are free, although he argues that we are not. Thus the determinist's beliefs refute his words.

What might a determinist reply to this argument? Is the argument sound? Why?

Compatibilism versus Incompatibilism

14. What premise accepted by libertarians and determinists alike is rejected by the compatibilist? If the compatibilist accepts *both* the doctrine of determinism and the doctrine of freedom, does this mean that he is committed to an inconsistent position? Why would the compatibilist deny that he is committed to an inconsistency?

15. The compatibilist defends his position by contending that causation is a constituent of action. How does the theory of volitions enter into his argument? In what way does the determinist object to this argument? How does the compatibilist's claim that actions are caused by something which is not itself an action help meet the objection raised by the determinist? What is the final determinist argument against this libertarian argument? Is it immune from doubt?

16. Consider the following incompatibilist argument:

The idea that volitions are caused is absurd. A cause, if it be genuine, must be described independently of its effects. Thus, for example, it will not do to say that the sleep-inducing capacity of a pill causes people to sleep, because the capacity, if it is a genuine cause, must be described independently of its alleged effect. Now suppose that a volition to raise my arm occurs within me. Such a volition cannot be a genuine cause of my raising my arm, because the volition is not described independently of its alleged effect, of my raising my arm. Thus, the volition to raise my arm, like the sleep-inducing capacity of the pill, is not a genuine cause; it is merely a pseudocause. Neither the pill nor the volition is described independently of the effect it is falsely alleged to produce.

Does this argument favor the libertarian or the determinist? Is the argument correct? Why?

17. What incompatibilist argument is derived from an analysis of the concept of determinism in terms of scientific explanation? How does the incompatibilist think this analysis demonstrates the

incompatibility of freedom and determinism? How does the distinction between causal determination and ancestral determination form the basis of the incompatibilist argument? How does the compatibilist answer this argument? Is the answer decisive?

18. Consider the following incompatibilist argument:

The compatibilist concedes that determinism involves universal predictability based on scientific laws. However, this notion of determinism is sufficient to prove the incompatibility of freedom and determinism. Let us first concede that free actions must at least sometimes result from decision. So decision is essential to freedom. One feature of decision is that no one can possibly know what his own decision is going to be before he makes it. Once a person knows what his decision is going to be, he has already decided. However, 'determinism' defined as 'universal predictability based on scientific laws' has the consequence that it is possible for anyone to predict anything. All one needs to know to make a prediction is the antecedent conditions and appropriate laws, and it is at least possible for a person to know this, even if in fact we do not. Thus, if determinism is true, it is possible for a person to predict what his own decision is going to be before he makes it. But if there are any decisions, as freedom requires, it is impossible for a person to know what his decision is going to be before he makes it. Therefore if determinism as defined is true, there are no free actions.

How might a compatibilist reply to this argument? How might he reply if he concedes that decision is essential to free action? Is the argument sound? Compare the article by Carl Ginet in the bibliography.

19. How does the compatibilist argue from the hypothetical analysis of 'could' to the compatibility of freedom and determinism? What example does the incompatibilist present in reply? How does he generalize from this example?

20. Consider the following compatibilist argument:

The compatibility of freedom and determinism is easily proved. Determinism tells us that everything is causally, and indeed, ancestrally, determined. But it does not tell us which things are not free. Therefore, suppose that I lift my arm and that, as freedom requires, I could have done otherwise. I could have left it at my side. What conclusion about this supposition can we draw from the thesis of determinism? All that we may conclude is (1) that I lift my arm is causally and ancestrally determined, and (2) that I could have done otherwise is causally and ancestrally determined. However, the fact that both of these things are so determined is perfectly compatible with their happening. Therefore what follows from determinism concerning free action is that the action and its being free are causally and ancestrally determined. This proves that free action and determinism are entirely compatible.

21. What is the final argument of the compatibilist? Do you consider it sound?

22. In the Finale, it is argued that we are free because we have control over our motives despite the fact that we live in a determinist world. How would you defend this argument against the following objection of the determinist:

The sense of control you have when you chose between your motives is an illusion. If determinism is true your "metachoice" is just as much determined as anything else you do. No matter how many choices, metachoices, metametachoices, etc., you make, every one of those choices is determined since the beginning of time. Ascending to ever higher levels does not get you one step closer to freedom. You are a puppet and you remain a puppet, no matter to which metalevel you rise.

23. Explain the notion of control to which the compatibilist appeals in his account of how it is possible for freedom and determinism to be compatible.

24. In the Finale, the compatibilist presents an argument against ancestral determination. What do you make of the following objection to this argument:

Of course the compatibilist is correct in saying that what you can do *now* depends on what powers you have *now*. But from this it does not follow that the causal chain that led to you having the powers you have *now* is irrelevant. Consider the following analogy: from moment to moment the Earth moves along in its path because of the position and the momentum it has *now*. Does this show that the movement of the Earth is not ancestrally determined? Surely not. The Earth could deviate from its path only if some condition in the past had been different.

In much the same way, what you do now depends on the powers you have now. But this does not show that you are not ancestrally determined. You could do otherwise now only if your powers were different; but for your powers to be different some condition in the past would have had to be changed. And that is beyond your control.

Suggestions for Further Reading

Historical sources

Hobbes, Thomas, *Leviathan* in Volume III of *The English Works of Thomas Hobbes*, W. Molesworth, editor (London: J. Bohn, 1839-45).

Holbach, Paul Henri Thiry, *System of Nature* (London: McDowell, 1850).

Hume, David, *A Treatise of Human Nature* (New York: Doubleday & Co., Inc., 1961).

James, William, *The Will to Believe and Other Essays in Popular Philosophy*, Frederick H. Burkhardt, Fredson Bowers and Ingas K. Skrupskelis, editors (Cambridge: Harvard University Press, 1979).

Locke, John, *An Essay Concerning Human Understanding*, A. C. Fraser, editor (Oxford: Clarendon Press, 1894).

Mill, J. S., *A System of Logic* (New York: Harper Brothers, 1843).

Reid, Thomas, *Essays on the Active Powers of the Human Mind* (Cambridge: MIT Press, 1969).

Schopenhauer, Arthur, *Essay on the Freedom of the Will*, translated by K. Kolenda (Indianapolis: Bobbs-Merrill, 1960).

Spinoza, Benedict, *Ethics*, translated by W. H. White and A. H. Sterling (Oxford: Oxford University Press, 1927).

Contemporary texts and collections

Ayers, M. R., *The Refutation of Determinism: an Essay in Philosophical Logic* (London: Methuen & Co., Ltd., 1968).

Berofsky, Bernard, *Determinism* (Princeton: Princeton University Press, 1972).

Berofsky, Bernard, editor, *Free Will and Determinism* (New York: Harper & Row, Publishers, 1966).

Campbell, C. A., *In Defense of Free Will, with Other Philosophical Essays* (New York: Humanities Press, 1967).

Davidson, Donald, *Essays on Actions and Events* (Oxford: Clarendon Press, 1980).

Dennett, Daniel D., *Elbow Room: Varieties of Free Will Worth Wanting* (Cambridge: MIT Press, 1984).

Feinberg, Joel, *Doing and Deserving* (Princeton: Princeton University Press, 1970).

Fischer, John Martin, editor, *God, Foreknowledge, and Freedom* (Palo Alto: Stanford University Press, 1989).

Fischer, John Martin, editor, *Moral Responsibility* (Ithaca: Cornell University Press, 1986).

Frankfurt, Harry, *The Importance of What We Care About* (Cambridge: Cambridge University Press, 1990).

Ginet, Carl, "Can the Will Be Caused?" *Philosophical Review* (1962) pp. 352-68).

Hampshire, Stuart, *Freedom of the Individual* (New York: Harper & Row, Publishers, Inc., 1964).

Hook, Sidney, editor, *Determinism and Freedom in the Age of Modern Science* (New York: New York University Press, 1958).

Kenny, Anthony, *Free Will and Responsibility: Four Lectures* (London: Routledge & Kegan Paul, 1978).

Lehrer, Keith, editor, *Free Will and Determinism* (New York: Random House, 1966).

Lehrer, Keith, *Metamind* (Oxford: Clarendon Press, 1991).

Melden, A. I., *Free Action* (New York: Humanities Press, 1961).

Morgenbesser, Sidney and James Walsh, editors, *Free Will* (Englewood Cliffs: Prentice-Hall, Inc., 1962).

Pears, D. F., editor, *Freedom and the Will* (London: Macmillan & Company, Ltd, 1963).

Thorp, J., *Free Will* (London: Routledge and Kegan Paul, 1981).

van Inwagen, Peter, *An Essay on Free Will* (Oxford: Clarendon Press, 1983).

Watson, Gary, editor, *Free Will* (Oxford: Oxford University Press, 1982).

Zimmerman, Michael J., *An Essay on Human Action* (New York: Peter Lang, 1984).

FOUR

The Mind-Body Problem

We may begin to formulate the mind-body problem by asking the question, "What is a person?" Clearly, a person is a complex being who can do many things. Unlike many other beings, a person can move himself, crawl, walk, and swim. These are all bodily activities. In addition, many events and processes take place within the body, such as the beating of the heart, the functioning of the kidneys, and the complex functioning of the brain. Such bodily processes are essential for keeping the person alive; in fact, we often describe the state of the person's body by stating the condition of such vital bodily processes. So it is clear that a person has a body which engages in various kinds of behavior, such as walking, and which has processes going on within it, such as brain functioning.

However, many other things a person can do seem not to be bodily activities. Persons think about various matters; decide on courses of action; hope for, desire, and dream about many different things. These all seem to be mental activities, quite different from bodily activities and processes. They seem to involve a mind rather than a body, a mind with states which are quite different from bodily states. So, a person seems to be not *merely* a complex body, but a being with a mind which is quite different from the body.

We do not merely describe a person in this way; we also try to explain bodily behavior and the workings of the mind. In doing so, we typically make remarks about the relationships between the person's body and mind.

For example, we might say that Mrs. Smith's uncharacteristic screaming at her children results from her splitting headache, or that the reason Mr. Smith will not climb mountains is because he is afraid of heights. In both cases we explain a bodily activity (screaming, refraining from climbing) by citing a mental explanation (headache, fear). We also reverse the order of such explanations. For instance, we might explain someone's pain, a mental condition, by citing as its cause some bodily injury, such as a cut on the finger. Or, much more radically, we might explain a change in a person's whole personality by referring to some brain surgery she recently underwent. So mental phenomena can affect the body, and bodily conditions can affect the mind.

Given these observations, we can formulate the mind-body problem by means of several questions: (1) *Are there* really minds and other mental phenomena such as mental events and states? (2) If so, are minds and mental phenomena actually *wholly distinct* from material bodies such as human bodies? (3) How are minds and mental phenomena *related* to material bodies? Philosophers and others have proposed different answers to these questions. Nearly everyone has agreed that we should answer YES to the first question, although one theory we shall discuss later, *eliminative materialism*, boldly answers NO. Assuming an affirmative answer to (1), many philosophers have also given an affirmative answer to question (2). These philosophers have adopted *dualism* as an answer to (2), for they have proposed that minds and mental phenomena are *different kinds* of things from material bodies. Below, we shall examine three dualistic theories: *dualistic interactionism, parallelism,* and *epiphenomenalism*. We shall also consider the theories that result from a NO answer to (2). Finally, there have been different answers to question (3). Some have said that the only relation between the mental and the bodily is that mental and bodily events occur in a parallel temporal order to one another. Others have claimed that causal relationships hold between the mental and the bodily, as people ordinarily suppose. And still others have said that mental phenomena *are* just bodily phenomena.

Some of these views are plausible, others are not. All face problems, but some problems are more damaging than others. Our task will be to evaluate critically the leading alternatives, with the hope that we shall be able to choose from among them one that can be shown to be more plausible than any other. We shall start by looking at dualist theories.

DEFINITIONS OF KEY TERMS

Before beginning the discussion of theories, we should first indicate how certain expressions containing the terms 'material' and 'mental' will be used. We have already discussed bodies (material objects) and minds (mental objects). We have also discussed events and states, both mental and material. We shall construe these different kinds of objects, events, and states as follows:

Material object: An object (such as a stone) that has size, shape, mass, and spatial and temporal position, and that can exist independently of any conscious being.

Mental object: An object that is either a conscious being, i.e., a being that is aware of things (such as a mind), or a being that cannot exist independently of some conscious being (such as a thought or sensation).

Material event: Something (such as the movement of an arm) that occurs over a period of time and consists only of material objects.

Mental event: Something (such as a dream) that occurs over a period of time and consists only of mental objects.

Material state: A condition or situation (such as an infection) of some material object.

Mental state: A condition or situation (such as a psychosis) of some mental object.

Notice that these definitions are *neutral* in the sense that they are consistent with all of the theories to be discussed below. For example, dualists, idealists, materialists and functionalists can all accept these definitions. Note also that we have used the word 'material,' rather than 'physical,' throughout. This is because the term 'physical' is somewhat broader in scope than the term 'material,' and the mind-body debate has generally concerned the relationships between the material and the mental. So, although for many purposes 'physical' would be an acceptable substitute for 'material,' we shall stick to the latter term in our discussion of the mind-body problem.

DUALISTIC INTERACTIONISM

The classical exposition of dualistic interactionism was given by René Descartes. According to Descartes, we can clearly distinguish between three different kinds of substance: one, the eternal substance or God, and the other two, substances created by God. He says: "We may thus easily have two clear and distinct notions or ideas, the one of created substance which thinks, the other of corporeal substance, provided we carefully separate all the attributes of thought from those of extension."[1]

Although there are these two radically different created substances, one that is extended and does not think (body), and one that thinks but is not extended (mind), Descartes claims that he is essentially a thinking substance. Yet he finds that he not only a mind, for he says, "I have a body which is adversely affected when I feel pain, which has need for food or drink when I experience the feelings of hunger and thirst, and so on . . . ."[2]

Nor are people merely minds that happen to have bodies. It would be better to call them *embodied minds*, for Descartes claims to have found

> that I am not only lodged in my body as a pilot in a vessel, but that I am very closely united to it, and so to speak so intermingled with it that I seem to compose with it one whole. For if that were not the case, when my body is hurt, I, who am merely a thinking thing, should not feel pain, for I should perceive this wound by the understanding only, just as the sailor perceives by sight when something is damaged in his vessel . . .[3]

These two kinds of substance which make up a person intermingle in such a way that they causally act upon one another. The mind does not interact with each part of the body separately; instead, Descartes' view is that the mind interacts only with the brain. So, strictly speaking, Descartes' theory is a mind-brain interactionist theory. The mind causally affects the movement of a person's arm, for instance, only in the sense that the mind affects the brain, and the brain sends the appropriate neural impulses to the arm muscles. The mind does not directly affect the arm.

Actually, Descartes thought he could be even more precise, for he thought he could pinpoint the exact place in the brain where the mind-brain interaction occurred. He said that there is just one point of immediate "contact" or interaction between mind and brain. He says, "the part of the

---

1. René Descartes, *The Philosophical Works of Descartes* (New York: Dover, 1955), Vol. 1: 241.
2. Ibid., 192.
3. Ibid.

body in which the soul exercises its functions immediately is in nowise the heart, nor the whole of the brain, but merely the most inward of all its parts, to wit, a certain very small gland which is situated in the middle of its substance . . . ."[4] He adds:

> The small gland which is the main seat of the soul is so suspended between the cavities which contain the spirits that it can be moved by them in as many ways as there are sensible diversities in the object, but . . . it may also be moved in diverse ways by the soul, whose nature is such that it receives in itself as many diverse impressions, that is to say, that it possesses as many diverse perceptions as there are diverse movements in this gland. Reciprocally, . . . the machine of the body is so formed that from the simple fact that this gland is diversely moved by the soul, . . . it thrusts the spirits which surround it towards the pores of the brain, which conduct them by the nerves into muscles, by which means it causes them to move limbs.[5]

This gland that Descartes thought to be the "seat" of the mind is the pineal gland. He felt that it functioned as the intermediary which transmits the effects of the mind to the brain and the effects of the body to the mind. Of course, we now think he was quite wrong about the function of the pineal gland, since it does not seem to be affected by all the brain processes which affect the mind. In other words, the brain affects the mind in many ways that bypass the pineal gland. So dualistic interactionists now would have to say something else about just where and how the brain affects and is affected by the mind. In fact, as more recent dualists have said, it is even wrong to talk of minds and brains interacting, because it is *events* that are causally related, not *substances*. So, although we will talk of minds and brains interacting, and also of mental events and brain events interacting, these statements should always be taken to mean that some brain event is causing a mental event, or that some mental event is causing a brain event.

So here is the theory in a capsule form: (1) There are material things (objects, events, states) as well as mental things. (2) Mental things are completely different *kinds* of things from material things. Mental things, according to this theory, are totally nonmaterial, so perhaps we could say that mental objects such as minds, on this theory, would be something like pure spirits. It is this second point that makes the theory *dualistic*. A theory is not dualist merely because it agrees that there are mental and material things, for as we shall see, nondualist theories accept that. We get dualism only when this claim is taken in conjunction with the further claim that the mental and the material are completely different kinds of

---

4. Ibid., 345.

5. Ibid., 347.

things. (3) Mental and material things causally interact, i.e., they causally affect one another. (4) On one common interpretation, dualistic interactionism holds that a person is not wholly a mental thing, nor wholly a material thing; rather, on this theory, a person is a composite being consisting of a mental object (a spirit-like immaterial mind) joined with a material body.

Descartes himself sometimes stated his theory in a somewhat different fashion, namely, by saying that the real person is *just* the immaterial mind, not the composite. True, the immaterial mind is joined to a material body in reality. But the person is not this combined being, Descartes sometimes said; instead, the person is the same thing as the mind. This version of dualistic interactionism characterizes minds and bodies, and relationships between the mental and the material, in the same way as the version expressed in the previous paragraph. It differs from the preceding version only on the question of which specific entity the person is said to be.

Is there any evidence in favor of dualistic interactionism? The interactionist part is certainly reasonable, even truistic. It seems obvious that my desire for something cold to drink is part of the cause of my going to the kitchen to get some water. And, equally obviously, my parched throat is part of the cause of my desire for something cold to drink. But what about the dualist part? Here, too, there are things to be said in its favor. First, immaterial minds (or souls) figure prominently in some religious doctrines. The mind or soul, it is said, survives bodily death and, in some cases, dwells eternally thereafter in heaven. To the extent that these religious doctrines are plausible, one might conclude, so also is the dualist account of the mind. Another argument for dualism was supplied by Descartes. He argued that he cannot doubt that he thinks, i.e., that he is a conscious being. On the other hand, Descartes maintains that he can doubt that he has a body. So he concludes that having a body is not essential to his existence, whereas having a mind is essential. Hence, his mind is not a material body. Notice that this argument supports the second version of the dualistic interactionist theory cited above, the one that identifies the person with the mind. A third argument for dualism derives from introspection. People are often introspectively aware of qualities of certain sensations, such as the aching or searing quality of some pain. These qualities of achiness or being searing, however, are not material properties, nor are they definable in purely functionalist terms. That is, a quality like achiness is not identical to a material property, nor does it seem to be *definable* solely in terms of typical causes and effects, which, as we shall see below, is the sort of definition offered by functionalist theories. Hence, a sensation such as a pain is not the same sort of thing as a purely material event or state, and neither is it a purely functional state of a person.

We thus have four different arguments in support of dualistic interactionism, one for interactionism alone and three for dualism. But are these arguments satisfactory?

Evaluation of the Arguments

We need not quarrel with the claim that mental and material (bodily) events causally interact. This seems to be a matter of simple common sense, which nearly every person can readily verify in his or her own daily life. The arguments for dualism, though, require closer examination.

Consider first the argument based on religion. It is certainly true that some major religions incorporate an immaterial soul or mind. However, not all major religions accept such an entity: Buddhism and Confucianism, for example, do not. Moreover, those religions that do accept souls generally give no evidence for the existence of such an object. Christianity and Islam, for instance, accept souls, but each of these religions was formulated centuries ago, at times when it would have been generally assumed that each person has a distinct immaterial soul. It was not thought necessary to provide evidence for such an assumption.

One might think, nevertheless, that such evidence exists. There have been numerous reports of so-called *out-of-body* experiences, in which a person is pronounced clinically dead by responsible medical authorities but, after a lapse of some time, the person "comes back to life." These renewed persons have then described the period of time during which they were presumed to be dead, and they have typically said that "they" left or went out of their bodies, that they hovered above or near the body, that they could see and hear medical personnel and grieving friends and relatives, that they could see their former bodies on the bed, though they could not be seen or heard or communicated with in any manner, and that they found this out-of-body condition quite pleasant and did not want to "return" to their bodies. The moment of "return" would then generally correspond to the moment when the person was revived, much to the astonishment of all present.

Cases such as these are not commonplace, but a fair number have occurred and been carefully documented and studied.[6] They provide evidence for dualism, because the entity that "leaves" the body is conscious; it is aware of the people and objects in the room; it can see, hear, understand, and, in general, have mental states quite independently of the body. Only an immaterial mind can do such things. So it looks as if we have hard empirical evidence for dualism. Indeed, cases such as these seem to show that having a mind is essential for life itself. Further, out-of-body experiences seem to support at least personal survival of bodily death—that is, the person seems to survive physical death, at least if we identify, as the person who has died, the being that is said to hover above the body and that is conscious of nearby people and objects. And personal survival of physical death is some evidence for the immortality of the person.

---

6. See Benjamin Walker, *Beyond the Body* (London: Routledge & Kegan Paul, 1974).

This very interesting argument is not wholly immune to criticism, though none of the criticisms is completely conclusive. We may note first that individuals who undergo such experiences may not be dead, even though they are pronounced dead by doctors at the scene. It is possible, and even quite likely, that these "dead" people are actually just barely alive, with brain function so weak that it escapes being monitored. Pronouncements of death, then, are simple errors, at least in many cases. Moreover, the out-of-body aspect of the experience can be explained as the brain *projecting* the person to some point in space, i.e., making it seem as though the person is at that point. Such occurrences are common in vivid dreams, and something similar seems to happen in out-of-body experiences. Also, the dreamlike character of the experience is reinforced when we note that the out-of-body being cannot speak or otherwise communicate to the living people in the room.

These observations go some way towards undermining this argument for dualism. They lead us to focus the issue by noting this: the fact that the revived person reports out-of-body experiences is some evidence that the person was never dead, despite the doctor's pronouncement. We might better describe these cases as *near-death* experiences. They are quite bizarre, but they do not resist explanation in purely medical, physical terms. They provide some evidence for dualism only insofar as we currently lack a complete medical explanation of the facts.

The second argument for dualism is some times attributed to Descartes; we can state it this way:[7]

1. I cannot doubt that I am a thinking thing.

2. I can doubt that I have a body, and so can doubt that I am a material thing.

Therefore,

3. I am essentially a thinking thing, and having a body or being a material thing is not essential to my being what I am.

To evaluate this argument we need to know something about Descartes's notions of doubt and thought. The latter is straightforward. Descartes used the term 'thinking' to cover all mental events and processes—believing, perceiving, sensing, and doubting were all understood by him as thinking, as was deliberating, the sort of thing we now normally regard as thinking. What Descartes meant by 'doubt' is not altogether clear, but he probably sometimes had in mind the logical possibility of false belief. Suppose that, while running in the forest, you trip on something and, upon looking down, you believe you see that you've tripped on a snake. This statement

---

7. Owen Flanagan, *The Science of the Mind* (Cambridge: MIT Press, 1984), 12.

would be doubtful, for Descartes, because although you believe it, it is logically possible that your belief is mistaken. Perhaps it was just an exposed tree root on which you tripped, something that at first glance looks like a snake. So, for Descartes, a statement S is doubtful (can be doubted) just in case it is logically possible to be mistaken in believing S. By contrast, S is indubitable (cannot be doubted) just in case it is logically impossible to believe S and be in wrong in this belief. So understood, the two premises of Descartes's argument amount to this:

1. It is logically impossible for me to be mistaken in believing that I am a thinking being.

2. It is logically possible for me to believe falsely that I have a body, and so logically possible for me to believe falsely that I am a material thing.

Taken by themselves, these premises are quite plausible. The second just amounts to saying that disembodied personal existence is logically possible, i.e., not logically contradictory. That is true. And premise (1) can be readily seen to be true by noticing that if I believe either that I am or that I am not a thinking being, it follows logically that I am one! We need only recall Descartes's way of understanding what thinking is to grasp this point.

What is questionable is whether the conclusion

(3) I am essentially a thinking thing, and having a body or being a material thing, is not essential to my being what I am.

follows from these premises. In effect, Descartes's argument assumes that what is indubitable and what is essential are somehow linked together. This is a mistake. To see this, notice that the Cartesian conclusion (3) implies that I am not a body. Hence, the two premises

(1) I cannot doubt that I am a thinking thing.

and

(2) I can doubt that I have a body, and so can doubt that I am a material thing.

should imply that I am not a body. The form of this argument would seem to be this:

I cannot doubt the existence of X.

I can doubt the existence of Y.

Therefore,

X is not identical to Y.

But this argument form is not valid. Consider this argument:

(4) I cannot doubt the existence of myself.

(5) I can doubt the existence of a person who spent a summer on a farm in rural Pennsylvania.

Therefore,

(6) I am not identical to a person who spent a summer on a farm in rural Pennsylvania.

But indeed, I (George Pappas) am a person who spent such a summer; so the premises are true, given Descartes's notion of indubitability, but the conclusion is false. Hence, the form of argument used here is not valid. Accordingly, neither is the Cartesian argument for dualistic interactionism valid.

The final argument for dualism is that based upon so-called introspection. It differs from the arguments already considered in that it does not attempt to establish the existence of an immaterial mind. Instead, it attempts to show that mental states and events have properties that are not material properties, so that mental states and events are not purely material in nature. To illustrate, suppose that you smell a rose. The olfactory sensation (or smell) that you experience will likely have certain features that will be difficult to describe in words. You may say that the smell is sweet, or delicate, or perhaps fragrant. The sweetness or fragrancy of a smell are certainly sometimes present as features of the smell; one can hardly deny the existence of such features. But it is also difficult to see how such features of the smell could be identified with material features, either of the rose or of the neural system of the person smelling it. One may experience the same sweetness or fragrancy in a smell even when no rose is present. So, even if it is true that the rose itself is sweet or fragrant, as many philosophers have claimed, the sweetness or fragrancy in the smell is not the same as the sweetness or fragrancy in the rose. And certainly the sweetness or fragrancy are not features of the neural system of the observer.

This is a strong argument for a limited form of dualism (limited because it does not pertain to immaterial minds). We are justified in believing that mental states and events have such features as sweetness or fragrancy in smells, and related features in sensations of other senses, because we often experience such features. However, a final verdict on whether this argument suffices to establish this limited form of dualism will have to wait until we look at how nondualist theories attempt to handle features of sensations.

THREE OBJECTIONS TO
DUALISTIC INTERACTIONISM

First Philosophical Objection: *Where* Does Interaction Occur?

For the dualist interactionist such as Descartes, mental events causally interact with brain events. So the interaction literally takes place *in* the brain. This seems to imply that the mental events themselves are located in the brain, since two causally related events are each located where the causal interaction occurs. Yet, according to dualistic interactionism, mental events have no material features except that of occurring at a time, and so they have no spatial location. Dualistic interactionism thus appears to be caught in a contradiction: interaction requires that mental events be located in the brain, but dualistic interactionism itself denies that mental events occur anywhere.

An immediate reply to this objection proceeds by questioning whether causally related events must be located in the same place. After all, we know of action at a distance, such as the gravitational pull of the moon on the ocean's tides. Here the gravitational force of the moon, if we can think of that as an event, is certainly not located where the motion of the water in the ocean is located. Nevertheless, this reply is only a temporary victory for the dualist. For although not located where the tides are, the moon's gravitational force has a location. So the real point is that causally interacting events have some, though not necessarily the same, spatial location. Thus, the contradiction in dualistic interactionism remains.

About all a defender of dualistic interactionism can do at this point is to question the assumption that if two events causally interact, then both have some spatial location. Merely to assert this, the dualist will say, begs the question against the theory. Hence, the contradiction is merely apparent, and this objection is not fatal to dualistic interactionism.

While we think this is the best response a dualist can make here, it is only partially effective. In all the cases we know about, causally related events have spatial location. So, though it may be logically possible for causal interaction to occur between non-spatially-located mental events and spatially located material ones, this interaction is very mysterious and puzzling, since it is unlike any other casual relationship we know about. This mystery and subsequent puzzlement, though not decisive, count against dualistic interactionism.

Second Philosophical Objection: *How* Can Interaction Occur?

The main point emphasized by the first objection is that, for the dualist, mental events and bodily events are radically different. Since this is so, these different kinds of events would seem also to have different kinds of causal abilities. Consider how material phenomena are causally affected: something exerts physical force upon them in some way. Now since physical force is a product of mass and acceleration, whatever can exert physical force must have mass and be capable of acceleration, i.e., change of rate of motion through space. But, according to the dualist, nothing mental has mass; nothing mental can accelerate, because nothing mental can travel from place to place. So, according to this objection, nothing mental can exert physical force; thus, nothing material can be causally affected by anything mental. Consider also how one material body causally affects something else. As already noted, the causal efficacy of a material body is the result of its physical force. But how can physical force be exerted upon that which has no mass, no size, no spatial location? If the dualist part of the theory is correct, and the mental and the material are different in kind, then the interactionist part of the theory must be incorrect. In short, if dualism is correct, there is no mind-brain interaction!

Notice that this objection is not based merely upon the absence of similar features, but ultimately upon the absence of features relevant to causal interaction. So the dualist cannot say here that simply because the mental and the material are very different, that fact does not preclude their causal interaction. True; mere difference does not rule out causal interaction. What rules it out is the kind of difference we find in the case of dualism; the mental and the material do not share any features that would facilitate causal interaction.

What can a dualist say in reply to this objection? His best strategy would be to rely on the comments of a modern interactionist, C. J. Ducasse. He says:

> The causality relation does not presuppose at all that its cause-term and its effect-term both belong to the same ontological category, but only that both of them be *events*.
>
> Moreover, the objection that we cannot understand how a psychical event could cause a physical one (or vice versa) has no basis other than blindness to the fact that the "how" of causation is capable at all of being either mysterious or understood only in cases of *remote* causation, never in cases of *proximate* causation. For the question as to the "how" of causation of a given event by a given event never has any other sense than *through what intermediary causal steps* does one cause the other.[8]

Ducasse is making two important claims in this passage. The first is that the matter of determining which things are causally related is completely empirical; the only restriction is that it be events that are causally related.

---

8. C. J. Ducasse, "In Defense of Dualism," in S. Hook, ed., *Dimensions of Mind* (New York: Collier Books, 1961), 88.

Before we examine specific situations, we can impose no restrictions upon what kinds of things can causally interact. Instead, we should find out by observation and experiment whether minds and brains interact, rather than proclaim that they cannot, just because they are very different in kind, or because they fail to share features we regard as causally relevant. The second point stressed by Ducasse is that when, we come to proximate or immediate causes, we must accept them as brute facts. One event E_1 is a *proximate* cause of another event E_2 when there is no additional event causally intermediate between them. E_1 directly affects E_2 rather than acting through some further event E_3. Ducasse's idea is that there is no way to explain proximate causation, because we explain how one event causes another only when the cause is remote and not proximate, that is, only if the cause brings about the effect by means of some intervening events. For example, we can explain why heating a gas causes the pressure on its container to increase by saying that increasing the temperature of the gas causes the molecules of the gas to move more rapidly and thus to hit the walls of the container with more force. But if an increase of temperature is a proximate cause of an increase in molecular speed, we cannot explain how this causal action works. Explanation comes to an end with proximate causation, and we must merely accept that such causes have the effects that they have. To bring the point back to dualism, we can explain how a desire for drink causes a person to reach for a glass of water by saying that the desire causally affects the brain, which by means of the nerves causally affects the arm. But we cannot explain how the desire affects the brain, because this is a case of proximate causation, something that must be accepted as a brute fact.

While this response enables the dualist to escape the full force of the objection, it makes mind-brain interaction even more mysterious and puzzling. We now have a theory which holds that wholly immaterial mental entities, with no spatial location and no known features that are relevant to causal interaction with material entities, interact causally with material entities at some place and in a manner which is entirely inexplicable. While these considerations do not refute dualistic interactionism, i.e., show that it is false, they certainly help to diminish the overall reasonableness of the theory. The theory can be weakened still further by consideration of a scientific objection.

A Scientific Objection:
Interaction Violates the Conservation of Energy Principle

The principle of the conservation of energy states that the amount of energy in a closed physical system remains constant. But suppose dualism is correct. Then, if there is a causal interaction between the mental and the material this principle is violated. When some bodily event causes an immaterial mental event, the physical energy involved in the bodily event is not transferred to anything else, and energy is *lost*. When a mental event causes a bodily event, the energy gained or lost by the resulting bodily event has not been transferred to anything physical, so that the total amount of energy is changed. So, because both bodies acting on minds and minds acting on bodies would violate the conservation of energy principle, we have good reasons for concluding that there is no interaction of the sort envisioned by the dualist.

We can illustrate this objection with a simple example. Suppose someone tries either to start or to stop the motion of a billiard ball merely by *willing* that it start or stop. Starting a billiard by an act of will would cause the ball to *gain* kinetic energy, which (because it was not transferred from anything physical) would constitute an overall gain in energy. Stopping a billiard ball by an act of will would cause the ball to *lose* kinetic energy, which (because it was not turned into heat or potential energy, or transferred to something physical) would constitute an overall loss of energy. But since the only relevant difference between stopping or starting a billiard ball and starting or stopping a brain event is the amount of energy involved, if doing the one violates the conservation of energy principle and is thus physically impossible, so is doing the other. Moreover, there is also a converse problem. If a rolling billiard ball suddenly stops only because it brought about a mental event, then because the kinetic energy of the ball is neither turned into heat nor into potential energy nor transferred to anything else, physical energy is lost and the principle is violated again. Again, because the only relevant difference between a rolling billiard ball causing a mental event and a brain process causing a mental event is the amount of energy lost, if one violates the principle then so does the other. But violating the conservation of energy principle is physically impossible; hence, causal interaction of the sort required by the dualist is also physically impossible. So dualistic interactionism is false.

Can the dualist effectively reply to this objection? As a start, he can point out that mind-brain causal interaction is at least *logically* possible, because nothing in the definition of the concept of causation entails that all cases of causation involve a transfer of physical energy. He can then argue that we really have two different cases to consider, and that they should be treated differently. The first is brain-mind causal interaction. Here the dualist can say that physical energy may not be required to bring about a mental event, because mental phenomena involve no physical energy. Thus, no energy would be transferred from bodily causes to mental effects, and so bodily causes of mental events need not behave like a ball stopping. Such bodily causes could retain their total amount of energy or perhaps transfer it to some other bodily event, thereby being a cause of a bodily event *and* a mental event at the same time. So there is no reason to think that brain-mind interaction involves a violation of the conservation of energy principle.

What about the converse, or mind-brain interaction? If we agree that mind-brain interaction is analogous to the billiard ball case, then we must reject mind-brain interaction. But we do not have to use this analogy. C. D. Broad, a leading twentieth-century defender of dualistic inter-actionism counters the billiard ball analogy with one of his own. He says,

Take the case of a weight swinging at the end of a string hung from a fixed point. The total energy of the weight is the same at all positions in its course. It is thus a conservative system. But at every moment the direction and velocity of the weight's motion are different, and the proportion between its kinetic and its potential energy is constantly changing. These changes are caused by the pull of the string, which acts in a different direction at each different moment. The string makes no difference to the total energy of the weight; but it makes all the difference in the world to the particular way in which the energy is distributed between the potential and the kinetic forms . . . .

Here, then we have a clear case even in the physical realm where a system is conservative but is continually acted on by something which affects its movement and the distribution of its total energy. Why should not the mind act on the body in this way?[9]

Broad's analogy brings out the point that one thing can causally affect the movement of another in two quite different ways. It can cause it to change speed, as in the billiard ball example, or direction, as in the pendulum example. The first kind of cause changes the total amount of energy involved; the second does not. If Broad's analogy is apt, then various mental events can be said to affect brain processes, not by starting or stopping them, but rather by affecting the course they take. If we assume for purposes of discussion that in each brain only one process occurs at a time and that it is started and stopped by other bodily events, then such a brain process is like a string pendulum which is started and stopped by the expenditure of physical energy. But after something hits the weight and begins its movement, where it goes depends upon the length of the string attached to it. Attaching strings of different lengths to the weight changes the course of the weight but in no way affects the overall amount of energy of the weight. According to this analogy, we are to take the causal role of mental events to be like the causal role of different lengths of string. There would thus be different results in the brain, which would in turn have different bodily results, so that the body would be affected in many different ways given the same input of energy.

This reply does show how the dualistic interactionist can avoid the objection based on the conservation principle. However, now a new

---

9. C. D. Broad, *The Mind and Its Place in Nature* (London: Routledge & Kegan Paul, 1925), 107–108.

problem crops up. How can there be a change of motion without a physical cause? This sort of change seems just as much a violation of scientific principles. Broad has an answer here as well. He says,

> [the facts] suggest that what the mind does to the body in voluntary action, if it does anything, is to lower the resistance of certain synapses and to raise that of others. The result is that the nervous current follows such a course as to produce the particular movement which the mind judges to be appropriate at the time.[10]

To the question, "How can a mental event change the direction a nerve impulse will take?" the answer we now get from Broad is that mental events do not really do this. Instead, they change distributions in the resistances at synapses, and it is the relative levels of resistance that cause nerve currents to take various directions.

Now we come to heart of the matter. How can mental events affect the relative levels of resistances at synapses? Once more, the only answer available to the dualist interactionist is to appeal to proximate causation, and to remind us again that proximate causation is not itself explicable but must merely be accepted for what it is. As with the first two objections, the mystery deepens regarding the nature of mind-brain interaction.

The conclusion we should reach is that the dualistic interactionist does not have the resources within his own theory to explain mind-brain interaction. He can only maintain that it happens in some inexplicable manner, and leave the matter there. Given such an outcome regarding interaction, and given that arguments in favor of the dualist part of the theory are not compelling, we really ought to abandon dualistic interactionism and search for a more satisfactory theory.

PARALLELISM

Historically, even in Descartes's lifetime, many philosophers came to a similar conclusion about interactionism. However, for the most part these philosophers wanted to retain dualism, it being regarded as obviously correct at the time. The natural thing was to drop just the interactionist part of Descartes's theory. This gives us parallelism, a different form of dualism.

Like interactionism, parallelism agrees that a person has both an immaterial mind and a material body, that there are mental and material events and states within a person, and that mental and material phenomena are radically different kinds of things. It differs from interactionism in that it

---

10. Ibid., 113.

denies causal interaction between minds and bodies. Mental events occur and material events occur, even in the same person, but they are causally independent of one another. Parallelists concede that certain bodily events, such as breaking an arm, *regularly precede* certain mental events, such as having pain; and they agree that certain mental events such as deciding, *regularly precede* certain bodily behavior, such as moving the pawn rather than the bishop in chess. But they deny that there is any causal interaction here. Having an arm broken does not *cause* pain, and deciding to move a pawn does not *cause* someone to move it. Such events merely parallel each other, in the sense that certain mental events are accompanied by certain bodily events and conversely. So parallelism does not face any of the three objections lately considered against dualistic interactionism.

An Objection to Parallelism:
It Cannot Explain Observed Regularities

If parallelism is correct, and mental and material events proceed completely independently of each other, then there is no reason for the regular relationships between them. There is no reason why what follows the breaking of an arm should not be pain one time and joy another. We can understand why the breaking of an arm should be followed by pain if bone breaks cause pain, but parallelists do not allow causes of this sort. It seems unlikely that regularities of parallel mental and bodily occurrences would happen merely by chance. So it is fair to demand an explanation for such regularities, but how can parallelists provide one? They cannot rely on a causal explanation, and no other seems available. Thus, the objection is that parallelism cannot explain what certainly needs to be explained, namely, the regularities between occurrences of mental and material events.

Two Replies: Occasionalism and Preestablished Harmony

Occasionalism, propounded by the seventeenth-century French philosopher Nicolas Malebranche (1638-1715), is the theory that, on the occasion that certain bodily events occur, God causes certain mental events; and, on the occasion that certain mental events occur, God causes certain bodily events. So, although there is no causal interaction between minds and bodies, we can still explain the regularity among certain mental and material events by stating that God, who has a most orderly and powerful mind, constantly causes the same kind of mental event each time a certain kind of bodily event occurs, and the same kind of bodily event each time a certain kind of mental event occurs.

The *preestablished harmony* theory, proposed by the seventeenth-century German philosopher Leibniz (1646-1716), claims that the procession of bodily events and the procession of mental events both proceed according to a preestablished plan of God's. Which material event follows a certain material event is predetermined; and which mental event follows a certain

mental event is also predetermined.   Also, there is a predetermined
harmony between these two independent series of events. That is, the two
series are so arranged that certain events in the material series are always
accompanied by certain events in the mental series, and vice versa.
Leibniz used the example of two clocks, one of which has a face and hands
but no bells to toll the hours, while the other has bells but no face or
hands. On noticing that each time the hands on the first clock were in a
certain position, the second clock struck once, and when the hands were
in a different position on the first clock, the second struck twice, and so
on, a person might suppose that there is some causal relationship between
the two clocks. But a closer look would show no causal connection at all.
It is just that some being regulated each clock and then set them running
in such a way that whenever the one's hands were in a certain position, the
other struck its bells a certain number of times. The two clocks run parallel
to one another and exhibit a joint regularity or harmony resulting from the
causal effect of some being who set the clocks to run in a certain manner.
Now, says Leibniz,

> put the soul and body in the place of these two timepieces. Then their
> agreement or sympathy will also come about in one of these three ways.
> The *way of influence* [interactionism] is that of the common philosophy.
> But since it is impossible to conceive of material particles or of species
> or immaterial qualities which can pass from one of these substances into
> the other, this view must be rejected. The *way of assistance* [occasion-
> alism] is that of the system of occasional causes. But I hold that God
> should help only in the way in which he concurs in all other natural
> things. Thus there remains only my hypothesis, that is, the *way of
> preestablished harmony*, according to which God has made each of the
> two substances from the beginning in such a way that, though each
> follows only its own laws which it has received with its being, each
> agrees throughout with the other, entirely as if they were mutually
> influenced or as if God were always putting forth his hand, beyond his
> general concurrence.[11]

Both Malebranche and Leibniz try to save parallelism from the objection
posed earlier by providing explanations of the regularities between mental
and material events.   And both postulate an unobservable being, which
they call God, in order to explain the observed mind-body regularities.
(We say only that they *call* this being God, because, as we shall see in the
next chapter, God has many important characteristics, and Malebranche
and Leibniz do nothing to show that their postulated being has those Godly
characteristics.)

---

11. G. W. Leibniz, *Philosophical Paper and Letters*, ed. L. E. Loemker (Chicago:
University of Chicago Press, 1965), 751.

Leibniz tries not only to justify his own postulation but also to rule out that of Malebranche. His idea is that interactionism cannot explain the regularities that need explaining, and occasionalism is not an *economical* or *simple* explanation. His point is that where postulation is necessary for explanation, we should postulate no more than is necessary to provide the needed explanation; i.e., we should use the simplest explaining device available. Malebranche's occasionalist theory requires God to be constantly intervening in the natural world, whereas Leibniz's own account requires only that God preprogrammed the universe so that mind-body regularities come about. Hence, Leibniz holds that his theory is preferable, and parallelism is vindicated.

A Problem for Parallelism: No Evidence to Reject Interaction
Parallelists argue that if we accept dualism but reject interactionism, we can escape the objections against the dualistic interactionist by postulating God as the cause of mind-body regularities. But why should we reject interactionism? We noted earlier that massive amounts of evidence seem to favor the view that mental and material (brain) events causally interact. We found no strong supporting arguments for dualism, but interactionism we found quite plausible, even truistic. Parallelists have given no evidence in favor of overriding our inclination to accept interactionism. Consequently, parallelists have gone too far in their reaction to the problems facing dualistic interactionism. They have rejected that part of dualistic interactionism which is most plausible and least open to objection, and have done so for no good reason. We should rather reject parallelism.

Another Objection to Parallelism: It Uses an Ad Hoc Hypothesis
Parallelists point to certain regularities or patterns in occurrences of mental events and bodily or brain events. A bodily injury is followed by pain; a desire is followed by action; and so on. Interactionists also hold that there are such regularities, and offer a simple explanation of them: an injury is followed by pain because the injury *causes* the pain; and a desire is followed by an action because the desire *causes* the action. In short, interactionists explain the regularities in terms of causal interaction. True, we have found their account of the nature of such interaction unsatisfactory, but this difficulty does not affect the point that causal interaction explains the regularities. Consequently, these regularities do not seem to be in *need* of explanation; they already have one.

Now consider the occasionalist or preestablished harmony hypotheses, both of which involve God's actions as the causes of mind-body regularities. Such hypotheses would have predictive power, and so be capable of being tested by observation and experiment, only if we could read God's mind and discover which of the kinds of mind-brain regularities not yet observed he will bring about in the future. But such mind reading is completely beyond our abilities. So, neither hypothesis has predictive power, nor is either testable by observation or experiment. This fact, together with the point that neither hypothesis seems to be needed to explain the regularities in question, leads us to conclude that each hypothesis is ad hoc and that the entity which each postulates (called God) is what Leibniz called a *deus ex machina*, that is, a theoretical entity the sole use of which is to enable its theory to explain what the theory otherwise could not explain. Hypotheses that are ad hoc in this fashion have no command on our attention.

EPIPHENOMENALISM

We should briefly consider one final dualist theory, the epiphenomenalist theory.   An epiphenomenon is a by-product of some process, so epiphenomenalism might be thought of as *by-productism*. On this theory, mental events are caused by bodily or brain events in the way that by-products are produced by more fundamental processes, but, according to this theory, mental events cause no bodily events.   Instead, mental events are causally inert, having no effects at all.

The twentieth-century philosopher George Santayana described the relationship between mental and material events for the epiphenomenalist by analogy with a mountain stream. The water of the stream runs over and around rocks and into pools, and in the process a babbling sound is produced. This sound is produced as a by-product of the water flowing over the rocks. It does not affect the course of the water, which speeds on its way affected only by the rocks and other objects in its path. Neither does the babbling sound at any one moment affect the sound that results at any later moment. Each moment's sound is caused by the action of the rocks and water, only to die out without a single effect of its own. Similarly, for the epiphenomenalist, each mental event is the causal by-product of some material event in the uninterrupted series of material events, and ends without causally affecting anything at all. Epiphenomenalism thus has *one-way causal interaction*. Material or brain events cause mental events, as by-products; but mental events cause nothing whatever. Thomas Huxley, a nineteenth-century defender of epiphenomenalism, explained the theory this way:

> All states of consciousness in us, as in [brutes], are immediately caused by molecular changes of the brain-substance. It seems to me that in men, as in brutes, there is no proof that any state of consciousness is the cause of change in the motion of the matter of the organism. If these positions are well based, it follows that our mental conditions are simply the symbols in consciousness of the changes which take place automatically in the organism; and that, to take an extreme illustration, the feeling we

call volition is not the cause of a voluntary act, but the symbol of that state of the brain which is the immediate cause of that act. We are conscious automata . . . .[12]

Epiphenomenalism might be considered attractive for several reasons. First, it fits in nicely with the theory of evolution. As more and more complicated physical processes evolve, it is not hard to conceive of consciousness evolving as a by-product that does not causally affect the basic evolving material processes. Also, epiphenomenalism might be attractive to people who value scientific controllability. If epiphenomenalism is correct we do not need to know anything about mental events to explain, predict, and control human behavior, because mental events would play no role in causally determining behavior. Thus, no hidden mental factors would be necessary for accurate predictions. Third, unlike parallelism, epiphenomenalism requires no *deus ex machina* to explain mind-body regularities, because it claims that each mental event is the causal by-product of a certain material event. Nevertheless, despite these potential attractions of the theory, epiphenomenalism is not very plausible.

Objection to Epiphenomenalism:
It Rejects the Effects of People's Minds on the Course of Events
If epiphenomenalism is true, then mental phenomena have no causal effect upon the history of humanity. None of people's hopes, desires, dreams, joys, or sorrows have in any way affected the course of human events. Nor is it correct to talk of psychosomatic illnesses, or to claim that psychological disturbances affect human behavior. We should not explain someone's behavior by referring to his neurosis or psychosis. Indeed, if epiphenomenalism is true, the entire course of human history is unaffected causally by any mental event. But surely this is an absurd conclusion. We can see this graphically in a simple example. Suppose a person accidentally touches a hot stove. Immediately the person will feel pain, perhaps he will yell OUCH or some other suitable phrase, and he will at the same time yank his hand away from the stove. Epiphenomenalism implies that the feeling of pain is not causally related to the verbal behavior of yelling OUCH, nor to the bodily behavior of pulling away one's hand. Yet it is hard to think of anything other than the pain that could be the cause of these two bits of behavior. We should, then, reject epiphenomenalism, because it conflicts with what plainly seems to be true.

12. T. H. Huxley, *Method and Results* (New York: Appleton-Century-Crofts, 1893), 244.

Another Objection to Epiphenomenalism:
It Requires Nomological Danglers

Herbert Feigl rejects epiphenomenalism, because he thinks it requires peculiar kinds of scientific laws. He says,

> It [epiphenomenalism] accepts two fundamentally different sorts of laws—the usual causal laws and laws of psychophysiological correspondence. The physical (causal) laws connect the events in the physical world in the manner of a complex network, while the correspondence laws involve relations of physical events with purely mental "danglers." These correspondence laws are peculiar in that they may be said to postulate "effects" (mental states as dependent variables) which by themselves do not function, or at least do not seem to be needed, as "causes" (independent variables) for any observable behavior.[13]

Feigl's objection to epiphenomenalism is that it requires that science include two very different kinds of causal laws. Usually causal laws state causal connections between events in the continuing series of causes and effects that causally determines what occurs at each moment. So the usual causal laws such as the law of gravity relate events which, although themselves caused, are themselves causal factors determining what occurs after them. If epiphenomenalism were true, however, psychophysical laws—that is, laws relating mental and physical events—would be quite different. They would express a causal relationship between physical events in causal chains and mental events that are neither part of a causal chain nor causally affect any chain. These mental events would be what Feigl calls "nomological danglers," that is, factors which, although integral components of certain laws, dangle uselessly, because they are unnecessary for the explanation and prediction of human behavior. The laws of psychology, which concern mental events, would generally be quite different from the laws of all other parts of science. If, by accepting some alternative theory of the mind, we can avoid having such peculiar laws, then that would be some additional reason to reject epiphenomenalism.

Comparison of Dualist Theories

If we had to choose only among the three dualist theories, which should we select? Dualistic interactionism clearly wins in such a competition. Both parallelism and epiphenomenalism conflict with the claim that there is mind-brain causal interaction, and this latter claim seems very well supported. Dualistic interactionism, of course, has no such conflict. The latter theory does face objections of its own, but, as we saw earlier, it at

---

13. H. Feigl, "Mind-Body, *Not* a Pseudoproblem," in Hook, ed., *Dimensions of Mind*, 37.

least has the resources partially to deflect their force, whereas neither parallelism nor epiphenomenalism has effective replies to objections facing them. Hence, in a competition to the dualist theories, interactionism is a narrow winner.

However, this is not to say that interactionism is the most plausible theory of mind overall, for we have yet to examine nondualist theories. Such *monistic* theories, as we shall call them, include both idealist and materialist versions. We shall begin with a very brief look at idealism.

IDEALISM

Materialism in its most general form is the thesis that all existing things are material: material objects, states, events, and processes. By contrast, *idealism* holds the opposite. In its most general form, idealism is the thesis that the only kinds of existing things are mental: mental objects, states, events, and processes. Idealists accept the view that minds and mental entities are wholly immaterial in nature. But what of material bodies, including human bodies and the human brain? They surely seem to be anything but mental in nature. The most well-known idealist answer here is that material bodies are groups or collections of mental entities, specifically of *sensations*. We can illustrate their idea with a simple example of perception. Suppose a person looks at a ripe, red cherry on a tree in early summer. When she does this, she gets visual sensations of redness, roughly spherical shape, and bulginess. If she were to reach out and touch or grasp the cherry, she would receive tactile sensations of various sorts; and if she were to eat the cherry, she would receive gustatory and perhaps olfactory sensations of certain kinds. All this seems relatively uncontroversial. Next, however, the idealist *identifies* the cherry with the group of sensations. That is, the cherry is said *to be* a group of sensations of redness, bulginess, spherical shape, tart taste, and the like. He then argues that certainly a sensation is something that exists when and only when it is perceived; hence, by our earlier definitions, it is certainly a mental entity. Thus, the cherry qualifies as a mental entity, too, for it is composed of entities all of which are sensations. George Berkeley, an eighteenth-century Irish philosopher, expressed these idealist views straightforwardly:

> I see this *cherry*, I feel it, I taste it: and I am sure *nothing* cannot be seen, or felt, or tasted: it is therefore *real*. Take away the sensations of softness, moisture, redness, tartness, and you take away the cherry. Since it is not a being distinct from sensations; a *cherry*, I say, is nothing but a congeries of sensible impressions, or ideas perceived by various senses:

which ideas are united into one thing (or have one name given to them)
by the mind; because they are observed to attend one another.[14]

If this argument works for cherries, then of course it would work as well
for all material bodies, including human bodies and even including human
brains. Each material body would be nothing more than a congeries or
collection of sensations, and so would really be a mental entity.

Why would an idealist philosopher think that a cherry is a collection of
sensations? For Berkeley, the answer was that he thought each perceivable
quality or feature of the cherry was a sensation; and he also thought the
cherry is best understood as a collection of its qualities. The latter claim
has some plausibility. What else might there be to the cherry than its
roundness, redness, spherical and bulgy shape, tartness, moisture, and so
on? So, although it is not entirely problem-free, we can grant the idealist
this assumption. But what is far from obvious is the claim that each
quality of the cherry is a sensation. To see how dubious this contention is,
we can focus on the spherical and bulgy shape of the cherry. If these
qualities were sensations, then each would exist when and only when it was
perceived or experienced. But we generally think that shapes and other
qualities of material bodies, such as their position and mass, are not
dependent on upon perception. Those qualities of the cherry would exist,
we typically suppose, in the complete absence of perceptions. So how
could they be sensations, since sensations exist when and only when
perceived?

Idealists such as Berkeley have taken the offensive here, and insisted that
this is precisely what holds for qualities such as shape: such qualities exist
when and only when perceived. To try to show this, Berkeley used what
we can call a *conceivability* argument. He challenges us to conceive or
imagine the shape of a cherry, or even the cherry itself, existing when *not*
perceived. If we try to do this, he says, then in that very process we will
be conceiving or imagining the cherry and its shape. So, in that very
process we will be perceiving the cherry and its shape. Hence, since we
cannot even conceive or imagine a cherry or its shape existing
unperceived, no such object does exist unperceived.[15]

It is easy to see the error in this argument. Of course, when a person
tries to conceive or imagine a cherry existing unperceived, the person will
think of a cherry. Berkeley is certainly right about this. But thinking of
a cherry or its shape is not the same thing as *perceiving* a cherry or its
shape! Berkeley's mistake is manifest: he supposes that thinking about a
material body or one of its qualities is the same thing as perceiving that

14. G. Berkeley, *Three Dialogues Between Hylas and Philonous*, ed. R. M. Adams,
(Indianapolis: Hackett, 1979), 81.

15. G. Berkeley, *Principles of Human Knowledge*, ed. K. Winkler (Indianapolis: Hackett,
1982), 32-33.

material body, and of course this is not so. If it were, then my presently thinking about Athens would be sufficient for me to be perceiving Athens, when all the while I am wholly present in the United States. Berkeley's argument surely fails.

Others have offered idealist arguments over the two centuries since Berkeley's time, but none has fared any better than his.[16] So we are justified in ruling out one form of monism, idealism, as implausible. We turn next to the remaining monistic theories.

MATERIALISM

Materialism is generally considered to be the chief opponent of dualism and idealism. It is the theory that whatever exists is material, and that what is taken to be mental either does not exist or is really identical with something material. The classical exposition of this theory occurs in the philosophy of Thomas Hobbes, a seventeenth-century British philosopher. At the center of Hobbes's materialism is his conception of *sense*, which he claims is the source of all of a person's thoughts, imaginings, dreams and remembrances, "for there is no conception in a man's mind, which hath not at first, totally or by parts, been begotten upon the organs of sense. The rest are derived from that original."[17] His materialism becomes clear when he says that sense is "some internal motion in the sentient, generated by some internal motion of the parts of the object, and propagated through all the media to the innermost parts of the organ."[18] For instance, one sort of motion within the sentient being—that is, the person—would be a purely physical event in the central nervous system; and for Hobbes, events of this very sort *constitute* sense, or what we would think of as sensation. They also constitute the whole realm of the mental, for, as we have noted, Hobbes holds that everything mental is either a part of sense or derived from sense.

To illustrate Hobbes's point, consider a specific mental event such as a pain. For Hobbes, the pain *is* a physical motion within the person, a motion within the nerve fibers. So Hobbes is certainly not denying the existence of the pain; on the contrary, he is telling us what he thinks it really is. Instead of denying the existence of the mental, Hobbes is trying to *reduce* the mental to the purely material. For him, everything we consider mental is actually a purely material entity internal to the person.

---

16. See W. T. Stace, "The Refutation of Idealism," *Mind* 43, No. 170 (1934): 145-155.

17. Hobbes, *Hobbes Selections*, ed. F. J. E. Woodbridge (New York: Scribner's, 1930), 139.

18. Ibid., 107.

Because of his reduction of the mental to physical motion, Hobbes can go beyond his claim of materialism to an assertion of *mechanism*. In his introduction to *Leviathan* he says:

> For seeing life is but a motion of limbs, the beginning whereof is in some principal part within; why may we not say, that all *automata* (engines that move themselves by springs and wheels as doth a watch) have an artificial life? For what is the heart but a *spring*; and the *nerves* but so many *strings*, and the *joints* but so many *wheels*, giving motion to the whole body such as was intended by the artificer?[19]

On this view, living things, including human beings, are no different from nonliving things. They are in principle just like a machine such as a watch, although much more complicated. We can explain and predict all the motions of machines and their parts by applying the laws of mechanics to our knowledge of the spatial locations and masses of the relevant material objects and the forces acting upon them. By similar uses of these laws, according to Hobbes, we can explain all the behavior of living things. He held that the science of mechanics is sufficient to explain and predict the behavior of absolutely everything, living and nonliving. Hobbes is thus not only a materialist but also a mechanist. However, Hobbes's mechanism is not essential to his materialism, because materialism does not entail mechanism. It is possible that everything is material and some events happen by chance. Chance events would not be explainable or predictable by the science of mechanics. So materialism can be true even if mechanism is false.

Reductive materialism, as in Hobbes, is not the only form of materialism. *Eliminative* materialism contends that there really are no mental entities—such entities can be eliminated from our conception of the world. This extraordinarily bold thesis goes considerably beyond reductive materialism. For eliminative materialists are not saying merely that there are no mental entities *as those are conceived by dualists and idealists*. Instead, the claim is that no mental entities exist *however conceived*; even the reductive materialist's claim that mental entities are material events inside the person is being denied by the eliminative materialist. He rejects outright the entire category of the mental.

Neither of these materialist theories seems initially promising. After all, as we noted at the outset, mental phenomena certainly seem to be radically different from material phenomena, so radically different that dualism seems initially very plausible. So, in saying that all mental phenomena are really material, the reductive materialist seems plainly to be saying that some things that are radically different from material phenomena are really material phenomena after all. This statement seems to be incoherent. On

---

19. Ibid., 136.

the other hand, the eliminative materialist's strategy of denying the existence of the mental seems truly desperate. For this amounts to denying that there are thoughts, feelings, desires, hopes, dreams, and even pains. Indeed, we would have to deny that anyone is ever conscious or aware of things, since these are mental states. Here the eliminative materialist is assaulting what seems most certain to us, namely our own feelings, sensations, hopes, and the like. Nevertheless, there are important arguments in defense of these positions, to which we must now turn.

ELIMINATIVE MATERIALISM

Three major arguments have been thought to provide good reasons for adopting eliminative materialism. The first, known as analytical or logical behaviorism, attempts to establish eliminative materialism by analyzing the meanings of psychological expressions of language in terms of purely physicalistic expressions. This elimination of the need for psychological terms has been held to justify a corresponding elimination of psychological or mental entities. The second and third arguments are both variations on a common theme, which claims that mental entities are not needed for certain explanatory purposes. That is, we need not refer to mental entities when we give explanations or accurate predictions of human behavior; so, it is maintained, we are fully justified in eliminating mental things, just as earlier scientists eliminated entities such as the ether and phlogiston. Each of these arguments deserves careful examination.

Analytical Behaviorism and Eliminative Materialism

Analytical behaviorism is the theory that all sentences using psychological or mentalistic terms are transformable by analyses of what they mean into sentences using no psychological terms, but rather only terms referring to some kind of bodily behavior. The theory claims that although some true sentences use psychological terms, we do not have to infer from this fact that there are mental things, because we can reformulate every one of those sentences in such a way that we use only terms that refer to material objects, events, and states. Thus, the analytical behaviorist admits that sentences such as "I like you," "Smith believes that it is raining," and "Jones suffers from inferiority feelings," are in many cases true. Hence, the theory is not committed to defending the implausible sentence, "There are no mental phenomena such as feelings and beliefs." Still, the analytical behaviorist claims that he can consistently be a materialist because to admit that a sentence is true is not to commit oneself to what it refers to. The analytical behaviorist says that what psychological sentences *really* refer to or are about are pieces of human bodily behavior.

The key to the analytical behaviorist theory is the concept of analysis which is adopted. We are here interested in what has been called *meaning analysis*, which we can think of as the linguistic method that analyzes the meaning of a linguistic expression (the *analysandum*) in either of two ways. The first is by providing another linguistic expression (the *analysans*) which is synonymous with the analysandum. The second way is by providing expressions such that (1) each is synonymous with certain key expressions *containing* the analysandum; and (2) none contains any expressions synonymous with the analysandum. The first kind of meaning analysis is explicit definition, and the second is contextual definition. Only the latter is relevant to analytical behaviorism, as some examples will show. We can give an explicit definition of the term 'human' by saying that 'human' equals by definition 'rational animal,' or, as we shall state it:

'human' $=_{df}$ 'rational animal'

We would explicitly define 'bachelor' as

'bachelor' $=_{df}$ 'unmarried adult male'

On the other hand, we could begin to give a contextual definition of the term 'existent' by seeing that a sentence such as 'Many strange things are existent,' can be analyzed as:

'Many strange things are existent' $=_{df}$ 'There are many strange things.'

Here in the analysans there is no word or phrase synonymous with 'existent.' Instead, a linguistic expression containing that term, namely the *sentence*, is said to be equivalent to some other sentence which does not contain 'existent' or a synonym for it. We shall have given a full contextual definition for the term 'existent' if, for *every* sentence using that term, we can give a synonymous sentence which does not use 'existent' or anything synonymous with it.

We can illustrate contextual definition, and see why it is important to analytical behaviorism, with an example. Consider the sentence

The average American family has 1.3 cars.

Let us assume that it is true, that we convince someone that it is true, and that he then exclaims that he had never before realized that there was in the United States a family with a fraction of a car. Of course, we will try to explain to him that he has misunderstood. We were not talking about or referring to a real family. Although the sentence is true, there is no such family. Our friend may then be completely puzzled. How can that sentence be true if there is no such family? What we have to show him is that the average American family is in an important way eliminable, unlike ordinary families. The problem of eliminating this average family is like that of the eliminative materialist. We cannot *identify* this average family with some ordinary family, for that would seem to imply that somewhere there really is a family with 1.3 cars. How can we eliminate this average family? We must try to restate the whole sentence in such a way that no expression in it seems to refer to the average family, but only to ordinary families. For this purpose, an explicit definition will not help. For suppose we replaced the term 'the average American family' with the following analysans:

the American family which has the average number of cars.

Here we have attempted to provide an explicit definition. Will it help our confused friend? Not at all, because the analysans we have given seems also to refer to that same strange family. We can help our friend, however, if we contextually define 'the average American family' by providing a sentence synonymous with the puzzling sentence but containing no phrase synonymous with 'the average American family.' We could use

The number of family cars in the United States divided by the number of American families equals 1.3.

Here we do not have 'the average American family' or any expression synonymous with it. We have only expressions that refer to ordinary families and cars, and no one need wonder about the strange family with its fractional car. We have "analyzed away" a very strange kind of entity with a contextual definition, because we have shown that we need no expression that seems to refer to such an entity. We only need expressions that refer to ordinary entities. The analytical behaviorist tries a similar strategy with psychological sentences. For example, he might try to analyze the sentence

Ms. Smith is now feeling abdominal pains.

solely in terms of Ms. Smith's behavior, perhaps with the sentence

Ms. Smith is now behaving in such-and-such ways.

The ways Ms. Smith behaves might be that she moans (verbal behavior) and clutches her stomach (bodily behavior). So the intended analysis might be

Ms. Smith is moaning and clutching her stomach.

This latter sentence certainly uses perfectly ordinary terms which refer to ordinary and publicly observable behavior of Ms. Smith. So, if it is really synonymous with the sentence "Ms. Smith is now feeling abdominal pains," then the analytical behaviorist would have shown that we *do not need to use* the term 'feeling abdominal pains' and hence we need not assume that it refers to anything mental. And, if we could do this for all mental sentences and all mental terms, then we could conclude that mental sentences do not refer to anything especially mental in nature. The analogy with the case of the average American family and the fractional car is complete.

Two Attempts to Justify Analytical Behaviorism
The argument we have just sketched can be stated this way:

1. Every mental sentence (sentence using mental terms) can be analyzed by, or shown to be equivalent in meaning to, a sentence that uses only behavior terms and other nonmental terms.

2. Hence, we need not use mental terms and mental sentences for purposes of describing human behavior.

3. Hence, we need not assume that mental terms refer to anything mental.

4. So we are justified in believing that there are no mental entities.

Pretty obviously, this argument squarely depends on premise (1), which is just a statement of analytical behaviorism. Why should we think that *it* is true?

One argument in its favor derives from the *logical positivists*, philosophers and scientists who wrote prolifically and enjoyed a great deal of attention from the 1920's through the 1950's. One member of that group, Carl Hempel, expressed confidence in analytical behaviorism:

All psychological statements which are meaningful, that is to say, which are in principle verifiable, are translatable into propositions which do not involve psychological concepts, but only the concepts of physics. The propositions of psychology are consequently physicalistic propositions. Psychology is an integral part of physics.[20]

An example of a psychological statement that Hempel claims to be verifiable, and so meaningful and translatable into a physicalistic sentence, is a statement "that Mr. Jones suffers from intense inferiority feelings of such and such kinds. . ."[21] Because this sentence can only be confirmed or falsified by observing Jones's behavior, the sentence "means only this: such and such happenings take place in Mr. Jones's body in such and such circumstances."[22]

To verify a sentence, as Hempel understands the matter, is either to confirm it (i.e., determine that it is true) or falsify it (i.e., determine that

---

20. C. Hempel, "The Logical Analysis of Psychology," in H. Feigl and W. Sellers, eds., *Readings in Philosophical Analysis* (New York: Appleton-Century-Crofts, 1949), 378.

21. Ibid.

22. Ibid.

it is false), by means of some observations. And how would we either confirm or falsify the sentence about Mr. Jones's inferiority feelings? Naturally, we would try to do this by observing Mr. Jones's behavior in different circumstances.

We can use the letter J to stand for the sentence about Mr. Jones's inferiority feelings. Then Hempel's argument can be put this way:

1. The conditions of the verification of J are Jones's behavior under such and such circumstances.

2. The meanings of sentences are the conditions of their verification.

3. Hence, the meaning of J is Jones's behavior under such and such conditions.

Because J is no different from other psychological sentences, this argument can be generalized to conclude that the meaning of any psychological sentence is the behavior of some person or persons under certain conditions. Thus, given the preceding argument, it follows that for each psychological sentence we can find a physicalistic sentence having the same meaning. These physicalistic sentences are about certain bodily events and states, so we can conclude that all psychological sentences can be analyzed into sentences using only behavioral terms—that is, analytical behaviorism is true.

Is Hempel's argument sound? Premise (1) is fairly plausible, because we do try to verify psychological sentences by observing people's behavior. But premise (2) is another matter, for this premise embodies a theory of meaning known as the verifiability theory of meaning (VTM for short).

The VTM divides all declarative sentences into those that have a truth-value, either true or false, and those that lack a truth-value. Those that have a truth-value are deemed meaningful, while those that lack a truth-value are deemed to be cognitively meaningless. The latter sentences might have some *other* kind of meaning, but they lack *cognitive* meaning. We all agree that some sentences lack truth-values. For example, interrogatives, exclamations, and imperatives are sentences that are neither true nor false. What about simple declarative sentences? Proponents of the VTM held that a great many of these sentences, too, lack a truth-value. Specifically, they held that only two sorts of declarative sentences have truth-values, namely, those sentences that are either *analytically* true or false, and those that are verifiable empirically, or by means of observation. Other declarative sentences that are neither analytically true or false, nor capable of being verified by means of observation, were held to be neither true nor false, and consequently meaningless. Instead, such sentences play some other role in our language.

Some examples may help to understand VTM. Consider these four sentences:

God created heaven and earth and all things.

We ought to help others.

This is a beautiful picture.

The mind is distinct from the body.

Here we have religious, ethical, aesthetic, and metaphysical declarative sentences. None is analytically true or false, and there seems to be no possible way to determine by observation that any one of them is either true or false. So none is verifiable, and consequently they all lack truth-value. So, by the VTM, each is cognitively meaningless. Such sentences were said to express certain feelings, desires, or hopes of speakers rather than to assert something true or false. In this way they are analogous to exclamations and imperatives.

On the other hand, what about mental sentences? Well, these can be declarative sentences that are verifiable by means of observation. So, they *do* have truth-values and *do* have meaning, and, according to Hempel, what they mean is just that certain behavior occurs in certain circumstances.

However, the VTM is quite dubious. The most serious problem is that it appears to be *self-defeating*. It claims that the only true sentences are analytic sentences and empirically verifiable sentences. Hence, the VTM itself, if it is true, must be either analytic or empirically verifiable. But it is not analytic because there is nothing self-contradictory about the statement that some nonanalytic, nonverifiable sentences are true. In fact, most people who are untutored in theories of meaning would reject the VTM as false, because they would think that many religious and ethical sentences are true. So the VTM does not seem to be a generalization based upon empirical observation of the ways in which people actually use and respond to sentences. So the VTM is neither analytic nor empirically verifiable. Hence, the VTM, by its own principles, would be cognitively meaningless! We should, then, reject the VTM, and with it premise (2) of Hempel's argument, which implies the VTM. The first attempt to establish analytical behaviorism fails.

The only other way to establish analytical behaviorism is to take a good sample of mental sentences and show that they really can be translated into behavior sentences. If we could do this for a good many mental sentences, then it would be plausible to generalize and say that the same can be done for all of them.

An Objection to Analytical Behaviorism:
It Cannot Analyze Belief Sentences
A leading critic of analytical behaviorism has been the American philosopher Roderick Chisholm. He rests his whole case on the failure of all attempts to analyze satisfactorily mental sentences of a specific sort,

namely those using 'believes.' In various articles Chisholm shows that all attempts hitherto made to analyze belief sentences into behavioral sentences have failed. So we should reject analytical behaviorism.

Chisholm's argument depends on examples. In each case he shows either that the analysans is not synonymous with the belief sentence, or that it has been made synonymous only by using some technical term that is not needed to describe merely bodily phenomena. The second part of Chisholm's attack is as important as the first, because some people have tried to avoid psychological language, not by translating it into behavioral language, but rather by coining scientific-sounding terms which seem to have only one function, namely, to avoid psychological terms. For example, some psychologists, instead of saying,

The subject of the experiment expects food.

say,

The subject of the experiment has an F-expectancy.

As Chisholm notes, such ploys cannot be considered as providing behavioral analyses of psychological sentences, because "in all probability . . . the psychologist has only one means of conveying what such expressions as 'F-expectancy' or even 'food-expectancy' might mean; namely, he can tell us that an animal may be said to have food-expectancy if and only if the animal expects food."[23] And of course, if these technical terms require the use of psychological sentences to explain their meanings, then analyses of psychological sentences by means of such technical terms are no help to the analytical behaviorist.

Chisholm considers four main behavioral analyses of belief sentences: the specific-response analysis, the appropriate-behavior analysis, the satisfaction analysis, and the verbal-response analysis. For each of these we can use the sample belief sentence

Jones believes that there is a fire nearby.

According to the specific-response analysis we might try to analyze this sentence as:

Jones exhibits fire-responses to his immediate environment.

But we have a technical term, 'fire-responses,' in this analysis. What does *it* mean? An analytical behaviorist might say that

Jones exhibits fire-responses.

---

23. R.M. Chisholm, "Intentionality and the Theory of Signs," *Philosophical Studies* Vol. 3, No. 4, (June, 1952), 58.

means

Jones is exhibiting the behavior which he exhibits when and only when there is a fire.

But this will not do, because it entails that Jones believes there is a fire when and only when there really is a fire. Yet Jones, like everyone else, sometimes believes what is false. Nor will it do any good to patch up the analysis by saying 'when and only when *he thinks* that there is a fire' because 'thinks' is a psychological term. In this way Chisholm refutes the specific-response analysis.

The appropriate-behavior analysis analyzes our sample belief sentence as

Under circumstances relevant to there being a fire nearby, Jones would behave in a way appropriate to there being a fire nearby.

Here we have a purely behavioral analysis containing no technical terms. But suppose Jones is involved in a fire drill, and he behaves just the way he would in a real fire. His behavior is certainly appropriate to there being a fire nearby. Imagine also that, unknown to anyone, a fire has broken out in the building just before the scheduled drill. Certainly, then, the circumstances are relevant to there being a fire nearby. Thus, the analysans is true. But Jones, knowing that this was merely the scheduled drill, believes that there is no fire nearby. Hence, the analysandum is false and this analysis fails.

The satisfaction analysis proposes

Jones is in a bodily state which would be satisfied if and only if a fire were to occur nearby.

as the analysis of our sample belief sentence. Here again we have a purely behavioral analysis with no technical terms, but we can conceive of numerous counterexamples to the claim that the two sentences are synonymous. Suppose that Jones has an uncontrollable urge to toast marshmallows over an open fire. He has the marshmallows on a stick and he needs only a fire. So he is in a bodily state that would be satisfied if a fire were to occur nearby and that would be satisfied only if a fire were to occur nearby. But suppose that Jones has no way to start a fire, and has searched everywhere for a fire but found none. He therefore believes that there is no fire nearby. Here the analysandum is false and the analysans is true, so that the two sentences are not synonymous. This proposed sort of analysis, too, should be rejected.

The last analysis we shall consider is the verbal-response analysis, which was once favored by Rudolf Carnap, a leading logical positivist. Carnap proposed to analyze our sample belief sentence as

Jones has relation B to 'There is a fire nearby' as a sentence in English.

The immediate reaction to this analysis is that it uses the technical term 'relation B,' which is needed only for analyzing away psychological terms. What might this technical term mean, and can its meaning be given without using psychological terms? Carnap does not answer this question. To see that the prospects are not bright, however, we may notice that, because it is not necessary that someone understand English in order to believe that there is fire nearby, what 'relation B' means cannot imply that Jones knows English. So, an equally good analysans for our sample sentence should be

Jones has relation B to 'Es gibt ein Feuer in der Nähe' as a sentence in German.

The most plausible explanation of what *this* analysans means is something like

Jones has B-responses to a sentence in his language synonymous with the English sentence 'There is a fire nearby.'

However, not only does this answer take us right back to the specific-response analysis, with its problems, but it seems that the phrase 'in his language' means 'in the language he understands,' and 'understands' is definitely a psychological term. So the verbal-response analysis does not avoid the use of psychological terms in its proposed analyses, and thus it, too, should be rejected.

We now have good reasons to think that belief sentences are not translatable into behavioral sentences. So we also have good reasons to hold that analytical behaviorism should be rejected, even though we have not tried to examine all of the behavioral analyses that might be proposed for other mental sentences. Consequently, the first attempt to establish eliminative materialism, via analytical behaviorism, should be regarded as a failure.

Another Attempt: An Analogy between Demons and Pains

Suppose someone goes to his doctor complaining of a sharp, throbbing pain in the stomach. The doctor asks various questions and conducts an examination, in which she pokes the person in the stomach at various points and asks, "Does that hurt?" after each poke. At one point, the patient answers, "Yes, that hurts a great deal." According to eliminative materialism, when the patient says this to the doctor, even in all sincerity and conviction, what he is reporting or actually referring to is *not* a pain (because, on this theory, there are no pains or other mental entities), but rather something like a purely physiological neural process. This contention, that the patient is not referring to a pain, is initially very implausible, and calls for some sort of explanation. Richard Rorty, who at one time defended eliminative materialism, has supplied an explanation in the course of arguing for his preferred theory.

Rorty sets up an analogy between the use of strange demons by a
primitive tribe to explain illness, and our present use of pains and other
sensations to explain human behavior. He describes this (imaginary) tribe
as follows:

> A certain primitive tribe holds the view that illnesses are caused by
> demons—a different demon for each sort of illness. When asked what
> more is known about these demons than that they cause illness, they reply
> that certain members of the tribe—the witch doctors—can see, after a
> meal of sacred mushrooms, various (intangible) humanoid forms on or
> near the bodies of patients. The witch doctors have noted, for example,
> that a blue demon with a long nose accompanies epileptics, a fat red one
> accompanies sufferers from pneumonia, etc. They know such further
> facts as that the fat red demon dislikes a certain sort of mold which the
> witch doctors give people who have pneumonia. If we encountered such
> a tribe, we would be inclined to tell them that diseases were caused by
> germs, viruses, and the like. We would add that the witch doctors were
> not seeing demons, but merely having hallucinations.[24]

He then uses the analogy to dispel the initial implausibility of claiming that
no one has pains:

> The absurdity of saying "Nobody has ever felt a pain" is no greater than
> that of saying "Nobody has ever seen a demon," if we have a suitable
> answer to the question "What was I reporting when I said I felt a pain?"
> To this question, the science of the future may reply "You were reporting
> the occurrence of a certain brain-process, and it would make life simpler
> for us if you would, in the future, say 'My C-fibers are firing' instead of
> saying 'I'm in pain.' In so saying, he has as good a *prima facie* case as
> the scientist who answers the witch doctor's question "What was I
> reporting when I reported a demon?" by saying "You were reporting the
> content of your hallucination, and it would make life simpler if, in the
> future, you would describe your experiences in those terms.[25]

Rorty is using two analogies, with the second based on the first. The first
analogy notes that the explanatory role of such things as demons in the
witch doctor's theory of illness has been replaced by that of entities such
as germs and viruses. Modern medicine has supplanted the witch doctor's
theory, and when we accept current medical theory as the explanation of
various illnesses we also suppose that the entities of the theory it
superseded do not (and never did) exist. The witch doctor theory has been
superseded, and we assume that the entities of that theory, namely demons,

---

24. R. Rorty, "Mind-Body Identity, Privacy, and Categories," *Review of Metaphysics*
Vol. XIX (September, 1965), 28-29.

25. Ibid., 30-31.

do not exist. Similarly with sensations and other mental things. Modern physiological theory is explaining more and more of what we now explain by appeal to sensations and other mental entities. So physiological theory is in this way analogous to medical theory. As physiological theory progresses, it will supersede mentalistic theories of human behavior, and so we will be justified in assuming that the entities of the superseded theory do not exist.

A second analogy is readily available in each case. The new theory, whether medicine or physiology, enables us to explain what a person is reporting when he says that he sees demons, or when he says that he experiences a sensation or other mental entity. In the first case, we can say that he is reporting the content of a hallucination; in the second, we can say that he is reporting the occurrence of various neural events, most likely events occurring somewhere in the brain.

Unfortunately, there is also an important disanalogy here. Rorty has provided the eliminative materialist with an answer to the question of what I report when I say that I have a pain, but, unlike the demon case, he has not provided any plausible way to explain why there is such a widespread mistake of believing and reporting that there are pains. Scientists explain why the witch doctors believe they see demons by stating that eating sacred mushrooms causes them to have hallucinations of demons, and these hallucinations are so vivid that they fool the witch doctors into believing that they are seeing actual demons. An eliminative materialist, however, cannot use hallucinations to explain why we mistakenly believe that we experience pains, because even if it would make sense to say that we hallucinate pains, these hallucinations would be mental entities rather than neural states, and so some mental things would not be eliminated. Furthermore, nothing else that an eliminative materialist can appeal to seems to explain our common error of believing and reporting certain occurrences, which are supposed to be merely neural processes, to be sharp, throbbing, and aching pains.

So, in simple terms, the objection is this: Rorty's story gives a good explanation of why the witch doctors report seeing demons. They have eaten certain mushrooms and these plants cause hallucinations. But he has provided no explanation of why people report having pains and other sensations, and some such explanation is needed. For the fact that nearly every person worldwide reports feeling pains and other sensations, is itself some evidence that there are sensations. Lacking an explanation of why people make such reports on such a systematic and ongoing basis, Rorty has given us nothing with which to override this evidence. So his two-part analogy does not suffice to establish eliminative materialism.

A Final Attempt:
Folk Psychology and the Explanation of Behavior

An important use to which we put mental entities is the explanation and prediction of behavior, especially human behavior. For example, we explain why Ruth has gone to Athens by saying that she *wants* to visit her relatives there; why she goes to Athens rather than Barcelona by saying that she *believes* that her relatives live in Athens and not Barcelona; why she flies rather than taking a ship by saying that she *knows* that a plane is both faster and less expensive than a ship. Here we have explained various pieces of her behavior by appeal to wants, beliefs, and states of knowledge. We might also make use of Ruth's hopes of finally meeting her relatives, as well as her fears, expectations, anxieties, and perceptions in the attempt to explain why she has gone off to Athens. We also predict behavior and, in the process, appeal to mental entities. We might predict that someone will pull off the highway at the next exit by citing the person's desire for food and drink, together with his perception of the appropriate sign indicating that a restaurant is located just off the next exit.

In making these explanations and predictions we rely upon our knowledge of various generalizations concerning what *causes* mental states (e.g., "People who tend gardens in the summer heat tend to feel thirsty."); concerning what some mental states themselves cause (e.g., "People who are happy tend to smile."); and more complex general statements, such as "If a person *desires* object O, and *believes* that method M is the best way to obtain O, then if the person has no other overriding desires, he will tend to try to obtain O by means of M." Generalizations of this kind, taken together, are often thought of as making up a commonsense, everyday *theory* about the mental, one that we all learn early in life and that we use every day. As one recent defender of eliminative materialism says:

> These familiar platitudes, and hundreds of others like them in which other mental terms are embedded, are what constitute our understanding of how we work. These rough-and-ready general statements or *laws* support explanations and predictions in the normal fashion. Collectively, they constitute a *theory*, a theory that postulates a range of internal states whose causal relations are described by the theory's laws. All of us learn that framework (at mother's knee, as we learn our language), and in so doing we acquire the common-sense conception of what conscious intelligence *is*. We may call that theoretical framework "folk psychology." It embodies the accumulated wisdom of thousands of generations' attempts to understand how humans work.[26]

However, despite its central place in the way ordinary people tend to think about the mental, folk psychology may well be a bad theory, or at

---

26. P. Churchland, *Matter and Consciousness* (Cambridge: MIT Press, 1984), 59.

least not as good as some rival. That is, folk psychology may give defective explanations, or no explanations at all, of some important human behavior. Paul Churchland thinks that folk psychology is defective in the latter way:

> The eliminative materialist will point to the widespread explanatory, predictive, and manipulative failures of folk psychology. So much of what is central and familiar to us remains a complete mystery from within folk psychology. We do not know what *sleep* is, or why we have to have it, despite spending a full third of our lives in that condition. (The answer, "For rest," is mistaken. Even if people are allowed to rest continuously, their need for sleep is undiminished. Apparently, sleep serves some deeper functions, but we do not yet know what they are.) We do not understand how *learning* transforms each of us from a gaping infant to a cunning adult, or how differences in *intelligence* are grounded. We have not the slightest idea how *memory* works, or how we manage to retrieve relevant bits of information instantly from the awesome mass we have stored. We do not know what *mental illness* is, nor how to cure it.[27]

Of course, folk psychology incorporates general statements about learning and memory, e.g., "Children learn by imitating adults' speech." and "We tend to remember best those things which are important to us." The problem is that these statements are so shallow and uninformative. There is far more to learning than mere imitation, particularly in first language learning; and, knowing that memory functions best with important items is of no help in showing us what memory is nor how it actually works in other cases. After all, people remember thousands of things that are of no importance, to them anyone else.

Is there a competitor to folk psychology, and, if so, does it do a better job of explaining and predicting human behavior? According to Churchland, the answer to both questions is *yes*. The competitor is not contemporary cognitive psychology, as one might expect, but rather *neuroscience*, i.e., the collection of sciences that study the composition, functions, and processes of neural systems—neurology, neuroanatomy, neuropharmacology, and neuropsychology. Perhaps neuroscience does not *now* provide better and more informative explanations of human behavior than folk psychology, at least not for the whole arena of human activity. But neuroscience is progressing at a truly remarkable rate, with dazzling successes in dealing with neural systems of lower animals, and such success is also to be expected in connection with humans. At that point,

---

27. Ibid., 45-46.

when neuroscience has matured to the point where the poverty of our current conceptions is apparent to everyone, and the superiority of the new framework is established, we shall then be able to set about *re*conceiving our internal states and activities, within a truly adequate conceptual framework at last. Our explanations of one another's behavior will appeal to such things as our neuropharmacological states, the neural activity in specialized anatomical areas, and whatever other states are deemed relevant by the new theory.[28]

By way of summary, then, we can state Churchland's eliminativist argument in the following way:

1. Our ordinary ways of thinking about the mental make up a theory (folk psychology) by which human behavior is explained and predicted.

2. Folk psychology provides only rough and in many cases completely defective or nonexistent explanations of human behavior (think of mental illness and sleep, respectively, as examples).

3. A mature neuroscience will provide more accurate and informative explanations of human behavior than folk psychology.

4. Hence, we are justified in believing that folk psychology is a defective theory, and so that the mental entities the theory incorporates can be eliminated. That is, eliminative materialism is justified.

Objection: We Cannot Eliminate What Is Not Posited

In some cases, when a theory is found to be defective in some manner, we conclude that the entities talked about in the theory do not exist. Suppose a theory is found to provide inaccurate explanations and predictions, and that some other theory in the same subject area provides much better and more accurate explanations and predictions. Frequently, the old theory is wholly rejected and the new theory is adopted. As an example, consider again *demon theory*, from early theories of medicine. People then believed that demons somehow entered a person's body and caused the person to become ill. To cure the person, one had either to make the demons leave the person's body or at least to appease them; and various methods were prescribed by those thought to be learned in demon theory to help bring about these cures. Modern medical theories, which talk of germs, however, provide much better explanations of the relevant illness. Moreover, attempts to cure the person typically proceed by attacking the underlying cause, such as the germ, and these methods, when successful, themselves help to confirm the germ theory. Modern germ theory has, of course,

---

28. Ibid.

supplanted the demon theory: we conclude that the demon theory is false and that the entities posited by the theory (namely demons) do not exist. Demons were eliminated by advances in medical theory.

This story of demon theory may be used to illustrate two epistemic points, as they pertain to entities posited by theories. In the demon case, if there are good explanatory reasons for referring to demons when trying to explain certain human disorders, then that alone is good reason to think there are demons. On the other hand, if there are no good explanatory reasons for referring to demons in attempting to explain certain human disorders, then that alone is good reason to think there are no demons. Shorthand versions of these two principles would be these: (1) if demons are good explainers, then that is good reason to think they exist; and, (2) if demons are bad explainers (or not needed for explanations), then that is good reason to think they do not exist.

Now what about sensations and other mental entities: are they analogous to demons in the ways suggested by these two principles? They are, with respect to principle (1): if sensations are good explainers, then that is good reason to think sensations exist. The same would hold for other mental entities such as beliefs or emotional states. But the second principle is a different matter. It would say: If sensations and other mental entities are bad explainers (or are not needed for explanations), then that is good reason to think there are no sensations and other mental entities. The reason for saying that this second principle as it applies to sensations and other mental entities is dubious is simple: there are *other* reasons, aside from explanatory virtues, for thinking that there are sensations and other mental entities. So, even if mental entities turn out to be failures, from the explanatory standpoint, there would still be these other reasons for thinking that mental entities exist. So, mental entities are not analogous to demons in quite the way supposed by the eliminativist. The only reason to think there are demons is if they should be good explainers. But explanatory success is not the only reason for thinking there are mental entities.

What this argument shows is that the inference from step (3) to (4) in Churchland's argument is not a valid one. Even if folk psychology is defective in the ways Churchland describes, that alone is not enough to warrant elimination of its mental entities. For explanatory success is not the only evidence for mental entities.

Reply: Appeal to This Other Evidence Begs the Question

We know what this other evidence in favor of mental entities amounts to: personal observation and introspection. How does one know about one's own pains, for example? The answer, of course, is by *feeling* them, a kind of perception. And if one attends to these pains carefully, one can discern that they are of various sorts: stabbing, aching, piercing, and so forth. One knows about one's own beliefs and desires by introspection; one attends to the contents of one's own mind. Observation and introspection constitute good evidence in favor of the mental.

It is precisely this appeal to such other evidence that Churchland finds question-begging. He says:

> The eliminative materialist will reply that this argument makes the same mistake that an ancient or medieval person would be making if he insisted that he could just see with his own eyes that the heavens form a turning sphere, or that witches exist. The fact is, all observation occurs within some system of concepts, and our observation judgments are only as good as the conceptual framework in which they are expressed. In all three cases—the starry sphere, witches, and mental states—precisely what is challenged is the integrity of the background conceptual frameworks in which the observation judgments are expressed. To insist on the validity of one's experiences, *traditionally interpreted*, is therefore to beg the very question at issue. For in all three cases, the question is whether we should *re*conceive the nature of some familiar observational domain.[29]

Churchland's point in speaking of the framework of folk psychology is that the way we conceive of observation and introspection, together with the ways we ordinarily think that such methods provide us with evidence—all that is itself part of folk psychology. Since it is precisely folk psychology that is being challenged, we have no right to appeal to some elements of folk psychology in the attempt to defend folk psychology. Such an appeal begs the question against the eliminative materialist. Even so, consideration of an additional objection to eliminative materialism may help to justify reliance on introspection and observation.

Another Objection: Futuristic Explanations and Neuroscience
Churchland's point is well taken, at least at first blush. But let us consider premise (3) of his argument more closely.

(3) A mature neuroscience will provide more accurate and informative explanations of human behavior than folk psychology.

Now, a mature neuroscience may provide explanations much superior to those currently given by folk psychology. However, neuroscience as it now stands is not "mature" in quite this way: neuroscience does not *now* provide better explanations than those of folk psychology, at least not for very many cases. True, neuroscience *may* develop to the point where it will explain all of human behavior and action, but this fact by itself is of no great significance. As an argument, it amounts merely to the claim that it is *possible* that neuroscience will develop in a certain manner, when what

---

29. Ibid., 47-48.

is needed is some evidence that the development actually will go in a certain direction and not in some other. Is there such evidence?

It must be conceded that there is some evidence of this sort. Neurological explanations of certain kinds of mental illness such as schizophrenia have led to improvements in our understanding of the nature of this illness as well as in its effective treatment. A similar comment is in order regarding some forms of depression. With these successes, it is a reasonable inductive inference that neuroscience will progress so that more and more conditions of a related sort will be effectively explained. However, we may note that neuroscience does not explain human actions very well at all today, and we presently have no evidence that neuroscience will someday explain actions.

To help see this point, consider the event of a person's arm going up, say a bicyclist's left arm rising to the horizontal position. Neuroscience can easily explain this event, by making reference to the appropriate neural activity, nerve impulses, and muscular contractions. But the event of one's arm going up is not the same thing as the *action* of signaling a left turn onto Elm Street. Reference to neural events, nerve impulses, and muscular contractions do not explain this action, for such bodily events do not help to explain why the person turned on Elm Street rather than some other street. In order to explain that, it seems that we need to make reference to the person's *belief* that Elm is the street on which his friend's house is located, or the street where the store is, or some such thing. Moreover, this is a very simple action. Neuroscience does even worse with more complex actions, such as raising one's hand to alert the police that the woman just behind you is a spy. To explain this action, reference at least to intentions and beliefs is required, and neuroscience is confined to explaining why one's hand goes up rather than why one has raised one's hand. The fact that neuroscience yields good explanations of conditions such as depression and schizophrenia is not of itself any reason to think that neuroscience will someday adequately explain human actions, either of the simple or the complex sort.

Given this current lack of evidence concerning the future development of neuroscience, we presently have no real alternative to folk psychology, at least for many explanatory purposes. Moreover, this fact shows that we have no reason at present to overthrow the whole framework of folk psychology. Accordingly, we have been given no good reason to jettison reliance on introspection and observation, as conceived within folk psychology, as methods of gaining knowledge of our own mental states.

With the failure of this last attempt, we can conclude that eliminative materialism should be rejected. The complete elimination of the mental, particularly sensations, remains implausible. Nevertheless, materialism itself has not been refuted, because reductive materialism remains unscathed. We need to consider this important theory.

REDUCTIVE MATERIALISM:
THE TYPE-TYPE IDENTITY THEORY

The crucial claim of a reductive materialist is that mental entities such as sensations are nothing over and above certain physical entities such as brain processes. This reductive claim states more than that each mental entity is the same thing as some brain (or neural) entity, because the phrase 'nothing over and above' also implies that mental entities have *only* the physiological properties of certain brain entities, together with some topic-neutral properties. Topic-neutral properties are neither mental nor material. For instance, if there are moral properties, then being morally good would qualify as a topic-neutral property: the fact that something, X, is morally good does not imply either that X is a mental thing or that X is a material thing. Thus, for the reductive materialist, mental entities have no mental properties, in spite of the way it may seem.

This reductive materialist position implies that each mental entity is identical to a purely material entity, namely a brain or neural entity of some type. This sort of theory is often called the *type-type identity theory*, because it identifies types of mental entities with types of material entities. Each mental entity type (e.g., pain, belief, desire) is held to be identical with a material (neural) entity type (e.g., an activation pattern of some complex of neurons). Such an identity theory should be distinguished from a close cousin, the *token-token identity theory*. The latter holds that each *instance* or *token* of a mental entity (e.g., the *particular* twinge of pain that a person feels at a certain moment) is identical with an instance or token of a material entity (e.g., a *particular* neural event in the person's brain). The differences between these two identity theories will emerge later when functionalism is discussed. For now we need only note that the type-type theory implies the token-token theory, but that the converse implication does not hold. The token-token theory is compatible with the falsity of reductive materialism. Not so for the type-type identity theory; it is required by reductive materialism.

A Defense: Central-State Materialism
One important argument for reductive materialism begins by construing mental states as inner causal states of a person—what are also called 'central states.' The idea is that mental states are inner—that is, they are states within the person—and they are causal states. To be a causal state is to be a state that (a) is itself typically caused in certain ways, and (b) is itself typically the cause of certain behavior, other mental states, and some physical states. As an example, consider a visual perceptual state. This is typically caused by certain inputs such as light rays reaching the eye and being processed by the rods and cones at the retina, and then further

processed in the visual cortex. These things constitute the typical causes of a visual perceptual state. Moreover, visual perceptual states typically are causes of behavior: they induce beliefs, or they make a person blink, or they induce one to turn left on Elm Street, and so on. Generalizing from this example, it has been held that mental states are states with a certain range of typical causes, and a certain range of typical effects. There will be different typical causes and effects for different mental states, of course. Perceptual states will doubtless have different typical causes and effects from emotional states, for instance. Even so, both perceptual and emotional states along with all other mental states, will be inner causal states.

Why should we think that mental states are inner causal states? The answer is that the concept of a mental state can be adequately defined or analyzed in terms of the concept of inner causal states. As one materialist says, "The definitive characteristic of any experience as such is its causal role."[30] If such a definition or analysis is correct, we may conclude from it that each mental state is an inner causal state. If we then look around for the states are most likely to be these inner causal states, we shall be led to central physiological (or neural) states, for these physical states have the definitive causal roles ascribed to mental states. So we could conclude that reductive materialism had been established. Here is the argument, succinctly stated:[31]

1. The concept of a mental state is analyzable (definable) as the concept of an inner causal state.

2. Hence, each mental state is an inner causal state.

3. Neurophysiological states have the causal roles ascribed to these inner causal states.

4. Hence, mental states are identical to, and indeed are nothing over and above, neurophysiological states.

Three Objections to Reductive Materialism

Although a great many objections have been lodged against reductive materialism, we shall concentrate on what we think are the most forceful. The first notes that, although the above argument provides some support for the type-type identity theory, it does not follow that reductive materialism is correct. The type-type identity theory allows that some mental entities, namely sensations, may have some purely mental proper-

---

30. D. Lewis, "An Argument for the Identity Theory," *Journal of Philosophy* LXIII (1966), 19.

31. This is the argument given by D. M. Armstrong, *A Materialist Theory of the Mind* (New York: Humanities, 1968); a very similar argument is given by Lewis, op. cit.

ties, so long as these purely mental properties are not *defining* characteristics of sensations. For example, suppose that the type of mental state *pain* is identical with some neural state type. Then the *defining* characteristics of pain are just those typical causes and effects of that type of neural state. But pain might also have other characteristics that are no part of its definition, such as the characteristics of being achy, or sharp, or stabbing. These are not material or topic-neutral characteristics. So, the type-type identity theory can be true even if reductive materialism is false. Thus, step (4) of the argument for reductive materialism overstates the case: at most what the argument establishes is the type-type identity theory.

A second objection builds on the first. A reductive materialist must claim that whenever anyone says, even with complete sincerity and conviction, "I have a sharp, throbbing, aching pain," what she is reporting is never a pain which is sharp, throbbing, and aching, but rather a pain which has only the purely material properties of the neural brain phenomenon with which it is identical (and perhaps some topic-neutral properties). So, unlike an eliminative materialist, the reductivist can agree that we often correctly report pains, but he must deny that we ever report something which has the purely mental properties of being sharp, throbbing, and aching, because pains never have those purely nonmaterial properties. But such a result is quite implausible. For, although we often do assign causal explanatory roles to sensations and other mental states, we also generally believe that in our own cases we immediately experience certain properties of sensations that they have whether or not they have any causal relationships to any of our bodily behavior or other typical effects. Hence, it is quite reasonable for each of us who has experienced a pain to think that some pains have nonmaterial properties of being sharp, throbbing, and aching because, in being aware of the pain, we are also aware of these properties.

A reductive materialist could try to avoid this criticism by claiming that such mental properties are actually reducible to purely material properties of the central nervous system. However, this strategy does not seem very fruitful, because a mental property of, say, achiness is not the same as those purely material properties which neurophysiologists discover or ascribe to brain phenomena such as neural impulses or molecular activity.[32]

A third criticism is aimed at the type-type identity theory, and by implication at reductive materialism. Both theories identify mental state types with *neural* state types, and in particular with the sorts of neural states found in persons and other higher mammals such as cats or dolphins.

---

32. For defense of this claim, see J. W. Cornman, *Perception, Common Sense, and Science* (New Haven: Yale University Press, 1975), Appendix.

This sort of theory seems to be *species chauvinist*, for it dictates that a creature feels pain only if that creature has a nervous system somewhat like that found in humans and higher mammals. This does not seem to be true, however, for creatures such as mollusks certainly seem to feel pain, even though they lack the complex nervous systems of higher mammals.[33] Moreover, other creatures, such as those that may be discovered in the future on some distant planet, might have no nervous system at all, but be constituted of completely different kinds of "stuff"—perhaps silicon chips and small wires—and yet these creatures could still have mental states, such as belief. For that to be true, these creatures need only be in states with the typical causes and effects associated with beliefs. So a mental state such as belief admits of *multiple realizations*: any entity, no matter what its constitution, can realize or have that mental state so long as that entity is capable of realizing (or having) the states which have the typical causes and effects associated with belief. Hence, we should reject the type-type identity theory, and reductive materialism along with it.

We can also conclude that we should reject materialism outright, because we have found that its two main versions—eliminative and reductive materialism—are implausible. Since we have also rejected the only other monistic theory, idealism, does this mean that we should accept dualistic interactionism after all, despite the fact that it faces formidable problems of its own? We are not quite forced to that position yet, for one other prominent theory deserves attention: a *functionalist* theory of the mind.

FUNCTIONALISM

We have seen that reductive materialists characterize mental states in terms of certain *causal relations*: to be in mental state M is to be in a state with such-and-such typical causes, and so-and-so typical effects. Functionalists accept this insight of reductive materialists such as Lewis and Armstrong. For the functionalist, being in M would amount to being in a state that is typically caused by such-and-such, that has so-and-so typical behavioral effects, and that typically causes specific additional mental states. We will refer to these defining causes and effects as "input-output relations." As described by N. Block,

> metaphysical functionalists characterize mental states in terms of their causal roles, particularly, in terms of their causal relations to sensory stimulation, behavioral outputs, and other mental states. . . . A . . .

---

33. This objection was first aimed at the type-type identity theory by H. Putnam, "The Nature of Mental States," in D. Rosenthal, ed., *Materialism and the Mind-Body Problem* (Englewood Cliffs: Prentice-Hall, 1971).

functionalist theory of pain might characterize pain in part in terms of its tendency to be caused by tissue damage, by its tendency to cause the desire to be rid of it, and by its tendency to produce action designed to separate the damaged part of the body from what is thought to cause the damage.[34]

We see, then, that functionalism has a strong resemblance to reductive materialism: both theories define mental states in relational terms. Why, then, do we not say that functionalism is itself a version of reductive materialism? The answer is that functionalism allows that many sorts of creatures can realize the input-output relations that define mental states; the creatures need not be entities with brains like those of humans and other higher mammals. As long as the relevant input-output relations are in place, the creature has appropriate mental states, regardless of whether the creature is a flesh and blood human or an extraterrestrial entity made of silicon chips and pieces of metal. Accordingly, functionalism is distinct from and incompatible with both reductive materialism and the type-type identity theory. Functionalism aims to be wholly species *non*chauvinistic.

A good way to see this is to note two kinds of entities that could have mental states if functionalism is true. In principle, a computer or robot could have mental states as conceived by functionalism. There need only be the appropriate input-output relations and, given the truth of functionalism, it would follow that this robot had beliefs or thoughts. Also, consider again dualistic interactionism according to which mental states occur "in" wholly immaterial minds. If such a mind is housed in a human body, as Descartes supposed, then such a theory is clearly consistent with functionalism. The functionalist characterization of pain, given in the passage quoted from Block, is perfectly consistent with dualistic interactionism. Hence, functionalism is not a *reductive* materialist theory.

At the present moment, functionalism is perhaps the most widely adopted theory of mind, and it is not difficult to see why. On the one hand, it gives a very plausible account of the nature of mental states. Equally importantly, it avoids nearly all of the objections facing other initially plausible theories. Nevertheless, one sort of problem causes serious trouble for functionalism: it does not seem to leave open the possibility of a certain kind of color-experience.

The Inverted Spectrum Problem
Recall that for functionalism, to be in a mental state is to be in a state characterized by such-and-such input-output relations. Suppose the input-output relations that obtain for Ruth, when she has sensations of red,

---

34. N. Block, *Readings in Philosophy of Psychology* (Cambridge: Harvard University Press, 1980), 172.

are the very same input-output relations that the great bulk of the population has for sensations of green. Neural stimuli (inputs) of a specific sort yield sensations of green in everyone except for Ruth. In her, those same sorts of neural stimuli yield sensations of red. In nearly every person, sensory discriminations are about the same. If asked to pick out green objects from some assortment, for example, they all pick pretty much the same objects. If Ruth is asked to pick out green objects, she, too, will pick out those very same things. Ruth, like everyone else, will say things like "The shades of green that one sees in landscapes in Ireland are simply marvelous," even though she is having sensations of red when everyone else is having sensations of green. So she will have the same typical outputs as the rest of the population despite the fact that her sensations are different.

Moreover, Ruth is not merely different with respect to green; she has a complete color inversion in the sense that she has sensations of green when everyone else has sensations of red; she has sensations of blue when everyone else has sensations of yellow; and so on, for each of the colors people typically see. In every case, Ruth has visual color sensations different from those had by members of the "normal" perceiving population, despite the fact that they are all looking at the same colors in the external physical world.

Ruth's mental state will then be *functionally* identical with that of every other person: the input-output relations will be the same. Moreover, since Ruth will make the same sensory discriminations as everyone else, the fact that her sensations are different will not be detectable. After all, nobody else can share Ruth's sensations. Now, according to functionalism, Ruth and all the other people are in the same *mental* state, because they are all in the same *functional* state. So, if functionalism were correct, a spectral inversion of the sort we find in Ruth would be out of the question, an impossible case. She would have to be having sensations of green, like everyone else, if she were really functionally isomorphic to the rest of the population. Or so a functionalist will say. Yet it seems entirely conceivable, and so possible, that Ruth should have sensations of red in the described situation, despite being in a state functionally identical to the one others are in when they have sensations of green. So functionalism is false, for it requires the impossibility of something eminently possible.

The Achilles' heel of functionalist theories is the *qualitative content* of some mental states, namely, sensations. In the case just discussed, the qualitative content of Ruth's visual sensations is that they are of red, and the qualitative content for everyone else's sensations is that they are of green. We have brought this up at several earlier points by noting that sensations seem to have some purely mental, nonreducible properties, even if other mental states such as beliefs do not. We need a theory that accommodates this seeming fact, in a way that eliminative and reductive materialism, along with functionalism, do not.

Back To Dualism?

Now we do seem forced to retreat to dualistic interactionism, because all of the major alternative theories of the mind have fallen victim to one objection or another. In a sense, we shall conclude that dualism is correct after all; however, the dualistic theory we finally adopt will differ in important ways from the interactionist version discussed earlier.

We have already noted a distinction between the type-type identity theory and the token-token identity theory. We found that the species chauvinism objection refutes the type-type theory, but has no effect on the token-token theory. The token identity theory can be stated in two ways, *wide* and *narrow*.

Wide Token Identity = The thesis that each mental state token is identical to some physical state token or other.

Narrow Token Identity = The thesis that each mental state token is identical to some neural state token or other.

The difference between these two theses should be clear: wide token identity requires only that each mental state token be the same as some physical state token, which *need not be a neural state*. So wide token identity is quite compatible with the thesis that some complex robots have mental states. Narrow token identity, by contrast, rules this out: robots have no neural states and so have no mental states. Of course, the narrow thesis implies the wide one, since neural states are physical states. It is the converse implication that fails.

Different animals have quite different neural systems. The neural system of a human, for instance, is quite different from that of a frog or a cat in many respects, and still more different from that of a lobster. So the narrow token identity theory should not be understood to assert that a specific neural configuration is pain, say, in all entities that have neural systems. The neural state token that is a token of pain in a human can be quite different from the neural state token which is a token of pain in a lobster. The narrow token identity theory implies only that each pain token is some kind of neural state token or other.

The narrow token identity does not say that each mental state is *only* a physical neural state, nor that a mental state is the same *type* of state as a purely material neural state. On the contrary, the narrow token identity theory can allow that mental states have some purely mental properties, such as (in the case of pain) those of being sharp, throbbing, and aching. In that case, some neural state tokens—namely, those that are identical with mental state tokens—would have *both* some purely mental properties and some purely material, neural properties. Not all neural state tokens would have mental properties, of course, only those that are identical with mental state tokens. We shall think of the narrow token identity theory as accepting the claim that mental states have both some purely mental properties and some purely material neural properties. In this way the theory escapes the main problem facing eliminative materialism, which implausibly denies that anything has mental properties, and also avoids the main problem facing reductive materialism, which claims that mental states have only purely material and some topic-neutral properties.

So construed, the narrow token identity theory is a form of dualism, namely *property dualism*. It differs from an interactionist form of dualism, because the latter holds that each mental entity is wholly distinct and different in kind from a material entity such as a neural event. For the interactionist, no mental state would have any material properties. By contrast, property dualism endorses the idea that mental states have both purely mental and purely material (neural) properties.

For all we now know, the narrow token identity theory is quite plausible. First, the thesis that mental states, and especially sensations, have some purely mental properties is supported by the introspective and observational evidence which we noted in our discussion of eliminative materialism. That is, it is supported by the fact that people certainly seem to be immediately aware of such properties of their own sensations. Next, consider how everything we regard as mental is *dependent* upon the neural. People who have strokes and lose certain brain functions also lose various mental functions as well. They may become aphasic, for example, and lose not only speech but thought and some memory in addition. Or consider how various drugs or alcohol produce changes in one's sensations, not to mention how they affect one's thoughts, emotions, and even beliefs. This sort of systematic dependence of the mental on the neural is just what one would expect if the narrow token identity theory were correct. Or, put another way, the theory nicely explains why we find the sort of dependence described above.

Note, too, that this dependence argument works for animals other than humans. If a dog or horse is anesthetized, for example, then it can have surgery performed upon it safely, just as a human can. We think that the anesthesia prevents the dog or horse from feeling pain from the surgeon's knife, just as humans feel no pain during surgery. The same would hold for any other creature with a nervous system; mental states in such creatures as lobsters and squid are also dependent upon the neural states of those creatures.

These facts about neural dependence make up a good piece of evidence for the narrow token identity theory. It might be objected, however, that this same sort of dependence is evidence in favor of dualistic inter-actionism. For suppose that theory is correct; then the mental and the material causally interact all the time, and do so via causal interaction between events in the mind and events in the brain. Given such a theory, we would expect that a dysfunction at the neural level will produce significant changes in one's mental life. So why should we say that the dependence argument favors the narrow token identity theory? The answer is that the latter theory faces considerably fewer problems than does dualistic interactionism. Let us see why this is so.

The problem of deciding *where* interaction takes place plagues the dualist interactionist, as we saw earlier. But this is no problem for the narrow token identity theory. On the latter theory, the problem is solved by finding where those brain processes that are identical to mental states occur. This poses no insurmountable problem. Neither is there any mystery about where mental events occur, given the narrow token identity theory, nor about how the mental and neural can causally interact. If it is granted that brain events are spatially located and interact with other bodily events—something we all concede—then there should be no worry about mental events, because they are identical with brain processes. The same point, furthermore, dispels the mystery of how the mental affects the body without violating any scientific principles. Each mental event affects bodily events in just the way any physiological event affects others. On all three points, then, the narrow token identity theory is superior to dualistic interactionism.

Further, the objections we found against parallelism are no threat to the narrow token identity theory. The crushing objection to parallelism is that it requires a *deus ex machina* to explain mind-body regularities. Also, by denying mind-body interaction, it denies what seems plainly true. The narrow token identity theory easily avoids both of these objections. Because mental events are identical with brain events and because brain events causally interact with other parts of the body, it follows that mental events causally interact with other parts of the body. And obviously no *deus ex machina* is needed to explain mind-body regularities, because they are completely explained by pointing out that underlying the regularities are identities.

The most important problem facing epiphenomenalism is that it denies what seems most certainly to be true, namely, mind and body interact. We have already seen above, in the discussion of parallelism, that the narrow token identity theory does not endorse such a denial. So the narrow token identity theory is certainly superior to epiphenomenalism.

However, before we conclude that the narrow token identity theory is the most plausible of those we have considered, we should ask whether this theory faces problems of its own, problems that may be quite distinct from those confronting alternative theories.

Objection: The Narrow Identity Theory Makes No Clear Sense

Many philosophers have argued that any identity theory of mind, and thus by implication the narrow token identity theory, must be incorrect because there are things which we can quite meaningfully say about mental states that we cannot meaningfully say about neural states, and conversely. We ascribe mental properties to mental states. To a pain we might ascribe properties such as being intense, sharp, aching, and unbearable. We also ascribe material properties to neural states, properties such as being located in the brain, conducting neural impulses, being publicly observable, and being constituted of molecules. Consequently, if each mental state token is identical to a neural state token, then sensations such as pains are located in the brain, are constituted of molecules, conduct nerve impulses, and are publicly observable. Also, we could conclude that some neural states are intense, throbbing, sharp, aching and unbearable.

The objection is that these attributions of properties are meaningless. The sentences, "My pain conducts nerve impulses" and "My nerve fibers are aching unbearably" seem to be like the sentence "Saturday is asleep in bed." This third sentence seems to be clearly meaningless, and therefore neither true nor false, because it makes no sense to say such a thing about Saturday. Hence, the first two sentences are also without meaning. But if the narrow token identity theory is correct, these sentences ought to be quite meaningful. So, the objection goes, we should reject this and any other identity theory of mind.

The best reply to this objection is to compare a sentence such as "My nerve fibers are aching unbearably" to a sentence such as "Would you please pass me the sodium chloride? I want to put some on my French fries." There was a time when a sentence such as this would have been considered quite odd and unusual; doubtless it would have been branded as meaningless. Nevertheless, we have by now become used to sentences of this type, and we now know that they are not at all meaningless. The point is that when a theory is in the initial stages of its development, many of its sentences will seem odd at first, and one will be tempted to suppose that they lack meaning. The passage of time, however, often shows that this would be mistaken. The analogy with the narrow token identity theory should be clear. These sentences concerned with pains and nerve fibers seem unusual to us now, when the theory has only recently been proposed. But it is reasonable to think that they will seem less odd as time passes. Indeed, to many people who have thought about such sentences, they do not seem at all odd or unusual, even now.

Conclusion about the Mind-Body Problem

With the rejection of the one objection we found to the narrow token identity theory, it is easy to see that it is the most plausible of the many proposed solutions to the mind-body problem. It avoids the problems unique to each of the alternative theories and faces none uniquely its own. We have, then, reason to reject the theory that our description of a person at the beginning of the chapter seemed to support, namely, dualistic interactionism. Nevertheless, that theory is correct about there being interaction, although it is wrong about the entities which interact. It is also correct about there being a dualism, although it is wrong about the two sorts of entities involved. There are no *purely* mental entities, because each mental entity token is identical to a neural state token. It is these neural state tokens that interact with bodily processes. Human beings, then, are different from purely material bodies, but not because they have minds or spirits in addition to their bodies. They are different because some of their material (neural) states have some nonreducible mental properties.

EXERCISES

Dualistic Interactionism, Parallelism, Epiphenomenalism, and Idealism

1. Using the characterizations of mental and material phenomena given in the text, classify the following terms. (Note that some of these are neither mental nor material and thus do not belong in any of the classes.) Give reasons for your choices.

the color blue	democracy
a loud sound	mirror images
bodily pleasure	afterimages
desires	fire
lightening	dizziness
the number 3	

2. Is Descartes right when he says that a person cannot doubt that he or she is a thinking being? That is, is it really true that a person cannot be mistaken in believing that he or she is a thinking being? What sort of evidence would even be relevant to help decide this question?

3. Give an example of proximate causation between events.

4. Broad claims that mental causes act on neural causal chains by varying the resistances of certain synapses to nerve currents. But if we think of a synapse as like an electrical circuit with a variable resistor, must not energy be expended in "turning the knob" that changes the resistance? That is, how can the "knob be turned" by something such as a mental event that has no energy to expand? How could Broad best reply to this?

5. Can you think of any human behavior that seems to be explicable only on the hypothesis that humans have immaterial minds? Consider falling in love, getting angry, telling a joke, writing poetry, dreaming, seeing a mirage. State whether you think that these or any other human activities require explanations in terms of immaterial mental phenomena, or whether you think no such explanation of any human behavior is needed.

6. Interactionists claim that certain material events are causally related to certain mental events, either as causes or as effects. Parallelists claim that no material events are causally related to mental events. Rather, some material events are constantly accompanied by mental events. Is there some way to decide by observation and experimentation whether there are any mind-body causal relations? Is there any way to decide between the two theories on the basis of experimental evidence? Can epiphenomenalism be experimentally distinguished from these two other dualist theories? If not, what do you think are the consequences for the mind-body problem?

7. Berkeley tells us that a cherry is nothing but a collection of sensations. What would Berkeley think a human body is? How would his account of a human body differ from that of an interactionist such as Descartes?

Eliminative Materialism:
Analytical Behaviorism and the Demon Analogy

8. What is the difference between reductive and eliminative materialism? Are they really different doctrines, or is one just a variant of the other? Explain.

9. Explain in your own words the difference between an explicit and a contextual definition. Give an example of each not given in the text.

10. Evaluate the following argument:

    Analytical behaviorism is merely a thesis about the contextual definitions of psychological terms. Consequently, it is not a metaphysical position, nor does it entail any, because such a (metaphysical) position is about what there is, not about the definitions of words. Therefore, we should not think that eliminative materialism can be established by derivation from analytical behaviorism.

11. According to the verifiability theory of meaning, which of the following are cognitively meaningful? Explain your answers.

    The planet Pluto is made of green cheese.

    Everything in the universe is today twice the size that it was yesterday.

    John is certainly a good son.

    Either God exists or he does not exist.

    Please drive carefully.

    There is life after death.

    There is no life after death.

12. Evaluate the following criticism of eliminative materialism.

According to eliminative materialism, there are no mental entities of any sort. Hence, if this theory is correct, there are no beliefs, and thus no justified beliefs. However, this means that no person can really justifiably defend the theory, for in order to do that one must have a justified belief that eliminative materialism is true. So we should reject this theory, since if it is correct, we cannot be justified in believing it.

Reductive Materialism and Functionalism

13. The following objection can be aimed at either the type-type or the token-token identity theory.

No one can see that I am in pain by looking at my pain, and therefore no one can see my pain. But neurosurgeons can see brain processes and states, so none of my or anyone else's pains is identical with a brain process or state.

Does this argument refute either form of the identity theory? Defend your answer.

14. According to functionalism, robots can have mental states, just as people do, provided the appropriate input-output relations obtain for the robot. This is so despite the fact that the robot is made of metal and plastic, and thus is no different in constitution than a radio or a VCR. But it is silly to think that a radio or a VCR has mental states; so why should we think any differently about purely mechanical robots?

Is this a good argument against functionalism?

15. Consider the following objection to the narrow token-token identity theory.

It is possible that human beings can think of any particular number. But there are infinitely many numbers. Thus it is possible for there to be infinitely many different human thoughts. But there is only a finite number of human beings throughout time, and there is only a finite number of discrete brain states for each person. Thus there are only a finite number of different human brain states. From this we may conclude that there are more mental states possible than there are brain states available in humans. Thus, a person might be in a mental state with which no discrete brain state is uniquely correlated. But then that mental state would not be identical with that brain state, and so the narrow token-token identity theory is false.

Critically discuss this objection.

Suggestions for Further Reading

Historical sources

Berkeley, George, *Three Dialogues between Hylas and Philonous*, R. Adams editor (Indianapolis: Hackett, 1979).

Descartes, René, *Meditations on First Philosophy*, translated by D. Cress (Indianapolis: Hackett, 1979).

Hobbes, Thomas, *Hobbes Selections*, F. Woodbridge editor (New York: Scribner's, 1930).

Leibniz, G. W., *Leibniz Selections*, P. Wiener editor (New York: Scribner's, 1951).

Malebranche, Nicolas, *The Search after Truth*, and *Elucidations of the Search after Truth*, translated by T. Lennon and P. Olscamp (Columbus: Ohio State University Press, 1980).

Plato, *Phaedo*, translated by G. M. A. Grube (Indianapolis: Hackett, 1977).

Contemporary texts and collections

Armstrong, David, *A Materialist Theory of Mind* (New York: Humanities, 1968).

Block, Ned, editor, *Readings in the Philosophy of Psychology*, Vols 1 & 2 (Cambridge: Harvard University Press, 1983, 1985).

Broad, C. D., *The Mind and Its Place in Nature* (London: Routledge & Kegan Paul, 1925).

Campbell, Keith, *Body and Mind* (New York: Doubleday, 1970).

Churchland, Paul, *Matter and Consciousness*, revised edition (Cambridge: MIT Press, 1988).

Cornman, James W., *Materialism and Sensations* (New Haven: Yale University Press, 1971).

Dennett, Daniel, *Brainstorms* (Montgomery, Vermont: Bradford, 1978).

Flanagan, Owen, *The Science of the Mind* (Cambridge: Bradford & MIT Press, 1984).

Hook, Sidney, editor, *Dimensions of Mind* (New York: Collier, 1961).

Lycan, William, *Consciousness* (Cambridge: MIT Press, 1987).

Lycan, William, editor, *Mind and Cognition: A Reader* (Oxford: Blackwell, 1989).

Popper, Karl, and Sir John C. Eccles, *The Self and Its Brain* (Berlin: Springer, 1977).

Rosenthal, David M., editor, *Materialism and the Mind-Body Problem* (Englewood Cliffs: Prentice-Hall, 1971).

Ryle, Gilbert, *The Concept of Mind* (New York: Barnes & Noble, 1949).

Shaffer, Jerome, *Philosophy of Mind* (Englewood Cliffs: Prentice-Hall, 1968).

Stich, Stephen, *From Folk Psychology to Cognitive Science* (Cambridge: MIT Press, 1983).

Wilkes, Kathleen, *Physicalism* (London: Routledge & Kegan Paul, 1978).

FIVE

The Problem of Justifying Belief in God

One of the most widespread beliefs is the belief in a supreme being, to whom we ordinary beings owe our existence, but whose own existence depends upon nothing else. Such a being we call God. We have previously examined quite different beliefs—that we have free will, that every event has a cause, that humans possess an immaterial mind as well as a body. In each case, we tried to become as clear as possible about what is believed; and we then examined the belief to see whether or not it is justified. These two tasks face us once again. We must first consider what is believed when someone believes that a supreme being exists; then we must try to discover whether or not this belief can be justified.

It may be objected here that the belief in a supreme being is unlike any of the others we have examined, because a supreme being is unlike any other being, so that this belief, unlike our others, is not open to scrutiny. It is true that a being we would be willing to call God would be different in many important respects from most beings we ordinarily believe to exist, but this alone does not warrant the claim that the belief in the existence of God should be exempt from scrutiny. Many fanciful beliefs, such as beliefs in the existence of witches, wizards, fountains of youth, are beliefs in things that differ importantly from ordinary beings. Yet we think that all such beliefs should be carefully scrutinized. So, initially, the belief in the existence of a supreme being seems open to the same sort of examination we apply to any belief. However, although this appears true initially, we also want to leave open the possibility that, after our examination, we might conclude the belief in a supreme being is, after all, *sui generis,* or unique, so that we could perhaps be justified in holding it even in the face of what seems to be contrary evidence.

EXAMINATION OF THE CONCEPT OF A SUPREME BEING

The first task mentioned earlier is that of becoming as clear as we can about the nature of the belief, and to do this we must become as clear as possible about the concept of God. We need to find those features or qualities of a being that we would be convinced is God. To begin, let us distinguish between the terms 'god' and 'God.' We can talk about one god or many gods, lesser gods, and false gods. That is, the term 'god' is a general term, such as 'person,' 'horse,' and 'stone,' and as such can apply to a whole range of entities. On the other hand, the term 'God' is usually used to talk about one specific being, namely, the one and only supreme being. Thus, we cannot talk about many Gods or lesser Gods, because if God exists, then there is exactly one being which is supreme. In line with this, we shall use 'God' to mean 'the supreme being,' and will use it interchangeably with 'the supreme being' throughout the following discussion.

The problem before us is to characterize adequately a being we would call God. We already have some idea where to begin, because the word 'supreme' is involved in the concept we are characterizing. Our question is the following: "Supreme in what regard?" Surely not supreme in evil, or merely in physical size or prowess, or even in physical beauty. We generally mean supreme in those characteristics or properties that make a being more perfect than it would be if it lacked them, so that we would call a being God only if it were the most perfect being of which we could conceive. Consequently, we would claim that the supreme being is one who is supreme in his ability to perform actions and to know what occurs, and who is certainly supreme in goodness. Thus we think of God as the being who is all-good, all-knowing, and all-powerful. That is, he is supreme in goodness, knowledge, and power. Let us then consider these three characteristics separately.

The Supreme Being Is All-Good

We can understand the statement that the supreme being is all-good to mean that whatever the supreme being wills or commands or does is the right thing to do. Thus whatever God decides, does, or commands is morally right. In addition, however, he always has good motives, for willing, doing, or commanding in the way he does, because he is a loving God who cares about the world and its inhabitants. Thus God does not do the right things with the wrong motives, nor does he have good motives but mistakenly do the wrong things. Let us take the statement 'God is good' to mean that God has good motives, and whatever he wills, does, or commands is morally right. There is, however, a problem about how to interpret this. We could interpret it to mean that if the supreme being wills or commands or does something, then *by definition* this is the right thing to do. On another interpretation, the statement means that if the supreme being wills or commands or does something, then *as a matter of fact* this is the right thing to do. Which interpretation should we use? It has been claimed that neither alternative is appealing, because each is faced with a problem. If we accept the first interpretation, then if the supreme being willed or commanded that someone wantonly inflict pain on innocent babies, or inflicted such pain himself, then inflicting pain on innocent babies would be defined as being the right thing to do. Although we shall not consider moral problems in any detail until Chapter Six, it surely seems that if wantonly inflicting pain on innocent babies is morally right, then nothing is morally wrong. We want to deny that this could be morally right. Yet, if a supreme being's doing or commanding it, which is surely possible, entails that it is right, we cannot justify such a denial. If it be objected at this point that God would not engage in or command wanton infliction of pain, we can ask, "Why not?" The answer cannot be that he could not because he is good and inflicting pain is wrong. For if he were to inflict pain, then, on this view, it would follow that doing this is right. Nor can we find a more helpful answer. This view, therefore, seems faced with an insoluble problem.

Let us turn to the second alternative. On this view, it is possible for God to do wrong, although as a matter of fact what he does always turns out to be right. Thus, although it is true that if God does or commands an act then it is right, it does not follow that if God were wantonly to inflict pain, then that would be right. We can say that in that case he would do wrong, but that, as a matter of fact, God never would inflict pain needlessly. Thus the second interpretation avoids the problem facing the first interpretation. However, some people have objected to one consequence of this view. It is claimed that if God does not prescribe the standard of what ought to be done, then there is a moral standard that exists independently of God, so that he can be judged by reference to it. Surely, it is argued, something has gone wrong with a view if it entails that we can judge the moral worth of the supreme being. However, it is not clear why anyone objects to a view that entails that it is logically possible to judge God's commands and acts by a standard. If the view entailed that it is not only logically possible but also morally permissible for a human being to judge God, then it might well be objectionable. But the view does not entail that statement. The second interpretation, then, seems to avoid the objection to it. Let us, therefore, define the sentence 'The supreme being is all-good' as 'All motives of the supreme being are good and all acts the supreme being wills, does, or commands are, as a matter of fact, the right things to do.'

The Supreme Being Is Omnipotent

The quickest way to define this statement is by saying that it means that the supreme being has the ability to do anything at all. But this definition is too loose, because it does not decide the issue of whether God can do something that involves a logical contradiction. Does God, for example, have the ability to make the mercury in a thermometer be one inch from the bottom of the thermometer at the same time that it is two inches from the bottom? Does he have the ability to make a lake frozen at the same time that there is no ice on it? Some have argued that if we claim that God does not have the ability to do something involving a logical contradiction, then we must conclude that he does not have the ability to do everything and thus is not omnipotent. However, there seems to be no reason why it would be limiting God's power to say that he is able to do anything that it is logically possible to do. This rules out nothing that has been claimed to be among God's acts, including creation out of nothing. It rules out only acts the descriptions of which involve a contradiction. Let us therefore try the following: 'The supreme being has the ability to do anything that it is logically possible to do' as the definition of the 'The supreme being is omnipotent,' (all-powerful).

At first glance this definition surely seems satisfactory, but we shall have to make another revision. Consider the act of sitting in a chair at a time when God is not sitting there. It is clear that you, I, and almost everyone are able to sit in a chair at a time when God is not sitting there. But is God able to do this? Is God able to sit in a chair at the same time God is not sitting there? Clearly not, and, because it is logically possible to do it (you and I do it), we must conclude by the preceding definition that God is not omnipotent.

It does not seem, however, that because neither God nor anyone else can both be at one place and not be there at the same time, this is any limitation on his power. It is, therefore, not the kind of inability that should be allowed to count against his omnipotence. Let us, consequently, revise the definition as follows: 'The supreme being is omnipotent' means 'The supreme being has the ability to do anything that it is logically possible that *he* do.' Using this definition we can avoid concluding that God is not omnipotent because of the above inability. The sentence

> The supreme being is sitting in a chair at a time when he is not sitting there.

is a self-contradiction, and so it is logically impossible that God perform this act.

The definition we have settled on not only avoids the preceding problem, but also allows us to solve an ancient puzzle. Consider a boulder so heavy that God does not have the ability to lift it. Does God have the ability to create such a rock or not? If he has this ability then there is something else God cannot do, namely, lift the rock. But either he has the ability to create the boulder or he does not. Therefore there is something God does not have the ability to do: both to create and to lift a certain boulder. Therefore God is not omnipotent.[1]

How might we refute this argument? First, notice that it contains two conclusions: that there is something God is unable to do, and, consequently, that God is not omnipotent. We must surely accept the first, simply because there are many things God cannot do (that is, whatever involves a logical contradiction). But because God's inability to do self-contradictory things does not limit his power, we should question whether we can draw the second conclusion that his inability both to create and lift this boulder limits his power. Using the preceding definition, the question is whether or not the statement that God does these tasks is self-contradictory. If his doing at least one of them is self-contradictory, then it is fallacious to draw the conclusion that God is not omnipotent. There seems to be no contradiction involved in saying that God creates a rock he is unable to lift, so we must insist that an omnipotent God is able to create the rock. The question, then, is whether it is logically possible that God lift such a boulder. That is, is it logically possible that God lift a boulder that *he* is unable to lift? The answer is clearly that it is logically impossible for God to perform this act, and, therefore, his inability to lift it does not limit his power. We can, therefore, avoid the conclusion that God is not omnipotent by agreeing that God is unable to lift such a rock, because such an inability does not limit his power.

The Supreme Being Is Omniscient

We can begin our definition of the sentence 'The supreme being is omniscient' as we did the previous definition—that is, by saying that it means that the Supreme Being knows everything. But again we must be careful, because not even God can be said to know a falsehood. Thus, it would be better to say that a supreme being knows all truths. There is, however, still a problem that should be considered. If God knows all truths, then he knows truths about the future, that is, he knows what will happen. But, it has been claimed, if God knows that something is going to happen before it happens—for example, that I will write the word 'thus' at the beginning of the next sentence—then it follows that I must write 'thus' there. Thus, God's foreknowledge, and hence his knowledge of all truths, is incompatible with my free will. Consequently, either no one has free will, or God cannot foresee all future events and he is not omniscient. Must we surrender our belief that human beings have free will in order to guarantee

---

1. For recent discussions of this problem, see G. Mavrodes, "Some Puzzles Concerning Omnipotence," *The Philosophical Review* LXXXII, No. 2 (April 1963), 221-23; and H.C. Frankfurt, "The Logic of Omnipotence," *The Philosophical Review* LXXXIII, No. 2 (April 1964), 262-263.

God's omniscience? We can avoid this because, in the premise "if God foresees that I do something then I must do it," the word 'must' indicates that the consequent follows logically from the antecedent. So the premise can be restated as "It is logically necessary that if God (or anyone else for that matter) foresees that I do something then I *will* so it." But it does not follow from the fact that I will do something that I *must*, in the sense of being coerced or forced to do it against my will. Thus it does not follow, from foreknowledge of what I will do, that I will not do it of my own free will.[2]

At this point someone might try a new line of attack. If someone has foreknowledge of what I do, then he can correctly predict what I will do. But he can correctly predict what I will do only if what I will do is causally determined and thus predictable on the basis of causal laws. Consequently, foreknowledge of what I do is not compatible with my doing it of my own free will. The first thing that can be said here is that the conclusion follows only if free will and causal determinism are incompatible. But we have previously found reason to deny this.[3] Secondly, there is no reason to think that someone can make a correct prediction only on the basis of causal laws. We often justifiably predict that, for example, Jones will decide to forgive his wife her latest infidelity because we know what he will decide. In addition, it is not clear that "foreknowledge" correctly describes God's knowledge of my future. It has been claimed that for God the whole of the temporal span of the universe—past, present, and future—is like a brief moment of time for us, and thus God knows what I will do in the way I know what I am doing now. No prediction is involved. Thus there are reasons for rejecting this second line of attack upon the compatibility of God's foreknowledge with our free will.

Before we move on, we should consider one other problem concerning God's omniscience. Let us say that at a certain time, t_n, God decides for the first time to do something (for example, create a particular universe). If at that time, t_n, God decides for the first time to create this world, then at no time before t_n did God know what his decision at t_n would be, because if he did, then he would not have decided for the first time at t_n. But if God is omniscient, then there is no time at which he does not know all truths; so if God is omniscient, then at every moment before t_n he knows what he decides for the first time at t_n to do. Thus, if God decides for the first time at t_n to do something, then God is not omniscient, for there is a time before t_n at which he did not know what he would decide. There are several ways to avoid this conclusion. One is to deny there is

2. For an argument for the incompatibility of free will and foreknowledge, see N. Pike, "Divine Omniscience and Voluntary Action," *The Philosophical Review* LXXXIV, No. 1 (January 1965), 27-46.

3. See Chapter 3, passim.

a time at which God first decides to do something. Two different reasons have been given for this. The first is that, no matter how far back in time you might go, God has already made all his decisions. The second is that, unlike us, none of God's decisions are made at some time, because God is not a member of the world of temporal objects.

There is another way to avoid this problem. This is to deny that it is impossible for anyone to know at t_n what he will do and at a later time, $t_n + 1$, to decide for the first time what he will do. Such a situation is odd, but, according to this proposal, it is not logically impossible.[4] It surely seems possible, for example, that Jones knows now that he later will decide for the first time to forgive his wife her latest in a series of infidelities, although he is firmly resolved not to forgive her now. He knows this on the basis of what he has done in the past, each time resolving not to forgive her but each time finally giving in. If Jones can know beforehand what he will decide to do, then surely God can. There is no contradiction here.

We can finally rest content with the definition of 'The supreme being is omniscient.' It means that the supreme being knows all truths.

Other Characteristics of a Supreme Being
We have discussed three essential characteristics of a supreme being—the characteristics of supreme goodness, omnipotence, and omniscience. The question now arises of whether there are any other characteristics an entity would have if he were the supreme being. There seem to be four additional properties. Because the supreme being is all-powerful, he can be neither created nor destroyed, and is therefore eternal. Furthermore, he is the creator of "heaven and earth and all things" who loves and cares about the creatures he creates. And, finally, God is holy. There is no problem about what it means to say that God is loving. In being all-good, he is not merely fair and just, but also benevolent and merciful toward his creatures, and deeply concerned about their welfare. The only problem about what is meant by calling the supreme being the creator of everything is whether this means that he created what there is *ex nihilo* (that is, out of nothing) or whether he created what there is out of some primordial chaos. Because there is disagreement about which is the correct interpretation, let us leave the question open by defining 'The supreme being is the creator of heaven and earth and all things' as 'The supreme being caused heaven and the physical universe to exist in their present form.' Thus we have not decided by definition whether nor not God's created everything *ex nihilo*.

---

4. For two opposing views on this point, see C. Ginet, "Can the Will Be Caused?" *The Philosophical Review*, LXXI, No. 1 (January 1962), 49-55; and K. Lehrer, "Decisions and Causes," *The Philosophical Review*, LXXXII, No. 2 (April 1963), 224-227.

There are two possible ways to interpret 'The supreme being is eternal.' The first is that *as a matter of fact* the supreme being never begins to exist and never ceases to exist. The second interpretation is that it is *logically necessary* that the supreme being neither begins nor ceases to exist. You will notice that neither interpretation begs the question of whether or not God exists, because his neither beginning nor ceasing to exist is consistent both with his always existing and with his never existing. There is, however, an important difference between the two interpretations. On the first interpretation, it is logically possible that God be created and destroyed, but on the second, it is logically impossible that anything create or destroy God. Let us characterize the two interpretations of 'The supreme being is eternal' by saying that, on the first, if he exists then he always exists, whereas on the second, if he exists then he necessarily exists.

Which interpretation shall we choose? Although some people have argued for the first interpretation, the following, which echoes the ontological argument that we shall consider later in this chapter, will justify our choosing the second. We have said that any being we would call God must be the being supreme in perfection, so that if we can think of a being more perfect than some particular being, then we would not call the latter one God. Furthermore, if it is logically possible that something create or destroy God, then we can think of a being more powerful and therefore more perfect than God, namely, a being that it is logically impossible to create or destroy. Therefore we can conclude that it is logically impossible that anything create or destroy God. We want, then, to characterize God in such a way that it is logically impossible that he be created or destroyed. However, if his eternality is merely a factual contingency, then it is logically possible that something create or destroy him. But if he is necessarily eternal, then this guarantees that it is not possible that anything create or destroy him. Therefore, in order to have this guarantee, let us use the second interpretation.

The last characteristic of a supreme being that we have to consider is that such a being is holy. It is perhaps the hardest of all the characteristics to define. When we say that God is holy we are trying to express something of our feeling that God is worthy, even more than worthy, of our full devotion, adoration, and reverence; that God is that being whom we should worship, honor, and obey. This characteristic is important for our purposes, because it can be used as a test of the adequacy of the sum total of the other characteristics that we have ascribed to the supreme being. If we have provided an adequate characterization, then the quality of holiness should really be redundant, because the total of the other characteristics should include all and only those that would make any being having them the being most worthy of our worship. In line with this, let us define 'The supreme being is holy' as 'The supreme being is that being who is most worthy of the complete devotion and reverence of humanity.'

We have characterized the supreme being as the eternal, loving, and holy being who created all things out of his omniscience, omnipotence, and supreme goodness, and we have analyzed what we are to mean by these terms. The question now before us is whether or not there is any reason to think that this concept of the supreme being, which we have carefully tried to analyze, applies to anything; that is, whether there *is* a supreme being in the sense we have described. We are taking this question as equivalent to asking whether there is any reason to think that God exists since, in the major Western religious traditions (Christianity, Judaism, and Islam), God is understood to be the supreme being we have just described and defined. Certainly many people believe that God, or the supreme being, exists. It is also true that many people deny that there is a supreme being. The question before us is which, if either, is the more reasonable.

A final clarificatory point is in order. Some people mean by the term 'God' such things as this: 'the force for love in the world,' or 'the original cause of things,' or 'that which sustains the physical universe,' or 'the transcendent object of ultimate concern.' Other similarly vague definitions of the term 'God' are often proposed. We are *not* asking the question whether God in any of these latter senses of the term exists. We are not even considering the question. We are concerned solely with whether God, considered as the supreme being, exists.

CAN THE BELIEF IN THE EXISTENCE OF A SUPREME BEING BE JUSTIFIED?

Generally, when we want to convince someone that something exists, we show it to him if we can. That is, we try to get him to see, or touch, or in some way experience the entity in question. Getting someone to experience something is the surest way to convince him of its existence. If, for example, someone doubts that there is a four-legged animal with a bill like a duck, the best way to convince him is to show him a duckbill platypus, and the next best is to have reliable witnesses tell him that they have seen such an animal. Similarly, the strongest proof for the existence of God would be one based on someone's experience of God. Let us, therefore, consider whether or not there are good reasons to think that someone has experienced God, because if there are, then we have excellent reason to believe that God exists.

APPEAL TO EXPERIENCE OF GOD

There have been repeated examples of people who in all sincerity claim to have experienced God. William James in his study of religious experience quotes the reports of several such people, including the following:

> I remember the night, and almost the very spot on the hilltop, where my soul opened out, as it were, into the Infinite, and there was a rushing together of the two worlds, the inner and the outer. It was deep calling unto deep—the deep that my own struggle had opened up within being answered by the unfathomable deep without, reaching beyond the stars. I stood alone with Him who had made me, and all the beauty of the world, and love, and sorrow, and even temptation. I did not seek Him, but felt the perfect unison of my spirit with His. The ordinary sense of things around me faded. For the moment nothing but an ineffable joy and exultation remained. It is impossible fully to describe the experience. It was like the effect of some great orchestra when all the separate notes have melted into one swelling harmony that leaves the listener conscious of nothing save that his soul is being wafted upwards, and almost bursting with its own emotion. The perfect stillness of the night was thrilled by a more solemn silence. The darkness held a presence that was all the more felt because it was not seen. I could not any more have doubted that He was there than that I was. Indeed, I felt myself to be, if possible, the less real of the two.[5]

Here, clearly, is a person convinced beyond all doubt that during a mystical religious experience he had come in contact with God. From this we can construct the following quick proof of God's existence:

1. If someone experiences an entity, then the entity exists.

2. Some people have experienced God.

Therefore

3. God exists.

Let us interpret what it is to experience an entity so that we can experience something only if it exists. On this interpretation premise (1) is true. This, however, does not also show (2) to be true, because there are many illusory experiences, in which people think they experience entities but are mistaken. Thus, although the person James quotes was convinced he had

---

5. W. James, *The Varieties of Religious Experience* (New York: Collier Books, 1961), 69.

experienced God, he may have been mistaken; his experience may have been illusory. Obviously, then, premise (2) is the crucial one. Have people experienced God?

People who think that premise (2) is true usually point to three different kinds of experiences to support their position—religious mystical experiences, revelations, and miracles. In these three cases, such people argue, what is experienced either is God, it is the direct result of something God does. There is, however, an important difference between religious mystical experiences and the other two. If in a mystical experience someone experiences God, then, as in the case quoted, he does so by being transported in some way beyond the natural world into the otherworldly presence of God. In the case of revelations and miracles, on the other hand, God participates by actually intervening in the ordinary course of the natural world. For example, the Ten Commandments were supposedly revealed to Moses by means of inscriptions on ordinary stone tablets. Miracles, such as turning water into wine, supposedly were witnessed by people in this the natural world. Because of this important difference between these kinds of religious experiences, we should consider their relevance to the argument from religious experience separately.

The Argument from Mystical Experience

We must begin by clarifying what we mean by 'religious mystical experience.' We have a choice in such a definition. We can define a religious mystical experience either as an experience in which, among other things, a person actually does experience God, or as an experience in which, among other things, a person believes that he experiences God. The difference is that on the first definition, many experiences that people believe to be mystical are not, because God is not actually experienced in them; whereas on the second definition, we can grant all such experiences to be mystical, but this implies nothing about whether God is experienced. Because in either case we must justify one claim—either that some experiences are mystical or that God is experienced in some mystical experiences —let us then choose the second kind of definition. This will allow us to define mystical experiences phenomenologically, without considering whether any entity is actually experienced.

In defining 'mystical experience' we can once again turn to William James. As a result of studying reports of mystical experiences such as the one quoted, James stated what he took to be the essential characteristics of such experiences. He said that mystical experiences are ineffable, transient, and noetic experiences in which the person involved is quite passive. Let us consider each of these characteristics.

1. *Ineffability*. The subjects of mystical experiences say that such an experience "defies expression, that no adequate report of the contents

can be given in words. It follows from this that its quality must be directly experienced; it cannot be imparted or transferred to others."[6]

2. *Noetic Quality.* Those who have mystical experiences claim that they have gotten or received deeply significant and important insights during the experiences. Thus, to the person who experiences mystical states, they seem to be states of knowledge. They seem to be "states of insights into depths of truth unplumbed by the discursive intellect."[7] In the case of the religious mystic (that is, a person who thinks he experiences God in his mystical experiences), the insights or illuminations the subject thinks he attains are believed by him to be the result of a direct confrontation or union with the supreme being. For those whose mystical experiences are not religious, the insights are thought to be the result of a new and more heightened way of experiencing the world around us, rather than a result of contact with anything supernatural.

3. *Transiency.* As James points out, "Mystical states cannot be sustained for long. Except in rare instances half an hour, or at most an hour or two, seems to be the limit beyond which they fade into the light of common day."[8]

4. *Passivity of the Subject.* Although a person can prepare himself for and help bring about mystical experiences, "when the characteristic sort of consciousness once has set in, the mystic feels as if his own will were in abeyance, and indeed sometimes as if he were grasped and held by a superior power."[9]

All four of these qualities are exemplified in the report quoted previously. The subject claims he could not fully describe the experience; that he became aware of, was even in unison with, his maker; that the ineffable joy and exultation which accompanied the experience lasted a moment; and that he did not seek unison with his maker, but passively felt it take place. This is, then, a clear example of a religious mystical experience. Our problem is to discover whether such an experience can be used to justify premise (2), the claim that some people have experienced God. The argument in which we are interested can be put as follows:

4. Some people have had religious mystical experiences.

5. In religious mystical experiences God is experienced.

---

6. Ibid., 300.

7. Ibid.

8. Ibid.

9. Ibid.

Therefore

2. Some people have experienced God.

If there is good reason to accept premise (5), then we can justifiably conclude that God exists. We surely must agree that religious mystics do have strange experiences very much like the one described, so that we can accept (4). But is there good reason for us to admit as well that during these experiences the mystics actually get insight into reality, that they experience God in ways that they cannot describe to us? Might a mystic not be like a person who is hallucinating, like one who *sees* a mirage and thinks that he is experiencing a real object? How are we to decide whether to accept at least very unusual illusory experiences? We cannot check the claims of mystics in the way we often check possible cases of illusory experiences, such as mirages, because we cannot observe whether or not there is an object experienced. We can, for example, go to the location in the desert where a person claims to have seen an oasis and carefully investigate the whole area, but we cannot in any comparable manner go to the "region" in which the mystic claims to have been aware of God.

Support for the Argument:
God Must Be Postulated as Experienced or as Cause

One type of obtainable evidence would make it reasonable to accept the mystic's claim. Suppose that some strange mystical experiences are totally inexplicable in terms of the natural causes that are the subject matter of natural sciences such as psychology, physiology, and biology. In that case, we might have some reason to think either that the entity experienced in such experiences is supernatural, or that the cause of the mystical experience is supernatural. We could then justify the existence of such a supernatural being the way we justify postulating explanatory theoretical entities such as electrons, protons, and neutrons. These theoretical entities are postulated to explain certain observable phenomena. Such postulation is justified only if there is no way to explain what is observed without postulating something or other. If satisfactory explanations can be made without postulating such entities, then, as we saw in Chapter Four, concerning the witch doctor's demons, we cannot justify belief in the existence of such entities.[10] The question, then, is whether there is any reason to think that some mystical experiences cannot be explained by means of natural causes, so that a supernatural cause is needed to explain them. If there is, then we may be able to use mystical experiences to justify premise (2). If there is not, then we shall have to conclude that whether or not the mystic experiences God, we have no grounds for claiming that he does and no way of using these experiences to justify premise (2).

---

10. See pp. 174-75.

We really have two arguments to consider. First, reports that people make of their strange mystical experiences are themselves exceedingly unusual. Such individuals report that they have merged with The One, or that they have in some manner been absorbed into pure unity, or similar utterly bizarre things. Nonmystics have no reason to think, generally, that such people are lying. Moreover, such reports as those just cited are common and consistently offered. Hence, the argument goes, the only way to explain these reports is to postulate the existence of some equally unusual entity such as a supernatural one. That is, the only way to explain the verbal behavior of the mystics, and perhaps other, nonverbal behavior of such people as well, is by postulating the existence of some supernatural entity that they have experienced. Then, given (a) that the assumption that they experience something supernatural *does* explain their behavior, verbal and otherwise, and (b) that this is the *only* effective way to explain this behavior, then nonmystics are justified in believing that the mystics experience a supernatural entity when they have mystical experiences. Hence, it would seem that we would have justified premise (5), "In religious mystical experiences God is experienced," and thereby have justified (2), "Some people have experienced God." Thus, since all else in the relevant arguments has been granted, we would have shown that the important step (3), "God exists," has been justified.

The second argument is similar. It claims that religious mystical experiences are so very strange that the only way to explain their occurrence and features is by the assumption that something supernatural is their *cause*. Then, again given the assumptions (a) that the postulation of such a cause *does* explain the occurrence and features of these experiences, and (b) that this is the *only* way to explain them, then we would have justified the claim that some supernatural entity exists and is the cause of these experiences. One major difference between these two arguments concerns what is to be explained. In the first, it is the behavior of the mystics that is said to be explained by the postulation of a supernatural entity; in the second argument, it is the actual occurrence and features of religious mystical experiences themselves.

Another significant difference is that it is not clear what support the second argument gives to step (5), "In religious mystical experiences God is experienced." This is because the second argument speaks of a supernatural *cause* of mystical experiences, rather than of a supernatural entity that is experienced in such experiences. However, we can bridge this gap in the argument. When we experience the effects of some cause, we may often be said to experience the cause as well. For instance, if I see certain footprints in the snow which were caused by raccoons, then in a sense I have experienced the raccoons, too. Of course, this is not the same as experiencing the animals themselves standing in front of me. It is, we might say, *indirectly* experiencing the raccoons. Still, this is a form of experiencing a thing. Hence, step (5) would again be justified and thus, via this second argument involving postulation, so would (2). Either way, then, the argument from the experience of God, when based on mystical experiences, would seem to have considerable plausibility even for us non-mystics.

Objection: No Need to Postulate the Supernatural

The weak point in the first argument comes in the claim that the *only* way to explain the behavior of mystics is via the assumption that they have experienced a supernatural entity. Consider how we explain the verbal and nonverbal behavior of persons who report sighting flying saucers and other strange UFOs. Ordinarily, it is noted that what they have seen are regular commercial or military aircraft flying in unusual weather conditions; or that they have seen falling meteorites. In a few cases, it is maintained instead that such individuals have experienced nothing at all, but rather have hallucinated in odd ways. These assumptions explain the behavior, verbal and nonverbal, of such people in a great many cases, indeed the vast majority, of alleged UFO sightings. It is similar in the situation of the mystics. Thus, in some cases where mystics claim that ordinary objects in their surrounding physical environment take on highly unusual features, one might plausibly contend that what is experienced is simply the surrounding physical environment seen under atypical lighting conditions or atmospheric conditions. In most other cases, where mystics claim to be absorbed into a union with pure being, or with the One, or something of the sort, one might plausibly explain what has been experienced is nothing at all; on the contrary, such people have had strange hallucinatory experiences. Their hallucinations could be exceptionally striking and perhaps vivid, and this would explain their subsequent behavior at least as well as the assumption that they have experienced a supernatural entity. Hence, the latter assumption is not *needed* for purposes of satisfactory explanations.

What about the second argument, in favor of the claim that we need to postulate the existence of a supernatural cause of mystical experiences? Many people claim that we can explain such experiences without any reference to a confrontation with anything supernatural or divine. They say that mystical experiences, like many other strange experiences, are really the result of abnormal states of mind, and, like other psychological abnormalities, they are the proper subject of physiology and psychology. Evidence in favor of this view comes from the fact that certain experiences that fit completely the description of mystical experiences given by James have quite natural explanations. Experiences which seem to provide indescribable insights into reality have been induced by inhalation of nitrous oxide (laughing gas), ether, and chloroform. It has also been found that certain drugs, such as mescaline and LSD, produce experiences with the phenomenological characteristics of mystical experiences. Surely, it is claimed, all these are merely abnormal experiences produced by natural causes.

Given all of this evidence, it is reasonable to conclude that many mystical experiences have quite natural causes. And, given the fact that we can explain the behavior of people who have mystical experiences without assuming that supernatural entities are experienced, we may conclude that the attempt to justify step (5), and with it premise (2), on the basis of mystical experiences does not succeed. We need to look elsewhere for an argument that justifies the belief in the existence of God.

It might be objected that this conclusion is a bit too quick, especially regarding the second of the two arguments just presented. After all, not all or even most mystical experiences are produced by drugs or other similar agents. Thus, nothing has been said to show that these mystical experiences lack a supernatural cause.

This objection misses the point of the argument. The crucial idea is that many experiences which are similar phenomenologically or, as we might say, internally, to mystical experiences, are caused by drugs, laughing gas, chloroform, LSD, and related agents. None of these agents, surely, is a supernatural one. Hence, since these experiences are just like mystical experiences phenomenologically, and since these experiences have quite natural causes, it is reasonable to think that mystical experiences also have quite natural causes, ones that will in time be discovered by the sciences of psychology and physiology. Thus, both the subsequent behavior of people who undergo mystical experiences and the actual occurrence of mystical experiences are explicable by means of perfectly natural causes. The argument from mystical experiences, while it might give the person who actually has the experience some reason to think that he or she has experienced God, provides no justification for us nonmystics to have a belief in God. Some other argument should be sought.

The Argument from Revelations and Miracles

Revelations and miracles both differ from mystical experiences in that in them God is thought to intervene in the ordinary course of the natural world. By 'God's intervention' is meant 'an occurrence in this, the natural world, which is not brought about by physical causes but is, rather, directly caused by God.' Thus, according to this definition, something is a revelation or a miracle only if it has a supernatural cause. Most people would probably agree that this is true of revelations, where, for example, a vision appearing in a bush which burns but which is never consumed, is said to reveal some word of God. There has been, however, much disagreement regarding miracles. No one denies that some miracles—such as the biblical miracles of turning water into wine, feeding a multitude from a few fish and loaves of bread, walking on water, and the vertical parting of the waters of the Red Sea—would be the direct result of supernatural causes, because in each case some law of nature would have been violated.

That is, if each of these events occurred, there has been a violation of some scientific law that has been repeatedly confirmed to hold universally. Thus, if we have reason to think that such events have occurred, then we have some reason to believe that God exists.

It has been claimed, however, that not all miracles involve a violation of a natural law otherwise confirmed to hold universally. R. F. Holland, for example, considers the case of a child who had wandered onto a railroad track unaware of a train approaching around a curve, so that there is no chance for the engineer to see the child in time to stop. The mother, watching from a distance and unable to help, sees the train approach and grind to a halt a few feet from her child.

> The mother thanks God for the miracle, which she never ceases to think of as such although, as she in due course learns, there was nothing supernatural about the manner in which the brakes of the train came to be applied. The driver had fainted, for a reason that had nothing to do with the presence of the child on the line, and the brakes were applied automatically as his hand ceased to exert pressure on the control lever.[11]

It was an amazing coincidence that a particular natural process culminated in his fainting at just the time he did.

Let us call any miracle, such as the preceding, that does not violate any law of nature a "coincidence-miracle," and the kind that does violate a law of nature, a "violation-miracle." Although these two concepts of miracles differ importantly, any miracle must have three features. First, whether or not he intervenes, God is in some way involved in and responsible for what occurs; second, what occurs is amazing and unusual; and, third, some disaster is avoided, or at least someone is aided, by what occurs. In both cases the feature that is most relevant for our purposes is that God is in some way involved in what occurs. Thus, if there is reason to think that either kind of miracle has ever occurred, then we are justified in believing that God exists. We are interested in the following argument:

6. Some people have experienced miracles.

7. Miracles are, by definition, situations in which God participates.
Therefore

2. Some people have experienced God.

In this argument, unlike the argument from mystical experiences, the point that can be questioned is whether miracles ever occur, and thus, whether

---

11. R. F. Holland, "The Miraculous," *American Philosophical Quarterly* 2, No. 1 (January 1965), 43-51.

people have ever experienced them. This is because miracles, unlike mystical experiences, occur only if God exists. Do we have any reason to think that miracles have occurred? Let us consider each kind separately.

Horrible disasters have often been averted by amazing coincidences. Do we have any reason to think that these are coincidence-miracles? We must also admit that incredible coincidences have often produced horrible disasters. How should we handle these? Is there any reason, in either case, to reject the claim that they are no more than very rare and most improbable coincidences? So long as each such event is explainable, each in its own way, in terms of a coincidence of individually quite ordinary occurrences, then there is no reason to regard the coincidence as anything more than that; there is no reason to think that something supernatural is involved. Given all the many chances for coincidences, it is not at all surprising that once in a while some very surprising things occur quite naturally. Thus, there is no reason to believe that coincidence-miracles have occurred.

The more usual attempt to justify a belief in God on the basis of miracles, however, is premised on the existence of violation-miracles. If there are grounds to believe that some law of nature confirmed to hold universally has been violated in such a way that some disaster has been averted, or someone aided, or some insight received, then this is surely some evidence for the claim that occasionally God has intervened in the natural course of things. Are there then, grounds for believing that there have been miraculous violations of laws of nature? The most celebrated attempt to deny such grounds is that made by David Hume.

Hume's Objection:
Belief in Violation-Miracles Is Always Unjustified
Hume says,

A miracle is a violation of the laws of nature; and as a firm and unalterable experience has established these laws, the proof against a miracle, from the very nature of the fact, is as entire as any argument from experience can possibly be imagined. . . . Nothing is esteemed a miracle, if it ever happens in the common course of nature. It is no miracle that a man, seemingly in good health, should die of a sudden; because such a kind of death, though more unusual than any other, has yet been frequently observed to happen. But it is a miracle that a dead man should come to life; because that has never been observed in any age or country. There must, therefore, be a uniform experience against every miraculous event, otherwise the event would not merit the appellation. And as a uniform experience amounts to a proof, there is here a direct and full proof, from the nature of the fact, against the existence of any miracle; nor can such a proof be destroyed, or the miracle rendered credible, but by an opposite proof, which is superior.[12]

Hume's point here is that we have grounds for believing that any particular event is a violation-miracle, or, similarly, a revelation, only if we have reason to believe that the event violates a law which has been confirmed to hold universally without exception. If a law is violated which is already in doubt, then the violation would provide further evidence that the law must be revised or replaced by another which accounts for the event that violated the first law. But once this is done, there is no reason to think a violation-miracle has occurred, because the event violates no acceptable law. Consequently, to be counted a violation-miracle an event must violate a law previously found to hold without exception. But, claims Hume, because all the evidence relevant to such a law has confirmed it as having no exceptions, all the evidence relevant to the event being a violation of the law counts against the event being a violation-miracle.

The crucial premise in Hume's argument is his claim that all the evidence relevant to the event counts as evidence against it being a violation of a law. It is true that all the evidence independent of the event itself counts against a violation; but evidence provided by the event itself might still count in favor of a violation. Surely, it might be claimed, if someone personally witnesses an event that, as he describes it, is a clear violation of a law, then we have good reason to think that a violation has occurred. If, for example, someone claims that he witnessed a violation of a natural law, such as a dead person restored to life, then we have eyewitness evidence which, it could be argued, outweighs the independent evidence. Hume, however, has an answer to this argument. He agrees that we should weigh the two conflicting sets of evidence. The question, then, is whether it is more probable that such an eyewitness is deceived about what he claims to have seen, or more probable that a dead person has been restored to life. Is it, as Hume asks it, more miraculous that what the person claims is false, or more miraculous that a dead person is restored to life? He answers,

I weigh the one miracle against the other; and according to the superiority which I discover, I pronounce my decision, and always reject the greater miracle. If the falsehood of his testimony would be more miraculous than the event which he relates, then, and not till then, can he pretend to command my belief or opinion.[13]

---

12. David Hume, *An Enquiry Concerning Human Understanding*, ed. by L. A. Selby-Bigge, rev. P. H. Nidditch (Oxford: Oxford University Press, 1975), 114-15.

13. Ibid., 116.

And because for any human the falsehood of his testimony, even when completely sincere, is less miraculous, that is, more probable, than that a law of nature is violated, we should, as Hume implies, believe the person is mistaken rather than believe that the violation-miracle occurred.

Following Hume, we can agree that the independent evidence outweighs the testimony of others. But what about a case in which someone himself experiences what seems to him surely to be a violation of a law of nature? This case is something like that of the mystic. It seems to both that they have experienced an event that in important ways is quite different from what has been established by uniform experience. Is it reasonable for a person who has had a certain kind of experience which seems to violate a law of nature to believe that a violation actually has occurred? We have seen that the person who has had a mystical experience may not be unreasonable in believing that he has experienced God, but we also saw that there is not sufficient reason to justify his belief. In the case of miracles, however, there is a great deal of evidence against the claim that a violation has occurred. Thus, not only is there not sufficient reason to justify a claim that a violation-miracle occurred, but there is surely a question of whether one should trust one's own testimony in the face of the overwhelming evidence against the violation he seems to have witnessed. In short, the reasonable conclusion is that what was experienced is the result of natural causes in spite of the way it may seem. Hume's argument, therefore, seems to be sound, and its conclusion is justified; that is, there are no grounds for believing in violation-miracles or revelations. We cannot appeal to violations of laws of nature, whether violation-miracles or revelations, to justify a belief in the existence of God. And because we have seen that we cannot appeal to coincidence-miracles, we must give up the attempt to justify God's existence by means of miracles and revelations.

A Third Argument from Experience

The arguments from experience already considered focus on quite extraordinary events: mystical experiences and reports of miracles of different kinds. However, some people have argued that God is experienced in all sorts of perfectly ordinary perceptual circumstances. Someone hiking in the mountains might see a great variety of beautiful wildflowers, and claim that seeing the wildflowers *is* seeing God, or perhaps that seeing the wildflowers enables him to see God. Or a person who participates in a religious service, and who thereby hears and sees many different things, may hold that these collective auditory and visual perceptions are, or provide the basis for, perception of God, an awareness of God's presence there in the religious service. Why should we think that experiences of these sorts serve to justify belief in the existence of God? According to William Alston, the answer is best provided by recognition of an important analogy. He says:

I want to explore and defend the idea that the . . . *perception* of God plays an epistemic role with respect to beliefs about God importantly analogous to that played by sense perception with respect to beliefs about the physical world.[14]

To help understand what Alston has in mind, we need first to consider what he says about perception.

Alston adopts a direct realist construal of sense perception,

> according to which I can be justified in supposing that my dog is wagging his tail just because something is visually presenting itself to me as (looks like) my dog wagging his tail; that is, it looks to me in such a way that I am thereby justified in thereby supposing it to be my dog wagging his tail.[15]

By 'direct realism' Alston means that people typically perceive physical objects directly, without the need to perceive any intermediate objects, especially intermediate mental objects such as sensations. We can here agree with this natural and commonsensical approach to perception. The core of Alston's idea can be illustrated by making use of his example.

Suppose I look at my dog, who is standing by the door. The dog appears to me to be wagging his tail; this is what Alston means by the statement that something presents itself to me as my dog wagging his tail. In such a situation, I will typically take it to be the case that I am seeing my dog wagging his tail; that is, I will typically believe that I see this. Furthermore, this belief will generally be justified. If we now ask what it is that justifies the belief in this situation, Alston's answer is that the appearance is the justifier. The fact that something appears to be my dog wagging his tail is what justifies me in believing that I see my dog wagging his tail. Moreover, the latter perceptual statement serves to justify the nonperceptual statement "My dog is wagging his tail." The example can be broken down into these stages:

a) Something appears to me as though my dog is wagging his tail.

b) On the basis of (a), I take it to be the case that I am seeing my dog wagging his tail.

c) The belief that I am seeing my dog wagging his tail is justified by the fact described in (a).

d) The belief that my dog is wagging his tail is justified (by the justified belief that I am seeing my dog wag his tail).

---

14. William Alston, "Perceiving God," *Journal of Philosophy* 83, No. 11 (November, 1986), 655.

15. Ibid, 656.

Two points deserve mention before we compare this ordinary perception case to the alleged perception of God. First, the usual case in which something appears to me as though it is my dog wagging his tail is one in which it *is* my dog. But this need not be so. I might be looking at a plant in the hallway which is slightly swaying in the breeze, and *this* might look like my dog wagging his tail. Even so, even when it is a plant and not a dog, I might nonetheless be justified in believing that it is my dog. The reason for this comes with the second point deserving mention: my belief that I see my dog is justified in the way here described *provided* I have no reason to believe that I am not seeing my dog. Following Alston, we can call this *prima facie* justification: it is the sort of justification that can be overridden by contrary evidence. For example, if I know that my dog is presently at the veterinarian's office, then the belief that I see my dog would not be justified. The justification that I would normally get for my dog-belief from the dog-appearance would be overridden by my knowledge that the dog is elsewhere. Still, when something looks to me as though it is my dog wagging his tail, then this confers *prima facie* justification on my belief that I see my dog, even if what I really see is a plant.

Now we can reconsider the case of the person who sees the beautiful wildflowers in the mountains. He might then take it that God is "speaking" to him in or through this perceptual experience. Of course, God is not literally speaking, because the person does not hear a real voice. He believes that God is somehow communicating with him. Why should Alston think that this belief is justified? It is because Alston holds that the wildflowers appear to the person as though God were "speaking" or communicating to him. It is here that the parallel between the perception of God and the perception of the dog is supposed to lie. In the one case, something appears as though it is a dog; in the other, something appears as though it is God communicating with a person. In the former case we say that the person sees the dog; in the latter, according to Alston, we should say that the person sees God. And, since visual perception of the dog provides *prima facie* justification for the belief that I am seeing my dog, so visual perception of God provides *prima facie* justification for the belief that the person sees God. We can see the intended parallel by again noting the stages:

e) Something appears to a person as though God were communicating to him.

f) On the basis of (a), the person takes it to the case that he is seeing God.

g) The person's belief that he is seeing God is justified by the fact described in (a).

h) The person's belief that God exists is justified (by the justified belief that he is seeing God).

It might not be God that the person sees, even though (e) is true. The God case would then parallel the situation in which a swaying part of a plant in the hallway appears as though it is the dog wagging his tail. And the justification one has for the belief that he is seeing God is *prima facie*; it can be overridden by other facts that the person might know about. For example, if something appears to the person as though God were communicating to him the message that ritual murders are permissible, then the justification for such a belief would be overridden by other things the person knows about God—in this case, that God is morally perfect, and so would not sanction ritual murders as morally correct.

Objection: Perception of Physical Objects and Perception of God Are Radically Dissimilar

If something appears to me to be my dog wagging his tail, but I am not sure, I can do things to check on the matter. I can walk over and try to touch the dog, or call the dog's name in an attempt to have the dog bark, or get someone else to have a look in the hallway. All of these things and many more besides are typical of ordinary perception of physical objects. However, we generally cannot do any of these things with cases of alleged perception of God. If, while looking at wildflowers, something (doubtless the flowers) appears to me as though God is communicating to me, I cannot check by touching God; I can only touch the flowers. Nor, in general, will I be able to get the testimony of others, for nearly anyone else I might ask would claim to see just flowers, but not God.

Moreover, there are additional dissimilarities. *Anyone* with normal perceptual capabilities can see my dog wagging his tail. In addition, people with all sorts of different beliefs, moral codes, political and religious ideas and values can all readily see my dog wagging his tail. People can be as different as you please, but it will make no difference to this perceptual event: they can all see the dog and his wagging tail. And the same is true for other senses—hearing, touching, and so forth. But this is not true in the case of perception of God. Not just anyone can perceive God; instead, such experiences happen to relatively few persons, and even with them on a relatively spotty, infrequent basis.

Now, Alston's point is that putative perceptions of God are sufficiently similar in relevant ways to perceptions of physical objects that each should have about the same epistemic status. So, since perceptions of physical objects serve to justify beliefs about the perception of such objects then, by analogy, perceptions of God will serve to justify beliefs about the perception of God. But if the claimed analogy, between perceptions of physical objects and perceptions of God, is weakened, then so is Alston's argument for the conclusion that belief in God's existence may be justified by perceptions of God. The above-described disanalogies do precisely this: they weaken the claimed analogy to the point where there is no good reason to think that belief in God may be justified by the sorts of perceptions of God Alston has in mind.

Reply: Arbitrary Double Standards and Epistemic Circularity

Let us call the all-pervasive daily activity of acquiring beliefs about the physical environment by means of perception 'SP' (for *sensory practice*) and, following Alston, use 'RE' to designate the practice of acquiring religious beliefs on the basis of religious experiences. Seeing my dog and thereby acquiring a belief about the dog qualifies as part of SP, and the wildflowers example qualifies as a case of RE. Now consider again how one would check on the perception of the dog in a situation of some uncertainty. One would rely on *other* instances of SP, either of one's own or of others. For instance, one would try to touch or hear or perhaps smell the dog, and these are all plainly more cases of SP. Or one might rely on the testimony of someone else, and here two different pieces of SP would be involved: first, the other person's perceptions, whatever they are, and second, one's own perception of the testimony of the second person. Once again, one would rely throughout on SP to check up on one instance of SP, namely, the original uncertain perception of the dog, for which a check was deemed desirable. Admittedly, this is a kind of circularity—what Alston refers to as 'epistemic circularity'—but what else is there? There does not seem to be any other way to check on instances of SP. Moreover, we do not take this sort of circularity to impugn the epistemic status of SP. That is, we do not think that SP is somehow made unreliable, as a source of justified beliefs about the physical world, just because checking on instances of SP by relying on other instances of SP involves us in epistemic circularity. Rather, we implicitly recognize that no other alternative is available.

If epistemic circularity is permitted for SP, then, Alston argues, it should also be permitted for RE. And, if it *is* permitted for RE, then the objection based on checking a potentially wayward perception can be overcome. For there are ways *within* RE to check on the putative perception of God when one looks at the wildflowers. Alston says:

> There is a long and varied history of experiential encounters with God, embodied in written accounts as well as oral transmission. This provides bases for regarding particular experiences as more or less likely to be veridical, given the conditions, psychological or otherwise, in which they occurred, the character of the subject, and the effects in the life of the subject.[16]

The point is that, within RE, a person can check on whether the putative perception of God in the wildflowers case is veridical, by discovering the

---

16. Ibid., 660.

effects on the subject, the character of the subject, the emotional and psychological (and perhaps intellectual) condition of the subject. We could ask, did the experience of God by way of the wildflowers produce any change in the person, perhaps by making him more religiously inclined? If the answer is *yes*, then from the RE standpoint, this constitutes a partial confirming check on the veridicality of the original perception. If someone protests that this is perfectly circular, the reply is as indicated above: this particular sort of circularity is unavoidable, and, more importantly, if it counts as a defect in RE it will also have to count as a defect in SP. Yet we do not admit the latter, so why concede the former? Doing so would mean arbitrarily imposing a double standard on RE.

The second objection, that perception of the dog can be accomplished by just about anyone, while perception of God cannot, Alston meets in a different manner: he denies the epistemic relevance of the objection. We all know that some aspects of reality, such as those studied by very specialized sciences, are graspable by only a very few highly trained individuals. But we do not think any less of the cognitive abilities of these individuals in these subject areas merely because their abilities are not shared by the majority of the population. Indeed, we think quite the contrary. This is enough to show that the mere fact that some facts are accessible only to a few persons, relatively speaking, is of no special epistemic import. Since that is just what we expect in many cases, it is hard to see why it constitutes an objection in the case of perception of God.

Two Further Objections:
The Fundamental Nature of Perception, and the Easter Bunny

An important difference between SP and RE has been overlooked. SP is not only all-pervasive, it is also fundamental in the sense that we make use of SP, in part, to check on practically all other belief-forming practices. SP functions as a kind of basic guide in judging the belief outputs of other practices, including RE. To illustrate, consider various areas of science where beliefs are formed by suitable individuals on the basis of various scientific practices: mathematical calculations, reasoning both deductive and inductive, occasional intuitive insights, and the like. Even beliefs so formed are generally ultimately supported or swept aside by being subjected to tests or observations of different types, usually in experimental situations. In this way, perception or SP is a fundamental arbiter even of belief-forming practices such as we find in the sciences. But how can SP be used to help support the deliverances of RE? As we noted earlier, if one individual claims to perceive God when he looks at the wildflowers, any (or practically any) other individual who looked would see just the wildflowers. But perception of wildflowers is not a confirmation of the claim that God has been perceived.

Or take a more familiar example, that of memory. I seem to remember having left my keys on the ledge next to the door, and this ostensible memory leads me to believe that my keys are on that ledge. I determine whether the memory is veridical or not by means of perception: I go to the spot by the door and look for the keys. In this way, one belief-forming practice, that of memory, has an important dependence on another, namely SP. Further, this is an epistemically relevant dependence: perceptions are used either to bolster or diminish the *prima facie* justification that accrues to my belief concerning the keys on the basis of the ostensible memory.

These considerations lead us to the view that we test many of the beliefs generated by RE by means of, or by utilizing, SP. In particular, perceptual beliefs produced by RE would seem most appropriate to be so tested, just as memory beliefs are tested in more familiar settings. Judged against such a test, the beliefs produced by RE would seem to fare poorly. It is precisely because we so often seem utterly unable to obtain perceptual verification of the beliefs produced by RE that we feel confident in at least being suspicious of claims to have perceived God.

It is perhaps true that we are here using a double standard in a way that Alston finds dubious. We are subjecting RE to an *external* check, using something outside of RE to test the products of RE. We do not do this for SP; instead, as earlier noted, we test SP by means of SP itself. The proper response is that this is as things should be, given the epistemically fundamental role that SP plays among belief-forming practices. We do not complain that SP should not be used as an external check on memory; rather, we find this completely appropriate and indeed essential, despite the fact that SP is external to memory. The fact that the checking procedures are external to the practice being examined is no objection to making use of those checking procedures.

On the other hand, if RE is insulated from all external checks, including that of SP, then another problem arises. Consider the story of the Easter Bunny, in which it is said that small children are brought various candies and other treats by a special rabbit, which appears only once a year. Of course, the children never literally see or otherwise perceive this rabbit. Nonetheless, there is an elaborate interrelated system of claims made about the rabbit, such as: that the rabbit hides during the year so that she will not be seen; that the rabbit does not want children finding out too much about her or her activities; that the rabbit can generally only be known by her effects; that "bad" children, in particular those who do not believe in the existence of the Easter Bunny, often do not receive Easter candy; and so on. In addition, especially after having been prompted by adults, children sometimes claim to have caught a fleeting glimpse of the Easter Bunny, perhaps behind the hedges or slinking between two houses. Now suppose that a child looks at some object, perhaps some flower arrangement similar to the decorations placed in the baskets children receive on Easter morning, and this object appears to the child as though the Easter Bunny is present, or this object presents itself as an Easter Bunny to the child. We can think of the practice of acquiring Easter Bunny beliefs as BB (for Bunny

Beliefs). And we can imagine that the child will acquire the belief that she is seeing the Easter Bunny on this occasion. She can check on her belief by consulting sundry other parts of BB, and she will likely find confirmation of her belief from that quarter. In that case, since her belief is not subject to any other sorts of checks, her belief is *prima facie* justified. True, her justification for this belief can be overridden, but, if it is, the defeat of this justification will come from within BB. But it is very unlikely in many cases that there will elements of BB which will defeat such *prima facie* justification.

Now there is absolutely nothing wrong with saying that the child's belief is *prima facie* justified in this example. After all, she does not have any other beliefs that would count *against* the belief that she has seen the Easter Bunny. So the point is not that insulating BB from all external checks permits a child to have justified Easter Bunny beliefs. Rather, the point to be drawn from this story is a little more subtle. It is this: there can easily be analogues of the Easter Bunny story, and analogues of BB, that do not apply merely to children but are equally farfetched. Imagine a group of people in Macedonia who revere Alexander the Great, perhaps the most famous Macedonian. These people have an elaborate system of beliefs about Alexander, somewhat on a par with the beliefs children have about the Easter Bunny, in that they hold that Alexander is still alive, that he hides in various parts of Macedonia, that he does not want much information about him to become known, and the like. Members of this group from time to time claim to perceive Alexander, dressed in his finest military uniform, in various hills; some have even claimed to have seen him on his horse, though this is a relatively rare event even for devoted members of the group. We can think of the practice of forming Alexander the Great beliefs as AG and, relative to AG alone, the beliefs people sometimes have concerning perceptions of Alexander and his horse are *prima facie* justified. The parallel with BB, the Easter Bunny story, and with RE, is straightforward, except for this: though we allow that the children are justified in their beliefs, the people in Macedonia are not. They are not justified because they have *defeaters* (contrary evidence) available to them that override the justification of their Alexander beliefs. For instance, they know or at least are fully justified in believing that human beings do not live for two thousand years and neither do horses. These latter justified beliefs override the alleged justification for the belief that Alexander and his horse have been perceived.

Notice that this overriding justified belief is *external* to AG; it comes from SP. And it is exactly what we would expect to count as a check on AG; we explain *why* we think the belief to have seen Alexander is not justified by noting some other justified belief, available to the people in Macedonia, that overrides the first belief. Lacking such an external overrider, we would have to conclude that the Alexander beliefs are justified.

The moral to be drawn from these considerations is that a dilemma faces the attempt to justify belief in God's existence via RE and perception. If no external checks are allowed on beliefs produced by RE, then by parity of reasoning it looks as though almost anything can count as justified—as in the AG case. There need only be a belief-forming practice with something like the structure of RE in order for this to occur. Hence, if beliefs about God's activities are justified by means of alleged perceptions of God, as in the case of RE, then beliefs about Alexander the Great being currently perceived would likewise be justified, in accord with AG. This certainly seems to be an intolerable consequence. On the other hand, if external checks are permitted for both AG and RE, then it would seem that the beliefs concerning putative perceptions of God and of Alexander the Great are in exactly the same boat—neither are justified. The reasons for this in the case of Alexander were already alluded to, and the same sorts of things hold for the case of God being perceived. Since we are generally unable to obtain perceptual verification of beliefs about God being perceived, we have no reason to suppose that these perceptions are veridical and thus no reason to accept the claim that God has been perceived.

We have been unable to justify belief in God by appealing to the experience of God. Can any other kind of experience justify the belief? Some people have claimed that certain facts that we experience in this world can justify the belief, although they are not experiences of God. We often justify belief in the existence of other entities in this way. For example, we justify belief in the existence of subatomic particles, such as electrons and neutrinos, not by experiencing them, but by inferring their existence from things we do experience, such as visible traces in cloud chambers. Others have claimed, however, that because a supreme being lies outside the realm of what we can experience in this world, we cannot justify belief in his existence by arguments that rely on what we experience. These people claim we must use what we can call, using the terminology of St. Thomas Aquinas, *a priori* proofs instead of *a posteriori* proofs. The difference between these two kinds of proofs is that an a posteriori proof is a proof in which at least one premise is an a posteriori statement, and an a priori proof is one in which no premises are a posteriori, that is, all the premises are a priori.[17]

---

17. For the distinction between *a priori* and *a posteriori*, see pp. 27-8, Chapter One.

THREE A POSTERIORI ARGUMENTS

The proofs we have already examined and dismissed are a posteriori. The question before us now is whether we might be able to use any other a posteriori proofs to justify belief in God. Aquinas, who thought that there are no a priori proofs of the existence of God, thought there were several sound a posteriori proofs. He produced five different a posteriori ways to prove that God exists, the most plausible of which we shall consider now. They are the arguments from motion and from causation (which we shall examine together as the first-cause argument), the argument from contingency, and the argument from design.

The First-Cause Argument

The first two ways of Aquinas have basically the same structure. The main difference between the two is that in the first way, the argument from motion, Aquinas begins with the a posteriori truth that some things are in motion, whereas in the second he begins with an *a posteriori* truth that there is an order of efficient causes. Because Aquinas takes motion to include not merely locomotion or change of spatial position, but all kinds of change, let us say that the first-cause argument, as we shall first construe it, is based on the empirical fact that there are changes and causes of change. This argument, then, starts with the a posteriori truth that there are changes taking place now which are caused. It goes on to consider what would be the case if everything that causes a change were itself caused to change by something else, and concludes that its chain of causes would be infinitely long. That is, no matter how many items in its causal chain had been enumerated, there would always be at least one that had not been enumerated. But, so the argument goes, such a causal chain cannot go on to infinity in this way, because without a first, or initiating, cause of change there would be no intermediate causes of change and thus no change now, contrary to the facts. Consequently, because there is change now, there is a first or initiating cause of change, which, as Aquinas says, we call God.[18] Let us lay out this argument in some detail so that we can examine it thoroughly:

1. There are now things changing and things causing change.

2. If there are now things changing and things causing change, and something causes change only if it is caused to change by something else, then its causal chain is infinitely long.

---

18. For Aquinas's statement of the first-cause argument, see St. Thomas Aquinas, *Basic Writings*, ed. by A.C. Pegis (New York: Random House, 1945), Vol. I: 22.

Therefore

3. If something causes change only if it is caused to change by something else, then its causal chain is infinitely long.

4. No causal chain can be infinitely long.

Therefore

5. There is something that causes change but is not caused to change by anything else, that is, there is a first cause, namely, God.

First interpretation: Temporally first cause

Before we begin to evaluate the argument we must settle the problem of interpretation. For most of us today, it seems obvious that the first-cause argument is concerned with causes that temporally precede their effects and thus with a causal chain stretching back into the past. On this interpretation, premise (4) asserts that a causal chain could not stretch back into the past over an infinite duration of time, because if there were no temporally prior, or first, cause of change then there could be no temporally subsequent causes of change and no change now. However, there are two reasons for rejecting this interpretation. The first is that premise (4) seems to be false on this interpretation. A series of causes stretching infinitely back into the past is not impossible. It is quite possible, and some people believe quite likely, that the raw material of which the universe in its present state is composed has existed in some state or other over an infinite period of time. Why could not change have been going on for an infinitely long period of time? It is only if at some time before now there was no change that we must postulate a temporally original cause of present change. But if change has always occurred, there was no temporally first cause and therefore no creator *ex nihilo*. Consider a phonograph record of a song being sung by a human voice. Let us assume that this record was recorded from another record, which was itself recorded from another record. Could this series of recordings go on to infinity? Some people might want to claim that somewhere in the past there must have been a human singer recorded. But it is surely possible that, no matter how far back into the past you go, you will always turn up another record. Consequently, if we are to make the argument as strong as possible, as we should always do before evaluating any argument, then we should look for a more plausible interpretation. Another reason for looking for a better interpretation is that the argument equates the first cause with God. But if by 'first' we mean 'temporally first,' there is no reason to say that the first cause of change, which existed at least many thousands of years ago, still exists now. Thus, there is no reason to equate God with a temporally first cause.

Second interpretation: Ontologically ultimate cause

Is there a more plausible interpretation available? F. C. Copleston, in his book *Aquinas* distinguishes two different ways in which one thing can be causally dependent on something else; consequently, he distinguishes two different kinds of causal orders, a temporal series of causes and an ontological hierarchy of causes. According to Copleston, for Aquinas the phrase 'first cause' does not mean first in the temporal order of causes, but rather supreme or first in the ontological order of causes.[19] This interpretation of 'first cause' as 'ontologically ultimate cause' rather than 'temporally first cause' allows us to avoid one of the problems facing the first interpretation. An ontologically ultimate cause would exist now, so that, unlike the temporally first cause, if we prove that there is such a cause, we have no problem concerning its present existence. We might illustrate the difference between a temporal series and an ontological hierarchy of causes as follows. Consider a room with perfect reflecting mirrors on two opposite sides. In the middle of the room burns a candle which is reflected in the mirrors. We can imagine that this candle has been burning for an infinite period of time. That is, for an infinite period of time light waves have been reflecting back and forth from one mirror to the other, causing images in the two mirrors. Thus causal action has been occurring over an infinite period of time. But—and here is where this example differs from the phonograph record example—at any one moment the mirror images exist only if the candle exists at that moment. Although a recording of a voice can exist after what has caused the recording no longer exists, mirror images cannot. Thus we might say that the candle is of a different ontological order from the images. They depend for their very existence at any and every moment on the existence of the candle, but the existence of the candle in no way depends on the images for its existence. On this interpretation, then, the argument asserts that God is to things in the world what the candle is to its reflected images.

There is one problem that faces the first interpretation that we have not yet applied to Copleston's interpretation. We saw that there is no reason why an infinite temporal series of causes could not occur so, that premise (4) seemed dubious. How does premise (4) fare on the second interpretation? Are there things in the world that, like the candle images, can exist at some time only if something else quite different also exists at that time? We know at least that any human being who exists for any period of time is causally dependent upon what might indeed be interpreted as a hierarchy of coexistent causes. For example, his existence is dependent upon the temperature of the earth remaining within a certain range, which in turn is dependent upon the earth's distance from the sun, which is dependent upon the gravitational and centripetal forces affecting the earth, which are

---

19. See F.C. Copleston, *Aquinas* (Baltimore: Penguin Books, 1957), 117-18.

dependent upon the masses of the earth and sun, which are dependent upon the chemical constituents of the earth and sun, which are dependent upon the atomic and subatomic makeup of the earth and sun. We have, then, for each human being not only a series of antecedently preceding causes, but an order of contemporaneous causal factors. This does not seem to be what Copleston means, however, because this order of causes leads neither to infinity nor to anything we would call God. It seems to go to basic subatomic particles. What might Copleston reply here? He might claim that the basic subatomic particles are no different from anything else in the world. They also are causally dependent on something for their existence, because their existence needs to be explained, just like anything else in the world. In other words, he might link causes and causal orders with explanations, as he did in a discussion of the topic with Bertrand Russell. He said, "Cause is a kind of sufficient reason. Only contingent beings can have a cause. God is His own sufficient reason; and He is not cause of Himself. By sufficient reason in the full sense I mean an explanation adequate for the existence of some particular being."[20] The point here is that if we are looking for the cause of something, we are looking for a sufficient reason for—that is, a *complete explanation* of—its existence. Perhaps, then, we should consider a first or ultimate explanation of why there are things like people, horses, stones, and even neutrinos, rather than considering temporally first or ontologically ultimate causes of change.

Third interpretation: Ultimate explanation of things

On the third interpretation we get an argument that is pretty much analogous to each of the steps in the first-cause argument. The argument can be stated this way:

1. There are now things existing and things explaining their existence.

2. If there are now things existing and things explaining their existence and each thing, X, that explains something else, Y, completely explains Y only if it, X, is itself explained by something else, then Y's complete explanation is infinitely long.

Therefore

3. If each thing that explains something else completely explains it only if it is itself explained by something else, then its complete explanation is infinitely long.

4. No complete explanation can be infinitely long.

Therefore

---

20. From a debate on the Third Program of the British Broadcasting Corp., 1948.

5. There is something that completely explains other things and is not explained by anything else, that is, there is something which is the ultimate explanation of things, namely, God.

It should be noted that, on this interpretation, the crucial claim in the argument is not that there would be an infinite number of different explanations, but that any complete explanation would be infinitely long. The idea here is that if the explanation of one thing requires reference to something else, which itself needs to be explained, then the explanation of the first thing is not complete unless the second is completely explained.

One important consequence of this stress on the completeness of the explanation of one thing is that a quite plausible argument supports premise (4). Consider that we would not call something an explanation unless we could completely express it, because the function of an explanation is to make what it explains intelligible, and something is intelligible only if it can be expressed. But a statement that is infinitely long is one that cannot ever be fully stated or expressed. Thus, no complete explanation can be infinitely long. Premise (4), then, no longer seems dubious. Can we now accept the argument as sound? Not yet, because we have not yet examined premise (2), which on this interpretation may be the dubious one.

A problem:
Are adequate scientific explanations complete explanations?
We can show premise (2) to be false if we can find an example where one thing is explained by reference to something else in such a way that even if we assume that each explaining thing must be explained by something else, the original explanation is, nevertheless, both complete and finite in length. If we find such an example, then even if an infinite number of different explanations were required to explain completely everything there is, some specific explanations of individual things would still be complete and finite, so that premise (2) would be false.

It seems quite easy to find many examples to show that premise (2) is false. Consider how we would explain that a high tide at a particular time and place. We would do it in part by reference to the position of the moon relative to the location of the tide. Although the resulting explanation might seem quite complicated, because it requires mathematical laws relating the relevant masses and the resulting gravitational attraction between the moon and the ocean, it is clearly finite in length. Furthermore, whether or not the position of the moon is to be explained by reference to something else, as it surely is, and even if the "chain" of separate explanations started in this way is infinitely long, the adequacy of the original explanation of the high tide is unaffected. It is a completely adequate scientific explanation as it stands, regardless of what else needs to be explained. The explanation of the high tide is finite in length and seems to be complete, even if we assume that each explanatory factor needs explaining by another. It seems, then, that premise (2) is false.

It is not hard to construct what the reply to this example would be. The idea behind this interpretation is that to explain something completely, everything referred to in the explanation must also be completely explained. But this clearly cannot be achieved if an infinite number of different explanations is required. Therefore, this reply would go, the explanation of the high tides is incomplete because it does not explain the position of the moon; thus the example does not refute premise (2). The important point to notice about this reply is that someone who makes it is committed to the position that a completely adequate *scientific* explanation of the high tide is, nevertheless, not a complete explanation. This is exactly the point Copleston makes at another place in his debate with Russell.

> *Russell*: But when is an explanation adequate? Suppose I am about to make a flame with a match. You may say that the adequate explanation of that is that I rub it on the box.
> *Copleston*: Well, for practice purposes—but theoretically, that is only a partial explanation. An adequate explanation must ultimately be a total explanation to which nothing further can be added.
> *Russell*: Then I can only say that you're looking for something which can't be got, and which one ought not to expect to get.
> *Copleston*: To say that one has not found it is one thing; to say that one should not look for it seems to me rather dogmatic.[21]

Who is right in this debate? Russell claims that science is our means of explaining facts about the universe. Whatever science cannot explain is, according to Russell, beyond the realm of explanation. But should we accept anything as beyond explanation? Consider the widely accepted principle that is called the "principle of sufficient reason," but that we might also call the "principle of complete explanation," that is, the principle that everything that exists or occurs can be completely explained. If this principle is true, then it would seem that nothing should be beyond the realm of scientific explanation, if science is the one means of explanation, as Russell claims. Two questions immediately arise here. First, is there something science cannot, in principle, explain? And second, is the principle of complete explanation true? Although there is no reason to think that science cannot come to explain each *individual* thing that occurs, there is another question it seems that science cannot answer. That question is, "Why is there any universe at all, rather than nothing at all?" Science may be able to explain why there is this particular universe by

---

21. Ibid.

reference, for example, to the big bang theory of the origin of the universe. On this theory, this universe resulted from the explosion of one primordial mass that sent bits and pieces in all directions and formed the various galaxies that make up the universe. But, for example, science could not explain why, rather than nothing at all, there was this primordial mass waiting to explode. Here scientific explanation comes to an end, for there is nothing in terms of which the existence of the primordial mass can be scientifically explained. Thus, if the principle of complete explanation is true, then it seems that there is at least one thing to be explained that science cannot explain. Copleston, then, might be able to begin a defense of premise (2) against the counterexample we have taken from scientific explanation.

Is there a reason to think that the principle of complete explanation is true? Copleston might attempt to turn the principle against Russell by claiming that it is certainly a presupposition of science, for scientific progress is premised on the doctrine that everything can be explained. We might agree that the achievements of science surely argue for a kind of justification of the principle as it is used by science, but must we then go on to agree with Copleston that science cannot do the complete job? Following Russell, we could interpret the principle so that it is sufficient for scientific purposes, but does not open the door to let in Copleston's nonscientific explanation. Science explains particular things and events; so the form of the principle needed for science is that there is a complete explanation of each particular event and each individual entity. This version of the principle, while allowing science all it needs, in no way states that the universe as a whole must be explainable independently of the particular explanations of each of the things that make up the whole universe. If we accept this version then we can agree with Russell that a completely adequate scientific explanation is a complete explanation and the high-tide example would falsify premise (2). There would, then, be no reason to claim that God is necessary to explain the world around us, no reason to postulate God as a theoretical explanatory entity. Science does not, however, answer questions such as, "Why is there something rather than nothing?" so perhaps we should agree that some kind of nonscientific explanation is required. It is not clear which position is more reasonable; thus we have reached an impasse on this point. We can, nevertheless, draw a conclusion about our main interest in explanation. Because we have not been able to resolve the debate about explanation in Copleston's favor, we can conclude that, although premise (2) may be true, it is open to reasonable doubt and therefore cannot be used to justify the conclusion that God exists. Thus, we should reject the third and final version of the first-cause argument. We cannot use it to justify a belief in the existence of God.

The Argument from Contingency

The third way of Aquinas is a most ingenious attempt to establish the existence of God. It begins with the a posteriori truth that there are contingent things, that is, things such that it is possible that they begin to exist and possible that they cease to exist, and concludes that there exists a necessary being, that is, a being such that it is impossible that it begin or cease to exist. Such a being is said to exist necessarily and is what we call God.[22] Aquinas moves from the premise concerning the existence of contingent things to his conclusion by adding that it is impossible that contingent things always exist. Thus, he says, if everything is contingent, then at some time before now, nothing existed. But if at some time before now nothing at all existed, then nothing exists now, which is plainly false. Therefore there is a noncontingent, that is, a necessary being, namely God.

As stated, the crucial claim in Aquinas's third way is the claim that if everything is contingent, then at some time before now nothing existed. Why would Aquinas believe this? Partly because he is assuming, for purposes of the argument, that time is infinite. As Copleston says, "Aquinas is clearly supposing for the sake of the argument the hypothesis of infinite time, and his proof is designed to cover this hypothesis."[23] Imagine that this is correct, and that time stretches back infinitely into the past. We may then ask whether contingent things have always existed, throughout infinite past time, or whether they have existed for only a finite amount of time. On either of these answers, two possibilities are open. Take infinite time and the assumption that contingent things have existed throughout an infinite past. This may mean either of two things:

a. At each and every moment, stretching infinitely back into the past, contingent things have existed.

b. Contingent things have existed at some times or other throughout infinite past time; that is, for *any* given moment of time in the past, some contingent things have existed at some time *before* that moment.

Thus, as an illustration of (a), imagine a line stretching infinitely back into the past from right now, where each cut on the line represents a moment of time, and each use of the letter c represents contingent things. As can be seen, at every moment of time there are contingent things in existence. If we were able actually to draw such a line as would be needed, drawn infinitely to the left of the page, it would have an infinite number of cuts for moments, and each cut would have a letter c below it. Thus, we would have represented (a) in the diagram:

---

22. For Aquinas's statement of the argument from contingency, see Aquinas, op. cit., 22-23.

23. Copleston, *Aquinas*, 120.

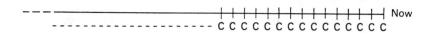

The difference between (a) and (b) is that (b) *leaves open the possibility* of there being at least one moment when nothing existed. It requires only that for any such moment when nothing existed, some contingent things existed before that moment. Thus, (b) leaves open the possibility of a situation such as that diagrammed in the following:

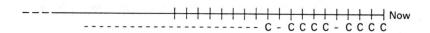

Now let us consider the other option, that contingent things have existed for only a finite amount of past time. Again we have two possibilities, namely:

c. At each and every moment, stretching back into the past up to time t_o, contingent things have existed.

d. Contingent things have existed at some times or other throughout past time back to time t_o, that is, for any given moment of time, back to $t + 1$, some contingent things have existed before that time.

Diagrams on lines can now be easily constructed for (c) and (d) based on the two given above for (a) and (b).

One reason why Aquinas's third way is so ingenious and fascinating is that it is designed to work no matter which option we choose, from (a) through (d). His central claim is that, given the assumption of infinite past time, then if either (a) or (b) or (c) or (d) is correct, then at some time before now nothing existed. And this, he thinks, is all he really needs to make the argument from contingency work. Notice that by arguing in this fashion, Aquinas need not actually assert and endorse any of (a) through (d). In our statement of the argument, the differences between (a) and (b) on the one hand, and between (c) and (d) on the other, are not explicitly stated. The argument is, as we said, designed to succeed whichever of those options we take. The argument, then, is this:

1. Either there have been things for an infinite amount of time, or there have been things for only a finite amount of time.

2. If there have been things for an infinite amount of time, then each different sum total of existing entities that can occur has occurred at some time or other before now.

3. If the only things that exist are contingent, then one possibility is that at some time before now none of them existed.

Therefore

4. If there have been things for an infinite amount of time, and the only things that exist are contingent, then at some time before now nothing existed.   (from 2, 3)

5. If there have been things for only a finite amount of time, and the only things that exist are contingent, then at some time before now nothing existed.

Therefore

6. If the only things that exist are contingent, then at some time before now nothing existed.   (from 1, 4, 5)

7. If at some time before now nothing existed, then nothing exists now.

Therefore

8. If the only things that exist are contingent, then nothing exists now.
                                                                              (from 6, 7)

9. It is false that nothing exists now.

Therefore

10. It is false that the only things that exist are contingent, that is, there is a necessary being, namely God.   (from 8, 9)

Although, in premises (2) and (3), the argument considers the consequences of contingent things existing over an infinite duration of time, it also, in premise (5), considers the consequence of contingent things existing only over a finite duration of time. Premise (5) states that if things have existed for only a finite duration of time before now, then there was some first moment at which something began to exist, so that at any time before that moment nothing existed. This is surely true, if we grant that time is infinite whether or not things have existed for an infinite duration of time. So, given the addition of this premise and premise (1), which is an obvious truth, we can conclude (6), which contains no reference to either hypothesis about how long things have existed. Thus if premises (2) and (3) are true, then, on this version of the argument from contingency, we can draw a conclusion that does not depend on which hypothesis is correct. This is why it was claimed that this is a stronger argument than one based on the assumption that things have existed for an infinite time. However, the major question is whether premises (2) and (3) are true. We can surely accept (9). Premise (7), although not a necessary truth, can be restated as a more general version of the principle of the conservation of mass-energy, which states, roughly, that in a closed system no amount of the energy, including that in the form of mass, can be either created or destroyed. Thus, if something new appears, this principle claims that it cannot have come from nothing, but requires a transfer of energy from something else. When premise (7) is considered in this light, it seems to be acceptable.

The crucial premises are clearly (2) and (3). Let us carefully consider both premises, beginning with premise (3), which is initially more plausible. If everything that has ever existed is contingent, then it is possible that each one ceases to exist at some time. Generally things cease existing at different times, so that usually at any one time some of them exist. But if we restrict our sample—for example, to the freshman class of a particular college—then, although the members of the class will cease to exist at different times, there will come a time when all of these contingent beings have ceased to exist. If we now enlarge our sample to include all people and indeed all physical objects, we can see quite clearly that in this age of nuclear armament it is very possible that there come a time when no persons and indeed no physical objects exist. Surely, then, if only contingent things have ever existed, it is possible that at some time, which may as a matter of fact have occurred before now, every one of those things that had previously existed had ceased existing and no new one had begun to exist. Notice that this is not to claim it *has* happened, but only that it is *possible* that it has happened, which is a much weaker claim.

Premise (3) seems to be acceptable. But is it? Consider once again the principle of the conservation of mass-energy, which we used as a reason for accepting premise (7). This principle states that if we take the universe to be a closed system, then no energy can be created or destroyed. But this looks familiar, because we can restate it to read that in the universe it is impossible that any amount of energy begin, or cease, to exist. Thus, given the truth of premise (9), once it is adapted to refer to energy, we must conclude that it is impossible that at some time before now nothing, including energy, existed. This will lead us to conclude that premise (3) is false unless we wish to claim that mass-energy exists necessarily rather than contingently, because it is something that can neither be created nor destroyed. But this is really not a viable way out, because when we characterized God as eternal, we decided that this should be interpreted so that it is *logically* impossible that he either begin to exist or cease to exist. Thus a necessary being is one that it is logically impossible to create or destroy. Therefore energy is contingent because it is logically possible to create or destroy it.

Objection: An Equivocation—Physical Versus Logical Possibility

Something has gone wrong. On the one hand, premise (3) seems acceptable; on the other, it seems false. It surely seems possible that nothing exist, but it also seems impossible because the energy there is now could not have been created and cannot be destroyed. It seems that we have a problem about what is possible and what is not. To solve it we must examine the concept of possibility. It is important to note that there are several different kinds of possibility, two of which are relevant to our problem: logical possibility and physical possibility.

A. *Logical Possibility*: Something is logically possible if and only if it does not violate the laws of logic, that is, it does not logically imply a contradiction when it is conjoined with any analytically true sentence and the laws of logic. By this definition it is logically impossible that there is a married spinster living somewhere.

B. *Physical Possibility*: Something is physically possible if and only if (1) it is logically possible, and (2) it does not violate the physical laws of nature, that is, it is false that it logically implies a contradiction when conjoined with any true sentence (with which it is logically compatible) and with the laws of physics and logic. By this definition it is physically impossible that some cow jumped over the moon from the earth with no help.

If we reexamine premise (3), we shall find that it is acceptable when we interpret 'possible' one way, but quite dubious when we interpret it the other way. Let us consider physical possibility first. Thus (3) becomes:

3a. If the only things that have ever existed are logically contingent, then one physical possibility is that at some time before now nothing existed.

We can quickly show that (3a) is false by referring to the conservation principle. Let us assume that everything that has ever existed is some amount of energy, whether in the form of mass or some other form such as heat. Consequently, the only things that have existed are logically contingent. None are such that it is logically impossible to create or destroy them. Nevertheless, it is not physically possible that at some time before now nothing existed. Energy, although logically contingent, is physically necessary, that is, it is physically impossible to create and destroy it. Consequently, (3a) is false. It was when we construed 'possibility' as 'physical possibility' that (3) seemed false.

At this point someone might object that this way of handling (3a) rules out completely the claim that God created the world *ex nihilo*, because the law of the conservation of mass-energy, as here interpreted to apply to the universe as a whole, entails that a certain amount of energy has always existed. It is true that applying the law in this way makes creation *ex nihilo* physically impossible, but this does not rule out creation. Such a creation is surely a miracle and, like all violation-miracles, involves the physically impossible. Thus, although we would agree with Hume that violation-miracles and *a fortiori* creation *ex nihilo* are highly improbable, on the basis of what has been repeatedly established, this does not rule them out completely. That is, it does not make it logically impossible that they occur, and, as we have also seen, it is only if miracles and creation *ex nihilo* were logically impossible that God would be unable to perform them.

Because (3a) using 'physical possibility' will not do, let us try 'logical possibility,' so that (3) becomes:

3b. If the only things that exist are logically contingent, then one logical possibility is that at some time before now nothing existed.

It can be quickly seen that (3b) is true. If we claim that it is logically possible for everything to cease to exist, then there is no logical contradiction in also claiming that nothing exists. We contradict ourselves only if we claim that something exists necessarily, that is, it exists now and it is logically impossible that it begin or cease to exist, and also claim that at some time nothing exists. We should then use (3b) in the argument from contingency.

Premise (2) is surely the most dubious of the premises, but we can make it seem somewhat more plausible by using an analogy involving coins. Consider two coins which are such that for each it is possible that it comes up heads and possible that it comes up tails. What are the possibilities available? There are 2^n possibilities, where n is the number of coins involved. Thus for two coins there are four possibilities: heads, heads; heads, tails; tails, heads; and tails, tails. If we are given an infinite number of flips of these two coins, we can surely conclude that at some time or other each of these possibilities will occur. Thus if premise (2) were stated as the flipping of two coins rather than the existence of objects, we could conclude that it is true. Furthermore, if we consider a million such coins, although there would be 2^{10^6} possibilities, nevertheless, given an infinite series of flips of all million coins, it would still seem likely that each of the 2^{10^6} possibilities would have occurred at least once at some time or other. Indeed, no matter how many coins we have, as long as the number is finite, it would seem that, given an infinite number of flips, each possibility would occur at least once. If we now apply the analogy so that we move from coins that can come up heads and can come up tails, to objects that can begin to exist and can cease existing, then we can see that, given an infinite amount of time, there may be some reason to claim that each possibility would occur at some time or other, and thus with premise (3) we would conclude, as in (4), that the one possibility of none of these objects existing would occur.

If, as the coin analogy implies, we might be able to accept premise (2), then the present interpretation of the argument from contingency may well be sound, because each premise is plausible and the argument is valid. One thing that should give us pause, however, is that the plausibility of premise (3) depends on which sense of 'possibility' is used. Which one have we used to make premise (2) plausible? To find out, let us consider another example, this time involving a roulette wheel. Given an infinite number of turns of the wheel, it would seem that the ball would stop at least one time at each number at which it is physically possible for the ball to stop, no matter how large the roulette wheel is. Would it also stop at each logically possible number? Consider a roulette wheel that is fixed so that it is physically impossible for the ball to stop at the number 1. In such a case, the ball would not stop at least once at each number at which it is logically possible to stop, because there is no logical contradiction in the claim about a roulette wheel that it is physically impossible that the ball stop at the number 1. Consequently, if the universe is more like a fixed roulette wheel than like one that runs randomly, then some things that are logically possible will not occur. Although it is logically possible that some day the cow will jump over the moon with no one helping it, it is surely physically impossible, so that we can conclude that it will not happen. It is physical possibility rather than logical possibility that it is important for what occurs. Furthermore, because the law of the conservation of mass-energy can be used to show that certain logically possible situations, such as the situation in which nothing at all exists, are physically impossible and thus will not occur unless miraculously, we must use 'physical possibility' in (2) if we are to make it at all plausible.

We must use 'physical possibility' in premise (2) to make it plausible, but we have to use 'logical possibility' in (3) to make it plausible. We need to use different senses of 'possibility' in these two premises for both to be plausible. The result is that we can make them both plausible only by equivocating in our use of the word 'possibility.' But this makes the argument invalid, because any argument to be valid must use all its terms univocally, with one meaning, throughout. Therefore the argument from contingency is faced with the following dilemma: If there is no equivocation on the word 'possible,' then at least one premise is false and the argument is unsound. If there is an equivocation on 'possible,' then the argument is invalid and, consequently, unsound. From this we can conclude that the argument is unsound. We cannot justify a belief in God using the argument from contingency.

The Argument from Design

One of the most discussed arguments that has been used to justify a belief in the existence of God is the argument from design, or, as it is called, the teleological argument. Although this argument is like those we have already examined in that it is an a posteriori argument, it differs from them in an important way. Unlike the previous arguments, which are all deductive, the argument from design is essentially an inductive argument. It is an attempt to construe the universe, or at least certain characteristics of the universe, as being like certain things humans have designed and created, so that we can inductively infer from this evidence of design that there is a designer or creator like the intelligent designers of human artifacts but, obviously, much more intelligent. At the core of the argument, then, lies an analogy between the universe and things we know to be designed and created by intelligent beings. The argument from design, then, is an analogical argument, and we should, therefore, briefly examine the form of an analogical argument. Let us assume that there is some object O_1 and that we want to find out whether it has some property P_1, but we cannot find this out in any direct way. If we compare O_1 with some other objects we know to have property P_1, and find that O_1 is like the others in several other respects but differs from them in no important respects, then we can conclude that probably O_1 has property P_1. It is important, of course, that all the available evidence be considered, because there may be differences which make it improbable that O_1 has property P_1.

Analogical arguments

We can state the general form of an analogical argument as follows:

1. Objects O_1, O_2, O_3, . . . , O_n have properties P_2, P_3, P_4, . . . , P_n in common.

2. Objects O_2, O_3, . . . , O_n have property P_1.

Therefore, probably

3. Object O_1 has property P_1.

We have said that all the available evidence must be considered if a statement such as (3) is to be justified in this way, because certain kinds of factors decrease the probability of the conclusion. Other factors, however, raise the probability, thereby strengthening the argument. Therefore, as with any inductive argument, the requirement to use all available evidence —called the requirement of total evidence—is essential. To see the importance of this requirement, consider the following example: Let us assume that O_1 is a car you wish to buy, that P_1 is the property of having a gas consumption of at least fifteen miles per gallon, and that you cannot test the car before you buy it. You can get some idea of the gas consumption of the car by comparing it with the gas consumption of other cars. The more cars you know about that get at least fifteen miles per gallon—that is, the greater number of cars included in $O_2, \ldots, O_n$ that have property P_1—the more probable it will be that car O_1 has property P_1. Furthermore, the more properties that these other cars have in common with car O_1 —such as the number of cylinders, the kind of transmission, the make of the car, the age of the engine, and the like—the more probable it will be that car O_1 will also get at least fifteen miles per gallon. However, if you find that many cars that have the same number of cylinders, the same kind of transmission, the same age engine, and so on, do not get at least fifteen miles per gallon, then the probability that the car you are thinking of buying will get fifteen miles per gallon will decrease markedly. Furthermore if, given the same information in your premises, you are interested in eighteen miles per gallon instead of fifteen miles per gallon, then the probability that your car will get eighteen miles per gallon is less than the probability that it will get fifteen miles per gallon.

From this example we can extract four different kinds of factors that will affect the probability of the conclusion. These and other relevant factors must be weighed in arriving at any final statement about the probability or improbability of a conclusion. The following two factors will strengthen the argument, that is, increase the probability of the conclusion:

1. The greater the number of objects included in $O_2, \ldots, O_n$ having properties $P_1, \ldots, P_n$, the more probable is the conclusion.

2. The greater the number of properties included in $P_2, \ldots, P_n$ that the objects $O_1, \ldots, O_n$ have in common, the more probable is the conclusion.

The following two factors decrease the probability of the conclusion:

3. The greater the number of objects that have $P_2, \ldots, P_n$ but do not have P_1, the less probable is the conclusion.

4. The stronger the claim made in the conclusion, relative to the premises, the less probable is the conclusion.

Let us return now to the argument from design. But let us also keep in mind these four factors that affect the probability or likelihood of the conclusions of analogical arguments, so that we do not overlook them and thereby fail to meet the requirement of total evidence.[24]

---

24. See I. Copi, *Introduction to Logic* 4th edition (New York: Macmillan, 1972), Chapter 11, for a more detailed examination of analogical arguments.

Two versions of the argument from design

The two most celebrated versions of the argument from design are found in Hume's *Dialogues on Natural Religion* and the fifth way of Aquinas. Aquinas states his version as follows:

> We see that things which lack knowledge, such as natural bodies, act for an end, and this is evident from their acting always, or nearly always, in the same way, so as to obtain the best result. Hence it is plain that they achieve their end, not fortuitously, but designedly. Now whatever lacks knowledge cannot move toward an end, unless it be directed by some being endowed with knowledge and intelligence; as the arrow is directed by the archer. Therefore some intelligent being exists by whom all natural things are directed to their end; and this being we call God.[25]

In the *Dialogues* it is Cleanthes—one of the *Dialogues'* fictional characters—who proposes the argument in the following way:

> Look around the world: Contemplate the whole and every part of it: You will find it to be nothing but one great machine, subdivided into an infinite number of lesser machines, which again admit of subdivisions, to a degree beyond what human senses and faculties can trace and explain. All these various machines, and even their most minute parts, are adjusted to each other with an accuracy, which ravishes into admiration all men, who have ever contemplated them. The curious adapting of means to ends, throughout all nature, resembles exactly, though it much exceeds, the production of human contrivance; of human design, thought, wisdom, and intelligence. Since therefore the effects resemble each other, we are led to infer, by all the rules of analogy, that the causes also resemble, and that the Author of nature is somewhat similar to the mind of man, though possessed of much larger faculties, proportioned to the grandeur of the work, which He has executed. By this argument *a posteriori*, and by this argument alone, do we prove at once the existence of a Deity and His similarity to human mind and intelligence.[26]

What both versions have in common is the claim that in the universe and among its natural parts there is evidence of a design or purpose, and that this design or purpose requires the existence of an intelligent being who directs the universe and its parts according to his purpose. However, we should consider two important differences between these two versions before we critically evaluate them. To see better what these differences

---

25. Aquinas, op. cit., 23.

26. David Hume, *Dialogues Concerning Natural Religion* (Indianapolis: Bobbs-Merrill, 1947), 143.

are, let us lay out the arguments formally. We can interpret Aquinas's version as follows:

1. The natural objects that make up the universe (that is, the nonsentient, non-man-made objects, such as trees, rocks, mountains, planets) act to achieve some end or goal.

2. If something acts to achieve an end, then it is directed toward that end by some intelligent being.

3. No natural objects are intelligent beings.

Therefore

4. There exists some intelligent being that directs the natural objects to achieve some end or goal.

5. This director is God.

Cleanthes' version can be stated as follows:

1. The universe is like a huge man-made machine made up of many lesser machines, except that the universe is much more complex than any man-made machine.

2. Like effects have like causes.

3. The cause of a man-made machine is an intelligent being.

Therefore, probably

4. The cause of the universe is an intelligent being.

5. This cause is God.

One difference, immediately evident, is that whereas Cleanthes' version is plainly an inductive analogical argument, Aquinas's version appears to be a straightforward deductive argument. Where is the inductive feature we claimed is essential to the argument from design? If we scrutinize the first premise of each argument, we can see the reason Aquinas's version seems to lack the analogical character of Cleanthes' version. Aquinas's first premise is surely much more dubious than that of Cleanthes, because whereas Aquinas claims that natural objects act for an end, Cleanthes claims merely that they are like things that we know to act for an end—for example, machines. What reason could there be to accept Aquinas's first premise? The obvious justification would require an analogical argument such as:

6. The natural objects that make up the universe are like things which act to achieve some end or goal.

Therefore, probably

1. The natural objects that make up the universe act to achieve some end or goal.

For Aquinas's argument, then, the analogy with things known to be designed seems to be what justified the first premise. And because this is the only dubious premise, premises (2) and (3) being acceptable, the analogy lies at the core of the argument. We can accept premise (2) because it surely seems that only a being with intelligence could set a goal to be achieved and set about achieving it by various means. Furthermore, because we have seen that by 'natural objects' we mean those nonsentient, non-man-made objects which make up the universe, we can grant that premise (3) is true by definition.

The second difference between the two versions is more important. Aquinas talks only of an intelligent being who directs natural objects to some goal, whereas Cleanthes talks about the author of nature. That is, Aquinas's version proves only that some very intelligent director or designer has planned the course of the universe, but Cleanthes' version proves that an extremely intelligent being created the universe in accordance with some plan or purpose. Before we examine the argument we must decide which conclusion to use. We know that Cleanthes' conclusion is stronger than Aquinas's because it claims that there is a creator and designer, whereas Aquinas's conclusion merely claims there is a designer. Thus Aquinas's conclusion will be more probable than that of Cleanthes relative to the same set of premises. However, the purpose of the argument is to establish the existence of God, and what we would call God is not merely the designer, but also the creator of the universe. Consequently, if we merely establish that there is a designer or architect of the universe, there is some doubt whether we are justified in calling such a being God. Let us, then, use Cleanthes' version for the purpose of a critical evaluation.

We can put Cleanthes' argument into the form of analogical arguments previously discussed by letting O_1 = the universe, $O_2, \ldots, O_n$ = various kinds of machines, P_1 = the property of having an intelligent designer and creator, and $P_2, \ldots, P_n$ = various properties O_1 has in common with $O_2, \ldots, O_n$. If we pick for an example of a machine, a watch, as used by another defender of the argument, William Paley, we can point out several properties in common.[27] A watch has gears, which revolve in a certain orderly way on certain axes, some of which affect others so as to cause the regular ticking off of the seconds, minutes, and hours. Similarly, we can observe the moon revolving around the earth and the earth revolving on its axis, and also around the sun, in a certain orderly way so as to cause the

---

27. See W. Paley, *Natural Theology; or, Evidence of the Existence and Attributes of the Deity*, 9th edition (London: R. Faulder, 1805).

regular rising and falling of the tides and the regular coming of day and night. The earth, moon, and sun in their various relationships to each other produce a regular temporal procession just as do the gears of a watch in their various relationships. And because a watch has property P_1 (that is, has an intelligent designer and creator), so also, most probably, does the earth and the rest of the universe. This, then, is the argument that we shall consider. However, this is not the only analogy possible. Although we have followed Cleanthes and likened the universe to a machine, there is also a design to be found in human works of art. The formal relationships of shapes and colors that go together to produce the beautiful design of a painting are much like the shapes and colors that go together to produce the quiet beauty of a sunset reflected in a mountain pool, or the brilliant beauty of a New England fall, with the colors of leaves contrasting with the white birch trunks. If we were to use this analogy, then God would be the supreme artist rather than the greatest inventor. We shall, however, continue to use Cleanthes' machine analogy, because there seems to be no reason to think that the art analogy is any better.

In evaluating Cleanthes' argument, we can do no better than to turn to his antagonist in the *Dialogues*, Philo, for the crucial objections. Philo's chief objections are aimed at two places: at the strength of the analogy and thus at the strength of the analogical justification of (4), and at the inference from (4) to (5)—that is, from the claim, supported by the analogy, that there is a cause of the universe, to the conclusion that this cause is God.

Objection to Cleanthes' analogy: Nonintelligent causes of design

Philo's objection to the analogical grounds of the argument is essentially an attempt to show that there is no reason to think that the universe resembles the creation of an intelligent being any more than the causal product of nonintelligent forces. In effect, Philo is trying to show that many objects have properties $P_2, \ldots, P_n$ in common with the universe, but do not have property P_1, that is, do not have an intelligent designer and creator. Philo, is then, applying factor (3) in order to decrease the probability of the conclusion to a point where it is no longer probable. Philo claims that, although what order and design we find in the universe might be attributed to intelligence, at least three other causes of order and design have equal claim. Consider the order and design that result from vegetable reproduction, animal reproduction, and instinct.[28] We can find intricate order, design, and beauty in a flower, bush, or tree, and all of these are brought about not by an intelligent being, but come from a seed in the ground which receives water and sunlight. In none of these four factors—seed, earth, water, sunlight—is there any hint of intelligence.

---

28. See Hume, *Dialogues Concerning Natural Religion*, 178-80.

Furthermore, consider a beautiful Persian cat, a peacock, exotic tropical fish, or even a particular human being. The orderly structure of such organisms, the interrelating functioning of their parts, and the beauty of many of them are all the causal result of the fertilization of an egg in an act of animal reproduction. Here again there is no reason to think that intelligence was at all relevant, not even in the case of humans, where intelligence is usually used to avoid fertilization. Think also of the marvelous order and design produced by instinct. The geometric precision of bee hives, the intricate pattern of ant tunnels, the functional design of birds' nests, and beaver dams, all seem to be effects of instinctive forces rather than the studied result of some intelligent planning. What grounds are there for picking one from among four quite different causes of order and design? It is no less reasonable to claim, and therefore no less probable, that the earth and the other parts of the universe have sprouted from some seed or matured from some egg fertilized eons ago, or are some residual part of the instinctive production of some animal long since extinct, than to claim that they are the planned result of some unseen being with great intelligence. Indeed, as Philo says, in countering Cleanthes' analogy with one of his own,

> Now if we survey the universe, so far as it falls under our knowledge, it bears a great resemblance to an animal or organized body, and seems actuated with a like principle of life and motion. A continual circulation of matter in it produces no disorder: A continual waste in every part is incessantly repaired: The closest sympathy is perceived throughout the entire system: and each part or member, in performing its proper office, operates both to its own preservation and to that of the whole. The world, therefore, I infer, is an animal; and the Deity is the *soul* of the world actuating it, and actuated by it.[29]

There are other ways that order and design can come about, one of the most usual being by purely physical forces. Millions of uniquely complex and lovely designs are found by examining snowflakes and crystals of certain salts. The flakes are the effects of temperature on water vapor and the crystals are the effects of supersaturation of a salt solution. In neither case do we find intelligence. All around us, order and design are produced in many different ways by many different forces. This may cause us to marvel at the wonder of it all, and, unable to believe that it could happen merely by chance, we sometimes are led to conclude that some guiding force must be behind it all. But if there is such a force it might be instinct, purely mechanical force, or indeed a combination of many varied kinds of forces, each producing its own kind of order and design. It will do no good to claim that all these other causes of order and design are the

---

29. Ibid., 170-71.

result of intelligence, or that they are evidence of some more basic originating intelligent force. Although this claim might be true, we cannot assume it, because it is what the argument is attempting to prove. Furthermore, there is no reason to think that it is true. Indeed, if we consider that part of the universe that we inhabit, as we must in drawing analogies from what we know, we find that each intelligent being was brought about by some particular act of animal reproduction, but that so far at least there is no reason to think that any cases of animal reproduction are the result of intelligence. Thus, on the basis of the available evidence, we should conclude that intelligence is probably not the originating cause of order and design; perhaps it is merely one of the resultant causes. This conclusion is bolstered by the theory of evolution, which claims that human beings, with their intelligence, have evolved as a result of the interplay of such nonintelligent factors as random mutation, food shortages, and the instinct for survival. If this theory is correct, then intelligence is a very recent addition to those forces that can bring about order and design.

From the preceding discussion we can conclude, with Philo, that because intelligence is only one among many things in this world that produce order and design, it is no more probable that an intelligent being, rather than something else, produced the universe. Consequently, although we can agree with Cleanthes that the universe is in several respects like a machine that has property P_1, we have also found that it is like many things that do not have property P_1, so that the probability that the universe has property P_1 is quite low indeed. It is surely too low to conclude that, from among all the kinds of causes of order and design, we can pick out intelligence as the probable cause of the universe.

Objection to inferring that the cause of the universe is God: Like effects have like causes

We have seen that the analogy essential to the argument from design cannot support the conclusion, statement (4): 'The cause of the universe is an intelligent being.' In a sense, then, it is superfluous to go on to show that even if statement (4) is granted, the move from (4) to (5)—'This cause is God'—is unsound. However, not only is Philo's objection to this move interesting in its own right, but it stresses another important point relevant to supporting conclusions about unknown things by means of analogies with known things. Philo points out that if we conclude (4) on the basis of the similarity between the universe and some human artifact, such as a watch or ship or house, then we must conclude, in accordance with the principle that like effects have like causes, that the causes of the artifacts and of the universe are equally similar. In other words, although the more similar the universe and human artifacts are, the more probable premise (4) is, it is also true that the more similar they are, the more similar are their causes. Thus if the similarity is sufficient to make (4) probable, then we must follow through with the analogy and conclude that probably the causes are much alike. But if this is so, and if we accept the inference from (4) to (5), then, as Philo points out, we would have to attribute some most ungodlike characteristics to God. Consider the following points made by Philo:

[1] Even if this world were perfect it must still remain uncertain, whether all the excellences of the work can justly be ascribed to the workman. If we survey a ship, what an exalted idea must we form of the ingenuity of the carpenter, who framed so complicated, useful and beautiful a machine? And what surprise must we entertain, when we find him a stupid mechanic, who imitated others, and copied an art, which, through a long succession of ages, after multiplied trials, mistakes, corrections, deliberations, and controversies, had been gradually improving? Many worlds might have been botched and bungled, throughout an eternity, ere this system was struck out: Much labor lost: Many fruitless trials made: And a slow but continued improvement carried on during infinite ages in the art of world making.[30]

[2] And what shadow of an argument, continued Philo, can you produce, from your hypothesis, to prove the unity of the Deity? A great number of men join in building a house or ship, in rearing a city, in framing a commonwealth: Why may not several Deities combine in contriving and framing a world? This is only so much greater similarity to human affairs.[31]

[3] But further, Cleanthes; men are mortal, and renew their species by generation; and this is common to all living creatures. Why must this circumstance, so universal, so essential, be excluded from those numerous and limited Deities?[32]

[4] And why not become a perfect anthropomorphite? Why not assert the Deity or Deities to be corporeal, and to have eyes, a nose, mouth, ears, etc.?[33]

Philo summarizes his point by saying that a person who adopts Cleanthes' analogy might perhaps be able to assert that the universe is the product of some designer, but he can go no further on the basis of the analogy.

This world, for aught he knows, is very faulty and imperfect, compared to a superior standard; and was only the first rude essay of some infant Deity, who afterwards abandoned it, ashamed of his lame performance;

---

30. Ibid., 167.
31. Ibid.
32. Ibid., 168.
33. Ibid.

it is the work only of some dependent, inferior Deity; and is the object
of derision to his superiors: it is the production of old age and dotage in
some super-annuated Deity; and ever since his death, has run on at
adventures, from the first impulse and active force which it received from
him. . . .[34]

In short, if the analogy with human artifacts is close enough to make it
probable that an intelligent being created the universe, it is close enough
to make the creator so much more like human beings than like God that we
must reject the claim made in (5) that the creator of the universe as
established in (4) is God.   We cannot establish (5) by means of the
argument from design.

We have found two objections to the design argument that are sufficient
to eliminate it as an inductive justification of the belief that God exists.
This is the last plausible a posteriori argument for the existence of God.
The natural move at this point is to reject a posteriori proofs and claim that
if the belief in the existence of God is to be justified it must be by some
a priori proof, some proof that uses no premises that are justified by
evidence gathered through the experiences human beings have in this
world.   Let us consider such a proof.

AN A PRIORI ARGUMENT

One of the simplest yet most intriguing and baffling arguments that has
ever been devised is the ontological argument.   From the time of St.
Anselm, in the eleventh century, to the present, it has been endlessly
discussed.   Time and time again, it has been thought to be refuted and
finally laid to rest, only to reappear, as troublesome as ever.   There have
been two classical statements of the argument, one by St. Anselm and one
by René Descartes.   We shall consider Descartes's version first, because
it is the simpler of the two and brings out more directly one of the central
points of contention.

The Ontological Argument: Descartes's Version
Descartes argues that

> Whenever I choose to think of the First and Supreme Being, and as it
> were bring out the idea of him from the treasury of my mind, I must
> necessarily ascribe to him all perfections, even if I do not at the moment
> enumerate them all, or attend to each.   This necessity clearly ensures

---

34. Ibid., 169.

that, when later on I observe that existence is a perfection, I am justified in concluding that the First and Supreme Being exists.[35]

We can lay out Descartes's argument in the following simple form:

1. All perfections are properties of the supreme being.

2. Existence is a perfection.

Therefore

3. The supreme being has existence, that is, exists.

Although the first premise is usually granted, the second has come under repeated severe attacks. One kind of attack on premise (2) has been to argue that if existence is a perfection, then it is a property or characteristic some things have and some things do not have; and if existence is a property of things, then the word 'existence' is a predicate, because properties of things are referred to by predicates. But the word 'existence' is not a predicate, so that existence is not a perfection. The obvious reply to this objection is that existence surely is a predicate, because it can be predicated of a subject in a sentence. However, those who use this refutation of premise (2) are not denying that 'existence' is a grammatical predicate. They put their point in several different ways, but the central claim of them all is that 'existence' is not a descriptive predicate. That is, it is not a predicate that can be used to describe things; it is not a predicate that can be used to refer to some property things might have. If it can be shown that 'existence' is not such a predicate, then there is good reason to conclude that existence is not a property and, therefore, not a perfection.

Kant's objection: 'Existence' is not a predicate

The classical and perhaps strongest attempt to show that 'existence' is not a predicate is based on the objection made by Immanuel Kant nearly two centuries ago. This has been considered by many people to be the objection which once and for all refuted Descartes's version of the ontological argument. The crucial part of his objection centers on the concept of a real predicate, that is, according to Kant, a predicate "which determines a thing." In other words, a real predicate is one that can be used to help define what something is. It is, then, what we can call a defining predicate. Kant argues as follows:

Being is obviously not a real predicate; that is it is not a concept of something which could be added to the concept of a thing. It is merely

---

35. René Descartes, *Philosophical Writings*, ed. E. Anscombe and P. T. Geach (Edinburgh: T. Nelson, 1959), 104-5.

the positing of a thing, or of certain determinations, as existing in themselves. Logically it is merely the copula of a judgment. The proposition, 'God is omnipotent,' contains two concepts, each of which has its object—God and omnipotence . . . . If, now, we take the subject (God) with all its predicates (among which is omnipotence), and say 'God is,' or 'There is a God,' we attach no new predicate to the concept of God, but only posit the subject in itself with all its predicates, and indeed posit it as an *object* that stands in relation to my *concept*.[36]

It will be helpful to interpret this argument as being concerned with how one term can be used to change the meaning of another. This will give us some better way to interpret what Kant means by one concept being added to another concept. For example, we consider that the term 'bachelor' is defined by the two predicates 'unmarried' and 'male.' We could, however "add" another predicate to the definition such as 'happy,' and so change the meaning of 'bachelor.' Any predicate which can help determine the meaning of a term in this way is a defining predicate. Thus a term can be a defining predicate whether or not it is ever actually used in a definition. The only requirement is that it be possible to use it in such a manner. We can construe Kant's argument as:

1. If a term is a real (defining) predicate, then it can be added to the meaning of a term to change its meaning.

2. The term 'exist' cannot be added to the meaning of a term to change its meaning.

Therefore

3. The term 'exist' is not a real predicate.

Premise (1) is surely acceptable, because if a predicate can be used to define a term, then it can be used to redefine a term and thereby change its meaning. Premise (2), however, is not so clearly true. Kant defends it by claiming that whenever we assert that something exists, although we predicate 'exist' of a term, we are saying, in effect, that the term *with the meaning it has* applies to something or other. Thus we do not ever change the meaning of a term when we use it to say that something exists. When we say, for example, that some happy bachelors exist, in no case are we trying to change the meaning of the phrase 'happy bachelor.' We are claiming instead that the phrase as given applies to some entities. If Kant's defense of premise (2) is sound, then it seems that he has established that 'existence' is not a real or defining predicate.

---

36. Immanuel Kant, *Critique of Pure Reason*, trans. N. K. Smith (London: Macmillan, 1958), 504-5.

Although this is a rather persuasive argument, at least two objections can be raised against it. First, even if the argument is sound, it is not clear how it shows that existence is not a property. The most it can show is that existence is not a *defining* property of anything. In other words, all it shows is that any statement which asserts that something exists is synthetic rather than analytic, but this is not enough to show that existence is not a property. Some people have argued that showing that no existence statements are analytic is sufficient to refute Descartes's version of the ontological argument. If so, then enough has been done for our purposes. This is wrong, however. Although in many passages Descartes can be interpreted as claiming that 'God exists' is analytic, his argument, either as quoted or as we have reconstructed it, does not imply that it is necessary that God exists. Consequently, the argument does not imply that 'God exists' is analytic. It is true that Descartes claims that God necessarily has all perfections, but he does not claim that it is necessary that existence is a perfection. Thus the argument is compatible with 'God exists' being logically contingent (nonanalytic). Descartes's argument, therefore, cannot be refuted merely by showing that 'exist' is not a defining or real predicate.

There is a reply to this first objection (to Kant's argument) that consists in adding some premises to Kant's argument. The premises are these:

1a. If a term is a descriptive predicate, then it is a defining predicate.

By combining (1a) and (1) we get, via hypothetical syllogism,

1b. If a term is a descriptive predicate, then it can be added to the meaning of a term to change its meaning.

then, by utilizing (1b) and (2) we get

3a. The term 'exists' is not a descriptive predicate.

We now need another premise, namely,

4. Existence is a property only if 'exists' is a descriptive predicate.

and by combining (3a) and (4), we get the conclusion Kant wants,

5. Existence is not a property.

The first formulation of Kant's objection to Descartes's argument led us to statement (3), which, we saw, was not sufficient to refute Descartes. With this amended Kantian argument we get a conclusion, (5), which, if correct, successfully undermines Descartes's ontological argument.

We already granted premise (1). Premise (1a) can be seen to be plausible once we note that if a term describes some entity (and so the term is a descriptive predicate) by referring to some property of the entity, then it can be used to help define some term which refers to that entity. Of course, (1b) follows from (1) and (1a), so that (1b) is likewise acceptable.

Moreover, let us grant premise (2) for the sake of the argument, on the grounds that verbs are not used to refer to properties of things and therefore are not real or defining predicates. They are not used in the kinds of definitions we are considering here. We are left, then, with premise (4) to examine.

The fact that the term 'exists' is conceded not to be a real defining predicate, gives us no reason to think that the adjective 'existent' cannot be used in definitions. But if the term 'existent' can be used in definitions, there is some reason to think that it is a real predicate, and likewise some reason to think that it is a descriptive predicate. Consider the following definitions:

> Let the term 'reggad' mean 'existent dagger' and the term 'nonreggad' mean 'nonexistent dagger.'

We can use these terms to say quite meaningfully, for example, that in his disturbed state of mind Macbeth saw a nonreggad which he thought was a reggad. And, because we can use 'existent' in such definitions of new terms, we can also use it to redefine terms already in use. Hence, we have found reason to suppose that the term 'existent' is a real defining predicate, and thus some reason to suppose that 'existent' is a descriptive predicate. But if 'existent' is a descriptive predicate, then it is reasonable to believe that existence is a property; descriptive predicates refer to properties of things. We have thus cast doubt on premise (4). For if the fact that 'existent' is a descriptive predicate is a *sufficient* condition *all by itself* for existence to be a property, then the term 'exists' being a descriptive predicate is not a *necessary* condition for existence being a property. Hence, Kant's attack on Descartes's ontological argument fails after all.

The reasoning here may be illustrated by consideration of a baseball example. Suppose that someone says a necessary condition of a batted ball turning out to be a home run in Veteran's Stadium in Philadelphia is that the ball carry a minimum of five hundred feet at the appropriate altitude. This person thus affirms,

> A batted ball is a home run in Veteran's Stadium in Philadelphia only if the ball carries at least five hundred feet at an appropriate altitude.

In fact, however, it is enough for a batted ball to carry four hundred feet at the appropriate altitude and be a home run in that stadium. The distance from home plate to the left field fence is less than four hundred feet. Hence, hitting the ball to left field, a distance of four hundred feet, at the appropriate altitude, is sufficient for its being a home run. Therefore, hitting the ball five hundred feet in that stadium is not a necessary condition for hitting a home run in that stadium. It is similar in our assessment of Kant's argument. If it is reasonable to believe that 'existent' being a descriptive predicate is sufficient for existence to be a property, then it is reasonable to believe that the term 'exists' being a descriptive predicate is not necessary for existence to be a property.

Another objection: Existence is not a perfection

We have found that the first kind or attack on Descartes's ontological argument fails. Let us consider another. The point here is that even if 'existence' is a predicate, even if existence is a property, existence is surely not a perfection. For our purposes here it will do to say that a perfection is a property an object has that goes together with certain other properties to make a being perfect. Thus we can compare two things and decide which one is the better or more nearly perfect. We would decide the issue by considering the perfections each had and each lacked. For example, someone might describe two different people in great detail but not tell us whether or not they exist. He then asks us which description more nearly approaches the *ideal* or perfect person. We decide on the basis of the properties he has described. Suppose that, after we have decided, he says that he forgot to give us one piece of information. The person we had thought less perfect is actually alive, but the other is merely a fictitious character. Should we reevaluate our decision in the light of this new evidence? It would seem not. The one person more nearly attains perfection than the other, whether or not he or she exists. Existence, then, is not a perfection.

There is surely some force to this argument. When we decide who is the greatest president or the ideal painter or the saintliest person, we do not need to consider whether he or she exists now or ever. We can evaluate both fictional and real people. Existence seems to be irrelevant to perfection, or to being an *ideal* thing of a certain type. Consequently, we should conclude that premise (2) of Descartes's version of the ontological argument is too dubious to support the conclusion.

The Ontological Argument: St. Anselm's Version

Let us turn to St. Anselm's version, which, as we shall see, is not so intimately reliant on the thesis that existence is a perfection. St. Anselm starts by saying that we understand the concept of supreme being.

> And whatever is understood, exists in the understanding. And assuredly that, than which nothing greater can be conceived, cannot exist in the understanding alone. For suppose it exists in the understanding alone: then it can be conceived to exist in reality; which is greater.
>
> Therefore, if that, than which nothing greater can be conceived, exists in the understanding alone, the very being, than which nothing greater can be conceived, is one, than which a greater can be conceived. But,

obviously this is impossible. Hence, there is no doubt that there exists a being, than which nothing greater can be conceived. . . .[37]

Although it may not be historically accurate, we can untangle some of the complexity of Anselm's argument by replacing 'can be conceived' with 'is possible' and 'does not exist in the understanding alone' with 'exists.' We can then state the core of the argument as follows:

1. If the greatest being possible does not exist, then it is possible that there exists a being greater than the greatest being possible.

2. It is not possible that there exists a being greater than the greatest being possible.

Therefore

3. The greatest being possible exists.

It should be noted that this argument claims neither that existence is a perfection nor that statement (3) is a necessary truth. Consequently, it seems to be open to none of those objections that we have seen launched against Descartes's version. However, Gaunilo, a contemporary of Anselm, offered a different objection, which we must consider.

Gaunilo's objection: The greatest island possible
Gaunilo asks Anselm to consider an island that is the most excellent of all islands and to consider the following argument:

And since it is more excellent not to be in the understanding alone, but to exist both in the understanding and in reality, for this reason it must exist. For if it does not exist, any land which really exists will be more excellent than it; and so the island already understood by you to be more excellent will not then be more excellent.[38]

Gaunilo's point here is that Anselm's argument proves too much, so that it is surely unsound. We can prove by this argument that the greatest possible object of any kind, whether it be island or scholar or athlete or dinner or whatever, exists, and this is surely mistaken. Anselm's reply was merely to say that the logic of his argument applies only to the greatest *being* possible and to no other.

Reply to Gaunilo: A being greater than the greatest island possible
Was Anselm's reply to Gaunilo justified? To see what both men were driving at, let us use variables in the premises instead of constants. However, there are two ways we can do this: (*A*) we can let 'being' be

---

37. St. Anselm, *Basic Writings* (LaSalle, IL: Open Court, 1962), 8.
38. Ibid., 151.

what replaces the variable X, or *(B)* we can let 'greatest possible being' be the substitute for X. The premises will differ accordingly. The premises of argument form A will be the following:

1a. If the greatest X possible does not exist, then it is possible that there exists an X greater than the greatest X possible.

2a. It is not possible there exists an X greater than the greatest X possible.

And the premises of argument form B will be the following:

1b. If X does not exist, then it is possible that there exists a being greater than X.

2b. It is not possible there exists a being greater than X.

We can substitute innumerable terms for X in A (1a) and (2a), so that we could prove that the greatest possible object of *any kind* exists. Surely something is wrong with this argument, as Gaunilo claims. However, the second argument form, B, supports Anselm's claim that his argument works only for 'the greatest being possible.' Premise (2b) is true when 'the greatest being possible' is substituted for X, but there is no reason to think it true for anything else such as 'the greatest island possible' because the statement:

It is not possible there exists a *being* greater than the greatest island possible.

seems to be false. Many beings, especially gods, are certainly greater beings than any piece of earth. Consequently, it would seem that Anselm had something like the second argument form in mind, and thus, as he claimed, his argument is not open to Gaunilo's objections.[39]

Another objection: The dirtiest being possible

Can we accept this version of Anselm's argument? It has avoided all the objections we have examined, and therefore we have found no reason to reject either premise. Furthermore, premise (2) is certainly acceptable. We can, however, find some reason for rejecting premise (1) when interpreted as (1b), a reason similar to Gaunilo's. Consider argument from C:

1c. If X does not exist, then it is possible that there exists a being more Y than X.

2c. It is not possible there exists a being more Y than X.

---

39. Mr. Lehrer should be given credit for this way of showing how St. Anselm can avoid Gaunilo's objection.

Here we have replaced 'great' in argument form B by the variable Y. In order for (2c) to be true X would have to equal 'the most Y being possible.' But we can substitute any adjective at all for Y and thus prove not only that the most *great* of any kind of being exists, as Gaunilo tried to prove, but also that a being that is superlative *in any way at all* exists. Thus we could prove by this argument that the happiest or saddest or cleanest or dirtiest, or fattest, or thinnest, or most absurd, or most evil being possible exists. In this case the two premises would be the following:

> If the most (dirty, absurd, evil, and so on) being possible does not exist, then it is possible that there exists a being more (dirty, absurd, evil, and so on) than the most (dirty, absurd, evil, and so on) being possible.

and:

> It is not possible that there exists a being more (dirty, absurd, evil, and so on) than the most (dirty, absurd, evil, and so on) being possible.

We can even prove that the being whose description involves the most contradictions possible exists. But it is not possible that a being whose description involves even one contradiction exists. Thus many arguments of the form C are unsound. But because the argument form is valid and the relevant premises of the form (2c) are true, it follows that the premises of form (1c) are false. Furthermore, because (1b) is (1c) with one less variable this surely casts doubt on premise (1) when taken as an instance of (1b). If at this point Anselm were to reply to us, similarly to the way he replied to Gaunilo, that his argument applies only to the one adjective 'great,' we could reply in turn that there seems to be no difference between the adjective 'great' and many others relevant to existence. If a defender of the ontological argument thinks that there is, then it is up to him to show it. It may be possible to do so, but so far no one has. Once again we have reached a point where we are unable to justify a premise. Thus, although the premise may be true, we are unable to use it in an argument to justify a conclusion. We should, then, reject the ontological arguments, as we have the others, as being inadequate to justify the belief that God exists.

A PRAGMATIC JUSTIFICATION OF
BELIEF IN THE EXISTENCE OF GOD

We have rejected the most plausible a posteriori and a priori proofs for the existence of God and thus have found no way to justify the belief that God exists. Unless we can find some other way to justify beliefs, we shall have to conclude that this belief is not justified. All the arguments we have examined have tried to justify the belief by giving reasons for thinking that the belief is true. However, such pragmatists as William James have tried to develop a different kind of reason for holding a belief. Some beliefs that we are unable to prove to be either true or false play such an important part in our lives that, according to James, we are justified in believing them under certain conditions. This "pragmatic" justification of certain beliefs, then, does not depend upon any evidence or reason in favor of the truth of what is believed. James, in his article "The Will to Believe," has applied this kind of justification to the belief that God exists. Let us examine what he says:

> The thesis I defend is, briefly stated, thus: Our passional nature not only lawfully may, but must, decide an option between propositions, whenever it is a genuine option that cannot by its nature be decided on intellectual grounds: for to say, under such circumstances, "Do not decide, but leave the question open," is itself a passional decision—just like deciding yes or no—and is attended with the same risk of losing the truth.[40]

The crucial phrase here is "genuine option," and James defines it to mean a choice between alternative hypotheses that is living, momentous, and forced. By a *living* option he means a choice between hypotheses at least one of which is of some interest to the person faced with the choice. Many options are not living, but are what James calls dead. The option of whether or not to believe that I have an odd number of hairs on my head is certainly of no interest to almost everyone.

We shall say that a *momentous* option is one where to decide for or against one of the hypotheses is to decide for or against something which is very important. The option offered an astronaut to accept or reject the assignment to be the first person to land on the moon is a momentous option. The last characteristic necessary for a genuine option is that the option be forced. A *forced* option is one in which there is no way to avoid a decision. A person held up at gunpoint, with no chance of escape, and given the choice, "Your money right now or your life," is faced with a forced option. He cannot avoid a decision by escaping, or by refusing to respond to the robber, because by refusing he would fail to hand over his money and thereby, in effect, agree to lose his life. However, the option to watch television or go to a movie is not forced because one can do neither—for example, by reading a book.[41]

The Religious Option and the Right to Believe

Having defined James's terms we can now lay out his argument as follows:

---

40. W. James, *Essays in Pragmatism* (New York: Hafner, 1960), 95.
41. Ibid., 88-90.

1. If someone is faced with an option which is genuine and cannot be decided by rational inquiry, then he is justified in deciding it according to his desires.

2. If the religious option is a living option for someone, then it is a genuine option for him.

3. The religious option cannot be decided by rational inquiry.

Therefore

4. If the religious option is a living option for someone, then he is justified in deciding it according to his desires.

James is arguing, then, that if someone has the will to believe, if he wants to believe, then he has the right to believe. Of course, if believing that God exists or that he does not exist is of no interest to someone, then James's argument does not apply to him. It applies to the person who wants to believe, the person for whom the option is live, but who withholds belief because he has no reason to think that the belief is true. Notice, incidentally, that not only the would-be believer but also the would-be atheist can justify his belief. Thus someone who wants to believe that god does *not* exist but has refrained because he cannot provide reasons for such a belief will also find James's argument helpful.

Some people have complained that James's argument provides us with an unrestricted license for wishful thinking, but if we look closely at the argument we shall see that this is not so. James's argument applies only to genuine options that cannot be decided by rational inquiry. This eliminates the great majority of our options, which can be decided by a rational investigation of the relevant facts. James's argument applies to a quite limited group of options. The question with which we are concerned is whether it applies to what James calls the religious option. For James, when we are faced with the religious option, the hypothesis in question is not 'God exists,' but rather something more complicated. James's religious hypothesis has two parts, the first of which I shall rephrase as 'God exists,' and the second as 'We are better off even now and surely later if we believe that God exists.' For James, then, the religious hypothesis is a conjunction of two hypotheses, and the religious option is the decision of whether or not to believe the religious hypothesis.[42]

Let us consider the premises. The first seems acceptable, because if someone wants to make an important decision, there is no way he can avoid making it, and there is absolutely no way to bring any evidence or reasons to bear on the decision, then surely he has the right to decide the way he wants. No argument can be used to condemn such a decision as

---

42. See ibid., 105, for James's way of stating the religious hypothesis.

irrational. He cannot avoid the choice, because it is forced; and he cannot just shrug it off, because it is important. In such a case, he is justified in doing as he wants. Nothing relevant to the decision overrides his desires.

The problem for the second premise is to decide whether or not James's religious option is momentous and forced. If it is both, then the premise is true. James says that

> we see, first, that religion offers itself as a *momentous* option. We are supposed to gain, even now, by our belief, and to lose by our nonbelief, a certain vital good. Secondly, religion is a forced option, so far as that good goes. We cannot escape the issue by remaining skeptical and waiting for more light, because, although we do avoid error in that way *if religion be untrue*, we lose the good, *if it be true*, just as certainly as if we positively chose to disbelieve.[43]

We can agree with James that his religious option is momentous, because to decide to believe the hypothesis is to decide in favor of extremely important benefits right now and also in the eternity of afterlife. However, it is not clear why James thinks that his option is forced. He seems to think that if we decide either to disbelieve or to refrain from believing his religious hypothesis, then we in effect have decided against attaining certain present benefits. But this is not so. We can reject his religious hypothesis, which is a conjunction, merely by rejecting just one of the conjuncts. Thus, if we reject the second conjunct, that believing brings us benefits, but believe that God exists, then we have not rejected the benefits, because receiving them requires only that we believe that God exists. Similarly, we can refrain from believing the religious hypothesis, without any risk of loss, if we only refrain from believing the second conjunct. Consequently, the religious hypothesis offered by James does not result in a forced option, and thus the second premise of James's argument is false.

However, we may be able to devise another religious hypothesis that will result in a forced as well as a momentous option. The simpler hypothesis that God exists will provide the forced option of whether to believe that God exists or not to believe that God exists. If I refrain from deciding, then, of course, I have in effect decided not to believe that God exists. This, of course, is different from deciding to believe that God does not exist. The option, however, is not momentous, as we have defined it. I have not decided for or against any present benefits if I either believe or refrain from believing that God exists—especially if I believe, for example, that if there were a God, he would reward me not for my belief in him, but for how I treat my fellow human beings. Thus, I may decide to treat others with love and respect and so decide in favor of the benefits. I may

---

43. Ibid., 105-6.

be wrong about what would bring benefits, but I face that risk no matter what I decide. The point, nevertheless, is that in deciding only about God's existence, I have not decided for or against the benefits. The following hypothesis, however, which I shall call *H*, avoids this problem:

> *H*. God exists and only those who believe the teachings of God (which include *H*) will receive certain important benefits now and also later.

In the case of *H*, we must believe both parts of the conjunction in order to receive the benefits, so that if we either reject or refrain from believing either part of the conjunction, we have in effect decided against the benefits. Thus an option concerning *H* is forced and is certainly momentous. Let us then accept the second premise of James's argument once we interpret the religious hypothesis as *H*.

We are left with the task of evaluating the third premise. We have found no sound arguments of God's existence, whether a priori or a posteriori. It may be thought that this alone is sufficient to justify premise (3), but this would be a mistake, for it might be refuted in one other way. Although there may be no good evidence *for* the existence of God, perhaps there is good evidence *against* the existence of God. If this is so, then premise (3) will be false. We need to consider this possibility next.

EVIL AS EVIDENCE AGAINST THE EXISTENCE OF GOD

The problem of evil is one of the most troublesome problems that faces anyone who believes that there exists an all-good, all-knowing, and all-powerful God who created the world we live in. We can begin to see the problem in the following way: If you were all-good, all-knowing, and all-powerful, and you were going to create a universe in which there were sentient beings—beings who are happy and sad; enjoy pleasure; feel pain; express love, anger, pity, hatred and fear—what kind of world would you create? Being all-powerful, you would have the ability to create any world that it is logically possible for you to create, and being all-knowing, you would know how to create any of these logically possible worlds. Which one would you choose? Obviously you would choose the best of all possible worlds, because you would be all-good and would want to do what is best in all that you do. You would, then, create the world containing the least amount of evil possible. And because one of the most obvious kinds of evil is suffering, hardship, and pain, you would create a world in which the sentient beings suffered the least. Try to imagine what such a world would be like. Would it be like the one that actually does exist, this world we live in? Would you create a world like this one, if you had the power and know-how to create any logically possible world? If your answer is "no," as it seems it must be, then you should begin to understand why the evil of suffering and pain in this world is such a problem for anyone who thinks that God created this world. This seems not to be a world that God would create, nor the kind of world he would sustain. Given this world, then, it seems we should conclude that God does not exist, and so did not create this world. The presence of so much evil in the world rules out the existence of an all-good, all-powerful, and all-knowing God.

The Argument from Evil: The Logical Version

One way to understand the argument from evil is in broadly logical terms. The existence of an all-good, all-powerful, and all-knowing God, it is said, is logically inconsistent with the existence of evil in the world. Hence, since we cannot deny that there is such evil, we should conclude instead that God does not exist. The argument here is straightforward. The two statements,

1. An all-good, all-knowing, and all-powerful God exists.

and

2. There is evil in the world.

are supposed to be logically inconsistent. That is, it is alleged to be logically impossible for both these statements to be true. But since (2) is surely true, (1) must be false. Hence, the existence of evil logically precludes the existence of God.[44]

Objection: The best world might contain evil

One way to see that statements (1) and (2) are consistent after all is to consider God's situation when he is about to create a universe. Presumably there is an infinite number of possible universes from which he might choose, and, as we noted above, if God is all-good he would certainly choose the best universe. Which one might that be? It is perhaps natural to answer that it is a universe that contains only good things, and no evil whatever. But think again: isn't it at least logically possible that a universe with some evil in it contains more total good than any other universe, including a universe with only good in it? Perhaps the presence of some evil in the universe augments the total amount of goodness in that universe to the point where the total goodness contained therein is greater than the amount of goodness in any other universe. We need not claim that this is the actual state of affairs, for we have no evidence that would support such a claim. But it is certainly logically possible that the universe with the

---

44. The logical version of the argument from evil has been endorsed by J. L. Mackie, "Evil and Omnipotence," and by H. J. McCloskey, "God and Evil," both reprinted in N. Pike, ed., *God and Evil* (New York: Prentice-Hall, 1964).

greatest amount of goodness in it contains some evil as well. Moreover, it is also at least logically possible that the best universe contains the greatest total amount of goodness, as opposed, say, to a universe in which there is less goodness but it is of a higher or better "quality." For these reasons, statements (1) and (2) are logically consistent. The existence of evil in the actual world does not logically rule out the existence of God, even when we assume that God creates the best possible universe.[45]

The Argument from Evil: The Probability Version

Perhaps the case has simply been overstated. The existence of evil in the world does not logically exclude the existence of God, but such evil might make it quite improbable that God exists. Statement (2), in other words, should be thought of as strong evidence against statement (1), evidence which makes (1) quite *unlikely* to be true. We shall call assertion the probability version of the argument from evil. From it we can conclude that belief in the existence of God is quite unreasonable.

Objection: Evidence available to human beings is insufficient

Although this conclusion seems warranted, there is one way it might be avoided. Many would reject the claim that people can gather evidence from what they know that will affect the probability or improbability of the existence of God. Consider the following analogy. Suppose that a young child is brought up in a primitive society in which the highest perfection is to be a great hunter with immense physical prowess. Suppose further that he is taken to a university where there is an acknowledged great mathematician. The child comes into contact with some of the effects of the mathematician's work. He sees strange markings left all over a blackboard, and he looks at pieces of paper with equally strange markings on them. Occasionally he hears people say how great this mathematician is, but never once do they mention hunting. He also hears others say that they cannot figure out what this woman is doing, and still others talk about her lack of physical exercise, and the fact that she continually sits at a desk. On the basis of these bits of information it would be quite natural for the child to think that this person is perhaps quite strange, but certainly not a great person. But we would not want to say that the child has an inductive justification for the claim that the cause of these effects he had seen is *not* a remarkable being. His information is so paltry that it is insufficient to justify any belief about the greatness of the person. Although the analogy is not perfect, it has been claimed that the information humans have about the ways of God is like the information the child has about the mathematician, except that it is even more paltry. How

---

45. Very detailed critical discussion of the logical version of the argument from evil can be found in Alvin Plantinga, *God and Other Minds* (Ithaca: Cornell University Press, 1967).

then could we think that the information we have obtained in our limited way is at all close to being sufficient to justify any belief, positive or negative, about the cause of the universe?

If we accept this analogy between our evidence relevant to God and the boy's evidence relevant to the mathematician, then, instead of concluding that it is improbable that God exists, we should conclude that no argument based on the evidence available to human beings is capable of affecting the justification of the statement that God exists or that God does not exist. We should also conclude that James is right in his claim that we are justified in believing the religious hypothesis even when there is no evidence to support it. Where there is no evidence against one hypothesis of a genuine option, we are justified in believing it. Thus, if we can accept the analogy, then even in the face of the seemingly contrary evidence provided by the evil in this world, there would be nothing irrational about believing that God exists.

Reply: Believe in accordance with the total evidence available

There is, however, an important difference between our situation relative to God and the boy's situation relative to the mathematician, and this difference vitiates the relevance of the analogy to our problem. When someone is attempting to justify a belief by means of a body of evidence, he may be said to have justified that belief only if he has considered the total amount of evidence available to him. The native boy clearly could have found more evidence relevant to the greatness of the mathematician, evidence that could have led him to revise his belief that there was nothing great about the person. We, however, at this stage of our discussion have good reason to think that we have examined, at least to some extent, practically all of the available evidence. Hence we, unlike the boy, can be said to have met the requirement of total evidence. Where someone meets that requirement, then, no matter how slight his evidence is, if it tips the scale in favor of one hypothesis, no matter how little, the rational course is to believe in accordance with the total evidence. In our present case, the total evidence seems to point in favor of the hypothesis that there is no God.

Objection: People are responsible for evil

The above argument is weakened once we notice that people are responsible for much of the evil we know about, so that God is absolved of responsibility for it. In that way, the mere existence of evil would not count against the idea that God exists, since God is not responsible for the evil, and so cannot be blamed for its occurrence. To see the import of this argument, we need only consider an example. We know from news reports that innocent people the world over suffer as a result of crimes and other deliberate acts which are committed by others. Certainly this undeserved suffering counts as evil, but God is not the cause of it, and so is not to be held responsible for it. The guilty parties are those who have committed the actions, namely other people. And this is true for a great deal of the evil that we know exists in our world. Accordingly, the probability version of the argument from evil, even when we take account of the total evidence available to us, does not suffice to make it improbable that God exists.

Reply: Moral versus natural evil

People are surely responsible for much of the suffering inflicted on others, but nevertheless there is much for which people do not seem at all responsible. To show this we can differentiate between what has been called moral evil from natural evil. Moral evil consists of all the evil in the world that is the causal result of the morally responsible agents (namely people) in the world. Natural evil includes all the other evil that there may be. So the massive suffering at Auschwitz is certainly a moral evil, whereas the immense suffering resulting from natural disasters such as earthquakes, floods, droughts, hurricanes, and the like, are not the causal result of any moral agent in the world. They are natural evils, evils for which no human being is responsible. We can then grant, for the purposes of this discussion, that much evil is moral evil and that God is not responsible for this. But this only means that the problem of evil can be redefined as the problem of natural evil, a problem no less easy to solve.

Objection: Satan as one cause of natural evil

Perhaps some or even all of the natural evil can be attributed to the work of Satan, rather than God. Maybe we should think that the natural evil that results from a terrible earthquake is Satan's doing: he causes the earthquake, and so he also is the cause of the resulting evil. In this way, Satan, not God, would be responsible for the suffering, and Satan rather than God would be properly held to blame for the suffering. And, if Satan causes most or all of the natural evils in this manner, then it would be reasonable to reject the argument from evil altogether. For people would be responsible for moral evil, and Satan for natural evil. God would not be a blameworthy agent, and so his supreme moral goodness would not be compromised by the existence of either sort of evil.

One might insist, though, that God is still responsible, even though Satan is the direct cause of the natural evil, because God *allows* Satan to do his awful deeds. Certainly God, being all-powerful, could act to stop Satan from bringing about events such as earthquakes and tornadoes with their resulting suffering. So, if we think that Satan is the immediate cause of such events, we should also suppose that God stands by and allows Satan free rein. So, one might argue, we can hardly *excuse* God from responsibility and blame, despite the fact that God is not the immediate causal agent.

But even this point can be overcome, if we just note that Satan, like people, has free will, and that God, having endowed Satan with free will, does not want to interfere, just as he allows so many moral evils because he does not want to interfere with any person's free will. Perhaps God does not want to interfere because free will is God's unique and most precious gift to all who have it. Such an attitude seems definitely admirable. Free will is so valuable that God allows it to be exercised by both Satan and people. True, some evil results. Still, with free will being so valuable, this evil needs to be tolerated in order to allow such a valuable commodity as free will to exist. God is absolved of the charge of responsibility, because there is an excellent reason why he does not interfere with Satan's activities.

Reply: Noninterference and natural causes
It is true that free will is a valuable thing, and in general we also think that it is best not to interfere with another's exercise of her free will. But in many cases we think otherwise, for example when we think that we ought to confine someone to a mental hospital or prison to keep him from harming other people. So, there are clear cases where it is morally a right thing to restrict someone's freedom, and this precisely because of the harm they would otherwise cause. Surely, then, by parity of reasoning, the morally right thing for God to do is to restrict Satan's free will by restricting his activities. An all-good being would certainly restrict Satan's actions, even though free will is a valuable thing to possess.

Moreover, we should ask whether there is any good reason to suppose that Satan *is* the cause of natural evil. On the contrary, it seems we have every reason to think that natural evils have purely natural causes. Take an earthquake as an example. We know from studies in seismology that these events are brought about by movements in the tectonic plates beneath the earth, so there is no reason to suppose that Satan is involved. Other events that bring about natural evils have natural causes, too. Flooding, for example, is typically caused by excessive rain, or from rapid snow melt in the mountains. Of course, we could try to justify belief in the existence and activity of Satan if the postulation of this creature were necessary to help explain what is observed, namely, natural disasters such as earthquakes, tornadoes, and the like. In this way, Satan would be a theoretical entity, much like the demons talked of by some witch doctors (as discussed in Chapter Four). But neither Satan nor the demons are needed to explain natural evil and aberrant human behavior, respectively. So postulation of these entities is not justified.

Compensation for victims: The prospect of an afterlife
It is widely held, by the major Western religions, that a person survives bodily death and, indeed, lives on forever and so is immortal. This "life

after life," or afterlife as we shall call it, is also sometimes described in such a way that people who have suffered natural evils are said to receive compensation for the pain they have suffered. The compensation, of course, is that these individuals spend eternity in heaven, a continual blissful state of presence with God. The situation in heaven, it is said, more than makes up for the ills such people suffered while on earth.

Notice that this objection concedes the existence and quantity of natural evil in the world. However, God's existence is claimed not to be improbable, given such evil, because God's omnibenevolence or moral perfection is not compromised by this evil. It is not compromised, in turn, precisely because God has set up a system in which those who have suffered most will later get their just rewards or compensation.

Reply: No good evidence of an afterlife

As a matter of incidental interest, it is by no means correct to suppose that *all* those who suffer natural evils will be compensated in an afterlife. Only those persons fortunate enough to spend an afterlife in heaven are to be so compensated. A great many people will not end up in heaven and thus will never be compensated. So, even if this objection to the claim that God's nonexistence is probable, relative to the amount of natural evil in the world, is fully correct, it will not suffice to refute the claim completely. A more important point is that this objection has force only if we have some good evidence to suppose that there is an afterlife and it is pretty much as described. Moreover, in the context in which we are operating, namely that of examining reasons for and against belief in the existence of God, the evidence for an afterlife would have to be *independent* evidence. That is, it would have to be evidence that did not itself depend on the assumption that God exists, for it is the reasonableness of that statement which is our present concern. But we do not know of any such independent evidence. True, there is the evidence of near-death, out-of-body experiences, which we discussed earlier in connection with dualism. But even if that evidence shows that a person survives bodily death, which is very doubtful, it does nothing to show that any person goes to heaven, nor anything to show that a person survives bodily death for any length of time, let alone an eternity. Accordingly, we should conclude that the appeal to a wonderful, heavenly afterlife, does nothing to show that the amount of natural evil fails to make God's existence improbable. Quite the contrary; it seems we should conclude that God does not exist, given the amount of natural evil in the world.

Objection: Natural evils are unavoidable

There is another attempt to avoid the problem of evil that we should consider. This position attempts to reconcile the evil in the world with the claim that this is the best of all possible worlds by claiming that the evils are all necessary or unavoidable, so that any other world would have more evils. The claim is often based on the view that the best world, for a being such as a person, is an orderly world in which he can predict the course of events with sufficient accuracy to guide his or her life safely and prosperously. Such a world must proceed in a lawlike way, and, according to the present claim, this requires a world which proceeds in accordance with causal laws. In any such universe, some degree of suffering and hardship is bound to result when people are faced with natural forces much too powerful for them. The claim, in brief, is that this is the best of all possible worlds, because all of its evils are necessary. This world has a minimum amount of natural evil consistent with a world which proceeds in accordance with laws. In this way, the probability version of the argument from evil can be overcome. We need only point out that any world not governed by causal laws would have a far greater amount of natural evil than the actual world.

Reply: Examples of avoidable evils

Let us once again turn to Philo, who lists several examples of what he thinks are avoidable evils. Philo is willing to grant that pain can serve a valuable function in warning sentient beings of bodily ills, and that it is better for people that the course of nature proceeds in an orderly way. But he finds no reason to think that pain is necessary for the purpose of warning sentient beings, or that causal laws are necessary for an orderly course of nature. He says,

> The *first* circumstance which introduces evil, is that contrivance or economy of the animal creation, by which pains, as well as pleasures, are employed to excite all creatures to action, and make them vigilant in the great work of self-preservation. Now pleasure alone, in its various degrees, seems to human understanding sufficient for this purpose. All animals might be constantly in a state of enjoyment; but when urged by any of the necessities of nature, such as thirst, hunger, weariness; instead of pain, they might feel a dimnuition of pleasure, by which they might be prompted to seek that object, which is necessary to their subsistence. Men pursue pleasure as eagerly as they avoid pain; at least, they might have been so constituted. It seems, therefore, plainly possible to carry on the business of life without any pain. Why then is any animal ever rendered susceptible of such a sensation?[46]

Some may disagree with Philo, thinking that some degree of pain is a much better way to implement learning than a mere dimnuition of pleasure. Yet it seems most unreasonable to believe that any animals need be as

---

46. Hume, *Dialogues Concerning Natural Religion*, 205-6.

susceptible to very intense pain as humans. A world like this one in all respects, except that animals are much less susceptible to pain, would be a better world, and one that seems quite possible. Thus pain, or at least certain intensities of pain, is an unnecessary or avoidable evil.

Concerning the necessity of casual laws in the best of all possible worlds, and thus in an orderly world, Philo claims,

> But a capacity of pain would not alone produce pain, were it not for the *second* circumstance, viz., the conducting of the world by general laws; and this seems nowise necessary to a perfect Being. It is true; if everything were conducted by particular volitions, the course of nature would be perpetually broken, and no man could employ his reason in the conduct of life. But might not other particular volitions remedy this inconvenience? In short, might not the Deity exterminate all ill, wherever it were to be found; and produce all good, without any preparation or long progress of causes and effects?[47]

Philo's point is that an omniscient and omnipotent being could control the course of events by particular acts of his will in as orderly a fashion as if all events were parts of continuous causal chains subject to causal laws. Consequently, causal laws are not necessary for the kind of orderly universe that is most helpful to human beings. God could, by an orderly procession of acts, avoid and eradicate much of the natural evil found in the world.

Furthermore, even in a universe in which the course of events is governed by causal laws, so many other factors are causally relevant to most events that, insofar as humans can tell, the events are more coincidences. As Philo says,

> A Being, therefore, who knows the secret springs of the universe, might easily, by particular volitions, turn all these accidents to the good of mankind, and render the whole world happy, without discovering himself in any operation. A fleet, whose purposes were salutary to society, might always meet with a fair wind: Good princes enjoy sound health and long life: Persons born to power and authority, be framed with good tempers and virtuous dispositions. A few such events as these, regularly and wisely conducted, would change the face of the world; and yet would no more seem to disturb the course of nature or confound human conduct, than the present economy of things, where the causes are secret, and variable, and compounded.[48]

Even if most events occurred as parts of continuous causal chains, and God only acted occasionally, he could do it in such a way that it would be

---

47. Ibid., 206.
48. Ibid., 206-7.

unknown to humans. They would find no break in the causal order; what would appear to them to be coincidence and accident could in many cases be the work of God, who could quite easily, by indiscernible coincidence-miracles, help humans more often than they are now helped by coincidences. Once again, certain features of the universe—unbroken causal chains that often result in pains—are avoidable.

Perhaps the most decisive example used by Philo concerns what he calls the "inaccurate workmanship of all the springs and principles of the great machine of nature."[49] He is willing to admit that certain parts of this universe may indeed be necessary for human welfare, but certain of the effects of these parts, which cause suffering, are by no means necessary.

> Thus the winds are requisite to convey the vapours along the surface of the globe, and to assist men in navigation: But how oft, rising up to tempests and hurricanes, do they become pernicious? Rains are necessary to nourish all the plants and animals of the earth: But how often are they defective? How often excessive? Heat is requisite to all life and vegetation, but is not always found in due proportion. On the mixture and secretion of the humours and juices of the body depend the health and prosperity of the animal: But the parts perform not regularly their proper function.[50]

In short, although wind currents, rain, a certain amount of heat, and such bodily fluids as blood may be necessary for human life, it seems quite unnecessary that there be hurricanes, tornadoes, floods, droughts, extreme cold or heat, or blood defects such as leukemia.

We have been investigating the idea that some natural evil is necessary because it is an unavoidable consequence of the fact that the universe is governed by scientific laws. But there are other ways in which natural evils might be deemed necessary, namely, when they are said to be necessary *for* something else, especially something of *value*. Let us turn to that important idea next.

Objection: Some evil is necessary for some knowledge

Consider what would be necessary for a person to prevent some occurrence of natural evil. Imagine that you decide to try to prevent an avalanche at a ski resort where you are working. You remove some snow, erect certain barriers, perhaps deliberately cause small avalanches, and the like. To know what action to take, you would certainly need some knowledge of prior avalanches—how they are caused, what effects they have, how they proceed down a slope, what sorts of conditions are often correlated with such events, such as time of day, temperature, wind speed, perhaps

---

49. Ibid., 209.
50. Ibid., 210.

barometric pressure, and doubtless much more. In general, to know what to do to prevent a future avalanche, you need knowledge of prior avalanches, and that requires that there have been some prior avalanches.

Of course, an avalanche may not qualify by itself as an instance of natural evil, because it may not cause any suffering to humans or animals. Surely many avalanches are of just this sort, occurring at very isolated and desolate locations. But some do cause human and animal suffering, and here is the point. You try to prevent future avalanches precisely to prevent future human and animal suffering. And, to know that future avalanches are apt to cause such suffering, one needs knowledge of prior instances of the very same thing; that is, knowledge of past cases of human and animal suffering caused by avalanches. In general, for people to know enough to prevent future cases of suffering or natural evils of type X, they need knowledge of past cases of natural evil of type X. Hence, there have to be *some* cases of natural evil of type X.

Another objection: Evils are necessary for there to be higher goods

Imagine the relatively mild suffering that a person endures when in the presence of someone who is arrogant, or rude, or obnoxious. Suppose, too, that this person is tolerant, and does not respond in kind, but instead manages to be kind and even pleasant to the rude or obnoxious person. For this person to be kind and tolerant, there have to be correlated evils, perhaps arrogance, rudeness, or obnoxious behavior. Or consider desirable actions such as compassion or forgiveness. For a person to forgive or be compassionate, there have to be appropriate evils. Tolerance, kindness, compassion, and forgiveness are not just good things, they are relatively rare among people, and they are so conducive to beneficial effects that it seems appropriate to think of them as higher goods. That is, they are somewhat more desirable than other good actions or character traits.

Of course, forgiveness and tolerance are generally directed towards instances of moral evil rather than natural evil. But compassion is also a higher good, and it often is directed at one who either inflicts or suffers natural evil. And the general idea is straightforward: for there to be instances of compassion, and doubtless other higher goods, there must be instances of natural evils. These evils are needed for there to be such highly desirable conditions as knowledge and higher moral and personal virtues.

Reply: Why so much natural evil?

Although it might well be questioned, we grant that some natural evils are necessary for people to have relevant knowledge and for the existence of appropriate higher goods. What is questionable is whether there has to be as much natural evil as there is for these effects to be achieved. Consider again the avalanche example. For people to have the appropriate knowledge concerning avalanche prevention, there need only have been one or at most a very few avalanches. Further, only a few people need have suffered as a result of an avalanche for us to know what it is we want to prevent (human death and suffering) when we try to prevent avalanches. Exactly the same considerations apply to cases of higher goods, but with the following added feature: for there to be many instances of compassion, there have to be correspondingly many instances of natural evils. But presumably we do not want to say that the greater the number of instances of higher good of compassion the better the world is overall. This would be saying that the greater the number of instances of natural evil of appropriate sorts, the better the world is overall. To see that we do not want to accept that, consider another higher good, mercy. We have in mind here the sort of mercy that a judge or jury shows to a person accused of a crime. For there to be a greater number of instances of mercy, there must also be a correspondingly greater number of crimes. But surely we do not want to say that the universe gets any better, merely because mercy is extended to someone more often, when this is achieved at the expense of an increase in the crime rate.

So it is not merely the simple existence of natural evils that works to make the existence of God improbable. Such evils may indeed be necessary to have other desirable items such as knowledge and higher moral goods. The improbability of God's existence derives from the overabundance of natural evils; the sheer quantity of natural evils far exceeds what would be needed to bring about the intended results in knowledge and higher goods.

Objection: Total evidence and probability

We noted earlier that we should base our conclusion concerning whether it is probable or improbable that God exists on the total evidence available. Defenders of theism, i.e., the claim that God exists, can rightly press for an identification of this total evidence, for it is that on which the claim of the improbability of God's existence is here based.

Certainly this evidence includes the claim that there is a great deal of natural evil, which we will represent as E (for 'evil'). There is, too, the failure of all the attempts we have examined that aim either to prove God's existence or to provide good inductive support for it. This claim we represent as F (for 'failed'). So the probability version of the argument from evil says that the existence of God is improbable given both E and F. But is this conjunction the *total* available evidence? We have been assuming that the answer is yes, but additional evidence may be available.

Here theists have an opportunity to mount a different attack on the probability version of the argument from evil. For instance, it might be said that God is an infinite being who exists for eternity, so it is to be expected that we would know little or nothing about many of God's actions. The same may be said of God's reasons for these actions; and, indeed, we can know little of God's reasons even for actions we can plausibly attribute to God. We can refer to these considerations as 'H' and represent it as follows:

H If God exists, then it is to be expected that we humans know little of his actions and of his reasons for his actions.

If we let G stand for the hypothesis that God exists and is omniscient, omnipotent, and all-good, then we can think of the probability version of the argument from evil as claiming that

The probability of not-G, given E and F, is high.

A probability is *high* in this context, we shall assume, provided the probability is greater than .5, or one-half. But now the theist will ask, what about the claim that

The probability that not-G, given E, F, and H, is high.

Is *this* claim true? The theist's answer is that it is not; the probability that God does not exist, given all of that evidence (E, F, and H) is not greater than .5. Accordingly, the theist urges the probability version of the argument from evil does not succeed.

The theist maintains, in effect, that E and F do not make up the total available evidence. Relative to *just* E and F, perhaps the probability of not-G is high. But E and F do not exhaust the relevant available evidence. When we add H to the evidence by conjoining it with E and F, we have a new evidence base, from which the probability of not-G does not come out high.

Another way to see the theist's point here is to contrast statement G ("An omniscient, omnipotent, and all-good God exists") with statement G*, which is,

G* God exists and has excusing reasons for his actions.

An excusing reason is one that absolves God of moral censure and blame for an action he either commits or allows to occur. Relative *solely* to E and F, doubtless we would say that the probability of not-G is greater than the probability of G*. But relative instead to the conjunction of E, F, and H, the probability of not-G is not greater than the probability of G*. Accordingly, we should reject the probability version of the argument from evil.

Reply: No knowledge of the probabilities

The theist's argument rests squarely on the assumption that we know the relevant probabilities. Only in this way can we reasonably claim that the probability of not-G is not greater than the probability of G* on the same (total) evidence. However, we can easily see the error in this line of reasoning when we notice that we can assign no actual number as the probability of either not-G or G* on the evidence. We cannot say, for example, that the probability of G* is .62, while that of not-G is .38; but neither can we assign any other actual probabilities to these statements. The reason is simple: the sort of evidence we have simply does not permit exact assignments of numerical probabilities; instead, we can make only the roughest of estimates of probabilities in this context. Hence, we can conclude that the theist has no grounds for claiming that the probability of not-G is not greater than the probability of G*.

Objection: Exact probabilities and comparative probabilities

The critic has misunderstood what is minimally necessary in the theist's argument. We do not need to know the exact numerical probabilities to know that one statement is more probable than another. We can and often do make well-founded comparisons of probability that are by no means exact, but are nonetheless adequate for some purposes. For example, if one has to travel from Philadelphia to New York to keep a business appointment at 10:00 A.M., we say that it is more likely that one will arrive on time if one takes the train rather than an automobile. We might defend this claim by noting the terrific amounts of traffic on the New Jersey Turnpike, on the bridges out of Philadelphia into New Jersey, and on those from New Jersey into New York. Here we are making a comparative probability judgment—getting to the appointment on time is more likely with the train than with an automobile—but we have no way to assign real numerical probabilities to either claim. We could not say, that is, that the probability of being on time with the train is (say) .75 and the probability of being on time with a car is (say) .45. We are in no position to assign these or any other numbers as probabilities to these respective statements. But we know, anyway, that an on-time appointment is more likely with the train than with an automobile.

Things are similar in the theist's argument. She is in no position to assign numerical probabilities to not-G and G*. This part of the objection is correct. But from this we cannot conclude that the theist is in no position to claim that not-G is no more probable than G* on the same evidence. For the theist is making only a comparative probability judgment here, one that does not require precise assignments of numerical probabilities. The theist is no worse off than the person making the comparative probability judgment about the train versus the automobile.

Can one object that things are not quite so favorable for the theist, because she is not even in a position to make the relevant comparative probability judgment? One might say that we have absolutely *no idea* whether G* is more probable than not-G given the evidence E, F, and H. That is, one might say that we just don't know what the probabilities are, not even in a rough-and-ready way. In that event, the theist's reply cannot gain a foothold against the argument from evil.

This sort of reasoning, however, curiously favors the theist. For if we have no knowledge even of whether G* is more probable than not-G, given E, F, and H, then we likewise do not know whether not-G is more probable than G* given that same evidence. Accordingly, the critic cannot carry through the probability version of the argument from evil, for the argument requires us to say straightforwardly that the probability of not-G is high, relative to the total evidence. If we cannot say this, then the argument from evil collapses.

CONCLUSION

What we think we have reached is at best a draw. Arguments designed to establish the reasonableness of belief in the existence of a supreme being have not been successful, but neither have arguments supposed to show that we are justified in believing that there is no such being. The positive evidence and the negative evidence are both inconclusive. What, then, should our overall conclusion be?

The best answer, based on the evidence we have considered, would seem to be that we should withhold belief; that is, we should believe neither that God exists nor that God does not exist. To do otherwise would be to go beyond the evidence as it has been presented here. Of course, there may be additional evidence, of a positive or negative sort, which we have not considered and which, were it to come to light, would tip the balance in favor of theism or its denial. Accordingly, the conclusion we have reached should be thought of as tentative, and subject to revision at some future time if additional pertinent evidence becomes available.

EXERCISES

The Concept of a Supreme Being

1. According to the characterization of God in the text, which of the following would God be able to do? Explain.

   Make hot ice.   Cause a triangle to have four angles.
   Make 2 plus 2 equal 5.   Destroy himself.
   Forget.   Inflict suffering sadistically.

2. Evaluate the following objection to the claim that God is omnipotent.

   It is possible that at time t someone, namely me, lifts the stone I lift by myself at t_1. But it is not possible that at t_1 God lifts the stone I lift by myself at t_1. Therefore, I can do something God cannot do and he is not omnipotent.

3. In the Gospels it is stated that Christ told Peter, "This night, before the cock crows, thou shalt deny me thrice," and that this happened, in spite of Peter's protests that it would not happen. This seems to be an example of divine omniscience. Explain whether you think Peter could have had free will given Christ's foreknowledge of what he would do.

Mystical Experience, Revelation, and Miracles

4. Discuss the following argument:

    Mystical experiences are ineffable; therefore they cannot be accurately described. Thus, any report of them must be misleading and hence unable to provide evidence for any claim. It follows that belief in God cannot be justified by appealing to mystical experiences.

5. Is there any possible situation in which you think a scientist should admit supernatural causes? If so, describe such a situation and justify your conclusion. If not, explain why not.

6. Do you think there is any historical evidence—scriptural or otherwise—that supports, at least to some degree, the claim that God has revealed himself to people? Justify your answer.

7. If you were to witness an event that you would feel certain is a violation-miracle, would this justify *you* in believing that God exists? Or would Hume's argument show that such a belief, based on what you have witnessed, would be unjustified, even for you?

The First-Cause Argument and the Argument from Design

8. Show which premises in the first-cause argument and in the contingency argument are a posteriori and which are a priori. Are the conclusions a posteriori or a priori? If they are a posteriori, explain what empirical evidence is relevant to them. If they are a priori explain how an a priori, and thus necessary, statement can be derived from premises some of which are a posteriori, and thus contingent.

9. The central question at issue in the third version of the first-cause argument is whether it is senseless to ask for an explanation of why there is something rather than nothing. One reason to think it is a legitimate question is that, because everything in the universe is contingent, so also is the universe. Thus, the existence of the universe must be explained, just like the existence of anything else.

Bertrand Russell's answer to this is that the error in the reasoning is the fallacy illustrated by the argument, "Every person has a mother; therefore, the human race has a mother." Evaluate these two conflicting positions.

10. It is often claimed that the theory of evolution has rendered the argument from design untenable. Yet Copleston, in his book *Aquinas*, (Op. cit.) says, "If Aquinas had lived in the days of the evolutionary hypothesis, he would doubtless have argued this hypothesis supports rather than invalidates the conclusion of the [design] argument." Explain how Aquinas might have used this theory to bolster the argument from design.

Other Arguments for Theism

11. Criticize the following argument:

God is a being who can do all things that it is logically possible for him to do. But a nonexistent being can do nothing at all, much less everything logically possible. Therefore, God exists.

12. The French philosopher Pascal proposed that the way to decide whether or not to believe in God is to discover whether belief or disbelief is the better and bet accordingly. This is known as Pascal's Wager. He tells us to consider the odds:

If we wager that God exists and he does then we gain eternal bliss; if he does not we have lost nothing. If we wager that God does not exist and he does, then eternal misery is our share; if he does not, we gain only a lucky true belief. The obvious wager is to bet God exists. With such a bet we have everything to gain and nothing to lose. This is far superior to a bet where we have little to gain and everything to lose.

Evaluate this attempt to justify belief in God.

Suggestions for Further Reading

Historical sources
Anselm, *St. Anselm: Basic Writings*, Translated by S. N. Deane (LaSalle, Illinois: Open Court, 1962).

Aquinas, Thomas, *Basic Writings*, A. Pegis, editor (New York: Random House, 1945).

Descartes, René, *Meditations on First Philosophy*, translated by D. Cress (Indianapolis: Hackett, 1979).

Hume, David, *Enquiry Concerning Human Understanding*, E. Steinberg, editor (Indianapolis: Hackett, 1977).

Hume, David, *Dialogues Concerning Natural Religion*, R. Popkin, editor (Indianapolis: Hackett, 1980).

James, William, *Varieties of Religious Experience* (New York: Longman's, 1902).

Kant, Immanuel, *Critique of Pure Reason*, translated by N. K. Smith (London: Macmillan, 1958).

Contemporary texts and collections

Alston, William, *Divine Nature and Human Language* (Ithaca: Cornell University Press, 1989).

Audi, Robert and William Wainwright, editors, *Rationality, Religious Belief, and Moral Commitment* (Ithaca: Cornell University Press, 1986).

Katz, Steven T., editor, *Mysticism and Philosophical Analysis* (New York: Oxford University Press, 1978).

Lewis, C. S., *Miracles* (New York: Macmillan, 1963).

Mackie, J. L., *The Miracle of Theism* (Oxford: The Clarendon Press, 1982).

Mavrodes, George, *Belief in God* (New York: Random House, 1970).

Neilsen, Kai, *Contemporary Critiques of Religion* (New York: Herder & Herder, 1971).

Pike, Nelson, *God and Timelessness* (New York: Shocken, 1970).

Plantinga, Alvin, *God, Freedom, and Evil* (New York: Harper & Row, 1974).

Plantinga, Alvin, *Does God Have a Nature?* (Milwaukee: Marquette University Press, 1980).

Plantinga, Alvin, and Nicholas Wolterstorff, editors, *Faith and Rationality* (Notre Dame: University of Notre Dame Press, 1983).

Ross, James, *Philosophical Theology*, 2nd ed. (Indianapolis: Hackett, 1980).

Rowe, William, *Philosophy of Religion* (Encino: Wadsworth, 1978).

Rowe, William, *The Cosmological Argument* (Princeton: Princeton University Press, 1975).

Rowe, William and William Wainwright, editors, *Philosophy of Religion: Selected Readings*, 2nd ed. (New York: Harcourt Brace, 1989).

Swinburne, Richard, *The Existence of God* (Oxford: The Clarendon Press, 1979).

Several journals regularly contain articles and reviews related to the material in this chapter:

Faith and Philosophy
International Journal for Philosophy of Religion
Religious Studies
Sophia

SIX

The Problem of
Justifying an
Ethical Standard

There is one kind of problem that continually confronts most people. At one time or another, we are faced with deciding what we ought to do. We also often wonder whether we have done the right thing, and we accuse others, as well as ourselves, of not doing what ought to be done. In many of these cases, we are making moral or ethical judgments, judging the moral worth of actions we or others have done or are thinking of doing. Think back about some of your past actions. Probably you can find some actions you think you shouldn't have done. Perhaps it was lying about your age to be served liquor in a bar, or taking a glance at the test paper next to you in an examination, or indefinitely "borrowing" a library book without signing for it. Even now, you may be thinking about some course of action in the future, whether to use the fraternity files for a course paper, whether to bury yourself in your work and avoid participating in social action, or whether to ignore an oft-proclaimed principle of your own to avoid some physical hardship. Where a person thinks about what she and others have done and are doing, rather than acting without thinking, there we find a person faced with making a moral judgment. And as with any judgment, when we make it we like to think we made the correct judgment, or at least that we are justified in the judgment we make.

How can we justify our moral judgments? When we decide what we ought to do, we would like to base our decisions on sound reasons, although, as in many other areas of human endeavor, we often decide without thinking. Usually, when we try to defend our moral decisions and actions, we do so by reference to some moral rule or standard, such as "Thou shalt not kill" or "Lying and cheating are wrong." That is, we often justify a claim that a particular action is right or wrong by reference to some ethical rule or standard which applies to the action. It is obvious, however, that we cannot show that an action is right or wrong by appeal to a standard unless we have appealed to the correct standard. For example, the attempt to absolve or excuse an adult who has abused a child, by appealing to the standard that no adult ought to be convicted of a crime when the victim is a child, fails to justify the act morally, because the standard appealed to is incorrect. On the other hand, attempting to eliminate acts of capital punishment by appealing to the standard that no person, or group of people, has the right to take the life of another person surely has some force. Those who defend capital punishment usually will not attack the standard but try to show that it must be modified to account for certain exceptions. An important part of justifying a particular moral decision, then, certainly seems to be basing it upon a correct ethical standard.

If we can justify a standard or a group of standards, then the only other particularly moral task we have left—probably the more difficult one—is the task of applying the standards throughout our lives. The second task faces us all, including philosophers, who are in no better position to achieve success than anyone else. Philosophers are particularly suited to the first task, however, because they are centrally interested in, and uniquely trained for, critical investigations of the arguments people propose to justify their actions and beliefs. In this chapter we shall examine the various leading theories that propose and defend particular moral standards, and we shall attempt a philosophical examination of each, with the hope that we can draw a justified conclusion about correct ethical standards.

EVALUATING ACTIONS
VERSUS EVALUATING PEOPLE

Before we move on to consider ethical *theories* (that is, theories that propose ethical standards) two points should be emphasized. The first is that we are interested in a standard that can be used to prescribe and evaluate particular courses of action, that is, a standard that can be used to prescribe what we ought to do and evaluate what we have done. We are, then, not interested in a standard for evaluating morally the people who perform the acts. We certainly use both kinds of standards, for we not only decide that what someone did was right or wrong, but we also praise or blame the person for doing it and sometimes judge him to be moral or immoral. Both kinds of standards are important, but they are different. It seems essential, in morally evaluating a person for what he does, that we consider his motives, his beliefs, and the particular circumstances surrounding his decision to act; but it is not clear that any of these are relevant to the evaluation of his action. For example, many people have claimed that it was wrong to drop the first atomic bomb on Hiroshima, and they have consequently blamed President Truman for ordering the bomb to be dropped. However, these are two quite separate issues. We might argue that it was morally wrong to drop the first bomb on a city because a less populated site might have been equally effective. Here we decide the issue without considering President Truman's motives, beliefs, and the pressures under which he made the decision. But in deciding whether to blame the President, we must consider his motive, his beliefs about the war and whether they were reasonable, and the external and internal forces playing upon the one person who had to make the decision. It may be, then, that the action he took was wrong, but he should not be blamed for it. Similarly, someone might do something that, contrary to what he intended, turns out to be right. In such a case, the action may be right but the person blameworthy. Consequently, we should remember to distinguish between these two kinds of standards, because we are considering only standards for evaluating moral actions and because failure to distinguish the two has often led to unjust accusations of blame and unnecessary feelings of guilt. Many actions are wrong but reflect no blame or guilt on the doer. Understanding rather than blame is often appropriate.

METHOD OF CRITICALLY EVALUATING ETHICAL THEORIES

The second point concerns the means we shall use to evaluate critically the various ethical theories. In general, we shall proceed as we did in Chapter Four, in which we considered various mind-body theories. That is, we shall try to elaborate each position clearly, consider the problems confronting each, and then decide which position is least troubled by serious objections. We must, then, elaborate and evaluate the most serious objections to each theory. We shall find, for example, that the standards proposed by some theories do not apply to all situations, and that other standards result in unresolvable moral conflicts when applied to certain situations. This last point is very important and deserves further comment.

We shall claim that someone has *some* reason to *reject* a standard that is clearly contrary to what, in an uncritical way, he or she *feels certain* is correct. A number of things must be said to clarify this idea. First, it is not enough for a person to be unsure whether what the standard prescribes is correct; he must be quite sure, or certain, that what the standard prescribes is not correct. Secondly, this sort of situation may occur in a number of different ways. For example, a given ethical standard might dictate that a specific action is obligatory, when a person feels certain that the action is morally permissible, that is, neither obligatory nor prohibited, or feels certain that it is forbidden. It is clear, too, that other conflicts of this sort between what an ethical standard prescribes and what a person feels certain is correct in a specific situation might arise. The term 'incorrect' was just used to cover each of these possibilities.

Imagine that a person tries to test an ethical standard by seeing whether it agrees in what it prescribes with what he or she feels certain is morally correct. Suppose, too, that this person finds considerable agreement on the matter. From this alone it will not follow that the ethical standard is *acceptable* for that person. All sorts of other things may be wrong with the standard. It does not even follow that the person has some reason to accept the standard. The problem is that a person might have inconsistent moral beliefs. Few people have self-consciously examined the whole spectrum of their moral opinions and decisions, and it is quite likely that many people are inconsistent. They decide differently at different times, even under similar circumstances, and especially when the action involves someone they love or hate. Where someone finds that he has inconsistent beliefs, then, even if he believes one of them quite strongly, he should not use it to test a standard. Consequently, a person should rely on his own intuitive opinions of what is right and wrong, obligatory, permissible, or forbidden, only when he feels quite certain of those opinions, and none of his other beliefs are incompatible with those opinions.

It can be objected, however, that it is a mistake to rely on this intuitive test of ethical standards, because people's ethical opinions, even their strongly held opinions, differ extremely widely about particular cases. For example, many Jews find obviously morally repugnant certain actions that many Nazis found quite acceptable. Also, there clearly are equally deeply felt disagreements between many pacifists and many military rulers. It surely is mistaken, according to this objection, to rely on a method of evaluation that allows Nazis and some of the most callous military rulers to be justified in holding a standard because they do not find that it prescribes anything morally repugnant, when so many other people find it clearly abhorrent.

This objection has some force, though not quite as much as one might initially expect. Reliance on the intuitive opinions of different people, as just described, will not by itself lead to different standards being *justified* for different people. At most, what will follow is that the way is left open for different people each to have *some reason* for accepting different standards. Nevertheless, it must be conceded that reliance, in part, on different people's intuitive opinions does allow that different people may each have some reason to accept ethical standards that are not only different but in conflict with one another. We think, however, that this much relativity of reasons (for different ethical standards) is inevitable. The critical questions are whether the proposed method sanctions justification for a person of a clearly mistaken ethical standard, and whether it allows for different standards to be justified for different people. There are three reasons why we believe that the proposed method will have neither of these consequences.

The first is that this intuitive test is but one of several tests or conditions for a satisfactory ethical standard. Many standards that meet this test for a particular person will fail because they do not meet the other conditions. Part of what we shall do, as we examine various proposed ethical standards throughout the chapter, is to try to uncover these important other conditions for a satisfactory standard. We shall do this primarily by examining the reasons we find for rejecting unsatisfactory proposals. By the time we have finished, it is hoped that we shall have found not only a satisfactory theory, but also the conditions and tests it has met in proving to be satisfactory.

The second reason is that we do not even expect widespread divergences among standards that meet the intuitive test. A standard is not shown to meet this test for someone, if he finds that he is not bothered by any of the actions it prescribes that most people find morally repugnant. He must find it meets this test in a wide variety of other cases as well. For example, many Nazis would find it morally repugnant for anyone to put loyal Nazis in gas chambers. But in certain conditions in different countries, such actions might well be prescribed by the same standard that he otherwise finds acceptable. Thus, a person is not to select in a biased way the cases he uses to test a standard. He must examine a wide range of possible as well as actual cases to see if it prescribes anything he feels quite certain is mistaken. Only when he has done this can he claim that a standard meets this particular test. And when he has done this, a person will find that many fewer standards meet the test than he might have expected.

A third and final reason is that we predict that there will be widespread agreement among different people that certain actions are morally repugnant, say, or morally right. The Nazi example used earlier may be used again here. We confidently predict that many people, indeed the great majority of people, will agree that Nazi torture and execution of millions of innocent people was morally wrong. Hence, if a given ethical standard were to allow such actions as permissible, the case for rejecting such a standard would be based, at least partially, on the fact that the great majority of people are quite certain that such actions are morally repugnant.

We may sum up this discussion of our method by saying that we shall be relying *in part* on two rules or tests:

1. If a person feels certain that a specific action is morally incorrect, and this belief is not inconsistent with any of his other beliefs, and an ethical standard dictates that this action is morally correct, then the person has some reason to reject the ethical standard.

2. If a person feels certain that a large number of actions are morally correct, and none of these beliefs is inconsistent with any of his other beliefs, and he has not been biased in choosing these actions for consideration, and he finds that an ethical standard agrees in all these cases with his beliefs, then the person has some reason to accept the ethical standard.

These are both complex rules but, we think, they are tolerably clear. Notice that they speak of having *some* reason to accept or reject an ethical standard. Thus, it is not claimed that if an ethical standard fails to measure up in the way described in (1), or does measure up in the manner described in (2), then one has conclusive evidence against or in favor of the standard. One would simply have one piece of relevant evidence, positive or negative, depending on the particular case.

THEOLOGICAL ETHICS

Much of our ethical training and learning takes place in a religious context. Indeed, ethics seems to be an essential part of religion. In both the Old and New Testament, and in most other religious documents, such as the Koran, there are ethical teachings. In the Old Testament, the Ten Commandments are central, and in the New Testament we have, among others, the teachings of the Sermon on the Mount. It is natural, then, to associate ethics and morality with religion, and to look to religion for the ethical standards we can use to prescribe and evaluate our actions. And if we think back to the discussion of God in Chapter Five, we might derive a standard from the goodness of the supreme being. That is, we might propose the following ethical standard:

Whatever God wills is what ought to be done.

If this is the correct ethical standard, then, whenever we are deciding what ought to be done or what ought to have been done, we should base our decision on what God wills.

To make this standard applicable to a specific situation, we need some way to discover what God would will in the situation. There are two ways to discover this. First, God might reveal his will to us by directly communicating with us, or he might reveal his will to someone else who relays it to the rest of us. For most of us, if God's will is revealed to us at all, it is only indirectly, with someone else as the intermediary. Consequently, if we are to apply the theological standard on the basis of God's will as indirectly revealed, we must be able to justify some particular claim about what God wills; for example, the Ten Commandments. But we have already seen, in Chapter Five, how difficult it is to provide grounds for thinking that any revelation of God's will has occurred, let alone show that any one particular claim is correct.[1]

Objection: We Must Justify Religious Claims by Ethical Claims

Let us assume someone claims that what God wills is that people obey the Ten Commandments. We now have an ethical standard that we can apply to particular situations. But how are we to justify the claim that this is the correct criterion? We cannot do so merely by claiming that God revealed the commandments to Moses. Consider what we would do if we read that Moses had returned with such commandments as "Make love to thy neighbor's wife," "Steal thy neighbor's goods," and "Take advantage of thy parents." We would decide that, whatever was revealed to Moses, it was not the will of God, because these are immoral commandments. We do not establish something is morally right by showing that it expresses God's will, because the only available way to evaluate conflicting claims about what God wills is by finding which one is in accordance with what is moral. Thus, we must use ethical claims, to justify religious claims, rather than ground ethics upon the claims of some religion.[2]

This is not to deny that religion is, for many people, the psychological basis of ethics. It may be that religion has an important psychological relationship to ethics. Nor is it to deny that God has willed or prescribed certain moral commandments. Everything just discussed can be accepted by someone who believes that whatever God wills should be done. Furthermore, nothing said so far gives any reason to think that the Ten Commandments do not express the revealed word of God. They might. If they do, they will also express at least part of a correct ethical standard. The only claim made here is that we cannot justify the claim that they or any other ethical standards are correct by appealing to the pronouncements of some particular religion, because we must justify the claim that these pronouncements express the revealed word of God by showing that they

---

1. See pp. 211-12.

2. For a clear argument against theological ethics, see Jeremy Bentham's discussion of the theological principle in *An Introduction to the Principles of Morals and Legislation*, in *The Utilitarians* (Garden City: Doubleday, 1961). John Stuart Mill also discusses theological ethics in *Utilitarianism*, also in *The Utilitarians*, 423.

are the correct moral pronouncements. Because our task here is to find and justify some ethical standards, we cannot stop with the pronouncements of some religion even if they are correct. We must find some way to show that they are correct, and this we cannot do by appealing to the religion itself.

We are in no better position if we try to ground an ethical standard on direct revelation. It may be that some day you will have a religious experience in which certain commands are issued to you. You may, as others have after similar experiences, uncritically accept these as revealing the word of God and proclaim them to all. But we are here interested not in what you might do, but in whether you would be justified in claiming that you had heard the word of God. That you have received these commands in a very strange and unique way is not enough. Many a person has followed his "voices" and committed ghastly crimes. We usually think such "voices" are the result of psychological disturbances. Furthermore, it is possible that not only God, but also the Devil reveals his will to human beings. Consequently, you could justify your claim that you had heard the word of God only if you could provide a reason to think that the word expressed a command of God rather than one of the Devil. You cannot do this by appealing to your religious experience. Thus, in the case of direct revelation as in the case of indirect revelation, justification of an ethical claim cannot be based on a religious claim.

The conclusion we have reached is that, although a religion may help us psychologically to decide what to do, it cannot help us justify what we decide to do. The justification of our ethical standards, and thereby our actions, proceeds independently of appeals to religion. Because of this, the existence of God is irrelevant to the justification of ethical standards. Thus, those who find they can no longer believe in God are not forced to the conclusion that nothing is right or wrong. There is nothing inconsistent in holding some particular ethical standard and also believing that God does not exist.

Nevertheless, there is a widespread view that if there is no God, then nothing is moral or immoral, nothing is right or wrong. This is the view that if anything is right and anything is wrong, it has been decreed so by God. Notice that this is a different claim from the one we previously examined. The previous claim is

If something is willed by God, then it ought to be done.

but the present claim is

If something is the right thing to do (ought to be done), then it is willed (proclaimed or commanded) by God.

Although the first statement is acceptable, the second is surely debatable. For one thing, there is no reason to think that all right actions are willed or commanded by God, because there is no reason to think that God issues commands covering every moral situation. It may be that *if* in a certain situation a particular action *A* is right, and *if* God were to command some action in that situation, then he would command action *A*. But it does not follow that if there is no God, then nothing is right or wrong. For compare: suppose action *B* is right in situation *X*; and imagine that if Charles de Gaulle were alive and were to command an action in *X*, then he would command action *B*. The fact that de Gaulle is not alive does not make action *B* anything other than right. Secondly, it is at least possible that we shall be able to justify some ethical standard as correct without reference to God. In that case, we shall have no reason to think that the correct ethical standard must issue from God. However, no matter what causes them to do it, many people talk of the breakdown of morality and the destruction of ethical standards, which they often blame on the decline of religion. The result of this, they claim, is that morality is relative, so that nothing is right or wrong, and what it is right for me to do is merely what I want to do. Although it is not unusual to hear such a claim, the claim itself is quite unusual, because it embodies three distinctly different ethical positions—ethical relativism, ethical nihilism, and ethical egoism. In one way or another these positions are prominent among the views about ethics expressed today. Consequently, each deserves individual attention here.

ETHICAL RELATIVISM

Ethical relativism seems to be expressed by the frequent claim

The right action for you is not always the right action for me.

This interpretation is often true, because two people are often quite different, but it does not imply ethical relativism. For example, if you are a good swimmer and I cannot swim, then in the same situation where each sees a child drowning, it is right for you to swim to help the child, but right for me to run off for help. But, although what each of us ought to do in this same situation differs, it is still true that both of us should do our best to help the child. There is nothing relative about this.

Action Relativism versus Standard Relativism
To avoid confusion here, we must distinguish between the relativism of ethical actions and the relativism of ethical standards.

Action Relativism: Actions are in some situations right and in some situations wrong.

Standard Relativism: Ethical standards are in some situations correct and in some situations incorrect.

We have seen a case of action relativism in the example of the drowning child, but this was not a case of standard relativism. Both you and I applied the same standard, that we ought to do our best to help the child. Thus there can be relativism of right actions without relativism of ethical standards. Consequently, as presently interpreted,

What's right for you is not always right for me.

expresses an action relativism, but, because ethical relativism concerns standard relativism, and because action relativism does not imply standard relativism, this often true claim does not imply ethical relativism. What may be confusing is that some ethical standards claim that certain acts are always wrong, such as "Thou shalt not kill," so it may seem that what we can call *standard absolutism* implies *action absolutism*. But in many other cases, such as one of the Biblical commandment, "Honor thy father and mother," no specific actions are forbidden. Thus, those who rebel against action absolutism are not forced to ethical relativism, because the correct ethical standard may allow that whether a specific action is right or wrong depends upon the specific circumstances in which it is done. How we honor our parents at some time depends upon them, us, and the particular circumstances.

Another interpretation of 'What's right for you is not always right for me' is the following:

What you think is right is not always what I think is right.

On this interpretation, the claim is surely true. But all it expresses is that you and I sometimes disagree about what we think is right, and this is quite compatible with standard absolutism. Thus, this interpretation does not lead to ethical relativism. To get to ethical relativism we need an interpretation that will make ethical *standards* relative. Another interpretation, which comes closer and is often thought to lead to ethical relativism, is the following:

The standard you are justified in accepting as correct is not always the standard I am justified in accepting.

This interpretation, although once again true, does not lead to ethical relativism, because someone can be justified in accepting something as correct when it is not. For example, we would certainly agree that someone who believed that the velocity of objects can be indefinitely increased was justified in his belief before Einstein propounded his theory. But we would also claim that, although he was justified, his belief is incorrect. Furthermore, as we have seen, our method of evaluating ethical standards, which uses each person's strongly held moral convictions as one of several tests, may result in some relativity in the justification of ethical standards. But, as with scientific hypotheses, although different people might be justified in accepting different standards, any one of them, indeed all of them, might nevertheless be mistaken. Thus, although there is a relativity of justification, this does not imply a relativity of correctness. Even though which beliefs are *justified* differs as people's knowledge changes, this does not affect which are the *true* or *correct* beliefs. The ethical relativist requires a relativity of correct standards. The kind of interpretation we need for ethical relativism is one such as the following:

> The correct ethical standard for you is not always the correct ethical standard for me.

This interpretation implies ethical relativism, because it implies that an ethical standard is correct relative to some situations and incorrect relative to others.   However, on this interpretation, the claim is no longer obviously true. We must consider what reasons there might be for accepting it.

Definition of Ethical Relativism
Let us define ethical relativism as follows:

> *Ethical Relativism*: Different ethical standards are correct for different groups of people.

This definition is stated broadly, to allow for various kinds of ethical relativism. For example, one species of ethical relativism, which some sociologists and anthropologists are tempted to accept, is *cultural relativism*, the theory that whether an ethical standard is correct depends upon the culture or society of the person concerned. There is also *class relativism* which, having its roots in Marxism, makes the correct standard relative to the economic class of the person. A relativism that appeals to historians, *historical relativism*, makes the correct standards relative to the particular times in which the person lived. None of these species of ethical relativism is any better justified than the general theory. Therefore, if we find a reason to reject this general theory, we shall be justified in rejecting each of its specific versions as well.

Let us begin the examination of ethical relativism by considering two of the main arguments used to justify it: the argument from differing ethical judgments, and the argument from different ethical standards.

The Argument from Differing Ethical Judgments
One of the most widely accepted facts relevant to ethics is that there is, has been, and probably always will be widespread disagreement about what is right and what is wrong. It is not merely that the judgments of people of one culture or time differ greatly from those of another culture or time. We find widely divergent ethical judgments even within one culture and at the same time.   Surely, this objection states, if, over centuries and throughout the world, people have continually made widely divergent and often contradictory moral judgments, then the ethical standards of people

must differ from place to place and time to time, relative to the situations in which people live. Therefore, according to this argument, correct standards are relative to the situations of the people who apply the standards. That is, ethical relativism is true.

Let us outline this argument so that we can critically evaluate it. It can be stated as follows:

1. The ethical judgments people make differ greatly, depending on where and when they live.

2. If the ethical judgments people make differ greatly, then the ethical standards people use differ greatly.

3. The ethical standards people use differ greatly.

Therefore

4. Ethical relativism is true.

Two objections can be raised against this argument. First, although premise (1) is acceptable, there is reason to doubt the second premise. We have already seen that action relativism does not imply standard relativism, and there is also little reason to think that a judgment relativism implies a standard relativism. Indeed, some anthropologists and sociologists who agree with (1) are not at all sure about (2). Many quite divergent judgments can be explained by pointing out that the people concerned have different beliefs about what the facts are, rather than different ethical standards. For example, in one society, the people had the custom of killing their parents when they began to grow old. In Western cultures, such an act is considered completely immoral. Most of us judge that killing one's parents is wrong, because we employ the standard that we should honor our parents. It may seem that the people of this society had no such standard, but this conclusion would be wrong. These people believed that each of us spends her afterlife in the physical state in which she dies. Thus, to allow someone to grow old and decrepit would not be honoring him. These people did what they thought best for their parents, and thus honored them by helping them obtain immortality in an enjoyable physical state.[3] In this example, they and we seem to use the same ethical standard, but, because we disagree about the facts of afterlife, the judgments we make differ greatly. Many differences of actual judgments can be explained in this way, without postulating different ethical standards. Some anthropologists hope to find that certain ethical standards are

---

3. This kind of example is discussed by Solomon E. Asch, in *Social Psychology* (Englewood Cliffs: Prentice-Hall, 1952), Chapter 13, especially p. 377, where he is trying to show how widely different ethical practices can result from divergent factual beliefs instead of different ethical standards.

universally believed to be correct. If this is so, it would certainly make premise (2) highly dubious.

However, even if the divergence of ethical standards is not as great as some people claim, the evidence presently available supports the claim that people often have different beliefs about which ethical standards are correct. Consequently, we can defend (3) interpreted as follows:

3a. The ethical standards believed to be correct by people often differ.

Thus, because we can accept (3a), we can also accept (4), if the inference from (3a) to (4) is valid. However, as it stands, the inference is invalid, because (3a) is a statement only about what people *believe* to be correct and (4) is a statement about what is *in fact* correct. This is the second objection to the argument from differing ethical judgments—it is invalid, because the inference from (3a) to (4) is invalid. We must find a premise that, with (3a), will allow us to infer (4). This takes us to the second argument for ethical relativism.

The Argument from Different Ethical Standards

It may seem to some that, although the inference from (3a) to (4) is, strictly speaking, invalid, it resembles the inference from 'Socrates is a human being' to 'Socrates is mortal'—what is missing is an obvious truth such as 'All human beings are mortal.' However, the dubious part of such an enthymematic argument is very often that missing premise. Let us examine the present case by constructing the argument as follows:

3a. The ethical standards believed to be correct by people often differ.

5. If the ethical standards that people believe to be correct often differ, then the ethical standards that are correct often differ for these different people.

Therefore

4. The ethical standards that are correct are often different for different people, that is, ethical relativism is true.

We have added statement (5) as the missing premise to make the argument valid. Consequently, because (3a) is acceptable, we should accept (4) if we can justify (5). Let us consider (5), which is a sentence of the form:

5a. If the x's which people believe to be correct often differ, then the x which is correct often differs for these different people.

Many sentences of that form are plainly false. For example, many people differ in their beliefs about the world around us, but this does not imply that in each case a different belief is correct. If I believe that the correct number of planets is eight and you believe that the correct number is ten, it is not that one number is correct for me and another correct for you.

Both you and I are wrong, both of our beliefs are incorrect, because there is one and only one correct number of planets, and that number is nine. In general, sentences of the form of (5a) are false. Furthermore, there is no reason to think that beliefs about ethical standards are relevantly different from those beliefs for which (5a) is false. We have, therefore, reason to conclude that (5) is false.

Because both arguments supporting ethical relativism are unsound, we have found no reason to accept it. Moreover, because it is clearly contrary to our ordinary conception of morality, we have some reason to reject it. When we claim that lying, cheating, and killing are wrong, we do not claim that these prohibitions are derived from standards that correctly apply to some of us but not to others. We think that an ethical standard is either correct or incorrect for one and for all, and, because we have found no reason to deny this, we can continue to accept it.

Ethical Relativism Defended: A Modified Argument

The case against ethical relativism as it applies to ethical standards certainly seems quite strong and compelling. But we may have overlooked some things in its favor. In particular, recall our earlier discussion of the method we shall use in this chapter, where two principles or tests were endorsed, one concerning reasons for rejecting an ethical standard, and the other concerning reasons for accepting a standard. Perhaps we can argue, in line with the latter of these tests, that different people have *some* grounds for accepting different ethical standards, and thus produce a new argument for ethical relativism. Such an argument might be the following:

3b. The ethical standards that different people feel certain are correct often differ from one another.

5b. If the ethical standards that different people feel certain are correct often differ from one another, then these different people have some reasons for accepting different ethical standards.

Therefore

6. Different people have some reasons for accepting different ethical standards.

Of course, even if statement (6) is established, we would not have established ethical relativism. But the argument could be continued with just one more premise, namely,

7. If different people have some reasons for accepting different ethical standards, then it is reasonable to believe that ethical relativism is correct.

Therefore

8. It is reasonable to believe that ethical relativism is correct.

There is reason to think that, when properly understood, this argument is sound. The expression 'reasonable to believe,' used in (7) and (8), must be taken to mean something like 'there is some reason in its favor.' When (7) is understood along these lines, it is quite plausible. Certainly premise (3b) is true. Premise (5b) might be suspect, however, since after all, people feel certain about all manner of things that are utterly absurd. However, (5b) can be bolstered if we understand it to mean that different people find that different ethical standards agree with what, in an unbiased way, they feel certain are correct actions, and in no case are the beliefs these people have about these actions inconsistent with their other beliefs. Then, according to principle or test (2), stated earlier (see p. 284), each of these people has some reason to accept these different standards. In other words, (5b) is plausible, provided that the reason such people feel certain about different ethical standards is that they have found, in accord with test (2), that these standards are in agreement with actions that these same people feel certain are correct. Hence, since everything in this argument is plausible, we have unearthed some positive support for ethical relativism.

Before we conclude that ethical relativism has been established, however, we should pay careful attention to just what this argument shows. Its conclusion asserts that ethical relativism is reasonable to believe and, as we just saw, this means that there is *some* reason in favor of it. Such a conclusion, though, is not at all the same as claiming that ethical relativism is *justified*. To understand why, we need only note that while there may be some reason in favor of ethical relativism, this is perfectly consistent with there also being some reason or reasons *against* it. And, indeed, this is precisely what we have just noted: ethical relativism runs against our ordinary conception of morality, what we ordinarily suppose about morality in our nonphilosophical moments. Such a conflict is by no means a decisive consideration against ethical relativism. However, it is *a* negative factor that is certainly relevant. And, when this negative factor is balanced with the positive factor provided by the argument just discussed, the negative factor goes some way to offsetting the positive. Hence, ethical relativism has not been *justified*, despite the acknowledged fact that some reason has been provided in its favor.

We should keep in mind, however, that no other ethical standard may prove any more reasonable than ethical relativism, and indeed all may prove less reasonable. If this latter turns out to be the case, then we shall have to settle for ethical relativism as the most reasonable ethical standard among available options. We shall reconsider this question later, when we have examined important *non*relativist theories.

The way seems open to search for an ethical standard we can justify as the correct standard for all. Our search, however, may be frustrated in another way. What reason have we for thinking any standard of right and wrong is correct either for some or for all? It is true that when we make moral judgments we act on the assumption that there is such a standard, but perhaps nothing is right and nothing is wrong; perhaps there is no correct ethical standard. If this is true, it is foolish to struggle to justify some standard. We should thus examine the claim of ethical nihilism before embarking on a critical examination of particular ethical standards.

ETHICAL NIHILISM

We can define ethical nihilism quite simply as follows:

Ethical Nihilism: There is nothing morally right and nothing morally wrong.

If this position is correct, it follows that nothing we do is moral and nothing immoral, that everything is permitted and nothing either morally forbidden or obligatory. It also follows that there are no correct ethical standards, because if there were, then the actions they required would be morally obligatory, and the actions they forbade would be morally prohibited. Such a view is quite contrary to our ordinary beliefs. Most of us feel quite certain that some actions are right and some are wrong. Consequently, unless there are cogent reasons for accepting ethical nihilism, we can reject it, as we did ethical relativism. Generally, the debate about ethical nihilism does not center directly on the question of whether any particular actions are morally right or wrong, because the issue can best be discussed by reference to ethical standards. If there is good reason to think that some ethical standard is correct, there is good reason to reject ethical nihilism. If there is good reason to think that no ethical standard is correct, there is some reason to doubt that any actions are right or wrong.

The Argument from Different Ethical Standards
Some people claim that it is wrong to infer ethical relativism from the widespread and enduring divergence of beliefs about which standards are correct. Such a disagreement, which has persisted for centuries everywhere, instead testifies that there really are no correct ethical standards. Such an argument, as you can probably see, is no better than the corresponding argument for ethical relativism. We can show this by presenting the argument as follows:

1. The ethical standards that people believe to be correct differ throughout the world and time.

2. If the ethical standards that people believe to be correct differ throughout the world and time, there are no correct ethical standards.

Therefore

3. There are no correct ethical standards.

As might be guessed, premise (2), which is like premise (5) in the corresponding argument for ethical relativism, is highly suspect. Premise (2) is of the form:

2a. If the x's which people believe to be correct differ, then there is no correct x.

And many sentences of this form are quite clearly false. For example, there are many divergent beliefs about life on distant planets, but this does not imply that none of these beliefs is correct. Some are correct and some are not. One often finds a wide range of beliefs on a difficult topic, most of which are wrong, but some of which are right. We can, therefore, reject this argument for ethical nihilism as no better than the corresponding argument for ethical relativism.

The Argument from the Lack of Justification

It becomes apparent, when critically evaluating the various leading candidates for the correct ethical standard, that none has overcome problems important enough to keep it from being justified. Thus, this argument goes, because no ethical standards are justified, all are unjustified, and therefore none is the correct standard. We can state the argument as follows:

1. No ethical standards are justified.

Therefore

2. All ethical standards are unjustified.

3. If all ethical standards are unjustified, then no ethical standards are correct.

Therefore

4. No ethical standards are correct (and thus ethical nihilism is reasonable).

There is a certain plausibility to this argument, because we can gather evidence to support (1), the immediate inference from (1) to (2) is certainly valid, and (3) appears true. That is, if no possible ethical standard can be justified as correct, so that all are unjustified, it certainly seems reasonable to conclude that none of them is correct. Thus, because both premises (1) and (3) seem acceptable, and the argument is valid, it seems that we should accept the conclusion. But think about it some more. We have accepted (1) on the grounds that none of the candidates has yet overcome problems, so that none has yet been justified. However, when we supported (3) we did so by talking about what is implied if no candidates can ever be justified. There is a difference between 'not yet justified' and 'cannot be justified,' for the first is compatible with a future justification but the second precludes any possibility of justification. The argument, then, seems to involve an equivocation of the word 'unjustified,' because (2) seems to require one sense of 'unjustified' and (3) a different sense. Thus the argument is invalid as it stands. We can bring out the equivocation and make the argument valid by replacing premise (3) with two other premises, namely,

3a. If all ethical standards are not yet justified, then all ethical standards are unjustifiable (cannot be justified).

and

3b. If all ethical standards are unjustifiable (cannot be justified), then no ethical standards are correct.

When we do this it is easy to see that (3a) is false and there is also some doubt about (3b).

In general, if we have not yet justified some of a group of alternative claims, it does not follow that no such claims can be justified. No particular claim about whether there is life on distant planets can now be justified, that is, there is not enough evidence to support strongly any particular claim. But this does not imply that no claim can ever be justified. Thus, in this example, as in ethics, if no position has been justified, we need not conclude that no position can be justified. We should reject premise (3a) and the argument containing it.

We have found no reason to think that ethical nihilism is true, so we have no reason to believe that nothing we or anyone else does is morally wrong. Furthermore, because certain actions clearly seem to nearly everyone who considers the matter to be morally right or wrong, we have some reason to reject ethical nihilism. Indeed, the mere fact that there is *some* evidence in favor of ethical relativism is itself evidence against ethical nihilism. Consequently, we should cast ethical nihilism aside.

THE "NO-STANDARD" THEORY

Earlier we distinguished between two forms of ethical nihilism, namely *action* nihilism and *standard* nihilism. We have focused attention on standard nihilism because it has been most often defended. But somebody could hold standard nihilism—that is, that no ethical standard is correct—and nevertheless agree that some actions are morally right and others morally wrong. The idea here is that people have the capacity to determine whether an action is morally right or wrong without relying on or appealing to any standard. Instead, people can somehow "sense" or "intuit" that an action is morally right or wrong. If people can discover that actions are sometimes morally right or wrong in this manner, then of course such actions *are* morally right or wrong, even though no ethical standards are correct.

This sort of theory, sometimes called *act-deontology*, we will call the *no-standard* theory. To illustrate how the theory is supposed to work, let us consider an example in which you witness a crime being committed, perhaps an armed robbery. This we would generally agree is morally wrong. The no-standard theorist asks what it is that you actually witness. You observe a person enter a store; the person is carrying a weapon; he says to the shopkeeper, "Give me all of the money in the cash register"; the money is given to the robber; and the robber leaves the store. This is what you see and hear. All of these things are nonmoral facts, the no-standard theorist will say. By itself, there is nothing especially morally right or wrong about entering a store, carrying a gun, demanding money, taking money, or leaving a store. By themselves, none of these items is any more morally right or wrong than is the color of the shirt the robber happens to be wearing. Thus, what you actually witness are many distinct nonmoral facts or events, indeed many more of them than we have listed here. By experiencing or observing a sufficient number of these nonmoral facts, according to the no-standard theory, you come to know that the action is morally wrong. You don't rely upon an ethical standard, such as "Thou shalt not steal." Instead, by first being aware of a sufficient number of relevant nonmoral facts, one becomes able to judge correctly that the action is morally wrong.

Of course, in some situations a person might rely upon an ethical standard, such as "Thou shalt not steal" to make a moral decision about an action. However, the no-standard theorist claims that one *need not* do this; one could have made oneself aware of enough of the nonmoral facts pertaining to that action in that situation and thereby been in a position to "intuit" or "sense" that the action was morally wrong. Ethical standards are real enough, naturally, but they are completely dispensable; we can make do without them. And since this is so, it is argued, actions are not right or wrong in virtue of their accord or lack of accord with an ethical standard.

The no-standard theory thus has two parts. The first is standard nihilism: no ethical standard is correct. The second part is that some actions are morally right and others wrong, and that in many cases we discover that they are by becoming aware of a sufficient number of relevant nonmoral facts pertaining to those actions. But, to support this theory, we need to find some better reason to accept its first part than we found in our earlier discussion of ethical nihilism. The no-standard theorist thinks he has such an argument.

The Argument from Exceptions

Consider again the ethical standard "Thou shalt not steal." In most cases people would agree with this principle; generally, one ought not steal and to do so is morally wrong. But imagine a situation in which a person and her family are nearing starvation. Perhaps she lives in the Eritrea area of modern Ethiopia, the crops have once again failed because of a lack of rain, and relief supplies are not getting through to Eritrea because of the civil war in that region. If this woman has the opportunity to steal food from the warehouses controlled by the rebel forces, just enough food to help ward off starvation for herself and family, then it seems clear that what she does is not morally wrong in this terrible situation. So here we have a plain example of an exception to "Thou shalt not steal."

Further, the same holds for any ethical standard one might propose. That is, any such standard will also have exceptions similar to this case of stealing. Nonetheless, in all these cases where there are exceptions, we do know that the exception qualifies as morally permitted. For instance, we do know that it is morally permissible in the circumstances for the woman in Ethiopia to steal food. We thus know without reliance on an ethical standard that in this situation stealing is not morally wrong. Hence, the no-standard theorist reasons, we establish both parts of the no-standard theory with a single argument.

Objection to the No-Standard Theory:
Not Every Ethical Standard Has Exceptions

Let us say that an ethical standard or principle is *specific* when it concerns a specific kind of action. Thus, "Thou shalt not steal" is specific in this sense, because it concerns one kind of action, namely, stealing. Other ethical standards are specific in just this way; they apply to just one kind of action, as in another of the Ten Commandments, "Thou shalt not kill." Now it is quite plausible that every *specific* ethical standard has exceptions. Here the no-standard theorist is onto a sound idea. However, ethical standards of the sort we are to consider are not specific in quite this way. Rather, they are very general standards which are supposed to apply to all kinds of actions; we can call them *general* ethical standards to contrast them with the specific sort. Consider theological ethics, already considered. It is a general theory, for its ethical standard states that what is morally right is what God has commanded, and what is morally wrong is what God has forbidden. But this standard does not specify *which* acts God has commanded or forbidden. Now, the objection to the no-standard theory is that, although we can concede that every specific ethical standard has exceptions, there is some reason to think that not every general ethical standard does. We shall consider later one theory designed to apply in all cases involving or requiring a moral decision, and since it accommodates all cases it would not have exceptions in the way the no-standard theorist imagines. At the least, the argument from exceptions is premature: it has not been applied to general ethical standards. And certainly, from the fact that every specific ethical standard has exceptions, it will not follow that every general ethical standard also has exceptions. We may conclude this later after an examination of relevant general ethical standards. But at this point we have no reason to accept such a conclusion.

A Second Objection to the No-Standard Theory: Nonmoral Agreement but Moral Disagreement

The no-standard theory says that people can discern the moral character of an action by becoming aware of a sufficient number of relevant nonmoral facts concerning that action. Suppose we have two perfectly normal, unbiased, competent adults who witness an action at the same time, and who are both aware of all of the relevant nonmoral factors regarding the action. The no-standard theory tells us that these two individuals will then agree in their moral assessments of the action, for they both engaged in what the no-standard theory says is the way people arrive at moral judgments. But it is notorious that people disagree about moral matters, even where they agree on all of the nonmoral facts. In this respect, ethics is no different from aesthetics, or the theory of artistic value. Two people observing the same painting, both of whom are quite aware of all of the nonaesthetic features of the object and the context, often will still disagree about the artistic merit or value of the work. We should, then, reject the no-standard theory since it implies something false: that there will be moral agreement between two or more people when they are all aware of the relevant nonmoral facts. This so often fails to happen that the no-standard theory is refuted.

ETHICAL SKEPTICISM

It seems we can begin our attempt to establish some ethical standard as correct. Before we do so, however, one other view relevant to our interests deserves mention, especially because it is often confused with ethical nihilism. It is the view that no ethical standards can be known to be correct, because no standard is more reasonable than all the others and consequently, none is justifiable as the correct one. We are, then, wasting our time trying. This is ethical skepticism, which is different from ethical nihilism in that it merely claims that no standard is known to be correct, or is justifiable as correct, rather than that no standard actually is correct. It is, then, a different claim from that of ethical nihilism. Moreover, it is by no means unreasonable. In fact, ethical skepticism might claim good inductive support, because it seems that, as of now, none of all the ethical standards proposed throughout history has been justified. Such evidence, if correct, makes ethical skepticism more reasonable than not, and if we must accept this evidence and can find no counterbalancing evidence, then it seems that ethical skepticism is the correct position for us to take. However, if we are to justify such a position, we must examine the evidence ourselves. That is, we must critically evaluate the various candidates for a correct ethical standard. Thus, although ethical skepticism may be correct, we cannot justify it until we have completed the task we have set before us.

ETHICAL EGOISM

Sometimes a person claims that no one has the right to tell him what to do, because he can do whatever he wants. Such a claim sounds like a statement of both ethical nihilism and egoism, and if he adds that anyone else can do what he wants also, it sounds like ethical relativism as well. But we must separate these three different claims, because taken together they are incompatible. The claim that each person can do what he wants is not a form of ethical relativism because it applies to one and all. (If the claim is that it is correct for me but not for anyone else to do what he wants, then it would be a form of relativism. But this is not what we are discussing.) The claim might be an assertion of ethical nihilism, if what is meant is that we are all permitted to do whatever we want, because nothing is right and nothing is wrong. But this claim, in denying that there is a correct standard, is incompatible both with ethical relativism, which states that there are several correct standards, and with ethical egoism, which claims there is just one, namely:

Ethical Egoism: Each person ought to act to maximize her own good or well-being.

Consequently, although we have cast doubt on both ethical relativism and nihilism, nothing we have said yet casts any doubt on ethical egoism.

Strictly speaking, if someone is expressing an egoistic ethical theory, when she says that she can do whatever she wants to do, it is more likely that she is asserting the species of ethical egoism known as egoistic hedonism, because she is talking about what she wants or desires. This brand of egoism often equates what is good with pleasure or happiness:

Egoistic Hedonism: What each person ought to do is to act to maximize her own pleasure or happiness.

Let us interpret this statement of egoistic hedonism as follows:

A person ought to perform an action in a situation if and only if she does it in order to maximize her own pleasure or happiness.

This will give us a standard we can use not only to decide what we ought to do, but also to decide what we have no obligation to do. On this interpretation, if I do something to maximize my pleasure then I ought to do it; if it is not something I do to maximize my pleasure then it is not true that I ought to do it (which means that it is morally permissible for me not to do it). Notice that the claim is that this interpretation provides a standard for what we are not obligated to do rather than a standard for what we are obligated not to do. This is an important difference because, for example, although we are not obligated to tie our left shoelaces before the right, this does not mean that we are obligated not to tie the left before the right. The first tells us that we have no moral obligations about the order of tying shoelaces, whereas the second states that we have a moral obligation not to tie them in a certain order, that is, we are forbidden to tie the left lace before the right. Using the standard of hedonistic egoism, we find out what we ought not do, what is morally forbidden or prohibited, by finding which actions are the contradictories of those actions we ought to do. For example, if I ought to tell the truth, then I am forbidden to fail to tell the truth, that is, I ought not lie. With these distinctions in mind let us examine the most widespread species of egoism, egoistic hedonism.

EGOISTIC HEDONISM

Before we begin a critical evaluation of this theory we must be sure of what it implies and what it does not imply, because certain objections to the theory have arisen from misunderstanding it. It is one kind of hedonistic theory and thus proclaims that pleasure is the one thing good in itself. That is, it proclaims that whereas certain things may be good as means to certain other things, pleasure is the one thing good as an end, the one thing to be sought for its own sake. Other things are to be sought only if they are means to pleasure. Thus, medicine is not good as an end, but it is good as a means, because it leads to pleasure by helping cure us of diseases. Pleasure, therefore, is what has been called the *summum bonum*, or the highest good. Some people have objected to equating the *summum bonum* with pleasure, because they equate pleasure with such bodily pleasures as those provided by sex, food, and drink. But a hedonist is not committed to such a position, because she can recognize what have been called the "higher" pleasures, such as aesthetic pleasures and the pleasures of contemplation, invention, and artistic creation. Consequently, a hedonist can aim at these "higher" pleasures and thus justify performing the activities that are the means to achieving them.

An egoistic hedonist is interested in doing what maximizes her own pleasure. Many people picture such a person as one who every minute is seeking immediate thrills and excitement without a thought for the future.

This, however, is wrong, because the amount of pleasure someone gets from an act depends not only on the present pleasures she receives, but also on the longer-range consequences of the act. A hedonist need not be shortsighted, because she can realize that by abstaining from pleasures now she might maximize the pleasure she gets throughout her life. A hedonist who, because of the present pain of the shots, refused a rabies shot after being bitten by a rabid dog would be a poor hedonist indeed, because the future pain of the disease far outweighs the pain of the shots. A hedonist, therefore, need not be one who lives for the moment and seeks sensual pleasures. She can aim at the intellectual pleasures by carefully planning her daily life, with her sights set on some future goals. Egoistic hedonism, then, is not what it might first appear to be. Nevertheless, it does seem contrary to our usual conception of morality, because it seems to condone a kind of selfishness. Consequently, unless there are good reasons for accepting egoistic hedonism, it is a theory that we should reject.

However, most people who profess egoistic hedonism are not disturbed by the challenge to defend their position, because they base it on a certain theory about the psychological abilities and limitations of human beings which they think is clearly true. Although there are several versions of this theory, many of them state that whether a person can do a certain action in a particular situation depends on which of her desires is strongest at that time; and furthermore, in any situation, a person's strongest desire is always to increase her own pleasure or happiness as much as possible. Thus, in any situation, a person acts to maximize his own happiness, regardless of anything else. This theory is psychological egoism, and can be defined as follows:

> *Psychological Egoism*: A human being is psychologically able to perform an action if and only if she does it in order to maximize her own pleasure or happiness.[4]

Notice how psychological egoism differs from ethical egoistic hedonism. The first states conditions for what we have the ability to do, whereas the second states conditions for what we have a moral obligation to do. They are, then, importantly different. The first is purely a factual statement, but the second expresses an ethical standard. Nevertheless, the factual, psychological claim is thought to provide reason for accepting the ethical claim.

---

4. This statement of psychological egoism should not be read as asserting that a person does everything he is psychologically able to do. It has the force of "A human being is psychologically able to perform an action if and only if he does it (if he does it at all) in order to maximize his own pleasure or happiness." We make use of the simpler version just stated for convenience.

The Argument from Psychological Egoism

The argument from psychological egoism can be stated as follows: The only actions a person is psychologically able to perform are those in accordance with her strongest desire, or, in other words, those she does to maximize her own pleasure. But surely we are under an obligation to do something only if we can do it. Therefore, the only things we ought to do are things we do to maximize our own pleasure. Egoistic hedonism is true.

Let us examine this argument by putting it in the following form:

1. A person has an obligation to do an action only if she is able to do it.

2. A person is able to do something only if she does it to maximize her own pleasure or happiness.

Therefore

3. A person has an obligation to do an action only if she does it to maximize her own pleasure or happiness.

Therefore

4. Ethical egoistic hedonism is true.

The first thing to notice is that the inference from (3) to (4) is invalid, because egoistic hedonism states not only that someone has an obligation to do something *only if* she does it to maximize her own pleasure, but also that she ought to do it *if* it is something she does to maximize her own pleasure. The second part of the claim is important for our purposes, because we are searching for a justifiable standard or criterion for deciding what we ought to do, which means that we want a sufficient rather than a necessary condition for moral obligation. Thus egoistic hedonist cannot be established merely by an appeal to the hedonistic psychological theory. However, because the inference from (1) and (2) to (3) is valid, an egoistic hedonist can, if (1) and (2) are true, establish that we have no obligation to do anything unless we do it to maximize our own pleasure. That is, this argument can establish, if sound, that any ethical standard would have to prescribe only actions that someone does to maximize her own pleasure, whether or not it also states that she ought to do those actions *because* they are the actions she does to maximize her own pleasure. The argument, then, although it does not establish egoistic hedonism, does provide us with a way of evaluating those ethical standards which compete with egoistic hedonism. And, because it seems clear that most other standards will sometimes prescribe actions that someone would not do to maximize her own pleasure, this argument, if sound, provides a powerful means of eliminating alternative ethical standards, perhaps to the point where only egoistic hedonism remains unscathed. It is important, then, to examine this argument.

Premise (1), often expressed as the dictum that "ought implies can," is a generally accepted principle. Generally we agree that no one has an obligation to do something if it is impossible for her to do it, for example, if she has some disability. Thus, in the example of the drowning child used earlier in Chapter Six, I have no obligation to jump into the water to save the child if I cannot swim. And if people blame me for not swimming out to the child instead of running after help, I can absolve myself of blame by telling them I could not swim. Thus, I had an obligation to swim to the child only if I could swim. Premise (1), then, is acceptable.

Objection to Psychological Egoism: People Sometimes Act Benevolently

The crucial part of the argument is obviously premise (2), the one derived from psychological egoism. Let us examine it. It might be claimed, however, that a philosopher has no business critically evaluating premise (2), because philosophers are not generally competent to evaluate empirical scientific claims. However, we shall find grounds for thinking that if, as claimed, psychological egoism is an empirical claim, then its falsity is so apparent that no special training is needed to show it.

We are assuming that, like any competing psychological theory, psychological egoism is an empirical scientific theory. As such, it should have one feature in common with other empirical theories, that is, it should be empirically falsifiable. There should, then, be some empirically ascertainable situation which, if it occurred, would falsify the theory. What we seem to need, to test psychological egoism, is a case where someone did not act in order to maximize her own pleasure or happiness. We can use, therefore, a case where someone acted to sacrifice her own happiness for the happiness of another, or, it would seem, any case of someone acting altruistically or benevolently. But surely cases of people acting benevolently are not uncommon. We hear of parents working many extra hours to help educate their children, of people donating a kidney to help a person dying for lack of one, of missionaries who risk their lives to bring help and knowledge to backward peoples. In these and many other cases, we surely seem to have people acting benevolently for others instead of acting for themselves. Thus it seems that we psychological egoism is not only falsifiable, but that it has been quite easily falsified. The argument we have used goes as follows:

5. If psychological egoism is true, then each person always acts to maximize her own happiness.

6. If each person always acts to maximize her own happiness, then no one acts benevolently.

7. Some people act benevolently.

Therefore

8. Psychological egoism is false.

Reply: People Always Act Out of Self-Love

Defenders of psychological egoism can be expected to reply with a counterargument, one which attacks premise (7). They will argue that people always act out of self-love or self-interest even when what they do helps others. They will insist that, although it is true that people often do *benevolent acts* (that is, acts that actually help others), nobody ever really *acts benevolently* (that is, *for the sake of* helping others). Why should we suppose that people never act benevolently? Those who adopt psychological egoism will no doubt answer that people always act on their strongest desires, and every person's strongest desire is for his or her own self-interest. It only seems to us that people act benevolently, because we confuse a benevolent act with acting benevolently. Once we make this important distinction, we see that premise (7) is false, and the argument that contains it does nothing to cast doubt on psychological egoism.

Final Objection: People Do Not Always Act Out of Self-Love

Our mistake was to stress examples of acting benevolently. We need, rather, to point out clear examples of people acting contrary to their own happiness, because, taking such examples with premise (5),

If psychological egoism is true, then each person always acts to maximize her own happiness.

we can clearly show psychological egoism to be false. Once again it seems we have a straightforward empirical question before us, and once again the answer seems to be that there are cases where it is most implausible to claim that a person is satisfying a desire for her own happiness. People sometimes seem to sacrifice their own happiness when they act out of a sense of duty to do what they think is right. Many patriotic soldiers are convinced by personal experience that war is hell, yet they volunteer for dangerous missions that surely are contrary to their own well-being and happiness. There have also been cases of people bent on revenge who plainly do not care what happens to them, as long as they destroy someone else. In such cases, it seems clear that these people are acting to satisfy other-directed desires rather than their desires for their own happiness. Consequently, once again it seems we should conclude that psychological egoism is false.

At this point, the almost invariable reply is that people act out of self-love even in those cases in which it seems evident that they do not act out of self-love. Once this move has been made, psychological egoism becomes like two other often heard claims (that is, people always act to satisfy their strongest desire, and people always act to reduce tension): even the most obvious contrary cases are not taken to count against the claim. That is, the theory has been made immune to empirical falsification. It is not merely claimed that no actual cases have falsified the theory, but rather that no case we could possibly conceive would falsify it. Psychological egoism is often held in this dogmatic way, but when it is, it is no longer an empirical scientific theory open to checking by observation. It has become consistent with anything we might observe, and thus it is no longer a theory of the empirical science of psychology. Consequently, it is no longer the kind of theory that can be justified by the findings of psychology, so that science will not provide a reason for accepting it.

Should we reject this nonempirical form of psychological egoism, as we have the earlier version? Unlike the previous version, it really does not matter what we do. Recall that the previous version, if acceptable, was to be used as a test of what persons can do and thus as a means for rejecting ethical standards which prescribe actions incompatible with it. It was, then, importantly relevant to ethics. But the present version has been made compatible with any behavior we could observe, and thus it cannot be used to test the actions prescribed by standards that compete with egoistic hedonism. Psychological egoism has been weakened to such a degree that it cannot help us decide among ethical standards. Thus any ethical theorist can accept it. We can, if we like, also accept this version of psychological egoism, but if we do, we can immediately ignore it because it has no relevance to ethics, or for that matter, to psychology.

We have found that the ethical egoist cannot rely on psychological egoism to help her justify her position. If the theory is empirical, it surely seems to be false, and, if it is nonempirical, it does not help provide reasons to choose ethical egoism instead of some other ethical theory. Consequently, the ethical egoist must find some other way to justify her theory. The only other remotely plausible argument is based on the fact that, when someone asks us why we did something, we often answer him by saying it was because we wanted to, and that settles it. For example, if you ask me why I went to the movies instead of studying last night, I might answer that I felt like going to the movies, or that I did not want to study, and when I reply this way, the question is answered. Now, the argument states, because such a question is a request for justification of my action, I have justified my action by answering the question. Thus, I have provided a good reason for what I did by reference to what I wanted, so that my doing what I want is justified and therefore is what I ought to do. Because this argument, which we can call the argument from good reasons, embodies two mistakes that are relevant to our current interests, we should examine the argument with some care.

The Argument from Good Reasons
The crux of the argument can be outlined as follows:

1. If I desire to do something (do something to get pleasure), then I can justify doing it by reference to the desire (pleasure).

2. If I can justify doing something, then I have a good reason for doing it.

3. If I have a good reason for doing something, then it is what I ought to do.

Therefore

4. If I desire to do something (do something to get pleasure), then it is what I ought to do.

This argument, like the previous argument, fails to justify ethical egoism, but for different reasons. First, it provides only a sufficient condition of obligation, whereas ethical egoism states a necessary condition as well. Admittedly, this is not a vital point, because we can design a parallel argument which would allow us to conclude that if I do not desire to do something, then it is not what I ought to do. The second reason is that ethical egoism refers to what maximizes my pleasure rather than to what merely gives me pleasure. We can fix this, however, by referring to what I most desire and what I do to maximize my pleasure. Let us assume, then, that from this argument, with the parallel negative argument, we can infer that ethical egoism is true. But is the argument sound?

Objection: Desiring To Do Something Does Not Justify Doing It
We have based premise (1) on the fact that we quite often can answer a "Why?" question once and for all by saying that we wanted to. Thus we often can satisfy a request for justification by such an answer. But we have inferred from this that we provide a justification for what we do, whenever we answer in this way. There are two reasons why this is a mistaken inference. First, when I reply to a question such as, "Why did you go to the movies instead of studying?" by saying, "I wanted to," or "I felt like it," my answer does not provide a good reason for what I did, but rather is used to refuse to give a reason or to claim that no reason is necessary. It functions more like "No reason," "I don't know," "Because," or even a shrug of the shoulders. Thus, when someone answers this way, he is not justifying his action, but rather is claiming that there is nothing to justify or is refusing to give a justification. Such an answer may stop the questioning, but it does not justify the action. This can be illustrated by a different example. Suppose you ask someone why he shot that old woman as she crossed the street, and he answers that he felt like it and will say no more. He might just as well have shrugged his shoulders, for in neither case would he justify what he did. In this example, we

are not satisfied with his answer, because here, unlike the first example, a justification is called for, and he has provided none. Thus, although we can sometimes answer requests for justification by talking about our desires and pleasure, we have not provided a justification for our actions, because such an answer is adequate only when no justification is required. Secondly, even if we were to agree that we can sometimes justify our actions in this way, the shooting example shows that many times we cannot. There are situations in which only I am affected, so that the only morally relevant factors are my own preferences. But where others are affected there are other morally relevant factors. Thus, we can reject premise (1) and with it this argument for ethical egoism.

Before we move on, we should also note that premise (3) is false, because this reemphasizes an important distinction. It is often true that if I have a good reason for doing something, then it is permissible for me to do it, that is, it is not wrong for me to do it. But it does not follow that it is always something I ought to do. Often, when we justify an action, we show that it is not prohibited rather than that it is obligatory. For example, it seems that people can often provide good reasons for not helping someone who is being attacked by a gang of knife wielders in the caverns of some large city. But, although such reasons show he has no obligation to help, and therefore is morally permitted not to help, they would not show that he had an obligation not to help. Once again we must distinguish between 'no obligation to' and 'obligation not to' to emphasize that, although the person who does not help in this case should not feel immoral, neither should he feel particularly moral.

Rejection of Egoistic Hedonism:
It Prescribes Morally Repugnant Acts

We have found no way to justify the species of ethical egoism we have called egoistic hedonism. Should we reject it? We have been operating on the principle that if an ethical standard prescribes certain actions a person feels certain are morally wrong, and these beliefs are not inconsistent with his other beliefs, then the person has some reason to reject the standard. In this case, in addition, no counterbalancing arguments favor egoistic hedonism. Moreover, some actions prescribed by this standard, we think, are ones that virtually anyone would feel are morally wrong. Thus, consider a sadist, or someone who hates a whole race of people. The catalog of sadistic pleasures found in *Justine,* by the Marquis de Sade, is enough to show that many actions that give people pleasure are nonetheless morally repugnant to virtually everyone who considers the matter. The pleasure some Nazis found in torturing, maiming, and killing Jews, the attitudes of thrill murderers, and the boastful and brash killings of some black persons by certain white Southerners all testify that egoistic hedonism would not only permit, but also make obligatory some of the most horrendous crimes ever committed.

We should, then, conclude not only that there is some reason to reject this standard, but also that egoistic hedonism ought to be rejected outright, because, by making each person's pleasure his or her guide to what is right and wrong, it prescribes the kind of selfishness that ignores the happiness and welfare of any other person.

NONHEDONISTIC ETHICAL EGOISM

We have rejected egoistic hedonism, which is one form of ethical egoism, but should we also reject ethical egoism in general? To answer this we must do the things we did in evaluating egoistic hedonism, that is, find out whether any arguments justify it, and it prescribes any actions we are convinced are wrong. We have defined ethical egoism as the theory that makes the following claim:

Each person ought to act to maximize his own good or well-being.

Corresponding to the standard we used for egoistic hedonism we have the following:

A person ought to perform an action if and only if he does it to maximize his own well-being (that is, if and only if he does it to maximize his own best interest).

We have come to this standard by substituting 'well-being' for 'pleasure.' Consequently, we can arrive at the arguments for ethical egoism by the same substitution. What we find, then, is an argument based on the theory that we always act for our own well-being or self-interest, and an argument based on the claim that we can justify our actions by reference to self-interest. We shall leave it to the reader to substantiate that the arguments in this form are no better than those in the previous form. Consequently, if the general theory of ethical egoism prescribes actions that we are certain are morally wrong, we can reject it with egoistic hedonism.

Objection to Ethical Egoism:
It Prescribes Morally Repugnant Acts
The first thing to note is that ethical egoism does not prescribe many of the specific actions prescribed by egoistic hedonism, because what provides me with maximum pleasure often is not what maximizes my well-being. This is especially noticeable if we identify our well-being and self-interest with mental and physical health and abilities. Some people have a choice between, on the one hand, a life of intense pleasures, in which their health deteriorates and they do not develop their abilities, and, on the other hand,

a restrained, often arduous and regimented life, in which they maintain their health and develop their abilities. It is not unlikely that the first life, even if considerably shortened by an early death—especially if it came quickly and painlessly—would contain more pleasure than the second. But the second would be more conducive to the well-being of the person. Thus, these two different standards might often differ in what they prescribe, so that the examples we used against egoistic hedonism cannot be used in their present form against ethical egoism. Nevertheless, examples can be devised that will provide grounds for rejecting ethical egoism. One example is the case where three people have a disease which is fatal unless they take certain pills. One of these people, unknown to anyone else, has the only three pills available, and he knows that if a person takes one he has a 90 percent chance of surviving the disease, if he takes two he has a 94 percent chance, and if he takes all three he has a 99 percent chance. What ought he to do? It seems clear that he ought to give each person one pill. But ethical egoism prescribes that he maximize his own well-being; that in this case he ought to take all three pills himself and let the others die.

CONCLUSION ABOUT ETHICAL EGOISM: IT SHOULD BE REJECTED

Because the general theory of ethical egoism seems no better justified than that brand of egoism we have called egoistic hedonism, we conclude that ethical egoism ought to be rejected. This is because no sound argument supports it, and because it prescribes certain morally repugnant actions. These are actions which, if we look back at the relevant examples, we find we have one morally relevant feature in common. In each case the action ethical egoism prescribes is morally repugnant, because the standard ignores the happiness and welfare of other people affected by the prescribed action. In short, the standard of ethical egoism seems to be misguided because it ignores one ingredient of morality that seems to be essential, namely, impartiality. In deciding what ought to be done, it seems that each person who is to be affected by the action should be taken into account. No one should be ignored, and no one should be given privileged status. Let us turn to a theory which explicitly incorporates impartiality into its standard.

UTILITARIANISM: BENTHAM'S VERSION

Utilitarianism is not only the name of a particular ethical theory, but the name of the doctrine that called for social reforms to be achieved by bringing the actions of persons and also governments into line with the ethical principle of utility. This principle, as an ethical and social weapon for reform, received its first eloquent expression in the writing of Jeremy Bentham, who defined it as follows:

> By the principle of utility is meant that principle which approves or disapproves of every action whatsoever, according to the tendency which it appears to have to augment or diminish the happiness of the party whose interest is in question; or, what is the same thing in other words, to promote or to oppose that happiness. I say of every action whatsoever; and therefore not only of every action of a private individual, but of every measure of government.[5]

As Bentham himself realized, it might be more perspicuous to call his ethical principle the greatest happiness principle, rather than the principle of utility, because the principle is to be concerned with happiness, pleasure, and pain of the parties affected by actions. And as he said in a footnote added later,

> The word 'utility' does not so clearly point to the ideas of *pleasure* and *pain* as the words 'happiness' and 'felicity' do: nor does it lead us to the consideration of the *number*, of the interests affected; to the *number*, as being the circumstance, which contributes, in the largest proportion, to the formation of the standard here in question; *the standard of right and wrong*, by which alone the propriety of human conduct, in every situation, can with propriety be tried.[6]

It is important, then, to note that utilitarianism, which is the theory proposing the principle of utility as the correct ethical standard, equates the utility of something with its tendency to produce happiness or pleasure. Thus, the word 'utility,' as we shall be using it here, is not synonymous with 'usefulness,' so that when we consider the utility of something we shall not be considering what use it has or how useful it is, but its relationship to the production of happiness.

---

5. Bentham, *The Utilitarians* 17-18.
6. Ibid., 291.

The Principle of Utility

Let us try to state the utilitarian standard clearly. A first approximation is the following:

An action ought to be done if and only if it maximizes the pleasure of those parties affected by the action.

This statement, however, can be made more precise by specifying what is to count as an affected party. It may seem evident that the reference is to persons, but Bentham realized that the state or community as a whole can be an interested and affected party. There are, for example, crimes against the state, and some heads of state have insisted that the interests of the state are distinct from those of its citizens. Thus leaders have called on citizens to sacrifice themselves for the fatherland, that is, sacrifice their own happiness, even their lives, for the state. Some people have claimed that the state is not only a distinct individual, but that it is an individual of more worth than any or even all of its citizens. It is surely important for our purposes, then, whether or not we are to count the state or community as a separate affected individual in formulating this standard. Bentham realized this and clarified what he meant by 'party.'

The community is a fictitious *body*, composed of the individual persons who are considered as constituting as it were its *members*. The interest of the community then is, what?—The sum of the interests of the several members who compose it.[7]

According to Bentham, then, we need not consider the state as a separate affected party, so that we can change the standard to read:

An action ought to be done if and only if it maximizes the pleasure of those people affected by the action.

This formulation is still ambiguous, however, because it might be interpreted as stating that an action is right only if the pleasure of each person affected is maximized. Not only is this not what Bentham meant, it is a standard which could rarely be met. In most situations, it is not possible to maximize the happiness or pleasure of *each* person involved. Usually, someone is going to be less than completely satisfied with what happens. What Bentham means is that the action that ought to be done in a particular situation is the one that maximizes the sum total of pleasure produced. Thus, although in many situations some of those affected will be made unhappy and made to feel pain, we might try characterizing right actions as those that minimize the number of people made unhappy and made to feel pain. However, even this modification is not quite right, because an action that causes several people to have a slight headache is

---

7. Ibid., 18.

better than an action in which, all else being equal, only one person suffers an almost unendurable pain. Thus, we must consider not merely how many people receive pleasure or pain from the action, but also how intense each pleasure or pain is. So let us take the principle to consider the total amount of pleasure and pain produced, where the amount is a function of intensity per person and number of people affected. We can now state the principle in the following form:

> An action ought to be done if and only if it maximizes the total amount of pleasure of those persons affected by the action.

We are not yet finished amending it. Although it may seem obvious that the feature of morality we saw was missing from ethical egoism—that is, impartiality,—is included in the preceding formulation of the utilitarian principle, there is still room for partiality. How we arrive at the total amount can be affected by many factors, including whether or not we give equal weight to each person affected. In any society where some people are considered second-class citizens, someone using the last version of the principle might weight the percent of the total pleasure or pain contributed by each person according to his status as a full-fledged or secondary citizen. It seems clear that pleasure and pain of black persons in many parts of some countries are not added in on equal grounds with white pleasure and pain. There are also examples where the pleasures of kings have been taken to count for more than those of their subjects. Bentham, however, wants no such fractionalizing, so we must state the factor of impartiality explicitly. This will give us the final version of the principle of utility:

> An action ought to be done if and only if it maximizes the total amount of pleasure of those persons affected by the action, counting each person as one and no person as more than one.

We shall use this statement in our critical evaluation of Bentham's standard, which we shall begin by examining the proofs that have been offered to support it.

Arguments for the Principle of Utility
As Bentham realized, two kinds of proofs can be offered in defense of an ethical principle—one he called direct proof, the other we can call indirect proof. The first kind of proof is a deductive proof in which the conclusion is the principle itself. Thus this kind of proof argues directly for the principle. In an indirect proof the principle is supported indirectly, by refuting objections to it and by showing that there are objections to the opposing alternatives. This is the way we argued in critically evaluating the various positions proposed as solutions to the mind-body problem, and it is the way we have been approaching the various ethical theories. Obviously, an indirect proof cannot provide an argument as rigorous, or

grounds as solid, as can a direct proof. Let us then begin by seeing whether any direct proofs support the principle of utility.

Direct Proofs for the Principle of Utility: Deriving 'Ought' from 'Is'

Bentham thought that there were no direct proofs of his principle, "for that which is used to prove everything else, cannot itself be proved: a chain of proofs must have their commencement somewhere."[8] Bentham's point here is that he is proposing the principle of utility as the ultimate or basic ethical standard. Therefore, although other ethical principles may be deducible from it, it is not deducible from any other ethical principle. Although we can deduce certain obligations from certain ethical standards, and perhaps those standards from others, the process of deduction must begin with one or more ethical principles that are not deducible from any others. These are the basic principles. For Bentham, as for most ethical theorists, there is only one basic principle, and this cannot be deduced from a more basic ethical principle.

It may occur to someone, that, although the basic ethical principle cannot be deduced from other ethical principles, this does not show that the basic principle cannot be deduced from some factual premises about the way things are. This has been tried. People have tried to deduce moral obligations from the nature of human beings, from the facts of evolution, or from facts about societies, cultures, and economic classes. In each case they have tried to deduce a normative ought-statement from a factual is-statement.

Hume's objection: No 'ought' is deducible from 'is'

One of the first to cast suspicion upon deducing 'ought' from 'is' was David Hume, who said,

> In every system of morality, which I have hitherto met with, I have always remark'd, that the author proceeds for some time in the ordinary way of reasoning, and establishes the being of a God, or makes observations concerning human affairs; when of a sudden I am surpriz'd to find, that instead of the usual copulations of propositions, *is*, and *is not*, I meet with no proposition that is not connected with an *ought*, or an *ought not*. This change is imperceptible; but is, however, of the last consequence. For as this *ought*, or *ought not*, expresses some new relation or affirmation, 'tis necessary that it shou'd be observ'd and explain'd; and at the same time that a reason should be given, for what

---

8. Ibid., 19.

seems altogether inconceivable, how this new relation can be a deduction from others, which are entirely different from it.[9]

Hume is making the straightforward logical point here that no ought-statement, that is, one that makes *only* an ought-claim and therefore no factual claim, is logically deducible from a factual is-statement, that is, one that makes *only* a factual claim and therefore no ought-claim. To see Hume's point here, consider any two propositions, P and Q, and imagine that Q is logically deducible from P. If it is, then an explicit self-contradiction will be deducible from the conjunction of P and *not* Q. For example, let P = 'It is raining and it is cloudy,' and let Q = 'It is raining.' It should be obvious that P entails Q or, put another way, that Q is deducible from P. After all, P is a conjunction and Q is one of the conjuncts. Now consider the conjunction P and *not* Q. In words it would be

It is raining and it is cloudy and it is not raining.

We can understand Hume's point by utilizing this key idea with respect to moral and nonmoral statements. Suppose we have a purely factual claim with no 'ought,' such as the proposition A, 'Helping others is maximizing happiness,' and a normative ought-claim, statement B, 'We ought to help others.' Now if A were to entail B, then an explicit contradiction would be deducible from the conjunction of A and *not* B. But consider that latter conjunction; it is

Helping others is maximizing happiness *and* we ought not help others.

This statement is not itself an explicit contradiction, a statement of the form P and *not-P*; and neither is there any contradiction we can deduce from this conjunction. Hence, reasoning just as we did above in the example about raining, we can conclude that A does not entail B.

We have not yet reached a conclusion about the principle of utility or any other ethical standard, because such standards typically include both ought-claims and is-claims (factual claims). However, we can use Hume's conclusion to draw one about ethical standards. Let us assume that O is some ought-statement, F is a conjunction of all true is-statements that make factual claims, and S is some ethical standard such that O or some other ought-statement is deducible from S, depending upon which factual statements are conjoined with S. Thus, if S were the principle of utility, and F includes the statement F_1, 'A is an action that maximizes the total amount of pleasure,' then we could deduce O, 'A ought to be done.' Now we have seen that no ought-statement is deducible from any purely factual

9. D. Hume, *A Treatise of Human Nature*, 2nd edition, ed. P. H. Nidditch (New York: Oxford University Press, 1978), 469.

statement. Consequently, O is not deducible from F alone, but, we can assume, O is deducible from S and F. From this we can conclude that S, which stands for any ethical standard, is not deducible from F alone, the conjunction of all true factual statements. Thus, no ethical standard is deducible from any or even all true factual premises.[10]

The reasoning here is somewhat intricate. However, it can be simplified in the following way: Suppose, that S is some ethical standard such as the principle of utility, F is the conjunction of all true factual claims, and that O is some ought-claim. Assuming that F includes F_1 as a conjunct, we have:

1. O is deducible from the conjunction S and F.

Now we already know, from an argument given earlier that no purely factual claim entails a purely normative ought-claim. Thus, we may say,

2. It is not the case that O is deducible from F. (Alternatively: It is not the case that F entails O.)

From (1) and (2), we want to conclude that

3. It is not the case that S (an ethical standard) is deducible from F (set of all true factual claims).

To see how to get this conclusion from (1) and (2), we may use an indirect proof or argument. That is, we may start by assuming the very *opposite* of (3), namely,

4. S is deducible from F.

Now we may certainly allow that

5. F is deducible from F.

But, if S is deducible from F, and F is likewise deducible from F, then so is their conjunction. That is, from (4) and (5), we get

6. The conjunction S and F is deducible from F.

Notice, though, that when (6) and (1) are taken together, we get directly,

7. O is deducible from F.

The move from (1) and (6) is just a type of hypothetical syllogism: If the conjunction S and F is deducible from F [= (6)], and O is deducible from the conjunction S and F [= (1)], then O is deducible from F [= (7)].

Statement (7), however, is the very opposite of (2). These two statements taken together amount to a contradiction, to the effect that O both is and is not deducible from F. We derived this contradiction by means of

---

10. See Chapter One, pp. 7-10, for a discussion of deductibility.

the introduction of (4), which, we may recall, is the very opposite of (3). So, we may conclude that (4) is, so to speak, the logical culprit here. From premises (1) and (2) and (4), we find that we can deduce a self-contradiction. Hence, using the very same reasoning we used earlier to discuss 'is' and 'ought,' we may conclude that (3) is deducible from the conjunction of (1) and (2).

A further objection: Naturalistic (definist) fallacy

We have seen that no ultimate ethical standard is deducible from any other ethical standard, and that no ethical standard is deducible from purely factual premises. It would seem, then, that we could conclude no direct proof is possible for an ultimate ethical standard. However, such a conclusion would be premature. Although no ought-statements and no ethical standards are deducible from a set of premises all of which are factual is-statements, it might be true nevertheless that with the addition of only certain analytic premises we can deduce some ought-statement or some ethical standard. If this can be done, then, because the additional premise is logically necessary, we can conclude that it is logically necessary that if the factual premises are true, then so also is the ought-conclusion. That is, the factual premise would entail the ought-conclusion, and, after all, 'ought' could be derived from 'is.'[11]

To see how this might be applied to 'ought' and 'is,' let us consider the following argument:

1. A is an action that maximizes the total amount of happiness.

Therefore

2. A ought to be done.

This argument with a factual is-premise and an ought-conclusion is invalid. But if we add as a premise

3. Whatever maximizes the total amount of happiness is what ought to be done.

then the argument is valid. And if (3) is an analytic statement and therefore necessarily true, then we can conclude that (1) entails (2). Consequently, someone might offer the preceding argument to show how 'ought' can be derived from 'is.' This, of course, raises the question of whether (3) is analytic, that is, a statement whose truth can be established by appealing only to logic and the meaning of its terms. Some people seem to have thought that it is, and the view has even been ascribed to Bentham, in spite of the fact that he thinks the principle of utility requires

---

11. See Chapter One, pp. 26-27, for a discussion of analyticity and entailment.

an indirect proof. We should, therefore, examine the claim that (3) is analytic, because if it is, then we need proceed no further in our search for a justifiable ethical standard.

Some might argue that (3) is analytic on the grounds that, first, it is analytic that what ought to be done is what maximizes what is good, and second, that the general happiness is, by definition, what is good. This is the way G. E. Moore interprets Bentham, when he claims that Bentham, like many others, commits what Moore calls the "naturalistic fallacy."[12] This fallacy, according to Moore, is committed by anyone who defines an ethical term such as 'good,' 'right,' or 'wrong' by terms that are purely factual or descriptive, and therefore have no evaluative force. Thus, the naturalistic fallacy is committed when someone defines ethical terms such as 'good' using only such empirical terms as 'pleasure,' 'happiness,' 'desire,' or 'interest.' However, the fallacy is not restricted to definitions that contain only naturalistic, that is, empirical, terms. It has been pointed out that this fallacy might better be called the definist fallacy because, as Moore says himself, it is committed whenever someone defines an evaluative term such as 'good' by any nonevaluative term.[13] Thus, not only naturalistic or empirical definitions, but also metaphysical and religious definitions would involve the fallacy. If Moore is right, to define 'good' as 'what God wills' is to commit the same fallacy as to define it as 'pleasure.'

Now we must ask why Moore thinks that any such definition is fallacious. His primary reason is that any such definition would make many open or debatable questions closed and trivial. For example, if someone were to define 'what is always good' as 'pleasure,' then the seemingly debatable question, 'Is pleasure always good?' becomes no more than the trivial question, 'Is pleasure pleasure?' It surely seems worth debating whether pleasure is always good, but no one would spend time debating whether pleasure is pleasure. Another way of seeing this is by realizing that many statements we use to command or condemn someone for doing something would become mere trivially true analytic sentences and lose their evaluative force. For example, if I tell someone that he ought to promote the general happiness because promoting the general happiness is promoting what is good, I mean to support a certain kind of action by commending it. But if 'what is good' means 'the general happiness' then all I have said is that he ought to promote the general happiness because promoting the general happiness is promoting the general happiness. This latter claim is not only absurd, but it is clearly not a case of supporting

---

12. See G. E. Moore, *Principia Ethica* (New York: Cambridge University Press, 1960), 5-21.

13. See W. Frankena, "The Naturalistic Fallacy," in W. Sellers and J. Hospers, eds., *Readings in Ethical Theory*, 2nd ed. (New York: Appleton-Century-Crofts, 1970), 54-62.

something by commending it.[14] I might just have said, "because killing is killing," or "promoting misery is promoting misery." But the original claim is not absurd. Therefore, the latter is not an adequate translation of the original claim, and any other translation that leaves out the evaluative, and thereby the moral, element will also be inadequate.

The consequences of this fallacy are important. We can now state that no ethical claim is derivable from factual premises, because none is entailed by any factual statement. Any such entailment would involve the naturalistic or definist fallacy. Therefore, we can also conclude that no ethical standard is entailed by any factual statement. In this way we have established what has been called the *autonomy* of ethics. That is, no ethical statements are derivable from any nonethical statements, so that no scientific findings entail any ethical principle, no metaphysical claims entail any ethical principle, and no (nonethical) religious claims entail any ethical principle. We cannot, then, hope to find a direct proof of the principle of utility or of any other ethical premises. We can conclude that Bentham was right: There is no direct proof of the principle of utility or of any other ultimate ethical principle.

Bentham's Indirect Proof of the Principle of Utility

Bentham uses just the kind of indirect proof we are using throughout this chapter. First, he claims,

> By the natural constitution of the human frame, on most occasions of their lives men in general embrace this principle, without thinking of it: if not for the ordering of their own actions, yet for the typing of their own actions, as well as those of other men.[15]

That is, according to Bentham, the principle of utility prescribes actions which, in their uncritical way, human beings believe to be right. Second, all principles which differ in what they prescribe from the principle of utility are confronted with objections sufficient for rejecting them. From these two premises, Bentham concludes that we are surely justified in accepting the principle of utility as the correct ethical standard.

Although, by and large, Bentham leaves it to the reader to investigate whether his principle is in line with our ordinary ethical beliefs, he does provide reasons for rejecting all opposing principles. He says that any principle different from his is either completely opposed to it or only sometimes opposed to it. The first opposing principle he calls the *principle*

---

14. See R. M. Hare, *The Language of Morals* (New York: Oxford University Press, 1952), Chapter 5, for a more detailed discussion of how the naturalistic fallacy results in the word 'good' losing its function of commending.

15. Bentham, *The Utilitarians*, 19-20.

of asceticism, which, he says, "like the principle of utility, approves or disapproves of any action, according to the tendency which it appears to have to augment or diminish the happiness of the party whose interest is in question; but in an inverse manner: approving of actions in as far as they tend to diminish his happiness; disapproving of them as far as they tend to augment it."[16] As Bentham points out, if such a principle were consistently followed, the earth would be turned into a living hell in a very short time. But Bentham's main attack is to point out that humans are incapable of consistently pursuing this principle. Consequently, because, as we have already seen, 'ought' implies 'can,' we can conclude that it is false that anyone ought to use such a principle. We can agree with Bentham that we should reject this principle.

All principles of the second kind opposed to the principle of utility, the kind that only in some situations opposes what the principle of utility prescribes, Bentham lumps together as various versions of what he calls the *principle of sympathy and antipathy*. By this he means

> that principle which approves or disapproves of certain actions, not on account of their tending to augment the happiness, nor yet on account of their tending to diminish the happiness of the party whose interest is in question, but merely because a man finds himself disposed to approve or disapprove of them: holding up that approbation or disapprobation as a sufficient reason for itself, and disclaiming the necessity of looking out for any extrinsic ground.[17]

Such principles, as Bentham points out, appeal to no standard independent of the feelings and sentiment of those who propose the principles. The appeal is in every case to what someone or other happens to approve or disapprove. Surely no justifiable ethical standard can be derived in this way. If Bentham is correct here, we should reject not only the principle completely opposed to his own, but also all those sometimes opposed. Only Bentham's principle would remain.

Objection to Bentham's proof: It does not disprove all opposing views
There are two points at which we can attack Bentham's proof: his reason for rejecting all principles that are in some situations opposed to the principle of utility, and his claim that no actions prescribed by his principle are morally repugnant. First, consider how Bentham characterizes all versions of the principle of sympathy and antipathy. No such principles, he claims, are standards independent of the feelings of people. He characterizes these rival theories as replacing an objective standard by a

---

16. Ibid., 21.
17. Ibid., 28.

mere reliance on feelings of approval and disapproval. Thus, according to Bentham, all these theories reduce to claims that we should make moral judgments merely on the basis of how we feel at the time.

We can agree with Bentham that all versions of the principle of sympathy and antipathy should rejected, but what seems clearly false is his claim that all principles sometimes opposed to his own are versions of the principle of sympathy and antipathy. Consider, for example, ethical egoism, which sometimes prescribes actions opposed to Bentham's principle of utility. It is clearly an objective standard applicable to all people at all times, and does not prescribe actions on the basis of what someone happens to find right or wrong at the moment. It is sometimes opposed to Bentham's principle, though it is not a version of the principle of sympathy and antipathy. Bentham's defense of his own principle fails, consequently, because he has not considered all rival principles.

Bentham might reply that principles sometimes opposed to his own also fail because they do not consider all people involved. But although this is true of egoism, it need not be true of all rivals to Bentham's principle, for they could be genuine rivals and consider all people involved, so long as they did not consider only the happiness of all involved. It will not do, of course, for Bentham to reject the opposing principles on the grounds that they do not consider only the happiness of all. If he did, he would only show that they differ from his own principle, but this is not a sufficient reason for rejecting them. Therefore, this part of Bentham's indirect proof fails, because he has failed to show that only the principle of utility and the previously rejected principle of asceticism are universally applicable principles that can be applied in an objective way.

The hedonic calculus

Although, as we have seen, Bentham has not shown that all principles different from his own can be rejected, this failure is not vital if, as Bentham thinks, his principle and his principle alone prescribes no actions that are morally repugnant to human beings. However, if we find situations in which what his principle prescribes is morally repugnant, then he is in serious difficulty. Let us, then, try to think of such a situation. To do so we must get some idea of how we are to arrive at a conclusion about what maximizes the total amount of pleasure in any one situation. The method proposed by Bentham is what has been called the *hedonic calculus*, because it proposes a way to calculate the total amount of pleasure by bringing in all the relevant factors. According to Bentham there are seven different relevant factors, which we can break down into three different basic categories. The first kind of factor includes the relevant characteristics of each pleasure and pain produced by the action being considered; the second kind includes the tendency of a particular pleasure or pain to be followed by more pleasure and pain; and the third kind is the method of including in the calculations all the pleasures and pains that result from the action being considered. Let us list these factors as follows:

Intrinsic Characteristics of Pleasure and Pain

1. *Intensity* of each pleasure or pain.

2. *Duration*, or length of time, of each pleasure or pain.

3. *Probability* that the pleasure or pain will occur after act.

This is affected by:

4. *Propinquity*, or nearness in time, of the pleasure or pain to the act.

Consequential Characteristics of Pleasure and Pain

5. *Fecundity*, or probability that the sensation will be followed by other sensations of the *same* kind.

6. *Impurity*, or probability that the sensation will be followed by other sensations of the *opposite* kind.

Summation of All Pleasures and Pains Resulting from Act

7. *Extent* of pleasures and pains.[18]

We can illustrate by a simple example how these factors might affect the sum total of pleasure and pain resulting from an act. Let us say that you, a person with barely enough money to eat, find a wallet containing $1,000 and cards identifying the owner as a multimillionaire. You plan to send back the wallet, but you are debating whether or not to send back the money. What should you do? To decide, you turn to the hedonic calculus. You calculate that because neither you nor the millionaire have any dependents no one need be considered but the two of you. You only have to weigh your pleasure and his pain if you keep the money against your pain and his pleasure if you send it back. We can surely assume that the intensity of pleasure you can obtain by using the money to buy food, drink, and entertainment far outweighs the intensity of the millionaire's irritation at not having the money returned. Furthermore, the duration of your pleasure will probably far exceed his irritation. We can assume that it is quite probable that you will get the pleasure and he will become irritated, so that factors (3) and (4) will not have much effect. We can also discount the effect of (5) and (6) in the case of the millionaire, because once his irritation is gone he will have too many more important things to think about. But if we assume that you will probably drink too much as a result of keeping the money we can say that the pleasure is somewhat impure, because of the hangover that follows it. Thus we must

---

18. Ibid., 37-40, for Bentham's statement of the hedonic calculus.

subtract some part of the total of your pleasure. And because such pleasures usually are not followed by additional pleasures as well as the pain of hangovers, we can conclude that your pleasure is not at all fecund. Nevertheless, it seems clear that if you keep the money your pleasure far exceeds the millionaire's displeasure, so that there is considerable overall increase in the total amount of pleasure. But if you return the money, the little pleasure the millionaire receives hardly outweighs the unhappiness you feel when you think of the good times you are missing. Given all this, the decision is easy. You should, if you apply the principle of utility, keep the money.

We have seen a simple example of how the principle of utility is to be applied in a specific situation. The question before us is whether there are certain situations in which the principle would prescribe morally repugnant actions. Someone might claim that we already have found such a situation, because we always ought to return lost items to their owner. However, there are exceptions to this rule, such as the one cited by Plato, where we should not return a lethal weapon to its rightful owner who has become a homicidal maniac. Furthermore, although the example we have used may seem to some to be a case where what is prescribed by the principle of utility is wrong, what it prescribes is not a clear-cut example of a morally repugnant act. It is by no means a clear counterexample to Bentham's claim that his principle generally prescribes actions in line with what we think is right. We need a stronger case to refute Bentham's claim.

An objection to Bentham's principle: Sadistic pleasures

We are to use the hedonic calculus to find out what we ought to do, so that if the calculus prescribes an obviously immoral action we can reject Bentham's principle. Let us take an example from the Marquis de Sade.[19] A roomful of men get extreme pleasure from the sadistic mutilation of the girl Justine. She suffers great pain, but all the men enjoy great pleasure, so that the sum total of pleasure in this case is greater than if the men forego their pleasure by allowing Justine to go her way unharmed. If we apply Bentham's principle, once again it is clear what ought to be done. The men should take their sadistic pleasures and Justine should suffer. But this is surely morally repugnant. Something has gone horribly wrong with a principle that prescribes such sadistic acts. It might be objected, however, that because the mutilation Justine suffers results in prolonged pain, whereas the pleasures of the sadists are short-lived, the total amount of pain outweighs the total amount of pleasure. This objection can easily be avoided by changing the situation to one in which this particular group always kills the object of their sadism at the end of the festivities by

---

19. Marquis de Sade, *Justine*, trans. Richard Seaver and Austryn Wainhouse (New York: Grove Press, 1965).

skillfully administering a drug that kills quickly and painlessly. Here murder, by cutting short sadistically inflicted pain, would, on Bentham's principle, remove an objection to willful injury.

Consider another example that illustrates again how emphasis on pleasure as the *summum bonum* can justify murder. Let us replace the sadists by a cult of people who hate pain but who get immense pleasure from mutilating a warm human body. This group carefully picks a victim who has no close family or friends and whose life is not particularly pleasurable. If they can, they try to choose someone who suffers from an illness so that they can eliminate pain. They kill such a person as skillfully and painlessly as the sadists; then they have their joyous rites. Such murders seem justified by Bentham's principle, but clearly they are wrong. Somehow, although the principle is, as we have seen, impartial, it still has omitted something essential to morality. We should, then, reject Bentham's principle of utility, as we have rejected ethical egoism before it, because we have found no reason to accept the principle, but we have reason to reject it.

This does not mean, however, that we have found reasons sufficient for rejecting utilitarianism, because Bentham's version is only one particular version. Another version, that proposed by John Stuart Mill, who followed Bentham in his ideas about social reform, is an explicit attempt to meet the kind of objection we have just raised. Let us turn, therefore, to Mill's ethical theory.

UTILITARIANISM: MILL'S VERSION

John Stuart Mill, whose father James Mill was a contemporary follower of Bentham, had ample opportunity to become acquainted with all the various objections raised against Bentham's theory. Consequently, in his book *Utilitarianism*, Mill set out to state and justify a version of the utilitarian principle. Like Bentham, he attempted to refute objections to the principle and to raise objections to opposing principles. Unlike Bentham, he tried to construct a less indirect proof of his principle, but his proof was far from satisfactory. In it Mill argued that the only proof that something is desirable is that it is desired. Hence, since pleasure and the avoidance of pain are surely desired, we could then conclude that these things are desirable. Now, if something is desirable then it is in some way worthy of being desired. So, Mill's proof would go some way towards showing that maximizing happiness and minimizing pain for the greatest number is worthy of desire and maybe also intrinsically good. The defect in Mill's argument comes in the first step; desirability does not follow from being desired. Presumably many Nazis desired to kill as many non-Aryans as possible, but from this it hardly follows that killing non-Aryans is desirable or worthy of being desired. So Mill's proof is a failure.

His proof aside, we are still interested in Mill's defense of utilitarianism, in particular, his refutation of the objection that if we treat all pleasures equally, as we must in applying the hedonic calculus, then sadistic pleasures as well as the merely bodily pleasures are to count on a par with the pleasures of contemplation, creation, discovery, and other so-called mental pleasures. That is, it is better to be a pig satisfied than a human dissatisfied; better in some situations that sadists are satisfied than that they are not satisfied. Mill answers this objection as follows:

> It is quite compatible with the principle of utility to recognize the fact that some *kinds* of pleasure are more desirable and more valuable than others. It would be absurd that, while, in estimating all other things, quality is considered as well as quantity, the estimation of pleasures should be supposed to depend on quantity alone.[20]

Quality versus Quantity of Pleasure

We should understand Mill here to be saying that we should understand the principle of utility to be consistent with qualitative distinctions among pleasures. He is thus significantly departing from Bentham's view. On Bentham's account, the only characteristics of pain and pleasure we are to consider in the hedonic calculus are their intensities and durations. No factor is available for distinguishing among different kinds of pleasures and pains. Just how radical a departure from Bentham Mill has undertaken can be seen by examining the criterion Mill proposes to distinguish between qualitative levels of pleasures. He says,

> Of two pleasures, if there be one to which all or almost all who have experience of both give a decided preference, irrespective of a feeling of moral obligation to prefer it, that is the more desirable pleasure. If one of the two is, by those who are competently acquainted with both, placed so far above the other that they prefer it, even though knowing it to be attended with a greater amount of discontent, and would not resign it for any quantity of the other pleasure which their nature is capable of, we are justified in ascribing to the preferred enjoyment a superiority in quality, so far outweighing quantity as to render it, in comparison, of small account.[21]

Mill's criterion tells us to decide which pleasures are qualitatively superior by what amounts to a poll of those who have experienced the pleasures in question. This seems to be an eminently democratic way to decide the

---

20. *Utilitarianism*, in *The Utilitarians*, op. cit., 408.
21. Ibid., 409

issue, but we shall see that it is not. The results of such a poll may show merely a wide range of disagreement or even a preference for "pig" pleasures. Mill, however, seems to dismiss this possibility immediately, for he assumes that the "verdict of the only competent judges" will be that "the pleasures derived from the higher faculties [are] preferable *in kind*, apart from the question of intensity, to those of which the animal nature, disjoined from the higher faculties, is susceptible . . . ."[22] It seems clear to Mill that the nobler pleasures, those associated with a person's intellect, will win the poll over the lower, bodily, or "pig" pleasures. Thus, for Mill, utilitarianism can avoid the objection that it is a pig philosophy. To understand why Mill is so certain of the outcome of such a poll we must concentrate on the key phrase, 'only competent judges.' In using this phrase Mill implies that the person who has savored the nobler pleasures but who prefers bodily pleasures is a backslider, a person of weak will who is not competent to judge. His vote, therefore, is not to be counted.

It may be that we can find some way to justify revoking the voting rights of the skid row inhabitants who have fallen from some previous higher estate, but it is not clear what grounds there would be. It is by no means clear, however, how we are to handle sadists, masochists, arsonists, voyeurs, and others who might prefer exotic pleasures to the "noble" ones. Perhaps we should call these people perverts, and allow only normal people to decide. But even if we could decide who is normal, in some way that is not question-begging, we would still find many men like D.H. Lawrence who, if they were asked to choose between intellectual pleasures and sexual pleasures, would without hesitation claim the latter should be chosen. It would be very hard to show that these people are backsliders or perverts. Furthermore, they often try to justify their choice on the grounds that, for example, without sexual pleasures people become isolated, lonely, hollow shells with no capacity to communicate with their fellow human beings. These people often argue that, in this age of alienation and automation, the one way to avoid dehumanization is through a passionate clinging together built upon the emotional base of the joys and pleasures of shared sexual acts. Many others, of course, including many philosophers, agree with Mill, but taking a poll hardly shows they are right. And what happens to the great number of people who, all their lives long, have little chance to experience the noble pleasures, through no fault of their own? On this issue these people do not count as one and, as a result, once a hierarchy of pleasures is decided, they might not count as one when applying the utilitarian principle.

A poll does not seem the way to decide the issue, but how else can it be decided? Very often when the issue is debated, the argument proceeds by referring to what the various pleasures are associated with or lead to. The

---

22. Ibid., 411-12.

qualitatively superior pleasures turn out to be those associated with what is better, for example, a person's intellect, or a person's love of his fellow human being. But once this line is taken utilitarianism has been abandoned, because the basic ethical principle is the one being used to distinguish the hierarchy of things which are good; and for this there is no need of a reference to pleasure. A utilitarian cannot take this line. If we are going to be utilitarians, we must agree either that all pleasures or else that only certain pleasures are the only things intrinsically good. If we take the first alternative, then the objection arises that utilitarianism implies that it is better to be a pig satisfied than Socrates dissatisfied. If we try the second, then we can only list the qualitative hierarchy of pleasures, without justifying the list by reference to anything else intrinsically good. Consequently, there will be no way to decide among alternative lists, and thus no basis for deciding what ought to be done in particular situations. Because neither alternative is attractive, perhaps we should abandon utilitarianism and with it the claim, which we have been considering since our examination of egoistic hedonism, that pleasure is the one thing intrinsically good.

AN OBJECTION TO UTILITARIANISM: SPECIAL DUTIES

Both Mill's and Bentham's versions face two additional serious objections. The first is based on the inability of utilitarianism to account for *special duties*. There surely seem to be duties or obligations that some people have because of their particular and special status, but that other people do not have. Consequently, these duties are different from the obligations we all have, for example, to maximize happiness. People who are parents, teachers, or judges have special obligations to their children, students, and defendants, respectively, obligations others do not have to these same people. Utilitarianism seems unable to account for these duties. When a teacher grades a paper or an examination, she does not decide the grade on the basis of what would maximize the overall happiness in this particular case. She tries to grade solely on the basis of the quality of the work done, even if the resulting grade produces more pain than pleasure. If she produces more pain, is she being immoral? Many students seem to think so, but it can hardly be right to adjust a grade according to how it affects the happiness of all those concerned. We can imagine a lonely student, unjustly despised by his fellow students, who would be handicapped unfairly relative to more popular students. Thus teachers seem to have, because of their special position, an obligation completely independent of the principle of utility. Special duties, therefore, present another problem for utilitarianism and for its central claim that only pleasures are intrinsically good.

We have just seen an example in which applying the principle of utility results in someone being treated unfairly. A similar problem could arise if a judge or jury were instructed to decide guilt on the basis of what maximizes the overall happiness. This would be unfair, unjust in many cases. This points to perhaps the most serious problem facing utilitarianism, the problem of fairness or justice. This seems to be a problem independent of the problem of special duties, because not only judges and juries ought to be just; it is an obligation each of us seems to have regarding our fellow human beings. It may seem strange that fairness should be a problem for utilitarianism, because we moved to utilitarianism from ethical egoism in search of an impartial standard. It is true that utilitarianism is impartial in counting each person as one and no one more than one regarding at least quantities of pleasure and pain, but this is not the only kind of morally relevant impartiality, and surely not the only kind that can be relevant to justice.

ANOTHER OBJECTION TO UTILITARIANISM: THE PROBLEM OF JUSTICE

The problem justice raises for utilitarianism is demonstrated by a scapegoat example. Imagine a town in which the young daughter of a prominent family had recently been kidnapped in broad daylight, then raped and brutally murdered. The police are completely baffled, and among the citizenry, aroused by the local newspaper, there is growing contempt for the police. It is becoming harder for the police to control the youth of the town, crime is on the increase, and fear is widespread. It seems that something should be done to restore confidence in law and the police. At this point the chief of police decides to find someone who can be accused of the crimes and brought to a speedy and decisive trial. The first hobo off the next through train is apprehended, and, with planted witnesses and carefully chosen jurors, quickly condemned to death. The town breathes easier, the police are praised, and happiness and tranquility are restored, except for one police patrolman who knew that the executed man was not guilty. But he is quickly reassured by the police chief, who, not previously known for his morality, gives him a quick course in utilitarianism and then shows how the overall happiness has been maximized.

This is an example of an obvious miscarriage of justice. Everyone, we believe, will agree that such cases should not occur, and certainly any ethical principle that prescribes them is clearly wrong. Thus utilitarianism, because it sacrifices justice to the overall happiness and thereby omits an essential ingredient of impartiality, should be rejected in favor of an ethical theory, that takes justice as an essential part of morality. To find such a theory, we shall turn to a standard that differs radically from any we have examined so far, in that it does not consider the consequences of an act as relevant to deciding its rightness. Such an ethical theory has been called "deontological": it stresses that morality is essentially based upon the relationship of an act to moral laws or principles rather than to consequences. That is, we are to consider a *nonconsequentialist* theory.

DEONTOLOGICAL ETHICS: KANT'S THEORY

Several of the ethical theories we have examined so far have had two things in common. They propose something as the *summum bonum* or highest good, and they prescribe that what ought to be done is to maximize whatever is the highest good. For example, both egoistic hedonism and Bentham's utilitarianism agree that, because pleasure or happiness is the one thing good in itself, it is the *summum bonum* and we ought to bring it about wherever possible. Where they differ is in their claims about whose pleasure each person ought to maximize. For such theories, what is morally important is whether or not our actions have consequences that bring about the highest good. Theories that emphasize the consequences of actions have been called "teleological" ethical theories.

The Highest Good: A Good Will

The great German philosopher Immanuel Kant propounded an ethical theory that is very difficult to interpret, but it has generally been construed as a prime example of a deontological theory. We shall follow this interpretation. Kant began his search for a basic ethical principle in the same way as Bentham and Mill. He too began by attempting to find the highest good. What he concluded, however, was so different from the conclusions reached by the others that on his theory the highest good can be realized regardless of the consequences of an act. To see how he arrived at this conclusion, we must understand the conditions he required of anything for it to be the highest good. According to Kant, the highest good must not only be good in itself, it must also be good without qualification.[23] This means that there are no situations in which the addition of the highest good makes the situation morally worse. Using this as his criterion, Kant can eliminate all the leading candidates for the highest good for the reason that each one when added to certain situations

---

23. Kant discusses what is good without qualification in the first section of *The Foundations of Metaphysics of Morals* (New York: Liberal Arts Press, 1959), 9-13.

makes them worse. He eliminates the "higher" faculties such as intelligence and judgment, because if a person with evil designs also has a high degree of intelligence, the results are worse. He eliminates traits of persons such as courage, resoluteness, and perseverance because "they can become extremely bad and harmful if the will, which is to make use of these gifts of nature and which in its special constitution is called character, is not good."[24] He rejects what he calls gifts of fortune, including power, riches, honor, and the utilitarian candidate, pleasure, because they too can make certain situations worse than if they were lacking. If, for example, we were to hear that the executioners at Auschwitz got pleasure from their horrible deeds and even if we agree that pleasure is good in itself, we would not think that this pleasure made the situation better. Instead we would think it made their deeds all that much worse. After rejecting these candidates Kant proposes the one thing he can find that meets his criterion. He says, in a famous passage:

> Nothing in the world—indeed nothing even beyond the world—can possibly be conceived which could be called good without qualification except a *good will*.[25]

Kant claims that the one thing good without qualification is a good will, but explaining what he means by 'good will' is far from easy. For our purposes it will be enough to begin by noting that, according to Kant, "the good will is not good because of what it effects or accomplishes or because of its adequacy to achieve some proposed end."[26] This is because what we do as a result of willing may, through chance, bungling, or interference by others, be quite the opposite of what we decided. We know of the well-intentioned bungler, and the villain who in spite of all he plans actually aids the hero. Kant says that the will "is good only because of its willing, that is, it is good of itself."[27] This means that whether a will is good does not depend on the consequences of willing but upon the manner of willing. This is brought out by the following definition we can use to express Kant's point:

S has a good will $=_{df}$ *S* acts out of respect for moral laws.

This is still only a beginning, because we have introduced two new terms Kant uses, both of which require explanation, 'act out of respect for' and 'moral law.' The first can be explained by distinguishing it from 'act in accordance with' in the following way:

---

24. Ibid., 9.
25. Ibid.
26. Ibid., 10.
27. Ibid.

S acts in accordance with principle $P =_{df} S$ does something that is consistent with what P prescribes.

S acts out of respect for principle $P =_{df} S$ does something solely for the reason that what he is doing is consistent with what P prescribes.

We can often act in accordance with a principle without even being aware of it or even when trying to violate it. Most of us when we drive a car, act in accordance with laws regarding speed limits, sometimes because we want to, other times without any thoughts or desires about it, and sometimes even when we try to break the law, if, for example, we mistakenly think the limit is lower than it is. In none of these cases do we act out of respect for the laws. We act out of respect for a law only when our decision to do something is based on, and only on, the reason that what we do is consistent with what the law prescribes. Thus to act out of respect for a law we must decide on the basis of reason alone, that is, without reliance on our inclinations and desires, to do what is consistent with what the laws prescribes. If we then act on the basis of our decision, we can be said to act out of respect for the law.

The Moral Law and the Categorical Imperative

The expression 'moral law' is more difficult to explain. We know three things:

1. A moral law prescribes what ought to be done.

2. What ought to be done is to bring about whatever is the highest good.

3. A will that acts out of respect for moral laws is the highest good.

From this we can conclude that a moral law prescribes just one thing, namely, that we act out of respect for moral laws. There are two important consequences of this. First, there is only one moral law, for there is only one thing prescribed. Second, because the moral law merely requires that we act out of respect for itself, it is unlike any previous basic ethical principle we have examined. They all prescribe what acts we should do, but this one prescribes how we should do any act. Therefore, it is not the particular actions a law prescribes that make it a moral law; that is, it is not the particular content of any law that makes it moral. And because any particular law consists only of some particular content embedded in a lawlike form, it must be this lawlikeness of a law that makes it moral. Thus, if we can find a law that expresses merely this lawlike form of laws, then we will have found the one and only moral law.

What is the form of all prescriptive laws? They can be distinguished from explanatory laws, such as scientific laws, in that they can be expressed as imperatives about people's actions. Thus legal prescriptive laws are often stated in the imperative mood, such as "Do not speed!" and "No smoking!" And because there is no restriction upon the moral imperative except that it expresses the form of lawfulness, there are no conditions that must be met for it to be applicable. It is then an unconditional or *categorical* imperative and an imperative with universal application. Thus the moral law, by requiring that we act out of respect for itself, requires that we act out of respect for universal and unconditional lawfulness. The moral law requires that, whenever we decide to do something, we should decide to do it solely for the reason that doing it is consistent with what universal and unconditional lawfulness requires. And, as we are interpreting Kant, universal and unconditional lawfulness requires that the principles we actually base our decision on, what Kant calls "maxims," should have the form of universal and unconditional laws. The moral imperative, therefore, requires that we are morally permitted to act on a maxim only if our decision to act on it is consistent with our willing to make the maxim a universal and unconditional law governing the actions of everyone, including ourselves. Kant formulates the moral imperative as

Act only according to that maxim by which you can at the same time will that it should become a universal law.[28]

The First Formulation of the Categorical Imperative

The preceding formulation of the categorical imperative is not the only formulation given by Kant, but it is the one he derives first. We shall examine his second formulation later, on p. 336. One thing both formulations have in common is that they prescribe principles, and therefore actions based on the principles, independently of the consequences of the actions. An ethical theory that takes this as its basic ethical principle is a deontological theory. This, like other ethical theories, faces objections, but before we assess them we must decide whether we should interpret Kant's principle as expressing both a necessary and sufficient condition of moral permission, or merely a necessary condition because of the word 'only.' That is, it seems equivalent to

You are permitted to act on a principle *P only if* you can will *P* to be a universal law.

Furthermore, if we try to interpret it as a sufficient condition as well, then immediate objections arise. If the possibility of someone willing that a principle be a universal law is a sufficient condition of the principle being one he ought to act on, then we get morally repugnant results. For example, a masochistic sadist might have no trouble willing that the principle, "Give Smith five lashes a day," be universalized to "Give everyone five

---

28. Ibid., 39.

lashes a day." But it should not be concluded from this that he is permitted to act on the principle of giving Smith five lashes a day. Therefore we should restrict the principle to stating merely a necessary condition.

Once we restrict the categorical imperative in this way, however, another objection arises. The restricted imperative is not helpful in cases where we can will a principle universalized, but are not sure of whether we ought to act on the principle. The most the imperative can tell us is that if we cannot will a principle to be universalized then we are not permitted to, that is, we ought not act on it. Consequently, Kant's imperative, although it may be an essential element of a basic ethical principle, cannot be the basic principle, because it is not applicable in many situations. Indeed, it might also be objected, it is not clear how it is applicable in any situation, because it is not clear how we can derive particular obligations from such an abstract principle. Kant tries to rebut this second objection by showing how to derive particular duties from his imperative. What he attempts to do is show that someone who does a particular act on the basis of a particular immoral maxim would become involved in some kind of inconsistency if he also willed that the maxim become a universal law. Thus what Kant means by "You cannot will the maxim you act on to be a universal law" is that if you do, then you will be in some way inconsistent, and thus your decision will be irrational. But making an irrational decision is contrary to acting out of respect for the moral law, because, as we have seen, we act out of respect for the moral law only if we decide on the basis of reason alone to act in accordance with it.

Let us examine two of Kant's examples to illustrate his method. One duty he derives from the first formulation is the duty not to make a deceitful promise, in order to borrow money, for example. In this case, according to Kant, the maxim would be

When I believe myself to be in need of money, I will borrow money and promise to repay it, although I know I shall never do so.[29]

If this maxim is universalized, we would have a law that whenever anyone needs money he makes a lying promise in order to get it. If this were a law governing everyone's actions, then, according to Kant, no one would believe a promise made in such circumstances, and no one would be fooled into believing the false promise. The result is an inconsistency between the intention of the liar to deceive others and his willing a universal law that eliminates the deception. We can conclude then that we ought not make a lying promise. Here is an ethical principle prohibiting specific acts so that, if Kant's derivation is sound, he has shown us how to apply his abstract principle to specific acts. No act of false promising is right.

29. Ibid., 40.

Another of Kant's examples concerns the person who decides not to help someone who needs help. In this example Kant understands the maxim to be the following:

I shall not help another person even when he needs help.

If we were to make this into a universal law it would be a law that no one is to help any other person who needs help. But, claims Kant, all of us desire that someone help us when we are in trouble, so that our desire for help would conflict with our willing this to be a universal law governing all human actions. Thus we have an obligation to help others in a specific situation when they need help.

Objection to first formulation: Which maxims to universalize?

We have seen from the preceding two examples that Kant's method of deriving specific duties from the first formulation of the categorical imperative depends upon deriving an inconsistency when certain maxims are universalized. There are two basic problems for this derivation. The first is the problem of applying the first formulation to maxims. To which is it to be applied and to which should it not be applied? The second is the problem of whether or not Kant can, as he claims, derive a clear inconsistency in applying the first formulation. To see the first problem, consider a wretched, starving person who makes a promise which he knows he cannot keep to an extremely wealthy person in order to get money for much-needed food and medicine. To what maxim are we to apply the imperative? Is it to Kant's quite general maxim or a more restricted one, such as:

Whenever I am starving and need food and medicine, and the only way to get it is to make a deceitful promise, I will deceitfully promise a wealthy person who can spare the money.

It is by no means clear that this is an immoral maxim even if the person's intention in acting on it is in some way inconsistent with his willing to universalize it.

Consider also a very sly universalizer who, whenever he makes a deceitful promise, claims that his maxim is something like the following:

Whenever anyone is six feet tall, has one blue and one brown eye, a three-inch scar on his left cheek, a bullet wound in his right palm, a gold ring in his left ear, and needs money, he is to borrow money and make a deceitful promise to repay it.

What makes this universalizer sly is that the only person who fits this description is himself. Furthermore, he claims that this maxim is universal as it stands, for it is of the form:

Whenever anyone is X, he is to do Y.

which is the form of Kant's universalized maxim. Indeed, the maxim applies to *everyone* who is X. It is only a contingent fact that only he is X. Consequently, our universalizer, who uses this form with the preceding description for all his maxims, finds that nothing is forbidden and nothing is obligatory, because all his maxims are universal. Thus, he can act on them and will them to be universal laws without inconsistency. The obvious reply is that some restriction must be placed on what we are allowed to substitute for 'X,' but it is not clear how to allow a phrase such as 'desperately in need of food,' but rule out the longer phrase invented by the sly universalizer.

Another objection: Cannot derive specific duties
The first is not the more serious problem, however, because it may be possible to place a satisfactory restriction upon the application of the imperative, but it is not clear how to avoid the second problem. It is essential for Kant to derive some kind of inconsistency. The most plausible example he gives is the case of deceitful promising, but even here his derivation fails. There is an inconsistency only if someone decides to deceive someone and also decides to do something that stops him from deceiving the person. But the deception would not be stopped if the *only* thing that were to happen is that the actions of everyone who needed money became governed by a law requiring them to make deceitful promises. If the person a liar was trying to deceive did not know that there was such a law or did not realize that this was a situation covered by the law about needing money, then there is a very good chance that he would be deceived, especially if the deceiver were clever. Even if this practice had been occurring universally for centuries, there is, as the saying goes, "a sucker born every minute." There is, unfortunately, very often little resemblance between what people are willing to believe and the truth.

The problem is more evident in the second example, for to arrive at the inconsistency Kant must claim that all of us desire someone to help us when we are in trouble. If someone did not have this desire, then his universalizing the maxim not to help another would not be inconsistent with any of his desires. He would consequently not be obligated to help others. Some people may not have this desire—people, for example, who claim they belong to that almost mythical breed of people known as rugged individualists. Kant can at most claim that we nonrugged people would become involved in an inconsistency, but even here problems arise. First there is, as before, the problem of restricting the application of the imperative. Even if we specify in the maxim merely the way in which help is needed, such as 'needs help crossing the street,' some of us are at least rugged enough not to desire this kind of help. Second, in absolving the rugged individualist from responsibility for helping others, Kant seems to condone what we might call the rugged individualist fallacy: Because I need no help, and everyone should be like me, I have no obligation to help anyone. Unfortunately, whatever we should all be, most of us are not rugged individualists. We sometimes need help, and therefore there are times others should help us whether or not they need help themselves.

Serious difficulties, then, face Kant's first formulation of the categorical imperative, difficulties that eliminate it as being itself the basic moral imperative. However, we should not reject it entirely, because it may be an important element in a satisfactory formulation of such an imperative.

The Second Formulation of the Categorical Imperative

Having rejected Kant's first formulation, why are we going to examine his second formulation and, indeed, why have we considered Kant at all, when our purpose has been to find an ethical theory that can accommodate justice? Although it is not obvious that the first formulation is related to justice, Kant, by requiring that the maxims we act on be universalized so as to be equally applicable to all, has incorporated into his imperative something essential to justice. When we get to the second formulation, however, we shall see clearly how Kant's theory overcomes the kind of difficulty justice poses for utilitarianism.

Kant, in stating his second formulation, gave expression to one of the greatest humanistic doctrines. It sums up in one short imperative the doctrine of the dignity and worth of the individual person:

Act so that you treat humanity, whether in your own person or in that of another, always as an end and never as a means only.[30]

There are two important prescriptions in this imperative. We are to treat people as *ends*, that is, we are to treat them as beings having intrinsic value in themselves, regardless of whatever value they may have or lack as a *means to some end*. We are also never to treat people as things that are *mere means*. That is, although we can, do, and often must treat people as means, in so doing we must also treat them as ends. Thus the farmer treats his plow and hired hands as means, a manufacturer treats his machines and laborers as means, and a student treats his books and teachers as means. But although it is all right to treat the plow, the machinery, and the books *merely* as means, the hired hands, laborers, and teachers must also be treated as ends. This implies that no person should be a slave or racially discriminated against or used as a scapegoat. Each person is an end in himself and must be treated that way. Here, surely, is the very essence of justice.

Kant claims that this formulation is just another way to express the very same moral law expressed by the first formulation. Although it is by no

---

30. Ibid., 47.

means clear why Kant thought this, perhaps the following will help explain what he had in mind. We have already seen that Kant holds that the good will is the highest good, so that a good will is an end in itself and should be treated as such. But we can treat a faculty of some being as an end in itself only by treating the being itself as an end. And because only a being who can act out of respect for law, that is, only a rational being, can possess a good will, it follows that we should treat rational beings with good wills as ends. Furthermore, because we cannot know from its effects whether a will is good, we cannot be sure whether or not any particular will is good. Consequently, in order not to omit any beings with good wills, we must treat all rational beings and therefore all human beings as ends in themselves. In this way, starting from the same premises as were used to arrive at the first formulation, we arrive by a slightly different route at the second formulation. In such a way Kant might have arrived at the second formulation and at the conclusion that it was equivalent to the first.

Another reason Kant might have thought that the two formulations are equivalent, and thus formulations of the same law, is that he thought the same duties could be derived from each. He illustrated this by deriving the same duties from each formulation. Let us examine how he derives the two duties previously discussed. We shall see that the derivation is easier and more plausible in this case. Kant derives the duty not to make deceitful promises from the prescription not to treat people as means only by arguing that anyone who intends to make such a promise "sees immediately that he intends to use another man merely as a means."[31] In this Kant surely is right, for deceiving someone to get something for ourselves is using the other merely as a means to our own gain. The obligation we have to help others is derived from the other prescription in the second formulation, that we treat people as ends. This means that we ought to further the well-being of people because this is how we should treat an end in itself. Consequently, it is not enough that we avoid treating people merely as means; we ought to do more.

Humanity might indeed exist if no one contributed to the happiness of others, provided that he did not intentionally detract from it; but this harmony with humanity as an end in itself is only negative rather than positive if everyone does not also endeavor, so far as he can, to further the ends of others.[32]

Although Kant is far from being a utilitarian, he arrives at an obligation which sounds quite utilitarian, that we ought to promote the happiness of others by treating each person as an end. Thus, Kant's second formulation

---

31. Ibid., 48.
32. Ibid., 48-49.

may provide a way to accommodate the greatest happiness principle and justice. However, in order to evaluate it we must see whether it faces other problems.

An objection to Kant's theory: It is not applicable in all situations

There are three objections that cast doubt on Kant's second formulation of the categorical imperative, but they can all be adapted to apply to the first formulation also; thus they are really objections to the whole of Kant's ethical theory. We have already seen the first objection as it applies to the first formulation: neither formulation is applicable in all situations. This problem arises for the second formulation in two kinds of situations. The first situation is one in which all the possible alternatives require treating someone as a means only, such as in the example of an overcrowded lifeboat where someone must be sacrificed as a means of preserving the others. Kant's imperative provides us with no way to decide. The second situation is one in which all the alternatives allow us to treat someone as an end, but each alternative involves different people. This is the problem confronting someone who is in charge of distributing welfare funds so limited that not everyone needing help can be aided. Kant's imperative does not provide a way to decide between, for example, a family with a talented child, another with a child needing medical attention, and another with a mentally disturbed child who terrorizes the neighborhood. Although in each of these kinds of cases the decisions are most difficult, a principle that would provide a way to distinguish among the alternatives would be superior in at least one respect to Kant's imperative.

A second objection: Absolute versus prima facie duties

The second objection is a more serious one. According to Kant the duties we derive from the categorical imperative are absolute duties. He is therefore committed to what we previously called action absolutism, that is, that certain acts are always right or always wrong. Thus, for Kant, the obligation not to lie is an absolute duty, so that we ought not to lie under any conditions. This, however, leads to some results that are surely morally repugnant. Assume that you are trusted by the local Nazi commander in occupied Holland, and that you are harboring an important Jewish refugee for whom the commander is searching. The commander comes to your door and, trusting you, asks if you are hiding the refugee. You know that he will go away without searching if you say you are hiding no one, and that saying nothing would amount to telling him the truth. It seems clear that you should lie in this situation, but a Kantian who remembers the absolute duty to tell the truth would say that you should admit you are hiding the refugee. Clearly such a Kantian is wrong.

It seems, therefore, that the duties derived from the categorical imperative should not be construed as absolute duties but rather as what have been called *prima facie* duties.[33]   That is, Kantian duties are duties we are required to perform unless they are overruled or overridden by something else required of us.   Thus the duty no to lie is not an absolute duty, but merely a prima facie duty, because in some situations it is overridden by some other prima facie duty, such as helping a deserving friend in distress. And, in any particular situation, that prima facie duty that overrides all others is our duty proper, that is, what we ought to do in the situation.

We can state the distinction between an absolute duty, and a prima facie duty by defining the key terms.

A has a *prima facie* duty to do *P* $=_{df}$ There is something C_1 that requires *A* to do *P*.

However, because a prima facie duty can be overridden and therefore might not be what we ought to do, we should also relate 'prima facie duty' to 'override' and to 'ought.'

A's prima facie duty to do *P* is *overridden* in situation *S* $=_{df}$ There is something C_1 that requires *A* to do *P*, but there is something else C_2 such that C_1 and C_2 together do *not* require *A* to do *P* in situation *S*.

This expresses what happens to the prima facie obligation to tell the truth in the refugee example.   In this situation there is something, for example, a Kantian rule, that taken by itself requires you to tell the truth, but that, when taken with the conflicting requirement to help the refugee, does not require that you tell the truth.   Furthermore, in this situation you surely seem to be required to do something instead of telling the truth.   What you are required to do, what you ought to do, what we have called a duty proper, is to lie.   Thus

A ought (*has a duty proper*) in situation *S* to do *P* $=_{df}$ There is something C_1 that requires *A* to do *P* in situation *S*, and there is nothing else C_2 such that C_1 and C_2 together do not require *A* to do *P* in situation *S*.[34]

Thus any prima facie obligation that is not overridden in some situation is a duty proper and we ought to do it in that situation.

We can now define 'absolute duty' as a duty for which there is no situation in which someone is required to do something instead of it.   It is, consequently, a duty that is never overridden.

A has an absolute duty to do *P* $=_{df}$ There is something C_1 that required *A* to do *P*, and there is *no* situation in which *A* is required to do something instead of *P*.

---

33. The concept of prima facie duty derives from W. D. Ross, *The Right and the Good* (New York: Oxford University Press, 1955), 18-20.

34. This way of defining these distinctions is derived from R. M. Chisholm, "The Ethics of Requirements," *American Philosophical Quarterly* Vol. 1, No. 2 (April, 1964), 147-53.

Once we see what is necessary for a duty to be an absolute duty, we can also see very few, if any, duties are absolute. There generally is some situation in which a duty is overridden, indeed, in which we are required to do something else. Most of our duties, therefore, are more properly called prima facie duties.

It seems that Kantian duties are more accurately described as prima facie duties than as absolute duties, for, as we have seen, there are situations in which they are overridden. We can handle the refugee example in this way, but if we do, we must conclude that Kant's theory is not adequate, because it cannot accommodate the concept of overriding. The problem is further emphasized by the third and most serious objection of Kant's theory.

A third objection: Kant's theory cannot resolve conflicts of duty

The refugee example not only shows that Kant's theory seems to prescribe morally repugnant actions in certain situations, but it can also illustrate the problem that conflicts of duty produce for his theory. In the refugee example, the person is faced with what is clearly a conflict of duties, for he has a duty to help the refugee and a duty to tell the truth. In this case, it should be easy to resolve the conflict, but Kant's theory cannot handle it. If, as Kant thinks, his theory prescribes absolute duties, then in this example the person ought to do two things he cannot possibly do together. Thus, not only is he obliged to do something he cannot do, but he is also unable to justify choosing one rather than the other. If we interpret the theory to prescribe prima facie duties, then, although the person is not obliged to do two conflicting things, he still has no way of deciding what to do. Consequently, Kant's theory cannot handle conflicts of duty. It seems that he has so divorced morality from the consequences of our acts that in a case like the refugee example, where the consequences seem most relevant, Kant's theory is unable to help us.

We have found three objections to Kant's deontological ethical theory which, taken together, constitute a sufficient reason for rejecting the theory as providing the basic ethical principle. Thus, we must continue our search. We should not, however, reject Kant's theory outright, because it embodies something that seems essential to any satisfactory basic standard. The question is how to include it. A recent and much-discussed answer is the theory called rule utilitarianism.

RULE UTILITARIANISM

Two of the main problems facing Kant's theory are that it cannot handle conflicts of duty, and that there are situations in which it is not applicable. Two of the main problems for utilitarianism are the problem of the lower pleasures and the problem of justice. Because Kant's theory can accommodate what causes the utilitarian trouble and utilitarianism can avoid what causes Kant trouble, it seems that if the two could be encapsulated in one theory which eliminated the weaknesses of both while maintaining the strong points of each, then we might well have a satisfactory theory. Kant's theory stresses the importance of moral laws that prescribe duties. This enables it to account for justice. Utilitarianism, on the other hand, proposes a standard that can be applied to every situation. It can also be applied to laws; that is, we can evaluate a law by deciding whether or not its enforcement tends to maximize the overall happiness. Indeed it has been claimed that the way to evaluate any legislation, newly proposed or in force, is to apply the principle of utility to it, because the purpose of government and thus of legislation is to maximize the general welfare.

Acts, Laws, Judges, and Legislators

The applicability of the utilitarian principle to legislation has led some philosophers to propose that the correct ethical standard should be constructed on an analogy with the way the utilitarian principle applies to legislation. To do this we must understand and distinguish between the relationship of a judge to a law and the relationship of a legislator to a law. P. H. Nowell-Smith claims,

> The duty of the judge is to pronounce verdict and sentence in accordance with the law; and the question "What verdict and sentence are laid down in the law for this crime?" As judge, he is not concerned with the consequences, beneficial or harmful, of what he pronounces. Similarly, the question "Was that a just sentence?" is one that cannot be settled by reference to its consequences, but solely by reference to the law.[35]

The judge, as Nowell-Smith points out, is concerned with deciding individual cases, and in doing so he can rely only on the laws in effect. He cannot use the consequences, whether for good or ill, to help justify his decision. The judge, therefore, because his decisions are bound by a network of laws, functions in a somewhat deontological way. As Nowell-Smith says, however,

> The duty of the legislator is quite different. It is not to decide whether a particular application of the law is just or not, but to decide what laws ought to be adopted and what penalties are to be laid down for the breach of each law. And these questions cannot be decided in the way that the judge decided what verdict and sentence to pronounce.[36]

---

35. P. H. Nowell-Smith, *Ethics* (Baltimore: Penguin Books, 1954), 236.
36. Ibid., 237.

The legislator should evaluate laws by their consequences rather than by some other set of laws, although, of course, what the consequences of a particular law are depends in part upon what other laws are already in effect. The legislator, then, because he evaluates not by means of laws but by consequences, functions in a somewhat utilitarian way. Using this analogy with legality, Nowell-Smith concludes,

> The obligation to obey a rule does not, in the opinion of most ordinary men, rest on the beneficial consequences of obeying it in a particular case in either the short or the long run, as utilitarians have almost always supposed. But the reasons for adopting a rule may well be of the kind that utilitarians suggest.[37]

In other words, Nowell-Smith is proposing an ethical theory that restricts the application of the utilitarian principle to rules of conduct rather than to particular actions. The particular actions we do and contemplate doing are to be evaluated by moral rules, which are in turn justified by the utilitarian principle. Let us call moral rules that are justified by the utilitarian principle "utilitarian rules." We have, then, what has been called both a *restricted utilitarianism*, because it restricts the application of the utilitarian principle, and a *rule utilitarianism*, because it restricts the principle to rules. This theory, therefore, differs from a theory that applies the utilitarian principle to acts. Thus, it differs from Bentham's and Mill's theories, which we have interpreted as versions of *act utilitarianism*. We can better understand this difference by stating a two-part principle containing the central doctrine of rule utilitarianism.

1. Someone has a prima facie duty to obey a *rule* of conduct if and only if having the rule in effect tends to maximize the overall happiness of those to whom it applies (that is, the rule is a *utilitarian rule*).

2. Someone has a prima facie duty to do an *act* if and only if the act is prescribed by a utilitarian rule.

SIX REQUIREMENTS FOR A SATISFACTORY ETHICAL STANDARD AND AN EXAMINATION OF RULE UTILITARIANISM

We have arrived at the rule utilitarian principle with the hope that it will incorporate the strengths of Kant's and Bentham's theories while eliminating their weaknesses. Let us, therefore, see how rule utilitarianism fares, but let us do so by bringing to bear upon it all the problems and

---

37. Ibid., 239.

objections we used to reject all the preceding theories, and what, as a result, we have found to be required for a satisfactory ethical theory. Any completely satisfactory ethical theory must provide a basic ethical principle which:

1. Is applicable in any situation requiring a moral choice. (Kant's theory and Mill's utilitarianism, which provide no justifiable way to evaluate pleasures qualitatively, fail to meet this condition.)

2. Accommodates special duties. (Act utilitarianism and ethical egoism fail here.)

3. Resolves conflicts of duty. (Kant's theory fails here.)

4. Guarantees the treatment of people as ends, and thereby guarantees justice and impartiality. (Act utilitarianism and ethical egoism fail here.)

5. Provides for consideration of the consequences of actions for human happiness. (Kant's theory seems to fail here.)

6. Prescribes no acts we feel certain are wrong. (Ethical egoism and Bentham's utilitarianism fail here.)

It is clear that rule utilitarianism meets condition (5), and there is no reason to think it cannot meet conditions (1) and (6), although it is hard to evaluate with regard to (1) and (6) because little work has been done concerning specific recommendations for utilitarian rules. Nevertheless, there seems to be no reason why there cannot be a utilitarian moral rule covering every situation, and no reason why any acts prescribed by these rules should be morally repugnant. At any rate, for the present let us assume that rule utilitarianism meets conditions (1), (5), and (6). It may seem that it cannot meet (2), (3), and (4), but rule utilitarians have concentrated on showing how their theory meets these conditions. They claim that the special duties of the parent, judge, and teacher can be handled because utilitarian rules impose these duties, that is, rules that can be justified as tending to maximize the overall happiness of those affected. Although this has not been established, it is at least plausible to think that the practices prescribed by such "special" laws have beneficial consequences for people. Therefore, we can also grant that rule utilitarianism seems to meet condition (2).

Condition (3) seems to raise a serious problem, however, because, as we have seen, when there are several moral rules there will be conflicts of duty. Rule utilitarianism is faced with conflicts of duties, and as we have stated its principle, it cannot resolve such conflicts. The rule utilitarian's reply to this is that the principle is incomplete as stated. A provision must be added to the effect that, when there is conflict between the prima facie duties prescribed by utilitarian rules, then the overriding duty, the one that ought to be done, is to be decided by direct application of the utilitarian principle to the *action*. Thus, when and only when someone faces a situation in which two or more conflicting prima facie duties are prescribed by utilitarian rules, he is to decide which action to do by the utilitarian principle. In all other situations the principle is to be applied only to rules. Thus condition (3) is met (and, incidentally, met in a way that justifies lying in the refugee example).

This brings us to the problem of justice, which causes the act utilitarian so much trouble. Is the rule utilitarian able to avoid the pitfalls of the scapegoat example? He tries to avoid it by handling justice in the same way he handles special duties. He claims that the obligation to be just follows from a rule that can be justified by application of the utilitarian principle. Thus the practice of treating people justly is prescribed by a utilitarian rule, because it is a practice having beneficial consequences for those affected. It seems, then, quite plausible to conclude that rule utilitarianism is a satisfactory ethical theory, because the basic ethical principle it proposes seems to meet all the conditions we have found to be required of any satisfactory ethical theory.

Objection to Rule Utilitarianism: No Guarantee of Justice

However, before we conclude that we have found the theory for which we have been looking, we should consider in more detail how the rule utilitarian accommodates justice. On this theory, justice is assured only as along as the general practice of being just tends to maximize the overall happiness. It is possible, therefore, that in some societies a rule requiring justice would not maximize happiness. It is possible that a law which forces people into slave labor might in certain circumstances tend to maximize the overall happiness, even counting the unhappiness of the slaves. In such a situation the guarantee of justice disappears. Thus, although rule utilitarianism can accommodate justice, whereas act utilitarianism cannot, there is no guarantee that it will. The kind of justification of rules required by rule utilitarianism depends so much on the particular circumstances that we cannot be sure any particular rule will be justified.

This is not the only way justice can be thwarted on the basis of the rule utilitarian theory. The rule of justice is merely one of many rules justified by the utilitarian principle. We have seen that where there is more than one of these rules it is likely that they will sometimes conflict, and when they do we are to apply the utilitarian principle directly to the action to determine what we ought to do. It is, therefore, likely that there will be occasions when the prima facie obligation to be just will be overridden, so that on those occasions we ought to be unjust. Consider, for example, a society in which one rule justified by the utilitarian principle is that respect for law enforcement ought to be maintained. What such a rule prescribes could quite easily conflict with the obligation to be just. In such a situation the principle of utility would be applied directly to the action and the scapegoat problem would arise again. Accordingly, even if a rule prescribing justice is justified, it may well be that in particular instances unjust treatment would be obligatory. Therefore, although rule utilitarianism seems preferable to the other theories we have examined, it still has a flaw. We should continue the search.

It seems that if we want justice guaranteed we must incorporate it in the basic ethical principle, rather than justifying it in some derivative way. The only theory we have found that does this is Kant's deonotological theory. If we can somehow make Kant's principle basic and also retain the features of rule utilitarianism, we shall have found a satisfactory theory.

We have seen that Kant's second formulation has two parts, one prescribing that we treat no person as a means only and the other that we treat all people as ends in themselves. If we can in some way give content to what it is to treat people as ends, we may be able to find the theory we want. And, although we only noted it in passing, we have already seen the hint we want in Kant himself. We know that in treating someone as an end, the minimum requirement is that we bring about and maintain the conditions necessary for his continued existence. But, as with anything that is an end, we should also promote his well-being. According to Kant (see pp. 337-338), we should also treat him in a utilitarian way; we ought to promote his happiness. This suggests that we should take Kant's principle, and thus justice, as basic, and use the utilitarian principle to help derive certain duties consistent with Kant's principle. What is wrong with rule utilitarianism is that it makes justice derivative instead of basic. Indeed, it is more reasonable to justify maximizing human happiness by some reference to the principle that humans should be treated as ends, that is, in a Kantian way, than to justify treating people justly by reference to the principle that we ought to maximize human happiness. Human happiness is morally important because human beings are important. It is not that humans are morally important because human happiness is.

A PROPOSAL FOR A SATISFACTORY STANDARD: A UTILITARIAN KANTIAN PRINCIPLE

Our job is to find some way to graft the utilitarian principle onto Kant's second formulation. We know two things: First, the basic prescription is, if possible, to treat no one merely as a means, but if this is not possible in a particular situation, then we should treat as few people as possible as mere means. The overcrowded lifeboat example illustrates a situation in which someone must be sacrificed, treated as a mere means, in order to save the others. In such a situation it is obvious that as few as possible should be sacrificed. Second, we should treat as many people as ends as possible. We have interpreted this to imply that we should actively promote the well-being of those affected by the action in question. However, because promoting the well-being of as many people as possible could conflict with treating as few people as possible as mere means, and because the most basic imperative is not to treat people as mere means, the second imperative must be restricted so that it is consistent with the first.

At this point an objection can be raised. We can avoid treating a person as mere means by doing nothing at all. Consequently, in any situation we can avoid treating anyone as a mere means. If we accept the preceding imperative as basic, we should sacrifice no one in the lifeboat example, because that would be to treat as mere means as few people as possible. But that would result in a needless loss of life. We must, then, find a different basic principle.

We can avoid the objection by construing the treatment of someone as mere means to include doing nothing to help him when he truly needs help, especially when his life is imperiled. Not to do anything to help someone in such a situation is to respond to him as something with no intrinsic worth. This amounts to treating him a mere means. We can, then, take the basic imperative to be

> In any situation, (a) treat as mere means as few people as possible, and (b) treat as ends as many people as is consistent with (a).

We have claimed that promoting someone's happiness is important for treating him as an end. We should, then, incorporate into our imperative a prescription to promote the happiness of those affected by an action. However, because promoting as much happiness as possible often conflicts with the previously stated basic imperative, any prescription to promote happiness must be restricted, so that following it is consistent with what our basic Kantian imperative prescribes.

Although this gives the essential skeleton of the principle, there is still the question how we are to relate the treatment of as many people as ends as possible to the promotion of happiness. The problem is that there are several conflicting ways we could do this. We treat one person as an end by promoting his happiness. We could, then, require the action that promotes to some degree the happiness of the greatest number of people, or we could be utilitarian at this point and require that it maximize the total amount of happiness, counting, of course, each one as one and no one more than one. Let us initially choose an act utilitarian interpretation that gives us the following principle:

An action ought to be done in a situation if and only if

1. Doing the action, (a) treats as mere means as few people as possible in the situation, and (b) treats as ends as many people as is consistent with (a), *and*

2. Doing the action in the situation brings about as much overall happiness as is consistent with (1).

As the reader can discover for himself, this principle seems to meet all of the first five conditions that any satisfactory ethical theory must meet, except for (3), which concerns special duties. By applying the act utilitarian principle to treatment of people as ends, we have allowed the problem of the special duties of teachers and others to arise again. However, because this problem can be handled by rule utilitarianism, we can accommodate special duties by applying the rule utilitarian principle. Here again we have a choice to make. We can assume, as a rule utilitarian does, that there are utilitarian rules covering every situation involving a moral choice. Or we can make provision for the existence of some situations not covered by these rules by requiring that the act utilitarian principle apply in these situations. Let us here, however, accept the rule utilitarian's assumption. What we can call the utilitarian Kantian principle will be

An action ought to be done in a situation if and only if

1. Doing the action, (a) treats as mere means as few people as possible in the situation, and (b) treats as ends as many people as is consistent with (a), *and*

2. Doing the action is prescribed by any utilitarian rule that (a) does not violate condition (1) in the situation, and (b) is not overridden by another utilitarian rule that does not violate condition (1) in the situation.

To help understand this principle, let us see what it would prescribe in one particular lifeboat example. Let us assume that you are the captain of a ship that has just sunk, and you are in charge of the one remaining lifeboat, which has too many people crammed into it and three others, who are taking their turns in the water, hanging onto the sides of the boat. Suppose further that a dangerous storm is quickly approaching, and the boat will capsize unless five people, at minimum, are cast adrift. You must decide what ought to be done. The utilitarian Kantian principle requires you to sacrifice some people, but as few as possible, in the situation in order to save the rest. In this way you would treat as few as possible as mere means, and as many as possible as ends in this situation.
Once this decision is made you are faced with the problem of finding a procedure for deciding who is to be sacrificed. One decision procedure which clearly treats no one as mere means is to draw straws, but another one is to ask for volunteers. The basic Kantian requirement expressed in condition (1) provides no way to choose between the two procedures. Thus, you must consider any relevant utilitarian rules. To see which rules apply, let us further assume that five people in the boat have publicly

volunteered to be sacrificed. Consider now the following rule: Whenever it is required that some people be sacrificed to save others, and some people have publicly volunteered to be sacrificed, then there is a prima facie obligation to sacrifice the volunteers. This rule clearly applies in this situation and it does not violate what the basic Kantian condition requires. Furthermore, it is reasonable to think it is a utilitarian rule, because its being in effect tends to maximize the overall happiness of those to whom it applies. Indeed, it is quite likely that if this rule were not followed when it applies, there would be great unhappiness, and strong resistance, or even mutiny, when those who did not volunteer, but know others did, are asked to take a chance on being sacrificed. And, given the additional plausible assumption that this rule is not overridden in this situation, your obligation is to ask for volunteers, rather than have the passengers draw straws.

The principle we have finally reached is complex. As can be seen from the preceding example, it requires of anyone that he consider and relate many factors in order to decide what he ought to do in any particular situation. In many situations, it is practically impossible to complete such a complex task. Each of us should, of course, do the best he can, and where anyone has done a reasonably good job but failed to decide correctly, no blame or guilt should attach to him. As brought out in the beginning of this chapter, the standards appropriate for morally evaluating actions are different from those appropriate for morally evaluating persons. Although we have not considered the latter kind of standard here, one thing is clear: Many actions that are quite clearly wrong do not reflect blame or guilt upon the doer.

CONCLUSION

Earlier, we conceded that ethical relativism does have some support. How does relativism fare in competition with the utilitarian Kantian principle? We can approach an answer to this question by considering how ethical relativism stands with respect to the six requirements we have unearthed from our discussion.

Suppose we consider ethical relativism in its cultural form. Then, for any given culture C, ethical relativism says that each person who is a member of C ought to do those actions which are prescribed by the moral rules of C. So, if the Inuit of northern Canada and Alaska make up one culture, then each person in that group ought to do what the moral rules of the Inuit culture prescribe. A similar claim would apply to persons in different cultures, such as in Papua New Guinea or Mongolia.

It is doubtful that these cultures will have moral rules that apply to all situations requiring a moral choice. This is because each culture will have and use groups of specific moral rules in the sense described earlier, rules such as those included in the Ten Commandments and many other specific rules. When novel situations arise, the moral rules of the culture will likely give no guidance to the person who needs to make a decision. Such a condition is now commonplace in the legal sphere, particularly in bio-medical areas. For example, in the United States, courts and government bodies have been trying to resolve questions concerning surrogate mothers who decide, following the birth of the baby, that they will not honor the contract and turn over the baby to the father. Legal questions about who has the right to keep and raise the child in such circumstances must be resolved, but existing laws did not help to resolve such cases in a com-pletely satisfactory manner. Legal cases of this kind appear in the news in countries around the world with some frequency, and legal systems have to find ways to contend with the problems raised. A similar point, only in the moral sphere, is being made regarding the moral rules used in a given culture. Cases are bound to arise that lie outside the scope of the existing moral rules. Hence, ethical relativism does not fare especially well with respect to the first of the requirements for a satisfactory ethical theory.

Nor need ethical relativism do very well with requirement (4), which concerns treating people as ends in themselves. To see this, consider a culture such as present day South Africa with its system of apartheid. In that culture (assuming we can identify a country, which is a political entity, with a culture), a majority of the population is treated as a mere means in many situations by the white minority, and this treatment is both legally and morally sanctioned by legal and moral rules ingredient in that culture. Ethical relativism thus guarantees neither justice nor impartiality, and so is no better off relative to this requirement than is ethical egoism.

It might seem, too, that requirement (6) will be readily violated by ethical relativism. A great many people outside the culture of South Africa feel certain that apartheid is morally wrong, for example, and yet ethical relativism sanctions this system of acts because it legitimizes a culture whose moral rules permit it. Defenders of ethical relativism reply to this sort of objection, however, by noting that one can only make moral judgments *within* a given culture. The claim that apartheid is wrong is made by people *outside* the culture of South Africa, and members of one culture with one set of moral rules have no business making moral pro-nouncements about the action of people in a different culture. Hence, ethical relativists can avoid the full force of this objection. Even so, by comparison with the most plausible nonrelativist theory examined, the utilitarian Kantian theory, relativism does not do especially well. For, although there are reasons in favor of relativism, there are also good reasons for rejecting it. Ethical relativism fails to satisfy adequately requirements (1) and (4), for instance, while there is reason to think that the utilitarian Kantian principle meets those requirements. So, on balance, and relative to all of the evidence we have considered in this chapter, the utilitarian Kantian principle emerges as the most plausible ethical theory.

We have not considered whether the utilitarian Kantian theory meets condition (6)—whether it prescribes no acts we feel certain are morally wrong. Consideration of this question is left to the reader. If she finds that it meets condition (6), that will be yet more reason to think that we have uncovered a satisfactory ethical theory. We think it is likely that further reflection will show that this theory does meet the sixth condition, because the most likely cases in which the theory would fail to meet it would concern instances of injustice. The addition of the Kantian part of the theory, in the form of Kant's second formulation of the categorical imperative, expressly deals with matters of injustice, so some confidence that the utilitarian Kantian theory satisfies condition (6) is warranted.

Earlier in the chapter, we found reason to reject many different ethical standards, but we left open the question of ethical skepticism. We decided that if by the conclusion of our examination of ethical standards, we found none satisfactory, we would have good inductive grounds for the claim of the ethical skeptic that there are no justifiable ethical standards. Although the examination is not completed, because we have not fully tested the utilitarian Kantian theory, even at this point we have some reasons to think that we have found a standard that at least approximates a justifiable one. We may be wrong, but even if we are, there are definite signs that progress has been made and is still being made. So we have grounds for concluding that ethical skepticism is wrong. Although the task of justifying an ethical standard is most difficult and often discouraging, we have found ample reason to suppose that success in this endeavor is within reach.

EXERCISES

Relativism, Nihilism, Skepticism, and Egoism

1. Which of the following do you think are moral judgments? Which are not? Explain your answers.

    All people have a right to liberty.

    God punishes those who break his laws, and rewards those who keep his laws.

    Thou shalt not steal.

    We should always obey the law.

    The use of cocaine is harmful to society.

    'Ought' implies can.

    Nothing is right or wrong, even though people believe the contrary.

2.   Which of the following are clear examples of ethical relativism as it is defined in the text? Explain your answers.

Polygamy is morally permissible in Egypt, but it is immoral in Western European countries.

What you claim is right is just your opinion, and so it is no better than anyone else's.

What is wrong is that which hurts society, so what is wrong in one society is often right in another.

The principle of utilitarianism may be all right for Western cultures, but it is surely wrong for Oriental cultures.

3.   Explain fully the difference between ethical nihilism and the non-standard theory. Is the latter really just a disguised form of ethical nihilism?

4.   Evaluate the following argument:

Causal determinism is true, from which it follows that no one has free will, and, consequently, no one is morally responsible for what she does. But if no one is morally responsible for what she does, then she cannot be obligated to do anything. That is, there is nothing she ought to do; nothing is right and nothing is wrong. Therefore, ethical nihilism is correct.

5.   Evaluate the following argument:

Ethical skepticism is correct because, in the last analysis, no person can do any more than follow his or her conscience in ethical matters, and nothing can be justified in that way.

6.   Suppose that someone named Jones had risked his life to save a drowning child. Discuss the following explanation of his action:

Jones did not really act unselfishly, that is, he did not risk his own life for the sake of the drowning child. Rather, Jones is the sort of person who gets satisfaction and pleasure as a result of helping others, and his desire for this kind of pleasure was so great it even outweighed his desire to protect his own life. Jones, therefore, was really acting to get the future pleasure, not to save the child.

7.   Egoistic hedonism was rejected on the grounds that there were no sound arguments in its favor and it prescribes morally repugnant acts. Suppose that an egoistic hedonist were to reply as follows:

My theory does not prescribe morally repugnant acts because such acts are clearly those that harm others and to harm another is to invite retaliation or punishment. Because it is obviously not in one's interest to bring injury to oneself, then on the basis of egoistic hedonism, the correct conclusion is that we should not harm others. My theory, therefore, does not prescribe morally repugnant acts.

Evaluate this reply.

'Ought' and 'Is'

8. Is the following derivation of 'ought' from a factual claim valid? Explain your answer.

   1. Mike says, "I hereby promise to help Smitty escape from jail."

   2. If someone says that he promises something, then he is obliged to do what he promises.

   3. If someone is obliged to do what he promises, then he ought to do what he promises.

   Therefore

   4. Mike ought to help Smitty escape from jail.

The Definist Fallacy

9. Which of the following clearly commit the definist fallacy and which do not? Justify your answers.

   What is good is what is commanded by God.

   The word 'good' means 'what ought to be maximized.'

   Pleasure is, by virtue of the meaning of words, the one and only thing good in itself.

   The good is, clearly, that at which all things aim.

   To say that something is good is to say that it is an object of human interest.

Utilitarianism

10. Bentham's version of utilitarianism assumes a "hedonic calculus," that is, a system by which various pains and pleasures can be added and subtracted as if they were oranges or apples. Thus we are supposed to be able to add the pleasure you get from making an important discovery to the pleasure I get from drinking fine wine, and get a result that is, let us say, three times the amount that Jones gets from calling a bluff in poker minus the headache Smith has. Surely, though, the very idea of such a calculus is absurd. Consequently, Bentham's principle of utility is absurd. Evaluate this objection.

11. Evaluate the following objection to utilitarianism.

According to the principle of utility we are to treat each person as one and no person as more than one. Thus, each person is to get equal consideration. But if we accept the principle of utility, we cannot do this, for some people are much more sensitive to pain and pleasure than others, and so when we "add" pleasures or pains, an extremely sensitive person would weigh more heavily in our calculations than normally sensitive persons. Thus, if we use the principle of utility, we cannot give all people equal consideration as the principle requires. The principle, therefore, is inconsistent, and should not be followed.

12. Consider the following objection to utilitarian ethical theories, and compare how an act utilitarian could reply to it with how a rule utilitarian could apply.

Jones is dying in great pain and has possibly a month to live with no hope of recovery. Jones has no relatives and no one who stands to gain or lose by his death. His doctor, a good utilitarian, decides upon a mercy killing. Jones, however, objects, and says that he wants to live as long as possible. Nevertheless, his doctor goes ahead and ends Jones's life. This seems to be an action which utilitarian ethical theories prescribe, but it is clearly wrong.

Kantianism

13. Smith, a Kantian, decides to make it his rule to eat dinner at 6:00 P.M. Accordingly, he universalizes his rule, that is, conceives of it as a universal law, and is horrified at the result. If everyone ate dinner at 6:00 P.M., essential services would go unmanned, patients would be left on the operating tables, airlines would crash, ships would run aground, and so on. Because he could not will this state of affairs, he concludes that he must reject this rule. Yet the same objection applies to a rule prescribing dinner at any other time, and he is faced with starvation. Has Smith made a mistake in employing the first formulation of the categorical imperative? If so, carefully explain it.

14. Suppose you want to decide whether to cheat on an exam. Find the maxim by which you would be acting if you did so and test it by means of each version of the categorical imperative.

The Utilitarian Kantian Standard

15. Ethical standards are used not only for moral evaluation of the actions of individuals, but also for moral evaluation of the laws of governments and societies. Is there some way to adapt the utilitarian Kantian principle to apply to laws? For example, consider and

critically evaluate the following, which is based on the thesis that no law should prescribe that any person or group of persons is to be treated as a mere means, and so the basic prescription is that laws, and indeed systems of laws, should be fair:

A law (system of laws) is morally just if and only if (a) what it prescribes is fair to all persons and groups to whom it applies, and (b) it is a utilitarian rule (system of rules) which is consistent with (a).

16. Consider this objection to the utilitarian Kantian standard:

An ethical standard that cannot be effectively used is worthless and ought to be rejected. The utilitarian Kantian standard is easily seen to be worthless, because it is so complex that in the attempt to actually use it to decide what to do, one would be caught in endless calculation. Hence, we ought to reject this standard.

Is this a reasonable objection to the utilitarian Kantian standard? Defend your answer.

Suggestions for Further Reading

Historical sources

Bentham, Jeremy, *Principles of Morals and Legislation*, in *The Utilitarians* (Garden City: Doubleday, 1961).

Hume, David, *Treatise of Human Nature*, ed. P. Nidditch, 2nd ed., (Oxford: The Clarendon Press, 1978).

Hume, David, *Enquiry Concerning the Principles of Morals*, J. Schneewind, editor (Indianapolis: Hackett, 1983).

Kant, Immanuel, *Grounding for the Metaphysics of Morals*, translated by J. Ellington, (Indianapolis: Hackett, 1981).

Mill, J. S., *Utilitarianism*, G. Sher, editor (Indianapolis: Hackett, 1978).

Plato, *The Republic*, translated by G. M. A. Grube (Indianapolis: Hackett, 1974).

Contemporary texts and collections

Aune, Bruce, *Kant's Theory of Morals* (Princeton: Princeton University Press, 1980).

Brandt, Richard, *A Theory of the Good and the Right* (New York: Oxford University Press, 1979).

Frankena, William, *Ethics* (Englewood Cliffs: Prentice-Hall, 1963).

Gewirth, Alan, *Reason and Morality*, (Chicago: University of Chicago Press, 1978).

Harman, Gilbert, *The Nature of Morality* (New York: Oxford University Press, 1977).

MacIntyre, Alasdair, *After Virtue* (Notre Dame: University of Notre Dame Press, 1981).

Mackie, J. L., *Ethics: Inventing Right and Wrong*, (Baltimore: Penguin, 1977).

Moore, G. E., *Principia Ethica* (London: Oxford University Press, 1903).

Nagel, Thomas, *Mortal Questions* (Cambridge: Cambridge University Press, 1979).

Quinn, Philip, *Divine Commands and Moral Requirements* (New York: Oxford University Press, 1980).

Rawls, John, *A Theory of Justice* (Cambridge: Harvard University Press, 1971).

Ross, W. D., *The Right and the Good* (Indianapolis: Hackett, 1988).

Smart, J. J. C., and Bernard Williams, *Utilitarianism: For and Against* (Cambridge: Cambridge University Press, 1973).

Author Index

The letter b following a page number indicates a bibliographical entry; the letter n refers to a footnote entry.

Subject Index